Metánoia (Repentance): A Major
Theme of the Gospel of Matthew

Metánoia (Repentance): A Major Theme of the Gospel of Matthew

ChoongJae Lee

FOREWORD BY
Jonathan T. Pennington

WIPF & STOCK · Eugene, Oregon

METÁNOIA (REPENTANCE): A MAJOR THEME OF THE GOSPEL OF MATTHEW

Copyright © 2020 ChoongJae Lee. All rights reserved. Except for brief quotations in critical publications or reviews, no part of this book may be reproduced in any manner without prior written permission from the publisher. Write: Permissions, Wipf and Stock Publishers, 199 W. 8th Ave., Suite 3, Eugene, OR 97401.

Wipf & Stock
An Imprint of Wipf and Stock Publishers
199 W. 8th Ave., Suite 3
Eugene, OR 97401

www.wipfandstock.com

PAPERBACK ISBN: 978-1-7252-6104-4
HARDCOVER ISBN: 978-1-7252-6105-1
EBOOK ISBN: 978-1-7252-6106-8

All rights reserved. The Southern Baptist Theological Seminary has permission to reproduce and disseminate this document in any form by any means for purposes chosen by the Seminary, including, without limitation, preservation or instruction.

Unless otherwise noted, all Scripture quotations are from the ESV® Bible (The Holy Bible, English Standard Version®), copyright © 2001 by Crossway, a publishing ministry of Good News Publishers. Used by permission. All rights reserved.

Manufactured in the U.S.A.   04/02/20

For the glory of God

Contents

Foreword by Jonathan T. Pennington | ix
Preface | xi
List of Abbreviations | xii

1. Introduction | 1
2. History of Research | 17
3. The Meaning of μετανοέω and μετάνοια | 34
4. John the Baptist's μετάνοια Preaching (Matt 3:1–12): Introducing the Thematic Significance of μετάνοια in Matthew | 48
5. The Thematic Significanc of μετάνοια Expressed in Matthew's Discipleship, the Great Commission, and Gentile Inclusion | 66
6. The Thematic Significance of μετάνοια Expressed in Matthew's Righteousness and Soteriology | 93
7. The Thematic Significance of μετάνοια in the Sermon on the Mount: The Contents of μετάνοια | 114
8. The Thematic Significance of μετάνοια in Matthew 10: Universal μετάνοια Commission for the Church | 139
9. The Thematic Significance of μετάνοια in Matthew 13: Explanation of Mixed Reception and Exhortation to μετάνοια | 162
10. The Thematic Significance of μετάνοια in Matthew 18: The Community Discourse of μετάνοια through Humility and Servanthood | 190
11. The Thematic Significance of μετάνοια in Matthew 23–25: The Last Discourse of μετάνοια | 205
12. Conclusion | 233

    Bibliography | 235

Foreword

MANY SCHOLARS OF THE wonder-filled Gospel of Matthew have reflected on that esoteric little verse in Mt 13:52—"Every scribe who has been trained for the kingdom of heaven is like a master of a house who brings out of his treasure what is new and what is old." (ESV)

This is an intriguing verse whose meaning remains somewhat shrouded in mystery. And that seems to be the point. A scribe trained in the Jesus way ("the kingdom of heaven") is one who regularly returns to the treasure-house of Holy Scripture and finds there riches both old and new. It is inexhaustible and often surprising. This is not because of a renegade cleverness of the scribe, but because of the infinite reward that is stored in Scripture for those who are willing to sell all to get it. The scribe's role is to be trained, to submit to a way of seeing and being in the world that enables him or her to be a conductor of treasures from the mysterious land of the Bible out into the broader world.

One such trained scribe is the author of this book, ChoongJae Lee. I had the great privilege of spending several years teaching and mentoring ChoongJae. But the credit goes to him for his diligence, carefulness, and Christian maturity through the long process of Matthean scribal training.

As a result, ChoongJae has brought forth a new treasure from the storehouse of Matthew. He has shown that the theme of repentance is more important to the theology and literary structure of Matthew than we have hitherto seen. Repentance is more than feeling sorry for sin and more than just the entry point into salvation. Repentance is an image, a metaphor, for the entirety of the Christian life. It is a comprehensive way to describe what it means to be a disciple.

This deepens our understanding of what Matthew is doing. Matthew is clearly the disciple-making Gospel, complete with its five major teaching blocks and its sophisticated presentation of Jesus as a model to be followed, not only a Savior to be sacrificed. ChoongJae Lee has helped us see that repentance is one of the macro-level means by which Matthew describes this vision for being a follower of Jesus. In repentance we turn from one way of seeing and being in the world to another way, the Jesus way, the narrow way that leads to life.

As I continue to teach and preach from Matthew I repeatedly find myself using what I have learned from ChoongJae. I suppose there is no greater testimony than that to the value of this trained scribe and to the riches of Holy Scripture generously given to us in the Gospel of Matthew.

Jonathan T. Pennington

Preface

THIS BOOK IS MY revised PhD dissertation, "μετάνοια (Repentance) as a Major Theme of the Gospel of Matthew" submitted to The Southern Baptist Theological Seminary in 2018. The first chapter appeared in *Reformed Journal of Theology* as "μετάνοια (Repentance) as a Major Theme," and is included here with permission. During the first seminar of the Sermon on the Mount with Dr. Jonathan T. Pennington at SBTS, I became interested in the theme of μετάνοια in the Gospel of Matthew. Jesus opens his public ministry with the commandment Μετανοεῖτε, ἤγγικεν γὰρ ἡ βασιλεία τῶν οὐρανῶν "Repent, for the kingdom of heaven is at hand" (4:17), but the theme of μετάνοια in Matthew has not been studied by scholars. I explore the theme of μετάνοια in the Gospel of Matthew as a significant theme. Special thanks to my supervisor, Dr. Jonathan T. Pennington, for his sincere help in my doctoral program and his labor with rough drafts of this dissertation. Thanks also to Dr. Robert L. Plummer and Dr. Brian J. Vickers for their careful reading. Special thanks to my advisors and friends at Gordon Conwell Theological Seminary, Dr. Ciampa for directing my study and for his encouragement, and many friends who make my life fruitful. Thanks to my teachers in Hapdong Theological Seminary, where I was stimulated by the study of theology and New Testament theology. Special thanks to my father and mother EulPyo Lee and OgBog Jun for their constant love and support. This dissertation is dedicated to my family, SangHee Kim, and Haram Christine Lee, whose support has allowed me to finish. *Soli deo gloria*.

ChoongJae Lee
Louisville, Kentucky
December 2018

Abbreviations

ABD	*The Anchor Bible Dictionary*
BDAG	*A Greek–English Lexicon of the New Testament*
BECNT	*Baker Exegetical Commentary on the New Testament*
CBQ	*Catholic Biblical Quarterly*
EBC	*The Expositor's Bible Commentary*
ExpTim	*Expository Times*
ICC	*International Critical Commentary*
JBL	*Journal of Biblical Literature*
JETS	*Journal of the Evangelical Theological Society*
JSNT	*Journal for the Study of the New Testament*
LXX	Septuagint
NA27	*Novum Testamentum Graece*
NIBC	*New International Biblical Commentary*
NICNT	*New International Commentary on the New Testament*
NIGTC	*New International Greek Testament Commentary*
NovT	*Novum Testamentum*
NTS	*New Testament Studies*
TDNT	*Theological Dictionary of the New Testament*
WBC	*Word Biblical Commentary*
WTJ	*Westminster Theological Journal*
WUNT	*Wissenschaftliche Untersuchungen zum Neuen Testament*

Chapter 1

Introduction

MATTHEW DESCRIBES THE BEGINNING of Jesus' ministry with the summary words, Μετανοεῖτε, ἤγγικεν γὰρ ἡ βασιλεία τῶν οὐρανῶν ("Repent, for the kingdom of heaven is at hand" (4:17). Matthew begins John the Baptist's ministry with the exact same phrase, Μετανοεῖτε, ἤγγικεν γὰρ ἡ βασιλεία τῶν οὐρανῶν (3:2). Why does Matthew use this command μετανοεῖτε at the beginning of their ministry? What do μετανοέω and μετάνοια mean? How does this opening commandment μετανοεῖτε function in the Gospel of Matthew and how does it relate to the rest of the gospel? Scholars have stated that μετανοέω in 4:17 has critical value for understanding Matthew because the verse functions as a summary statement (or key phrase) of Jesus' public ministry and teaching.[1] This opening statement shows the thematic significance of μετάνοια (repentance) in the Gospel of Matthew. Even though Matthew locates μετανοέω and μετάνοια at the beginning as an important message of John the Baptist (3:2–12), and Jesus and some scholars recognize its critical importance, no work has been done on Matthean

---

1. France, *Gospel of Matthew*, 143. Allison, "Structure of the Sermon on the Mount," 423–45. Talbert, *Reading the Sermon on the Mount*, 143–44. France explains the role of Jesus in the Sermon on the Mount as eschatological judge (7:13–27) demanding repentance (4:17). And he states that the sermon shows the contents of repentance. See also Keener, *Gospel of Matthew*, 149. Keener mentions that the Sermon on the Mount is connected to 4:17 as "the repentant lifestyle," or "the nature of the ethic of repentance." He rightly observes their close relationship. In Luz, *Matthew 1–7*, 198, Luz argues that the repentance message is "the entry gate" to the greater righteousness of the sermon and *dominates* it. In Scaer, *Sermon on the Mount*, 49, 64, Scaer also argues that especially 4:17, which points to the beginning of Jesus's public ministry, is a characteristic summary of Jesus' common message, especially the sermon. One of his supporting ideas is the appearance of agricultural parables in both John and Jesus (3:17, 13:24–30). In Runesson, *Divine Wrath and Salvation*, 119, Runesson notes repentance as a key motif in Matthew. See also Chamberlain, *Meaning of Repentance*, 51; Carlston, "Metanoia and Church Discipline; Nave, *Role and Function of Repentance*, 95–99. Morris, *Gospel according to Matthew*, 83.

μετάνοια as a significant theme of the book.[2] Even the general theme of μετάνοια (repentance) within biblical studies has not received sufficient scholarly interest over the last fifty years.[3]

The theme of μετάνοια (repentance) has not been sufficiently discussed in Matthean scholarship for three possible main reasons. First, the infrequent occurrence of μετανοέω and μετάνοια in Matthew limits one's ability to recognize the theme of μετάνοια. Scholarship has not paid sufficient attention to the theme because the word group of μετανοέω and μετάνοια occur only seven times in Matthew (3:2, 8, 11; 4:17; 11:20, 21; 12:41).[4] Does the small number of occurrences indicate Matthew forgets about μετάνοια right after this opening phrase? Or does Matthew express μετάνοια in other ways? The infrequent use of the terms and μετάνοια's location as the opening summary in Matthew leads back to the question of how this phrase relates to the whole of Matthew.

A second reason the theme of μετάνοια has not been developed in Matthean study is due to the misunderstanding of the lexical idea of μετανοέω and μετάνοια. The common understanding of repentance based on the Greek terms μετανοέω and μετάνοια is to regret or feel remorse for past sins and stop doing them, or simply to change one's mind. Therefore, μετανοέω and μετάνοια have been understood as an emotional event or just a change of mind. About a century ago, A. T. Robertson already noted the problem with the English translation "repent," when it is understood to mean "to be sorry again." He argues that instead μεταμέλομαι in Matthew 27:3 has the idea of "being sorry again"/"repenting," and this is different than μετάνοια.[5] Georg Strecker similarly argues that Luther mistranslated μετάνοια into Buße and notes that μετάνοια does not mean to feel remorse

---

2. There are some works on the theme of repentance in Matthew. However, these works do not argue for the theme of repentance as a significant theme in Matthew, but simply a theme in Matthew. See n. 1 above.

3. For the history of research on the theme of repentance, see Boda, 'Return to Me.'

4. Davies and Allison, *Matthew 1–7*, 388–89. Davies and Allison say repentance is not a key theme of the Gospel of Matthew since it appears two times in noun form and five times in verb form. Also, they think that Matthew understands repentance as entrance into the Christian community. However, recent research shows that repentance is not just entrance to the community, but is the purpose of community. In Matthew's Gospel, repentance is not a one-time event, but a lifelong experience/commitment/way of being.

5. Robertson, *Word Pictures*, Matt. 3:2. See also Silva, *New International Dictionary*, 3:290–91; Thompson and Martens, *New International Dictionary*, 4:55–59; Merklein, *Exegetical Dictionary of the New Testament*, 2:417–18. Kittel and Friedrich, *TDNT* 4:975–80.

or intellectual change of mind.[6] This misunderstanding of μετανοέω and μετάνοια hinders their being seen as a significant theme of Matthew and fails to emphasize the first phrase of Jesus' public ministry (4:17) as a significant Matthean theme or message. The English translations of "repent" and "repentance" do not match the body of Matthew, because the body of Matthew communicates a deeper/bigger idea of turning one's heart and life than just feeling remorse and changing one's mind. The English translations "repent" and "repentance" should be reconsidered. What then do μετανοέω and μετάνοια exactly mean? How does their correct meaning govern the body of Matthew?

The third reason μετάνοια is underappreciated in Matthean studies is the insufficient recognition of the location of μετάνοια in Matthew's narrative and structure. Μετανοέω and μετάνοια in summary statements (3:2, 8; 4:17) are powerful motivations for the rest of the Gospel of Matthew. Many scholars divide the introductory section from 1:1 to 4:23 or 25, naming it "Jesus' early history" or "preparation for public ministry," with Jesus' public ministry beginning at 5:1.[7] Some regard μετάνοια as a one-time entrance event to the Christian community since it appears at the beginning of the gospel.[8] As a result, 4:17 is divided from Jesus' public ministry and its close connection to the rest of the book is lost.

Thesis

This book will argue the thematic or even paradigmatic significance of μετάνοια in Matthew. Μετάνοια toward Jesus and the kingdom of heaven is a significant message of Matthew that John the Baptist and Jesus begin their public ministry with (3:2; 4:17), which also summarizes Jesus' teaching, especially the five major teaching blocks. The lexical idea of μετανοέω and μετάνοια involves a change of mind (or heart, will, thinking) and behavior, and so in turn of one's whole being and life. This opening commandment of turning (μετανοέω), especially the concept, the essence, and the contents is fully revealed throughout the body of Matthew in various ways, demonstrating the thematic significance of μετάνοια in Matthew.

---

6. Strecker, *Theology of the New Testament*, 224.

7. For example, Davies and Allison, *Matthew 1–7*, 425–43; France, *Gospel of Matthew*, 143.

8. Davies and Allision, *Matthew 1–7*, 388–89.

Summary of the Entire Argument

This thesis will be established through the following supports. First, Matthew's summary of Jesus' teaching in 4:17 (cf. 3:2) shows the commandment of turning (μετανοέω) in view of the imminent coming of the kingdom of heaven to be a significant theme of Jesus' teaching in Matthew, while 11:20–21[9] denotes μετάνοια as the aim of Jesus' wonderwork ministry. The highly structured Gospel of Matthew should be read through the commandment of turning (μετανοέω) because Matthew locates it as a summary at the onset of Jesus' public ministry and teaching (4:17) and John the Baptist's preaching (3:2). Based on location alone, this Matthean opening summary of Jesus' ministry and teaching emphasizes the significance of μετάνοια even though it does not occur many times in the book.[10] This location should be emphasized, especially when taken together with the last phrase of Jesus' ministry, the Great Commission (28:18–20). In comparison, the last words of Jesus have earned much interest as a main argument of the book because of their location at the end.[11] In terms of structure, some scholars argue that 4:17 begins a new section as the summary statement for Jesus' public ministry and governs the first of Jesus' teaching blocks, the sermon.[12] In reality, 4:17 serves as the beginning of Jesus' ministry in Matthew, and so its emphasis should be highlighted as a significant theme of the whole book.

Second, the lexical meaning of μετάνοια is a turn (or a change) one's mind (or will, heart) and conduct so whole life and this meaning of μετάνοια is paradigmatic in the body of Matthew.[13] Strecker explains it as "a total

---

9. Matt 11:20–21: "Then he began to denounce the cities where most of his mighty works had been done, because they did not repent. 'Woe to you, Chorazin! Woe to you, Bethsaida! For if the mighty works done in you had been done in Tyre and Sidon, they would have repented long ago in sackcloth and ashes.'" Matt 11:25–27 says that God himself has hidden truth from the unrepentant people, but hardness of heart does not excuse the hardhearted. They still should have repented.

10. See n. 1 above.

11. Brooks, "Matthew 28:16–20," 2–18; Kingsbury, "Composition and Christology," 573–84; Keener, "Matthew's Missiology," 3–20. For a contrasting argument, see Sim, "Is Matthew 28:16–20?," 1–7.

12. Kingsbury, *Matthew*, 29–30 suggests 4:17 as the beginning of a new section. Talbert, *Reading the Sermon on the Mount*, 11, argues that the sermon begins at 4:18. Also, Carter, *Matthew*, 141–43 argues 4:16 ends Jesus' origin and identification section, and 4:17 begins Jesus' public ministry. Nolland, *Gospel of Matthew*, 170 argues for 4:13–25 as the establishment of Jesus public ministry.

13. Thompson and Martens, *New International Dictionary*, 4:55–59. Silva, *New International Dictionary*, 3:290–91. Merklein, *Exegetical Dictionary of the New Testament*, 2:417–18; Cremer, *Biblio-Theological Lexicon*, 792. BDAG 640 defines μετανοέω "to change one's mind, feel remorse, repent, be converted." See note 16 and my next chapter for more lexical studies of this term. Μετάνοια (repentance) in Matthew therefore is

reorientation of human existence, a radical change in human life, a turning from self to God. . . it combines internal and external transformation." He suggests "return" or "turn around" as the proper translation.¹⁴ Louw–Nida's semantic domain for μετανοέω and μετάνοια places them under "changing behavior" and defines μετανοέω and μετάνοια as "change [in] one's way of life as the result of a complete change of thought and attitude with regard to sin and righteousness."¹⁵ Robertson suggests "to return" and points out that John and Jesus did not mean "to be sorry, but to change their mental attitudes and conduct."¹⁶ Μετανοέω and μετάνοια refer to a change (or turn) of mind and behavior, and thus of one's whole being and life. Μετάνοια contains not only a negative aspect of being sorry and stopping a sin but also a positive aspect of reorienting one's whole being and life toward Jesus Christ. Thus, this opening commandment of turning (μετάνοια) naturally necessitates following a detailed explanation of what this μετάνοια looks like. If such is not the case, this commandment will lose its meaning and intent and remain empty. This meaning of μετάνοια governs the body of Matthew, which emphasizes turning from a wicked mind and conduct to the right mind and right conduct.¹⁷

---

not legalistic because it means to change one's mind (or heart or will) and according conduct. Legalism means to have good conduct only. Also, μετάνοια (repentance) is a lifelong relational concept between Jesus and his disciples. Μετάνοια (repentance) in Matthew is based on divine initiative and grace. Matthew's Immanuel theme in 1:18 and 28:20 indicates divine initiative—grace supports repentance. Also, John the Baptist's identification of Jesus as the Holy Spirit baptizer for repentance (3:11) indicates so. Moreover, 11:20–27 show that the acceptance of Jesus' μετάνοια is dependent on God's election, not legalism that God hides Jesus from the wise and intelligent but reveals him to infants whom Jesus wills to reveal.

14. Strecker, *Theology of the New Testament*, 224.

15. Louw and Nida, *Greek-English Lexicon*, 510.

16. Robertson, *Word Pictures*, Matt. 3:2. In this paper, to avoid confusion, I will continue using the terms "repent" and "repentance." Even earlier seventeenth-century English commentators such as Dickson, Leigh, Lightfoot, and Henry Hammond defined μετάνοια as changing both internal mind and external conduct. See Lanser, "Repent Ye," 279–96. Hammond said μετάνοια is "a change mind. . . conversion. . . and reformation" (quoted in Lanser, "Repent Ye," 285).

17. Morris points out Matthew's emphasis on good deeds and the importance of 3:2 and 4:17b for a leading idea of the Gospel of Matthew and its relationship to grace of God in Matthew: "Such preaching (4:17b) is a clarion call to action, not a recipe for slothful complacency. We should not overlook that importance of this call to repentance at the very beginning of Jesus' ministry; everything else follows from that. Matthew has often been seen as one who stresses the importance of good works, and of course he does. But this must not be held in such a form that his emphasis on grace is missed" (Morris, *Gospel according to Matthew*, 83).

The term μετανοέω has a strong bond to the Hebrew term šub in the Old Testament (OT) prophets which means to turn or return from sin to a faithful relationship with God and obedience to the law of God with one's whole mind and deed (Deut 30:2, 10; Hos 2:7; 3:5; 6:1; 11:15; Amos 4:6, 8–9; Isa 6:10; 9:13; 31:6; Jer 2:27; 3:10, 12, 14, 22; Ezek 14:6; 18:30, 32). Therefore, μετανοέω in the first words of Jesus' public ministry involves a change of mind (or thinking, heart, will) and also a change of behavior which produces fruit.[18] Specifically, Jesus' commandment to obey the law and the prophets as he teaches in the sermon (5:17; 7:12, 21; 22:40) parallels the OT prophets' command to turn/repent (šub) and obey the law of God. Jesus commands μετάνοια in 4:17 and immediately begins to teach about the true meaning of the law and the prophets embodied in μετάνοια. This parallelism shows that Jesus' teaching and ministry calls

---

18. For more discussion, see Boda, 'Return to Me,' 192–93. Boda states that biblical repentance is "a fundamental return to covenant relationship with the triune God." Matthew attaches Jesus' call to follow (4:18–23) to Jesus' call to repent (4:17b) and keeps saying discipleship (16:21–28 and so on). Another helpful concept study of the theme of repentance in the four gospels, especially the Fourth Gospel, is Croteau, "Repentance Found?," 97–123. This work provides three main views of μετάνοια as "(1) a turning away from one's sins (not just a willingness or resolve to do so); (2) the intention, resolve, or willingness to turn from sins; (3) to change one's mind (about something). μετάνοια does not mean 'to be remorseful,' 'to be sorry,' or 'to regret'; that is the primary meaning of μεταμέλομαι" (104). Croteau defines repentance as "a change in the mind and conduct, which involves a turning away from sins and turning to God, which produces demonstrable results" (105). He also argues that repentance is not opposed to salvation by faith because repentance is a gift and a God-enabled human response (Acts 11:18; Rom 2:4; and 2 Tim 2:25) and faith includes repentance (Matt 12:41 with Jonah 3:5; Acts 3:19; 10:43; 11:21; 20:20; 26:20). For the last half of the article Croteau examines the concept of repentance in the Fourth Gospel (107–23). For more information about the meaning of μετάνοια, see Thompson, "Metanoeō and Metamelei"; Dirksen, New Testament Concept of Metanoia; Chamberlain, Meaning of Repentance; Chamberlain, "For Deliverance and Freedom," 271–83; Boda and Smith, Repentance in Christian Theology; Nave, Role and Function of Repentance; Porter, "Penitence and Repentance in the Epistles," 127–52; Humphrey, "And I Shall Heal Them," 105–26; Schnabel, "Repentance in Paul's Letters," 159–86. David Sterns argues that μετάνοια denotes "change your mind, have a complete change of heart" based on the underlying Hebrew concept of teshuba, which means a religious behavioral "turning" from one's sins and "returning" to God. He emphasizes that μετάνοια includes both turning "from" sin and turning "to" observant ways of the manner of life prescribed by Orthodox Judaism. In addition, he states that the Jewish concept of μετάνοια "requires God's grace to be able to do it—'Turn us to you, O Adonai, and we will be turned' (Lamentations 5:21)" (emphasis his). Repentance is not a one-time event, but a lifelong event. For more background study, see Nitzan, "Repentance in the Dead Sea Scrolls," 145–70; Jason, Repentance at Qumran. Fuller note and discussion of the correct meaning of μετανοέω and μετάνοια (repentance) will follow in a later section.

for μετάνοια. The following arguments will demonstrate that this lexical meaning permeates the narrative.

Third, even though μετανοέω and μετάνοια occur infrequently, the Gospel of Matthew uses the concept of μετανοέω and μετάνοια throughout the book in its meaning, a turn (or a change) of one's mind (or heart or will) and conduct or of one's whole being and life. This correct understanding of μετανοέω and μετάνοια is significantly expressed in the body of Matthew. Word count alone does not seem to support μετάνοια as a Matthean emphasis. However, recent New Testament (NT) scholarship has realized the limits of word counts and is now emphasizing instead concept–based study, which includes literary context, synonyms, antonyms, images, similar language with the same meaning, and paraphrasing statements. A few works on the Four Gospels and the Pauline writings do recognize their emphasis on μετάνοια as not only terminological but also conceptual.[19] Matthew also uses widespread conceptual themes, images, and language related to μετάνοια and fruit worthy of μετάνοια. For example, synonyms and terms delivering similar meanings of μετάνοια and μετανοέω occur in the body of Matthew demonstrating that the theme of μετάνοια appears throughout the body of Matthew: στρέφω occurs in 18:3, ἐπιστρέφω occurs in 13:15, μεταμέλομαι occurs in 21:29, 32.[20] In addition, righteousness, doing the will of God, discipleship, changing one's heart, and fruit-bearing images and parables all illustrate the essence and the contents of μετάνοια and show the significance of the opening commandment of μετάνοια (4:17, cf. 3:2, 8) and fruit worthy of μετάνοια (3:8) in the body of Matthew. The opening commandment of turning (μετανοέω) in 4:17 and the Great Commission, in

---

19. Chamberlain, *Meaning of Repentance*; Wilkin, "Repentance as a Condition"; Nave, *Role and Function of Repentance*; Bailey, "Repentance in Luke-Acts"; Schnabel, "Repentance in Paul's Letters," 159–86; Kintu, "Repentance in the Sermon on the Mount"; Boda and Smith, *Repentance in Christian Theology*. Croteau, "Repentance Found?," 107–23 has done a concept study of the theme of repentance in the four gospels, especially the Fourth Gospel, and Croteau examines the concept of repentance in the Fourth Gospel. Even though the terms μετανοέω and μετάνοια do not occur throughout the NT but mostly in the four Gospels and Acts, the concept of repentance is throughout the NT.

20. See Louw and Nida, *Greek-English Lexicon*, Domain 41, 510. Louw and Nida's semantic domain for μετανοέω and μετάνοια places them under "changing behavior." It includes στρέφω, "change one's manner of life, with the implication of turning toward God," ἐπιστρέφω and ἐπιστροφή, "change one's manner of life in a particular direction, with the implication of turning back to God," μετανοέω and μετάνοια, "change one's way of life as the result of a complete change of thought and attitude with regard to sin and righteousness," γεννάω, ἄνωθεν and παλιγγενεσία, "experience a complete change in one's way of life to what it should be, with the implication of return to a former state or relation," and ἀμετανόητος, "pertaining to not being repentant."

concept and nature, frame Jesus' ministry, and thus emphasizes the significant ideas of Matthew: turning (μετάνοια) to Jesus with one's whole being and life to enter the kingdom of heaven, or in other words, following Jesus by becoming a disciple and keeping what he commands in order to enter the kingdom of heaven. The following arguments relate to this conceptual illustration of the theme of μετάνοια in Matthew.

Fourth, the first discourse block of Matthew, John the Baptist's commandment of μετάνοια (3:2–12), first introduces the significance of μετάνοια in the Gospel of Matthew. Specifically, μετάνοια appears in the idea of bearing fruit worthy of μετάνοια (3:8, 10), and the images about bearing good fruit in the body of Matthew (7:16–20; 12:33; 13:8, 26; 21:19, 34–43) consists of μετάνοια. John the Baptist's μετάνοια preaching block is important for understanding Matthew because it introduces μετάνοια and its significance at the beginning of the whole book. The fact that Jesus' first words in public ministry in 4:17 are the same as John the Baptist's (3:2) indicates that Jesus' preaching and ministry parallel John the Baptist's and that μετάνοια is significant in Jesus' teaching and ministry. Matthew 3:2–12 begins with the commandment of turning (μετανοέω) and introduces several significant aspects of μετάνοια, which repeatedly appear in the body of Matthew: the commandment of turning (μετανοέω) (3:2), bearing fruit worthy of μετάνοια (3:8), the need for μετάνοια (3:7), the reconstitution of the people of God as both Jew and gentile through μετάνοια (3:9), judgment (3:7, 10, 12), and Jesus' Holy Spirit and fire baptism for μετάνοια (3:11). These ideas appear thematically and verbally throughout the book of Matthew creating a unique Matthean parallelism between John the Baptist and Jesus Christ, thus indicating the significance of the commandment of turning (μετανοέω) in Matthew.

Moreover, Jesus' baptism of μετάνοια before his public ministry shows Jesus' life is a model of the good life of repentant people. Jesus' life as a model or fulfilling of a worthy fruitful life of the repentant expresses the theme of μετάνοια. Jesus is not only the incarnation of God but also the one entrusted with what it means to live a life of the repentant people of God. In addition, John the Baptist's identification of Jesus as one who will baptize with the Holy Spirit and fire for μετάνοια as John baptizes with water for μετάνοια (3:11–12) indicates that Jesus' ministry will be a μετάνοια ministry. The baptism with the Holy Spirit and fire (3:12) reveals Jesus as one who enables μετάνοια through the Holy Spirit and as the one who has authority to punish the unrepentant sinner with fire. In this sense, Jesus is the fulfiller of the OT prophetic call of μετάνοια represented by John the Baptist. Jesus fulfills it through the Holy Spirit and fire. This eschatological μετάνοια by the Holy Spirit and fire indicates that Matthew will display

Jesus' teaching and ministry through the lens of μετάνοια and the judgment of the wicked, leading to the end of the old era and the establishment of the new people of God and thus the beginning of the new era (3:8–9; 8:11–12; 21:28–32, 39, 43; 22:1–14).

Fifth, Matthew's widespread discipleship language and image show the significance of μετάνοια because they express the concept and the essence of μετάνοια and echo the commandment of turning (μετανοέω) (4:17). The injunction to follow Jesus by carrying one's own cross and observing Jesus' teachings (4:18–23; 11:28–30; 16:24; 28:18–20) illustrate the concept and the nature of the opening commandment of turning (μετανοέω). Most importantly, the narrative sequence of the commandment of turning (μετανοέω) in 4:17 and Jesus' calling of the disciples and their turning to follow Jesus in 4:18–22 closely connects μετάνοια and discipleship. Matthew begins Jesus' public ministry with the summary phrase of μετάνοια in 4:17 and then the next scene, 4:18–22, unpacks μετάνοια. Matthew 4:17–22 shows a perfect definition of μετάνοια. Jesus' calling of the disciples and their turning illustrate μετάνοια when μετάνοια is correctly defined as turning one's life to follow Jesus by leaving everything behind. This scene shows that μετάνοια is not a negative feeling of remorse or regret for the past sins but a positive action of turning one's whole life, including both mind (or will) and conduct. This μετάνοια is relational[21] as human beings turn to follow Jesus with their whole life (4:17–23).

Matthew's teaching on discipleship continues to reflect his idea of μετάνοια in other passages as well, showing the significance of the commandment of turning (μετανοέω) in the beginning of Jesus' ministry (4:17). Jesus' call to discipleship in 11:28–30 and 16:24–28 illustrate Matthew's idea that μετάνοια is turning one's mind and conduct to follow Jesus by giving up one's life to obtain rest and eternal life.[22] In addition, the Great Commission's

21. Boda, 'Return to Me,' 192. Boda states that biblical repentance is "a fundamental return to covenant relationship with the triune God." Matthew attaches Jesus' call to follow (4:18–23) to Jesus' call to repent (4:17b).

22. Matthew 4:17 and 16:21 make up Kingsbury's well-known structure shift for the Gospel of Matthew (Kingsbury, *Matthew*, 29–30). It is interesting that Peter appears in both places (4:17 and 16:21) positively and negatively, as do stories about discipleship. For a more detailed examination of Kingsbury's structure, see Neirynck, "Apo Tote Ērxato," 21–59. Kingsbury argues 4:17—16:13 deal with Jesus' preaching ministry and 16:21—28:20 deal with Jesus' suffering, death, and resurrection. Neirynck revises Kingsbury by proposing that 4:17 and 16:12 clearly divide Matthew, but that Jesus' preaching does not end at 16:12 and instead goes through 28:20, and that Jesus' suffering, death, and resurrection are added from 16:12. I think Jesus' preaching ministry from 4:17 is about repentance. Another work on Matthean structure based on Kingsbury is Weren, "Macrostructure of Matthew's Gospel," 171–200. He argues that 4:12–17; 11:2–30; 16:13–28; 21:1–17; and 26:1–16 are hinges of the Gospel of Matthew

discipleship theme, making disciples and teaching them to observe what Jesus has commanded (28:19–20), illustrates what μετάνοια is echoing in the opening commandment of turning (μετανοέω) in 4:17 and indicates the significance of μετάνοια in Matthew. Other discipleship language in Matthew, such as being "doers of the will of God" (7:21; 12:50), "being whole" (5:48; 19:21), "being righteous" (10:41; 13:43, 49; 20:4; 23:28–29; 25:37, 46; 27:19), "being followers of Jesus," and "being persecuted/carrying one's own cross," (5:10; 10:38; 16:24),[23] comprise the essence of μετάνοια and fruit worthy of μετάνοια showing the significance of μετάνοια.

In addition, the widespread stories of universal repentant people—both Jew and gentile as well as unrepentant people—demonstrate the significance of μετάνοια, a key component in discipleship. For example, the turning of the disciples (4:18–22; 9:9), the unrepentant generation in comparison with the repentant people of Nineveh and the Queen of the South (12:41–42), the Canaanite woman (15:21–28), and the feeding of 4,000 gentiles (12:33–38) all express the universal μετάνοια theme of Matthew. Jesus' universal returning sayings in 8:11–12, 12:17–21, and 24:14 especially point to the universality of μετάνοια in Matthew. These frequent universal μετάνοια stories demonstrate the significance of μετάνοια in Matthew.

Sixth, the last words of Jesus, the Great Commission (28:16–20), which are also a summary of Matthew, conceptually share the essence of μετάνοια idea—turning one's whole being and life toward Jesus by making disciples and teaching them to observe all Jesus' commandments. Jesus' disciples also preach a message of turning to Jesus and keeping what he has commanded. The entirety of the Great Commission includes what Matthew has described as μετάνοια throughout his book and culminates in the theme of μετάνοια throughout the Gospel of Matthew. In this respect, 4:17 and the Great Commission create μετάνοια conceptual inclusio. This μετάνοια conceptual inclusio demonstrates the significance of μετάνοια that frames the whole book of Matthew in which he spurs the listener to turn to Jesus by becoming a disciple and keeping what Jesus taught. In a sense, the Great Commission elaborates the theme of μετάνοια as meaning to be baptized in the name of the Father, the Son, and the Holy Spirit. This baptismal formula in the Great Commission has as its backdrop John the Baptist's μετάνοια baptism and Jesus' baptism with the Holy Spirit. This baptism idea connects μετάνοια and the Great Commission. Also, both 4:17 and the Great Commission command universal μετάνοια. The Isaiah 9:1–2 citation in

---

that connect, not divide, the Gospel of Matthew. Matthew 4:12—26:16 includes the five discourse blocks (5–7; 10; 13; 18; 23–25).

23. For more information of Matthean discipleship, see Wilkins, *Discipleship*.

4:12–16 near to 4:17 denotes that Jesus' summary statement commands the universal μετάνοια paralleling the universal range of the Great Commission. The Matthean gentile inclusion theme also reflects universal μετάνοια from the beginning of the book to the end.[24] Specifically, the centrality of the Great Commission in Matthew demonstrates the centrality of μετάνοια in Matthew. Scholars argue that the Great Commission is the summary of the whole Gospel of Matthew and impacts the structure of the book.[25] Since the Great Commission conceptually parallels the commandment of turning (μετανοέω), the Great Commission-centered reading of Matthew points to the significance of μετάνοια in Matthew.

Seventh, Matthew's emphasis on righteousness (3:15; 5:6, 10, 20; 6:1, 33; 21:32),[26] doing good works (5:16), doing the will of God (6:10; 7:21; 12:50; 18:14; 21:31; 26:42) and changing one's heart and mind (5:3, 8, 28; 6:21; 9:4; 12:34; 13:19; 15:8, 18, 19; 18:35; 22:37; 24:48) express the essence of μετάνοια and the contents of fruit worthy of μετάνοια (3:8), expressing the significance of turning (μετανοέω) in Matthew.[27] These themes also point to outward expressions of μετάνοια based on the meaning of turning (or changing) one's mind (will and heart) and conduct toward Jesus echoing 4:17.[28]

---

24. Schnelle, *Theology of the New Testament*, 456. Schnelle states, "The universal mission to all nations is the theological matrix in which Matthew and his church live." He mentions numerous examples of this widespread universalistic direction: 24:9, 14; 25:32; 28:19; 12:21; 13:38a; 24:9–14; 26:13. He also argues that Matthean community was not within the frame of Judaism but under the universal lordship of Jesus Christ.

25. Brooks, "Matthew 28:16–20"; Kingsbury, "Composition and Christology"; Keener, "Matthew's Missiology." For a contrasting argument, see Sim, "Is Matthew?," 1–7.

26. Strecker, *Theology of the New Testament*, 364. Strecker titles the Gospel of Matthew the book of "the way of righteousness." Strecker defines righteousness (3:15; 5:6, 10, 20; 6:1, 33; 21:32) as "the comprehensive term for the right conduct of the disciples in general, and thus for the whole Christian community, that must be different from that of the Pharisees and scribes (5:20)." Jesus' righteousness involves the inner and outer righteousness. Strecker argues that Matthean righteousness is "the human answer to the redemptive act of God." It is a demand, and not a "gift" obtained for human beings by Jesus' suffering as atonement or substitutionary death. For a history of research on the law and righteousness in Matthew, see Deines, "Not the Law but the Messiah," 53–84. In Pennington, *Sermon on the Mount*, 87–90, Pennington defines righteousness in Matthew as "whole person behavior that accords with God's nature, will, and coming kingdom." And the righteous person is "the one who follows Jesus in this way of being in the world . . . the *whole/teleios* person (5:48) who does not just do the will of God externally but from the heart" (in contrast to the Pharisees) (91, emphasis his).

27. See, Luz, *Matthew 1–7*, 198. Luz notes that the repentance is "the entry gate" to the greater righteousness of the sermon and *dominates* it. Also, in Gundry, *Matthew*, 46–47, Gundry notes that this fruit points to genuineness righteousness. This righteousness is of the true Abrahamic descendant in contrast to the wicked Pharisees and Sadducees (3:7–9).

28. They are also related to the Matthean eschatological judgment theme, along

The opening commandment of Jesus in public ministry, μετανοέω governs the theme of righteousness, doing good, and doing the will of God as outward expressions or fruits of μετάνοια. The close location of 4:17 and Jesus' sayings about righteousness in 5:17-20 implies that "the demand for repentance is a demand for righteousness. Righteousness in Matthew is about how one lives in relationship to God in terms of God's will for what is right."[29] The worthy fruit of μετάνοια in 3:8 implies that Matthean language of doing good and doing the will of God comprise μετάνοια as significant theme in Matthew. Also, since μετάνοια denotes a change of one's mind and works, the Matthean emphasis on changing one's heart (5:8, 28; 6:21; 9:4; 12:34; 13:15; 15:8, 18, 19; 18:35; 22:37) also demonstrates the essence of μετάνοια. Specifically, "all righteousness" (3:15) and "higher righteousness" (5:20) show the essence of the worthy fruit μετάνοια to change both mind and conduct. In these conceptual ways Matthean μετάνοια dominates the book.

Eighth, Μετάνοια appears as a significant Matthean soteriological theme because the summary phrase 4:17 states that μετάνοια is required in the coming kingdom.[30] The first words of John and Jesus in Matthew 3:2-12 and 4:17 govern the soteriological theme and language, expressed in ideas such as entering the kingdom of heaven (5:20; 7:21, 18:3; 19:23, 24; 23:13; 25:10, 21, 23), eternal life (7:14; 18:8, 9; 19:17), and judgment such as "being thrown into hell, eternal fire or darkness" (3:10, 11, 12; 5:22, 29, 30; 7:19; 8:12, 29; 10:28; 13:40, 42, 50; 17:15; 18:8, 9, 34; 22:13; 23:15, 33; 24:51; 25:30, 41). Theses expression show the significance of the summary phrase 4:17 which commands μετάνοια and the coming kingdom of heaven. Scholars have noted righteousness, doing good, and doing the will of God in the Matthean salvation structure.[31] As noted above, these ideas are outward expressions of μετάνοια demonstrating the significance of μετάνοια in the Matthean salvation structure. Matthean soteriology demonstrates the significance of μετάνοια in the Gospel of Matthew.

---

with 4:17, such as entering "the kingdom of heaven" or life (5:20; 7:13, 21; 18:3, 8, 9; 19:17, 23, 24; 23:13; 25:10, 21, 23) or eternal fire (3:10, 11, 12; 5:22; 7:19; 13:40, 42, 50; 17:15; 18:8, 9; 25:41)."

29. Nave, *Role and Function of Repentance*, 92.

30. See Runesson, *Divine Wrath and Salvation*, 119.

31. See Marxsen, *New Testament Foundations*, 231-48. For covenantal nomism's understanding of the Matthean salvation structure, see Luomanen, *Entering the Kingdom of Heaven*; Mohrlang, *Matthew and Paul*; Runesson, *Divine Wrath and Salvation*. Some scholars argue for divine initiative grace based on human works; see Kupp, *Matthew's Emmanuel*. See also Talbert, *Matthew*, 13-27. Some argue that both indicative and imperative are present in Matthew but that Matthew does not systematically develop a clear relation between the two (see Luz, *Matthew 1-7*, 201-2).

Ninth, each of the five major discourse blocks of Matthew (5–7, 10, 13, 18, 23–25) show the significance of μετάνοια in Jesus' teaching. Following John the Baptist's introductory μετάνοια preaching block in 3:1–12, the five major Matthean discourse blocks (5–7; 10; 13; 18; 23–25) continue to communicate the theme of μετάνοια in a variety of ways, thus demonstrating the significance of μετάνοια. In detail, the proximity of 4:17 and the sermon indicates that the sermon elaborates the theme of μετάνοια, showing μετάνοια's nature, contents, its necessity, and its corresponding judgment. In the sermon, Jesus proclaims that Israel, who thought themselves righteous, are sinners who need μετάνοια. The Beatitudes consist of the contents of fruits worthy of μετάνοια (5:3–12). The repeated occurrences of the term "good" in 3:8, 10 and 5:16 shows the Beatitudes are the contents of good fruits worthy of μετάνοια. Matthew 5:16 denotes that the characters in the nine Beatitudes are the essence of good works or characters that the disciples have to have. The term "good works" in 5:16 also occurs in 3:8 as "fruit worthy of μετάνοια" and 3:10 "good fruits." These repeated occurrences of the term "good works" and "good fruits" indicate that the nine characters of the Beatitudes consist of good fruits worthy of μετάνοια.

The reverse, the antitheses, also reveals μετάνοια (5:20–45). In the Antitheses, Jesus reinterprets the Torah and rebukes Israel and her leaders for their sinful nature. Each Antithesis comprises the contents of μετάνοια. Matthew 6–7 also shows the contents of μετάνοια in terms of hypocritical law keeping, prayer, faith, and judgment. The final remark of the sermon (7:16–29) includes a commandment to bear good fruit worthy of μετάνοια for entering into the kingdom of heaven, a rephrasing of 4:17: "Not everyone who says to me, 'Lord, Lord' will enter the kingdom of heaven, but the one who does the will of my father who is in heaven" (7:21).[32] And the parable of the house on sand and rock (7:24–27) reasserts the opening commandment of turning (μετανοέω) and its implications proclaimed in the sermon.

Matthew 10 functions as a universal μετάνοια commission. The context and redaction of Matthew 10 and the parallel universal μετάνοια conceptual materials indicate this passage serves as the commissioning of the twelve apostles (10:2) for the universal μετάνοια mission. Jesus commands his apostles to preach what he preached (4:17 and 10:7) to Israel (10:5–6) and gentiles (10:8, 17, 18, 34). In fact, Matthew 10 expands the Great Commission that sends the apostles to the world for the universal μετάνοια commission. Matthew 10:5–6 indicates the church's priority is to

---

32. See Donahue, *Gospel in Parable*, 90–91. Donahue states that "fruit is a metaphor for repentance, conversion, and actions that manifest such conversion. John proclaims to the Pharisees and the Sadducees, 'Bear fruit that befits repentance' (Matt 3:8) and says that every tree 'that does not bear good fruit is cut down and thrown into the fire'" (3:10).

preach the gospel to Jewish people rather than Jesus' restriction of gentile mission. In addition, Matthew 10 includes teachings on the life of μετάνοια. The language of being "worthy" (ἄξιος) in 10:11, 13, 37, 38 connects the worthy fruit of μετάνοια (3:8; 22:8) and the language of "receiving a prophet" in 10:14, 40, 41 conceptually refers to receiving John and Jesus' message of μετάνοια as well. Matthew10:37–39 especially explains the nature of the fruit worthy of μετάνοια in relation to Jesus—one must love Jesus more than one's biological family and take one's cross and follow Jesus. Jesus explains what μετάνοια looks like in each of these passages.

In Matthew 13, Jesus and the kingdom of heaven receive a mixed reception. He then uses parables to describe this mixed reception and encourage μετάνοια in view of the coming kingdom.[33] Jesus hides the mystery of the kingdom of heaven and his previous message of μετάνοια through parables for those who reject his teaching. However, he privately explains the message of μετάνοια and the kingdom of heaven in the parables for his followers. A near- and larger-context study of the chapter demonstrates the significance of μετάνοια in Jesus' parables. Matthew 13's opening phrase in 12:50 illustrates μετάνοια the same way as in 7:21, indicating that the theme of μετάνοια is found throughout the parables. In addition, Matthew 13 includes many parallel concepts related to μετάνοια and corresponding judgment: bearing good fruit (13:8, 32, 33, 44, 46), entering into the kingdom of heaven, eternal life, or eternal fire (13:30, 42, 43, 48–50), and so on. Specifically, the fifth and sixth parables exactly match 4:17. First, the presence of the kingdom of heaven in 4:17 is perfectly expressed in the images of the hidden treasure found in front of a man and the pearl of great value found in front of a merchant. Second, the commandment of turning (μετανοέω) is perfectly described in the image of the man and the merchant selling all they have and buying the treasure and the pearl, which refers to turning one's whole life to Jesus by believing in him and following his commandments.

Matthew 18, the community discourse, begins with the commandment, "turn and become like children" (18:3–4). This passage is a rephrasing of 4:17 because it uses στρέφω, "to turn," a synonym of μετανοέω. In other words, Matthew 18 commands μετάνοια in the community. This opening commandment of turning (μετανοέω) shows the significance of μετάνοια in the community discourse. Matthew 18 also includes parallel μετάνοια and corresponding reward and judgment language (18:3, 6, 7, 8, 9, 14, etc.) echoing the commandment of turning (μετανοέω) in the beginning of

---

33. See, Davies and Allison, *Matthew 8–18*, 374–77. See ch. 9 for a survey of scholarship.

Jesus' ministry (4:17). In particular, the parable of the lost sheep (18:10–14) explains the heavenly value of one who sins (or wanders) but turns back (μετανοέω). Matthew 18:15–20 deals with role of the instituted church in carrying out μετάνοια. Jesus' teachings on unlimited forgiveness (18:21–22) in the church, and the unforgiving tenants (18:23–35) encourage sinners to turn (μετανοέω) because they will be forgiven.[34]

Matthew 23, in contrast with the nine blessings of μετάνοια in Matthew 5, deals with seven woes as the negative content of μετάνοια. The judgment language in Matthew 24 is a warning and consequence of eschatological universal μετάνοια. The two parables of the kingdom of heaven in Matthew 25 insist on a wise and faithful life as a way to be ready for the second coming of Christ. As John the Baptist commands μετάνοια in preparation for the coming of the Christ, Matthew 25 also commands believers to be ready for the coming of the Christ through wise and faithful life of μετάνοια in humility and servanthood (23:11–12; 25:34–46).

Conclusion

In conclusion, this overview introduction chapter tries to show the significance of μετάνοια in Matthew. The lexical idea of μετάνοια means a change of mind (or heart, will, thinking) and behavior, and so in turn of one's whole being and life. The Gospel of Matthew begins Jesus' public ministry with the commandment of μετάνοια (4:17) to emphasize the significance of μετάνοια in Matthew. This opening commandment of turning necessitates further explanation and the contents of μετάνοια. The contents of μετάνοια is fully revealed throughout the body of Matthew in various ways. In sum, John the Baptist's μετάνοια preaching (3:2–12) first introduces the thematic significance of μετάνοια and the fruit worthy of μετάνοια in Matthew. Discipleship, the language of righteousness, doing the will of God, changing one's heart and mind, the Great Commission, and Matthean soteriological theme convey the essence of μετάνοια and the contents of the fruit worthy of μετάνοια. The five major Matthean discourse blocks (5–7; 10; 13; 18; 23–25) restate the theme of μετάνοια in a variety ways. The Sermon on the Mount comprises the nature of μετάνοια and fruit worthy of μετάνοια. Matthew 10 charges the apostles to proclaim μετάνοια. Matthew 13 illustrates Jesus' μετάνοια ministry and its mixed reception and exhorts μετάνοια through parables. Matthew 18 commands μετάνοια through humility and servanthood using its synonym στρέφω, "to turn" (18:3). Matthew 23–25

---

34. See Runesson, *Divine Wrath and Salvation*, 119–36 for the inseparable relationship between repentance and forgiveness.

shows the negative contents of μετάνοια (Matt 23), proclaims the judgment of the coming kingdom (Matt 24), and directs listeners to be ready for the second coming of Christ (Matt 25) paralleling John the Baptist's ministry of μετάνοια and its worthy fruit as preparation for the first coming of Christ (3:2–3). I suggest when one asks when or what is one's turning point or what and who leads one and one's life change, Christians should be reminded of the significance of Matthean Jesus' calling of μετάνοια, turn and change your entire life to follow the Son of the living God, who brings his kingdom of heaven to the earth.

Chapter 2

History of Research

BIBLICAL RESEARCH ON REPENTANCE (μετανοέω and μετάνοια) has only recently received interest from scholars. The greatest effort to research the biblical theme of repentance is found in Mark Boda's several works. Boda recently published a book about a biblical theology of repentance, *'Return to Me': A Biblical Theology of Repentance*, which follows his editing work for *Repentance in Christian Theology*. In his section on the history of literature on the biblical theme of repentance, Boda emphasizes that there has been no interest in the theme of repentance within biblical studies for the last fifty years.[1] And no work has been done on Matthean repentance as a significant idea within Matthew's Gospel.

This section first gives an overall history of research on the theme of repentance (μετάνοια), then, looks at a chronological review of the biblical theological works on μετανοέω and μετάνοια in the Gospels and Matthew. Since this book does not have independent chapters for the background study of μετάνοια but focuses on the Matthean μετάνοια theme, this second part will provide a basic background study of μετάνοια in the OT, NT, and Second Temple literatures.

Overall History of Research of the Theme of Repentance (μετάνοια)

In general, few works were found in the early twenty-first century that focused on a lexical and background study of repentance (μετανοέω and μετάνοια) in the OT, Second Temple literature, or secular Greek literature.[2] Likewise, few works are available from the mid-twentieth century that

---

1. Boda, *'Return to Me.'*
2. Thompson, "Metanoeō and Metamelei"; Dirksen, *New Testament Concept*; Bhem, *TDNT*, 4:975–80; Würthwein, *TDNT*, 4:980–88; Thompson and Martens, *New International Dictionary*, 4:55–59.

examine repentance (μετανοέω and μετάνοια) as a NT theme.³ Including Boda's, several works have recently been written in the biblical guild including biblical theology, the Sermon on the Mount, Luke-Acts, Johannine writings, and Pauline letters.⁴ Specifically, recent works on Luke-Acts repentance (μετανοέω and μετάνοια) argue for repentance as one of the driving ideas of Luke-Acts.⁵

These works show that μετανοέω and μετάνοια do not mean to regret and stop past sins but refer to a lifelong change of heart and behavior, or of one's whole being and life. They also show a trend to study repentance (μετανοέω and μετάνοια) not only through word statistics but also conceptually, including synonyms, different repentance languages, images, and so on. This book deals conceptually with repentance (μετανοέω and μετάνοια) as one of the driving ideas of the Gospel of Matthew.

Repentance (μετάνοια) in the Gospels and Matthew

William D. Chamberlain argues for the importance of repentance in the Gospels and the need to restudy the term's biblical meaning. He first asserts the importance of repentance because the Synoptics report it at the front of both John the Baptist's and Jesus Christ's ministry. Secondly, Chamberlain asserts the need for retranslation of μετανοέω and μετάνοια. The English words "repent" and "repentance" cause a shallow understanding of repentance as "emotionalism or sacramentarianism," and this translation causes the church to lose its proper practice in the world.⁶ Chamberlain criticizes Tyndale's English translations of "repent" and "repentance" because it only emphasizes regret, remorse, and morbid introspection.⁷ Thirdly, Chamberlain revisits the Reformers' teachings on repentance, in which their emphasis "on the transformation of the whole mind, heart, and will

---

3. Chamberlain, *Meaning of Repentance*; Chamberlain, "For Deliverance and Freedom," 271–83; Vos, "Meaning of Repentance," 98–104.

4. Boda and Smith, *Repentance in Christian Theology*; Wilkin, "Repentance"; Etzioni and Carney, *Repentance*; Merklein, "Die Umkehrpredigt," 29–46; Nave, *The Role and Function of Repentance*; Bailey, "Repentance in Luke-Acts"; Kintu, "Repentance in the Sermon on the Mount"; Schnabel, "Repentance in Paul's Letters," 159–86; Porter "Penitence and Repentance in the Epistles," 127–52; Humphrey "And I Shall Heal Them," 105–26.

5. Nave, *Role and Function of Repentance*; Bailey, "Repentance in Luke-Acts"; Dupont, "Repentir et Conversion," 137–73; Michiels, "Conception Lucanienne de La Conversion," 42–78.

6. Chamberlain, *Meaning of Repentance*, 17.

7. Chamberlain, *Meaning of Repentance*, 29.

of man" contrasts with the Catholic emphasis on penitential practices.[8] "A transformation of the mind transforms the man; a transformation of the man transforms his conduct."[9] Fourth, Chamberlain points out Paul's use of μετανοέω and μετάνοια in which "repentance is more than godly sorrow for sin (2 Cor 7:8-10)."[10] Fifth, he points to the failure to distinguish μετανοέω from μεταμέλομαι, which is also translated "repent" in the King James Version (Matt 21:29, 32; 27:3; 2 Cor 7:8; Heb 2:7), because the former means to change one's mind and life, and the latter means "regret or sorrow for what has been done."[11] Finally, Chamberlain briefly studies the history of interpretation of those who have protested the misunderstanding of μετανοέω and μετάνοια and concludes that "Repentance is a pilgrimage from the mind of the flesh to the mind of Christ."[12]

Chamberlain examines the Gospels' emphasis on repentance. Chamberlain again asserts that the location of repentance at the beginning of Matthew (Matt 3:2; 4:17) indicates that repentance reverberates throughout the whole NT.[13] Chamberlain defines repentance in John the Baptist's preaching in Matthew 3:2-8 (and Luke 3) as "reformation in conduct, and transformation of mental outlook"[14] because John demanded the fruit of repentance and destroyed the ethnic privileges of Israel. Jesus elaborates on repentance in relation to "happiness, righteousness, the nature of God and

---

8. Chamberlain, *Meaning of Repentance*, 22.
9. Chamberlain, *Meaning of Repentance*, 22.
10. Chamberlain, *Meaning of Repentance*, 25.
11. Chamberlain, *Meaning of Repentance*, 30-31.
12. Here is Chamberlain's history of interpretation: "(1) Tertullian said μετανοέω was not to confess a sin but to change one's mind. . . . (2) Lactantius (A.D. 260-330) and Theodore Beza with him said μετανοέω was 'a return to a right understanding' so 'a recovery of one's mind.' . . . (3) The Geneva Bible translated μετανοέω 'Amend your lyves.' . . . (4) John Calvin defined μετανοέω as a 'change of mind and intention,' in other words, 'the change of the life design: the whole life pattern is changed; the goal of life is different; the aspirations are different.' . . . (5) Jeremy Taylor (seventeenth-century bishop) said, 'To repent is to 'turn' from darkness to light, from the power of Satan to God, doing works worthy of amendment of life, for the forgiveness of sins, that we may receive inheritance among them that are sanctified by faith in Christ Jesus.' . . . (6) George Campbell translated μετανοέω and μετάνοια 'reform' and 'reformation.' . . . (7) Coleridge suggested 'transmutation,' which refers to 'a transposed mind which thinks new thoughts, aspires for better things and acknowledges a new sovereignty—God's will, not one's own.' . . . (8) Matthew Arnold said, 'The main part of μετάνοια is active and fruitful, the setting up of an immense new inward movement for obtaining the rule of life'" (Chamberlain, Meaning of Repentance, 36-47).
13. Chamberlain, *Meaning of Repentance*, 35.
14. Chamberlain, *Meaning of Repentance*, 52.

of his kingdom," especially in the sermon.¹⁵ From the Four Gospels Chamberlain briefly examines Mark 6:12; 8:35; Luke 5:32; 10:13; 11:32 and John 10:10 and summarizes repentance as a change to a new center of life, "Not my will, but thine, be done,"¹⁶ in other words, a change of the mind of the flesh to the mind of Christ. He says repentance is the purpose of God for all nations and that the Acts of the Apostles is a story of apostles carrying repentance to all nations.¹⁷

Chamberlain's work is important for opening a discussion on repentance and it reveals the need for restudy of repentance (μετανοέω and μετάνοια). My thesis affirms Chamberlain's definition of repentance (μετανοέω and μετάνοια). Repentance is not a gloomy feeling of regret or remorse but a bright life of turning to the light of the world, Jesus Christ. We should think of repentance with a picture of Jesus' disciples turning and following Jesus, leaving everything behind when he called them. In particular, Chamberlain's comment on the negative understanding of repentance that leads to the church's lack of proper action in the world is reasonable. This indicates the importance of the restudy of repentance in the church today where people become Christians with a cheap gospel. Also, his brief history of the protest against the misunderstanding of repentance is helpful for revealing the need for restudy of repentance (μετανοέω and μετάνοια). However, Chamberlain's work does not deal with repentance (μετανοέω and μετάνοια) as a leading idea of any NT book but reveals its importance in NT study overall. Chamberlain hints in his book that the Gospel of Matthew includes repentance, but I further say that repentance (μετανοέω and μετάνοια) is a significant theme of the Gospel of Matthew.

Similarly, C. E. Carlston argues the significant point that the Synoptic Gospels do not include μετανοέω and μετάνοια many times, but the prominent location of these words strongly indicates that Jesus' ministry is a repentance ministry, especially in terms of his teaching.¹⁸ All the Synoptic Gospels summarize Jesus' ministry with repentance (Matt 4:17; 10:7; Mark 1:15; 6:12; Luke 5:32; 24:46). Repentance with eschatological pressure (*the Psalms of Solomon* and *Jubilees*) emphasizes one's allegiance more than one's ethical standing.¹⁹ John the Baptist's repentance is an

---

15. Chamberlain, *Meaning of Repentance*, 54.
16. Chamberlain, *Meaning of Repentance*, 59.
17. Chamberlain, *Meaning of Repentance*, 60–61.
18. Carlston, "Metanoia and Church Discipline."
19. Carlston, "Metanoia and Church Discipline," 3. Carlston examines Philo's understanding of repentance as "change of mind and regret and also conversion from sin to God" (3) without an eschatological emphasis. And Josephus's repentance is simply "obedience to the Law" (3). Qumran documents emphasized eschatological repentance

eschatologically urgent, motivated prophetic demand including judgment on Israel and forming a separate Baptist sect.[20] Carlston distinguishes Jesus' repentance calling as more than John the Baptist's calling since Jesus inaugurated the future kingdom.[21]

Robert Nicholas Wilkin argues that repentance in the Gospels is a condition for salvation and requires a change of thinking and attitude concerning oneself, Jesus Christ, idols, and God to avoid eternal judgment.[22] Also, he argues that repentance does not require good deeds as a precursor but appropriate fruit, and it requires the absolute lordship of Jesus in one's life. And repentance in the Gospels does not require acts of penance nor sorrow over one's sins.[23] He suggests an English translation of μετανοέω as "to change one's mind (or thinking)."[24]

While Wilkin's study is mainly limited to the places where the term μετανοέω and μετάνοια occur (3:2–15;[25] 4:17;[26] 12:41), he widens it a bit to conceptual repentance: (1) In Matthew 9:13 and 11:20–21, Jesus declares that he came to call sinners, not the (self) righteous; (2) in 18:1–4, στρέφω occurs; (3) in 21:28–32, the parable of two sons is conceptual repentance.[27] Wilkin's study of Matthean repentance only examines how Matthew

---

and the division between sectarians, the true Israel, and outsiders. Repentance in Rabbinic literature emphasizes "the life of the pious Israelite" (3) including the genuine abandonment of sin, contrition, confession, and restitution. Rabbinic repentance is a daily rather than once-for-all act as the prerequisite of blessing.

20. Carlston, "Metanoia and Church Discipline," 7.
21. Carlston, "Metanoia and Church Discipline," 7–8.
22. Wilkin, "Repentance as a Condition."
23. Wilkin, "Repentance as a Condition," 197–203.
24. Wilkin, "Repentance as a Condition," 207.
25. Wilkin examines John the Baptist's preaching as likely being rabbinic preaching of *teshuba*, which "calls Israel to turn from sins and to commit wholeheartedly to obeying God." He interprets 3:2–15 by saying that John mainly preached repentance by commanding Israel to put down self-righteous attitudes and favoritism as a seed of Abraham but to confess their sins, bearing fruits worthy of repentance and believe Jesus Christ. John enforced his repentance preaching with strong judgment language (Wilkin, "Repentance as a Condition," 96).
26. Jesus' repentance preaching in the beginning of his public ministry in 4:17 is "a call for people to change their attitude and thinking about themselves (i.e., to give up self-righteous thinking and instead to recognize one's sinfulness and need of forgiveness)" (Wilkin, "Repentance as a Condition," 102).
27. Wilkin, "Repentance as a Condition," 95–117. Wilkin exegetes 18:1–4, another example of Matthean repentance in that one must realize their smallness before God. I think "to be a child" means to be the least in the world as a worthy fruit of repentance. Lastly, in the parable of the two sons he explains religious leaders' need to change their self-righteous attitude. It explains true repentance with fruits worthy of repentance.

understands repentance, which is helpful to define Matthean repentance, but his work does not deal with repentance as a main theme of the Gospel of Matthew, and he limits his work to word occurrence.

Helmut Merklein has done work on the repentance preaching of John the Baptist and Jesus.[28] He notes that μετανοέω plays a major role in the Gospels. Its concept is in all the Gospels through a line of ministry from John the Baptist and Jesus to the apostles. μετανοέω appears almost exclusively in the context of the ministry of John the Baptist and Jesus. Merklein's basic understanding of μετανοέω is that studying its semantic roots in the Greek is not sufficient, but the OT and Jewish tradition are also needed. In the German "umkehren," "umkehr" (reverse, reversal) are best suited.[29] He says the repentance message of John and Jesus is radical and eschatological. He mostly deals with Lucan repentance material. Repentance is not what the son can do before forgiveness, but what he can do after forgiveness.[30]

Jacques Dupont examines the theme of repentance and conversion in the Acts of the Apostles.[31] Dupont's work is important because it deals with the theme of repentance and conversion in a particular NT book. As the title indicates, Dupont sees the NT concepts of repentance and conversion as equal. He notes that the Septuagint (LXX) uses ἐπιστρέφω to translate šub, but the NT uses μετανοέω as its counterpart. While he tried to distinguish conversion and repentance in Acts by proposing that ἐπιστρέφω is related to "convert" and μετανοέω to "repent,"[32] the text does not clearly distinguish them. It is rather understood that the meaning of μετανοέω changed to šub during the intertestamental period.[33] Dupont also argues that Jesus' death and resurrection are key aspects of the theme of repentance because they appear together many times in the preaching of the apostles.[34]

---

28. Merklein, "Die Umkehrpredigt," 29–46.

29. Merklein, "Die Umkehrpredigt," 29–30.

30. Merklein, "Die Umkehrpredigt," 44. From Luke 13:3–5 he says turning away is the basic character of repentance: repentance requires distance from everything. From Luke 10:13–15 and 11:31 he declares that Jesus' miracles are for repentance. He also interprets the parable of the prodigal son in Luke 15 through the repentance theme. He warns against reading the return of the son as being the same as repentance, but focuses instead on the action of the father running to his son with joy and hugging and kissing him as signs of forgiveness before his son confesses his fault.

31. Dupont, "Repentir et Conversion," 137–73.

32. Dupont, "Repentir et Conversion," 138.

33. *ABD* 6:654–73.

34. Dupont, "Repentir et Conversion," 149.

Robrecht Michiels has written a work on the Lucan concept of conversion, based on μετανοέω and ἐπιστρέφω.³⁵ Michiels notes μετανοέω in the Synoptic Gospels as an eschatological concept continuing the OT prophetic call to conversion or condemnation. μετανοέω is total conversion, once for all. It conveys a total change, particularly a return to God to escape his wrath and to enter his reign.³⁶

Jon Nelson Bailey argues that repentance is most prominent in Luke-Acts based on word statistics because μετανοέω and μετάνοια occur in Luke-Acts more than in any other of the NT books.³⁷ He also notes that repentance appears conceptually without these terms in Luke-Acts, arguing that the concept of "conversion" is not different from repentance. He says, "For Luke, repentance is a change of attitudes and actions, resulting in a life of faith and ethical righteousness."³⁸ This is the same in Matthew, as I will argue.

Bailey's helpful contribution is his thorough examination of the religio-historical background of repentance μετανοέω and μετάνοια from

---

35. Michiels, "Conception Lucanienne de La Conversion," 42–78. Michiels examines almost every Lucan passage where μετανοέω and ἐπιστρέφω appear. He argues that Acts especially proclaims repentance for Jesus' death (47) and includes the concept of repentance through moral content (49) and gentile repentance from the sin of idolatry (53). Michiels also emphasizes the content of repentance in apostolic preaching: moral behavior, sin, Jesus' murder, and the impiety of idolatry. He also notes that Luke refers to μετανοέω as a permanent moral disposition of the Christian life (Luke 3:8; 17:3, 4; Acts 26:20), which is related to the new life of Christians (76). Finally, he argues that the theme of repentance in Luke-Acts is universal and this universal repentance is dominant throughout Acts, with the apostle Paul's repentance mission ending in Rome, the very center of the pagan world (77–78).

36. Michiels, "Conception Lucanienne de La Conversion," 75–76.

37. Bailey, "Repentance in Luke-Acts." The 22 occurrences of μετανοέω and μετάνοια in Luke-Acts is relatively frequent compared with the other Synoptic Gospels (seven times in Matthew, three times in Mark). This frequency indicates that Luke-Acts is driven by repentance theme.

38. Bailey, "Repentance in Luke-Acts," 285. Bailey distinguishes between two kinds of repentance in Luke-Acts: Jews' and gentiles.' For the Jews, repentance involves acknowledging their rejection of Jesus and his death and believing in him for salvation and eternal life. For the gentiles, repentance requires turning from idols to the risen Jesus, the true God. Bailey also argues that different NT authors have different understandings of repentance. Specifically, Luke develops his own view on repentance by combining ideas from the OT, early Judaism, early Christianity, and Hellenistic ideas of repentance μετανοέω and μετάνοια, which were related to gentile Christians' prior religious conversion and moral transformation. Bailey says, "Lukan Repentance is a transformation of belief, involving faith in God and in Jesus as the Messiah and risen Lord. Repentance is also a change of behavior involving a life of ethical righteousness in the Christian community" (4).

OT,[39] the Qumran documents,[40] Rabbinic Judaism,[41] and the Hellenistic idea.[42] Bailey's great work on the background study provides evidence that μετανοέω and μετάνοια involve both a change of mind and deeds, thus one's being and whole life.

39. Bailey, "Repentance in Luke-Acts," 32. He briefly explains repentance as "a religious reorientation in which people turn away from sin, and turn to God and a life of righteousness," a physical action of turning, moral, spiritual, or religious turning; "turning from evil and turning to God" (Jer 3:6–25; 4:1; 5:3; 15:7; 18:8; 26:3; 36:3; Ezek 3:19; 18:21–32; 33:7–16; Hos 3:5; 5:4; 6:1; 7:10; 11:5; Amos 4:6–13) (30–32). Deuteronomy 30:10, for example, indicates that repentance is "a change not only in what the Israelites believe, think, and feel, but also a change in how they live (Isa 1:16–20; 58:5–14; Mic 6:6–8)" (31). In addition he points out that Jonah 3:5–10 emphasizes the repentance of gentiles or non-Israelites to God. Bailey also emphasizes the role of the prophetic spokesperson in returning to righteousness and restoring the covenantal relationship (32). Bailey further explains that OT repentance includes prophetic spokespersons demanding change and reactions: regret, sorrow, or shame, expressed as fasting, weeping, mourning, offering sacrifices, confessing sins, wearing sackcloth, sitting in ashes (Deut 8:11–20; 11:1–28; Judg 20:26; 1 Sam 7:3–6; 2 Sam 1:11–12; 12:16–23; 1 Kgs 21:27–29; 2 Kgs 19:1–2; 2 Chr 20:3–12; Ezra 9:1–15; 10:1; Neh 1:4–11; 9:1–37; Job 1:20; 2:8; 16:15–16; 42:5–6; Pss 32:5; 35:13–14; 44:1–26; Isa 1:10–15; Jer 6:26; Dan 9:3–19; Joel 1:5–14; 2:12–17; Jonah 3:5–8), and fasting and confession on the Day of Atonement (Lev 16:29–34; 23:27–32; Num 29:7). Bailey points out that in the LXX μετανοέω and μετάνοια indicate "a change of one's beliefs and behavior, a transformation of one's attitudes and actions. . . . It is required of all people throughout the world, and not just the Israelites" (35). From the Pseudepigrapha he concludes μετανοέω/μετάνοια is an intellectual and emotional change with penitence toward a life of righteousness by a sinner as the way to avoid God's judgment (41).

40. Bailey, "Repentance in Luke-Acts," 35. Bailey points to repentance as essential for the Qumran sect. Qumran repentance was not only penitence but also "a change of beliefs and behavior resulting in a new social and religious identity as a member of a separate sect of Judaism" (35). He also emphasizes that the "Teacher of Righteousness" was crucial for the repentance of the sect, which thought it was the true Israel in a new covenant with God (35).

41. Bailey, "Repentance in Luke-Acts," 49. For Rabbinic Judaism, repentance was not only feeling remorse for past sins, but also the reforming of life, cessation of all evil behavior, and restitution of wealth earned through sinful deeds. b. Ta'an 16a; b. B. Qam. 66a, 94a–b; b. B. Bat. 88b; b. Sanh. 25a–b; b. 'Abod. Zar. 17a–b. In addition, the need for repentance extends beyond Israel to all nations (Song Rab. 5:16.5), and the Messiah will come and guide people from all nations in the way of repentance (Song Rab. 7:5.3) (49).

42. Bailey, "Repentance in Luke-Acts," 95. The Hellenistic idea of μετανοέω and μετάνοια expresses various changes in the mind, will, emotions, and even behavior. These changes usually denote specific sins but also "a change of one's entire orientation or way of life" (94). Bailey includes Philo: "For Philo, these two terms are associated with the conversion of Gentiles to Judaism and denote turning from sin (especially idolatry) to God to begin a life of virtue. However, these terms also describe the change of attitude and actions by anyone, even a Jew, who turns to God from a life of ignorance, incontinence, injustice, or immorality. And for Philo, μετάνοια is actually considered a virtue in the life of a wise person" (94).

While Bailey argues for the conceptual appearance of repentance in Luke-Acts, he seems not to examine the concept of repentance in the Gospel of Matthew. Based on word statistics, Bailey does not find the Matthean significance on repentance. Bailey's Lukan understanding of repentance does not differ from the Matthean understanding. Bailey argues that Matthean repentance (Matt 3:2, 8; 4:17) is a one-time act, not a continuing act of community life, because Matthew does not give a full explanation of the fruits worthy of repentance (3:8) or the content of the repentance.[43] Bailey says that Matthean repentance applies only to Jews to avoid judgment and to accept Jesus as the Messiah.[44] However, the sermon is a fuller explanation of repentance than any Lucan discourse. Matthew 18, which has been known as "Community Rules," actually deals with a continuing life of repentance. In addition, Bailey's OT background argument also parallels repentance in the Gospel of Matthew. For example, gentile repentance in Jonah clearly shares the gentile repentance theme of the Gospel of Matthew. Also, Bailey's study on the Second Temple literature and Classical and Hellenistic Greek usage supports the whole person change understanding of Matthean repentance.

Guy D. Nave says that even though the terms μετανοέω and μετάνοια occur primarily in the Four Gospels and Acts, the concept of repentance is found throughout the NT. While the traditional understanding of μετανοέω and μετάνοια does not agree that they were influenced by the pre-Christian Greek meaning but only derived from the OT, Nave argues they were influenced by contemporary Greek concepts of μετανοέω and μετάνοια, which meant "a fundamental change in thinking that leads to a fundamental change in behavior and/or way of living."[45] The biblical terms μετανοέω and μετάνοια were influenced by Hellenistic ideas of μετανοέω and μετάνοια and show that repentance involves life transformation.[46]

43. Bailey, "Repentance in Luke-Acts," 65.

44. Bailey, "Repentance in Luke-Acts," 66.

45. Nave, *Role and Function of Repentance*, 89. I think that not only secular Greek usages of μετανοέω and μετάνοια of that time carry the meaning but also references from the OT.

46. Nave, *Role and Function of Repentance*, 69–70. From Classical and Hellenistic Greek literature (HGL), including from the fifth century BCE (Epicharmus and Democritus); fourth century (Xenophon); third centurym (Stoic Chrysippus, according to fifth-century author Stobaeus); second century (Polybius); first century (Diodorus Siculus); and others (Dio Chrysostom, Appian, Lucian, Pausanias, Chariton, Plutarch, Antiphon, Timaeus of Tauromenium, Epictetus, Marcus Aurelius, and so on), Nave analyzes μετανοέω and μετάνοια: (1) They did not merely denote "thinking afterwards" but instead "change in thinking," (2) "to think differently, to change one's mind or view, to form a different opinion, plan or purpose," (3) "A sense of regret and or remorse is implied as part of the meaning of them, which suggests an emotional change of feeling and or belief as well as an intellectual change of mind," (4) They include "a sense of

Terms of μετανοέω and μετάνοια in the pseudepigrapha denote "moral, ethical, and religious transformations in the lives of idolatrous and sinful human beings."[47] While non-Jews' repentance involves turning from idols and false gods and turning to the God of Israel, Jews' repentance involves a return to God from wicked and sinful behavior, especially mistreating other human beings, in other words, "a moral and ethical transformation."[48] Nave concludes his interpretation of μετανοέω and μετάνοια with one phrase

---

regret and/or remorse because the past action or way of thinking is often later perceived as having been wrong, inappropriate, or disadvantageous," (5) They were expected to those who sin against divine being and human, (6) They "often occurred as a result of chiding, both divine and human, took placed in the form of speeches and/or messages of exhortations," (7) They provided a means for escaping judgment and punishment, (8) "Deeds had to accompany any and all claims of repentance. Genuine repentance was manifested by a demonstrable change of behavior," and (9) "Ultimately, the change in behavior resulting from μετανοέω led to forgiveness and reconciliation between estranged parties." Therefore, he concludes that non-Christian Greek thought influenced Christian μετανοέω and μετάνοια (69-70).

47. Nave, *Role and Function of Repentance*, 110. The following is a summary of Nave's definition of μετανοέω and μετάνοια in the pseudepigraphical documents. (1) *Jos. Asen.* - A fundamental change in the life of non-Hebrews; (2) *Sib. Or.* - Repentance is a moral and ethical transformation; (3) *Let. Aris.* - "you will convert them from evil and bring them to repentance"; (4) *Pr. Man.* - Repentance entails a sense of sorrow and remorse over sin. It is God's mercy and grace that leads sinners to repentance and that makes repentance available to them and secures their salvation; (5) *Apoc. Mos.* - Adam says "let us repent and offer prayer for forty days." Adam fasted for forty days and stood in the Jordan River praying and crying aloud to God that God might forgive him and Eve and have mercy upon them (29:11-14); (6) *T. Ab.* - "my heart is moved for sinners, so that they may convert and live (ἐπιστρέφω) and repent (μετανοέω) of their sins and be saved (σώζω)" (12:1-13); (7) *T. 12 Patr.* - Repentance is an appropriate response to sin and evil deeds; (8) Sir 17:24; 48:15; Wis 11:23. From these works the time of fulfillment had arrived with the expectation of divine judgment that is found in antecedent and contemporary Jewish literature.

48. Nave, *Role and Function of Repentance*, 110. Nave also examines Josephus and Philo. Josephus uses μετανοέω and μετάνοια seventy-seven times. Josephus uses these terms for human-God and human-human relationships. Nave explains that Philo's usages of μετανοέω and μετάνοια express the general notions of regret, remorse, and changing one's thinking and/or purpose. They mean to break sin and wrongdoing and to change one's behavior and conduct. In conclusion, Nave emphasizes that repentance in Philo expresses works and actions in an individual's entire lifestyle, one's way of life, and a virtuous and harmonious life (95-96).

For early Christian literature, Nave deals with *1 Epistle of Clement to the Corinthians* (1 Clem. 1-6; 7.2—8.5; 57.1-2; 65:1-2), Ignatius of Antioch (Ign. *Smyrn.* 4:1; 5:1-3; 8:1—9:1; Ign. *Phld.* 3:2; 8:1), *Epistle of Barnabas* (Barn. 1:5; 16:1, 6, 7-10) and *Didache* (Did. 10:6; 15:3). He concludes that they all entailed the Christian understanding of μετανοέω and μετάνοια, "a change in thinking and behavior that sought to address and correct one's relationship with God and Jesus, one's relationship with other human beings, and—as was the case in the late first and early second century—one's relationship with the church" (144).

from his background study: "a change in thinking that usually leads to a change in behavior and or way of life."[49] This definition is not different from Matthean μετανοέω and μετάνοια.

Nave also argues that only Luke-Acts develops the repentance theme throughout the book, according to word statistics (thirty-five occurrences in the Synoptics and Acts, twenty-five in Luke-Acts). The Lucan preaching of John the Baptist includes universal salvation through repentance (Luke 3:6) and gives specific behavioral demands (3:10–14), which will be further developed as Lucan social justice. Nave argues that Mark and Matthew do not explain the meaning or content of repentance.[50] However, Nave still argues that the location of the occurrences of μετανοέω and μετάνοια in Mark and Matthew, as a summary phrase in the beginning of Jesus' ministry (Mark 1:4, 15; 6:12; Matt 3:2; 4:17; 10:7), signifies how important repentance is to the ministries of John the Baptist, Jesus, and the apostles.

Nave correctly observes that Matthew demands a change in thinking and living in Jesus' teachings, especially in the sermon. He says that the close location of 4:17 and Jesus' sayings about righteousness in 5:17–20 implies that "the demand for repentance is a demand for righteousness. Righteousness in Matthew is about how one lives in relationship to God in terms of God's will for what is right."[51] The perfect corresponding parable, Nave points out, is the parable of two sons (Matt 21:28–32).[52] Matthew, I submit, actually develops 5:17–20, that is, the demand of the higher righteousness than of the Pharisees, by contrasting the Pharisees' interpretation of the Law with Jesus' reinterpretation of the Law in 5:21–48. Nave says 5:21–48 is Jesus' demand of "a fundamental change in thinking regarding what it means to live righteously."[53] He points out that Matthean righteousness is to live for others as Matthew declares twice the sum of the law and the prophets in 7:12 and 22:37–40: "In everything do to others as you would have them do to you;" "the first and the greatest commandment is to love God and the second is love your neighbor as yourself." Therefore, μετανοέω and μετάνοια is not only a private matter between God and an individual but also a public matter between the Christian and society (that is, one's neighbor).[54] The fruit-bearing images in the Gospel of Matthew (Matt 3:7–10) are part of the

---

49. Nave, *Role and Function of Repentance*, 145.
50. Nave, *Role and Function of Repentance*, 95–99.
51. Nave, *Role and Function of Repentance*, 92.
52. Nave, *Role and Function of Repentance*, 93.
53. Nave, *Role and Function of Repentance*, 93.
54. Nave, *Role and Function of Repentance*, 101.

repentance theme because repentance requires not only a change of thinking but also a change of behavior.⁵⁵

Even though Nave argues that only Luke-Acts develops the repentance theme, the sermon and the following teaching blocks in the Gospel of Matthew fully explain and demand repentance, possibly more than Luke-Acts does. Matthew does not use μετανοέω and μετάνοια directly, but conceptual references and similar repentance language are everywhere in the Gospel of Matthew. Matthew also includes the universal salvation theme through repentance and behavioral demands of repentance more than Luke-Acts does. The Gospel of Matthew, which is full of Jesus' teachings and miracles that prove the authority of his teachings, should be read with repentance in mind.

The Gospel of Matthew teaches that μετανοέω and μετάνοια are a matter between God and an individual, but it is always expressed in a public manner, that is, by doing good for neighbors. Likewise, the concept of repentance is dominant in the Gospel of Matthew. In fact, Nave's Lucan repentance helps to reveal Matthean repentance in which repentance always includes behavior change—good deeds—according to a change of one's heart. Also, the repentance-centered ministry of the Acts of the Apostles following Jesus' ministry proves that repentance was at the center of Jesus' public ministry.

Edith M. Humphrey's work looks at repentance in the Fourth Gospel.⁵⁶ I include this work because it shows the conceptual study of the theme of repentance. Humphrey begins her article by questioning the absence of μετανοέω and μετάνοια in the Fourth Gospel in comparison

---

55. Nave, *Role and Function of Repentance*, 94.

56. Humphrey, "And I Shall Heal Them," 105–26. Humphrey says that John does not use μετανοέω and μετάνοια but στρέφω (12:40) to remove the emotional aspect ("sorrow" or "regret") of one's turning to Jesus (109). Humphrey argues that "turning," which includes the physical action of turning, represents the theme of repentance in the Fourth Gospel (109–10). Here is Humphrey's explanation of the conceptual expression of μετάνοια in the Fourth Gospel. "Light comes into the world, and shines; we expect certain reactions to the light, and will not be disappointed. Before our eyes the world is divided into those who face light and follow, and those who turn away. Networks of metaphors spin the story, depicting those who stand, follow, come and see (1:35), who 'believe' (2:23–24) and 'come to the light' (3:20–21), who 'believe and obey' (3:36), who 'hear and believe' and so pass from death to life (5:22–24), who turn from food that perishes to food that endures (6:27), who come and drink (7:37), who are divided one from the other (7:40, 44), who are healed and told to sin no more (8:11), who follow and walk in the light (8:12), who hear the shepherd's voice and follow (10:1–4), who have bathed but must continue to wash (13:10), and who must as branches be 'pruned' (15:2)" (109–10). This analysis shows conceptual images and language of repentance in John. There are shared images and language in the Synoptic Gospels and especially in the Gospel of Matthew.

with the Synoptic tradition. She explains this phenomenon as one example of the Johannine tendency to present crucial themes indirectly rather than explicitly.[57] The Fourth Gospel highlights repentance with the concept of following Jesus, just as the Gospel of Matthew does (Matt 4:17–23). Overall, Humphrey's article is a good example of conceptual analysis of repentance in the NT.

Mark J. Boda also traces the repentance theme in the Gospels according to the succession of ministries from John the Baptist to Jesus and to the apostles (disciples). He deals with several passages in the Synoptic Gospels and Acts where μετανοέω and μετάνοια occur. Boda explains that John the Baptist's repentance "does not merely involve a shifting of inner orientation toward God but rather impacts outward behavior, as John declares in Luke 3:8: 'bear fruits in keeping with repentance.'"[58] Also, he emphasizes the close relationship between repentance and the Holy Spirit baptism in Matthew 3 and Acts 2, and between repentance and faith in Mark 1:15, "repent, and believe in the gospel" (also Acts 11; 20:21). Boda points out that Jesus calls for repentance in order to escape destruction (Luke 13:1–5).[59] In the book of Acts, Luke constantly reports the apostles' repentance ministry (Acts 2:38; 3:19, 26; 15:19; 17:30; 26:18, 20). For Peter, James, and Paul "repentance clearly means turning from one orientation of life with its attendant behavioral patterns to a new orientation of life that impacts actions."[60] Boda also extends his study from these terms to related larger literary contexts, images, forms and concepts. He looks for the concepts of repentance in the Synoptics and Acts that do not contain μετανοέω or μετάνοια: Jesus' invitation to follow him (Matt 4:18–22; Mark 1:16–20; Luke 5:10–11); Zacchaeus (Luke 19:1–10); Paul's conversion (Acts 9; 22; 26); the lost son (Luke 15:11–32); the rich man and Lazarus (Luke 16:19–31); the two gates image (Matt 7:13–14);

---

57. For example, neither Jesus' baptism, the transfiguration, the Lord's Supper, nor the ascension are present in the Fourth Gospel but they are all indirectly presented (Humphrey, "And I Shall Heal Them," 107). She examines many materials as indirect expressions of μετανοέω and μετάνοια (repentance): John's disciples' turning and following the Lamb; Nathaniel's changing his mind; Nicodemus's conversion (3:2–15; 19:39–42); the transformation of the Samaritan woman from cynic to evangelist (4:29); the paralytic's changed life (5:11); the recommitment of offenders (6:60–69); the charge to the adulterous woman not to sin again (8:1–11); the blind man's restored sight (ch. 9); Lazarus's sisters' belief in Jesus after his resurrection (ch. 11); Thomas's doubt turned to belief; Mary's move from grief to joy; and Peter's betrayal, restoration, and commission by Jesus (107–8). Humphrey argues for continuity between Hebrew piety and the NT μετανοέω and μετάνοια repentance, especially from the stories of Nicodemus, Lazarus's sisters, and the Samaritan woman.

58. Boda, 'Return to Me,' 164.

59. Boda, 'Return to Me,' 164–66.

60. Boda, 'Return to Me,' 165.

carrying the yoke and dying to oneself (Matt 11:28–30; 16:24–25; 18:4; Mark 8:34–35). This analysis helps to study repentance in the Gospel of Matthew where μετανοέω or μετάνοια occur few times.

Finally, Moses Kintu gives a conceptual study of repentance in the sermon.[61] Kintu argues that the closeness of summary statement 4:17 to the sermon hints that the sermon includes the concept of repentance. He argues that the sermon is a commentary on this summary phrase. Despite the fact that the term "repent" does not appear in the sermon, the repentance concept is in the sermon. This study eventually aims to contribute to the biblical concept of repentance from the Gospel of Matthew. Kintu's dissertation is important since it is the first work done on the repentance theme of the Gospel of Matthew. However, it is limited to the sermon only and does not solve the problem of limited word occurrence. He does not clearly analyze repentance in the sermon and his main section on the sermon is a typical verse-by-verse exegesis. Also, he skips the antitheses (5:17–48), which is Jesus' most important repentance teaching. The Antitheses parallels the Zadokian interpretation of the Law by which the teachers of the righteous lead repentance of the Qumran sect.[62] Through the Antitheses Jesus plays the same role, "reinterpreting the law and the prophets" for repentance. In the Antitheses Jesus interpretation of the law and the prophets reveals Israel's sin and the need to repent. Israel thought themselves righteous following their own interpretation of the OT law, but Jesus reveals them as sinners through his new and correct interpretation. The strong judgment language in the Dead Sea Scrolls (DSS) matches the Gospel of Matthew.

Kintu's background study is helpful and worth including here. In the prophets, Kintu finds the Deuteronomic pattern of repentance in which God gave rules, Israel sinned, God called them to repent, and Israel returned. Also, he concludes that repentance in Second Temple literature does not differ from the OT prophets. Kintu's background from the DSS points out that in the Qumran repentance means "entry" and "continuing membership" in the community. This concept became the forerunner of NT repentance.[63] Kintu concludes that Qumran's repentance and Jesus' repentance are similar

---

61. Kintu, "Repentance in the Sermon on the Mount."

62. For the full argument on parallelism between 4QMMT and Matt 5:21–48, see Foster, *Community, Law, and Mission*, 80–93. Foster argues that "both documents contain a series of antithetical halakah and they understand the performance of the legal rulings, as interpreted by respective groups, as pertaining to righteousness" (83). Foster distinguishes that while Qumran antithetical halakah invites the opposing group to their practices, Matthew dismisses the opposing group as "hypocrites and unrighteous" (Matt 6:1) (86).

63. Kintu, "Repentance in the Sermon on the Mount," 343.

in that they both call people to repent in view of the incoming kingdom of God (Matt 4:17) and expect "bearing fruit worthy of repentance" (Matt 3:8).[64] He concludes, in the DSS "repentance engaged the whole person, demanding a change in thinking and behavior" (1QS I, 1–3) (115). Kintu emphasizes that the Qumran sect's purpose was "a life of repentance" (1QS V, 1–VI, 23; 1QS V, 1–6:23).[65] "Repentance encompassed both the initial change in thinking and behavior and an ongoing mechanism to live out the initial act of repentance."[66] Also, he explains that Qumran repentance involved confession of one's sin and guilt both individually (CD IX, 13) and communally (1QS I, 24–2:1), restitution (CD XV, 4–15), and a commitment not to sin again (1QS II, 11–20).[67] In short, "Repentance involves 'walking perfectly in all God's ways'" (1QSIII, 9).[68]

The most important point is that "the goal of repentance is to return to the pure observance of the Torah as interpreted by the community."[69] Repentance is to "take upon his soul by a binding oath to return to the Torah of Moses, according to all which he has commanded with all heart and with all soul, according to everything which has been revealed from it to the sons of Zadok" (1QS V, 8–9), echoing OT repentance (Deut 9:29–31; 30:2–3; 1 Sam

---

64. Kintu, "Repentance in the Sermon on the Mount," 131.
65. Kintu, "Repentance in the Sermon on the Mount," 115.
66. Kintu, "Repentance in the Sermon on the Mount," 119.
67. Kintu, "Repentance in the Sermon on the Mount," 115.
68. Kintu, "Repentance in the Sermon on the Mount," 118. "Repentance was comprehensive in scope, beginning with one's entry into the community and going on throughout one's membership, and covering one's thinking, attitude (1QS V, 4–5) and behavior (1QS VII, 1–25). It involved confession of sin (1QS I, 24–II, 1) and commitment to obey the Law (1QS I, 6–18)" (Kintu, "Repentance in the Sermon on the Mount," 129). It "incorporated into the community's liturgical prayers (4Q504 II, 1–10) (130) related to OT penitential prayer in Dan 9; Ezra 9; and Neh 9." And "the judicial aspect (1QS V, 25–VI, 1; CD IX, 2–8, 16–22) looks back to the OT (Lev 19:17; Deut 19:15) and forward to the NT (Matt 18:15–17)" (130). Kintu also gives some comments on the relationship between repentance and water purification (1QS III, 9–10 to be sprinkled "with waters of purification" and to repent). Kintu quotes Nitzan who notes that in the "Qumranic philosophy, repentance 'with faith and wholeness of heart' is regarded as the highest virtue a human being can attain, for a person who is clean from any sin and impurity may be equal to the angels (1QHA 16:17–18; 17:14–15; 12:20c–24)" (115). "In Community Rule 1QS I, 24–II–1: repentance includes a confession of sin; a commitment to obey all God's commandments (1QS 1:16–18); divine forgiveness after the confession (1 QS II, 2–4); covenant entry ritual (1QS V, 12–14): their ancestors, followed OT model in Neh 9:33–34 and Dan 9:4–8; sincere and whole-hearted (1QS II, 5–10), if not the severe curses calling as the lot of Satan; strong curse for halfhearted or insincere repentance (1QS II, 11, 17) (115–17).
69. Kintu, "Repentance in the Sermon on the Mount," 120.

7:3; 1 Kgs 8:47-50; 2 Kgs 23:25; 1 Chr 22:29; Jer 29:13-14; and Joel 2:12).[70] In other words, Qumran repentance had to be according to the interpretation of the sect done by teachers of righteousness.[71]

Kintu concludes that in the Matthew μετανοέω and μετάνοια have three aspects: (1) the original once-for-all turning away from sin and to Jesus and all that he stands for; (2) the small turns otherwise known as "penance," a description of the change in thinking and behavior in response to failure by those who are already Jesus' disciples; (3) an expectation for the disciples of Jesus that they "bear fruit worthy of repentance" (Matt 7:15-20).[72] Regarding repentance in the sermon he says, "The Sermon has a dual audience of disciples and crowds. For the disciples, repentance means turning away from specific sins ('penance') and bearing fruit worthy of repentance. For the crowds who were part of the audience, repentance means the once-for-all turning from sin to Jesus, a commitment to be Jesus' follower."[73] Kintu also studies Matthean repentance outside of the sermon. He deals with some passages in the Gospel of Matthew where the terms μετανοέω and μετάνοια (3:2; 4:17; 10:7; 11:20-24; 12:38-45) and their synonym στρέφω (18:1-4) are used. His repentance study outside of the sermon is limited to occasions where repentance vocabulary is used. μετανοέω and μετάνοια do not occur many times in the Gospel

---

70. Kintu, "Repentance in the Sermon on the Mount," 120.

71. See Nitzan, "Repentance in the Dead Sea Scrolls," 2:150-51. Nitzan says this Zadokian interpretation was "the hidden matters in which all Israel had gone astray (CD 3:13-16, cf. 1QS 1:13-15)" and only allowed to sectarian members. Repentance for sectarians was "to turn from the corrupt way of performing the Law that the majority of Israel were misled to do. Hence, the sectarian authorities ruled out as incorrect, or as false repentance, the laws as interpreted by other authorities of Israel. . . . The abandoning of the Torah was considered a sin, the sectarian writings from Qumran also considered its incorrect performed as a sin (1QS 5:11; CD 1:14-16; 4QpHosa 2.5)." "The Qumran writing mainly blame the Pharisees for misleading the children of Israel by false interpretation of the Law (see for example, CD 1:14-20, and the *Pesharim* scrolls mentioned above). On the other hand their opponents, the Pharisees, blame those who disbelieve their interpretations of the Law, such as Zaddok and Baitos." "They considered themselves as 'the men that have entered the new covenant,' as promised in Jer 31:30-32 (CD 6:19; 8:21), which meant that the Community was regarded as the congregation of the "new covenant."

72. Kintu, "Repentance in the Sermon on the Mount," 7.

73. Kintu, "Repentance in the Sermon on the Mount," iv-v. Kintu's explanation of two kinds of repentance based on the dual audience of the sermon seems an unlikely interpretation. Rather, one kind of repentance through one's whole life is more likely. Repentance is life-changing and life-giving. In other words, repentance is a one-time but ongoing event. Repentance always conflicts with everyday challenges from the sin nature, but Jesus allows one to ask forgiveness if one fails.

of Matthew, but Kintu suggests some different repentance concepts—the parable of the two sons (21:28–32)—being one example.

Conclusion

In sum, the history of research on repentance (μετανοέω and μετάνοια) largely reveals four things: (1) μετανοέω and μετάνοια have been ignored for a long time but have recently earned the interest of a few scholars. No one has done a μετανοέω and μετάνοια study from the Gospel of Matthew as a significant theme. (2) All literature mentioned above argues that μετανοέω and μετάνοια repentance includes a religious and moral change of one's whole being and life. This change should be according to Jesus' interpretation of the OT, which reveals the need for and the content of repentance. (3) The word statistics-based study of μετανοέω and μετάνοια should be widened to a conceptual study including literary context, synonyms, antonyms, images, and similar language with the same meaning or paraphrasing statements. Recent works on repentance in the NT mentioned above prove that μετανοέω and μετάνοια (repentance) appear conceptually throughout the NT even when the terms do not. (4) NT μετανοέω and μετάνοια (repentance), especially in the Gospel of Matthew, is not legalism or moralism but emphasizes a change or transformation from heart to behavior. Most of the time eschatological salvific judgment language and images follow it.

Chapter 3
Meaning of μετανοέω and μετάνοια

Introduction

IN THIS CHAPTER WE examine the meanings of μετανοέω and μετάνοια in search of a proper definition and understanding, shed additional light on the significance of μετανοέω in Matthew 4:17 as thematic or paradigmatic in Matthew, and explore the Matthean understanding and translation options of μετανοέω from various commentators and dictionaries. We begin with the OT background of the term. Kittel focuses on lexical methodology and critical scholarship. Many scholars criticize Tyndale for translating the Greek word μετανοέω as "repent" because that definition only entails the negative meaning of feeling remorse or regret and to stop sinning,[1] but neglects its positive meaning to change one's mind, conduct, and life.[2] This reductionism of μετανοέω to emotional remorse and refrain from sin obstructs the right understanding of the first word of Jesus Christ in Matthew and therefore

---

1. The English word "repent" means only to stop doing sin, or to change one's mind. According to the *Oxford English Dictionary*, repent, made up by *re* and *penitire*, means first "to affect with contrition or regret for something done," second "to cause to feel regret," third "to feel contrition, compunction, sorrow or regret for something one has done; to change one's mind with regard to past action or conduct through dissatisfaction with it or its results," and fourth "to view or think of with dissatisfaction and regret." Repentance is "the act of repenting or the state of being penitent; sorrow, regret, or contrition for past action or conduct" (*Oxford English Dictionary*, 637). This meaning of "repent" does not correspond to μετανοέω. *Webster's Third New English Dictionary* first explains that repent is a compound verb "*re + pentir* "to be sorry" from the Latin *paenitere* "to be sorry," and means "to turn from sin out of penitence for past wrongdoings . . . to cause to feel regret or contrition for a past action, course of conduct, or decision" giving an example of Luke 13:3 (*Webster's Third New International Dictionary*, 1444).

2. For example, Louw and Nida, *Greek-English Lexicon*, Domain 41, 510; Robertson, *Word Pictures*, Matt. 3:2; Hendriksen, *New Testament Commentary*, 196–97. Broadus, *Commentary on the Gospel of Matthew*, 33–35. See later section in this chapter for more recent scholars' comments.

obscures its importance as a driving idea of the Gospel of Matthew, which emphasizes changing one's mind and conduct of life.

Repentance (μετάνοια) in the OT

The most important background to understand the term μετάνοια in Matthew is the OT, since as we will see in the next chapter Matthew includes the last prophet, John the Baptist, preaching of μετάνοια (Matt 3:2), and Jesus as prophetic Messiah parallels John and continues his μετάνοια ministry.

Ernst Würthwein provides the OT prophetic concept of the theme of repentance as an origin for the NT μετανοέω and μετάνοια. It includes penitential observances, external forms of fasting, mourning, sackcloth, sitting in ashes, crying, wailing, and confession of sin (1 Kgs 21:27; Isa 58:5; Neh 9:1; 1 Sam 7:6; Dan 9:4). In addition the OT prophetic concept of conversion conveys a personal view of sin (Hos 1–3; Isa 1:2; Jer 1:16) and a personal view of repentance as turning to Yahweh (Hos 2:9) by obedience to Yahweh's will (Hos 6:1–6; Jer 34:15), trust in Yahweh (Hos 14:4; Jer 3:22–23; 25:5; Isa 10:20), and turning from everything ungodly (Jer 26:3; 36:3).[3]

Here I will briefly summarize Mark J. Boda's recently published book on the biblical theology of repentance in the OT and briefly in the NT.[4] This work is a good source for the OT repentance study. He chooses the main Hebrew terms for repentance in the OT: (1) *šub*, "turn," "return,"[5] "turn to God or righteousness,"[6] "turn away" from evil;[7] (2) *šubâ, sûr* "turning

---

3. *TDNT* 4:980–88. See also Thompson and Martens, *New International Dictionary*, 4:55–59. They explain that *šub* firstly indicates a physical motion of "returning" or "changing directions." Secondly, it denotes reestablishing of broken relationships between husband and wife (Jer 3:1) or king and citizen (1 Kgs 12:27). Thirdly, in a religious sense, it is a central word of the theme of repentance "a turnabout to Yahweh" (2 Kgs 17:13; 2 Chr 30:6; Isa 44:22; Hos 14:1–2). Jeremiah 3:22—4:2 includes the detailed process: acknowledging God's lordship (3:22); admitting wrongdoing (3:23); including a verbal confession (3:25); addressing the shame (3:25); and affirming and adhering to new conduct (4:1–2).

4. Boda, *'Return to Me.'* See also, Boda and Smith, *Repentance in Christian Theology*.

5. E.g., Isa 6:10; Hos 3:5; 11:5; Zech 1:6b; Ps 78:34; Lam 5:21; 1 Kgs 8:47; 2 Chr 6:37.

6. With preposition *'el*: 1 Sam 7:3; 1 Kgs 8:33, 35, 48; 2 Chr 6:24, 26, 38; 2 Kgs 23:25; Isa 10:21; 44:22; 55:7; Jer 3:10; 24:7; 37:41; Hos 5:4; 6:1; 7:10; Joel 2:13; Zech 1:3; Mal 3:7; Prov 1:23; Ps 51:13; Neh 1:9; 2 Chr 30:6; 36:13. With *'al*: 2 Chr 15:4; 30:9. With *'ad*: Deut 4:30; 30:2; Isa 9:13 [Heb 9:12]; 19:22; Hos 14:2; Joel 2:12; Amos 4:6, 8–11; Job 22:23; Lam 3:40; Hos 12:6. Boda, *'Return to Me,'* 25.

7. *min*: 2 Kgs 17:13; Isa 59:20; Jer 18:11; 26:3, 13; 35:15; Ezek 3:19, 22; 13:22; 14:6; 18:21, 27–28, 30, 32; 33:9, 11; Jonah 3:8, 10; Zech 1:4; Dan 9:13; Neh 9:35; 2 Chr 7:14; in *hiphil* Ezek 14:6; 18:30, 32; 33:9, 19. Boda, *'Return to Me,'* 26.

aside from or putting aside foreign gods or sinful behavior,"[8] (3) *nhm*, "turn" (mostly divine shift, but also human: Job 42:6; Jer 8:6; 31:19).[9] Also, a few Greek terms refer to repentance in the NT: μετανοέω, μετάνοια, στρέφω, ἐπιστρέφω, ἐπιστροφή, and possibly μεταμέλομαι. Boda examines the traditional understanding of the two main Greek terms of repentance, μετανοέω and μετάνοια, by saying, "Although μετανοέω can refer to a change in inner disposition (Acts 8:22), it is regularly connected to a change in external activity (2 Cor 12:21; Rev 2:5, 21, 22; 9:20, 21; 16:11)."[10]

Boda picks Zechariah 1:16 and Acts 26:16–20 as representative passages on repentance in which biblical repentance means "a (re)turn to God and away from that which is contrary to God and which also involves a shift in behavior,"[11] or in other words, "a turn or return to faithful relationship with God from a former state of estrangement."[12]

Boda's references to and discussions of repentance in the OT are very helpful for a correct understanding of NT μετανοέω and μετάνοια. Boda correctly finds that the OT prophetic tradition parallels Jesus' prophetic repentance ministry and the OT understanding of repentance is key to reading the Gospel of Matthew through μετανοέω and μετάνοια.

Boda's analysis of the OT prophetic background of μετανοέω and μετάνοια is helpful to understand repentance in the NT. The first important prophetic repentance call is found in Deuteronomy 4 and again in 30 where Moses predicts Israel's fall and asks them to return to God, reminding them that God is merciful. Moses emphasizes two things: heart (30:29) and deeds (30:40), along with the list of covenant blessings and curses (30:27–28). In Deuteronomy 4 and 30, Moses predicts the future fall of Israel and commands them to repent in their heart and repent of their deeds. Repentance in Deuteronomy 4 and 30 emphasizes the behavioral and affective dimensions of repentance, exhorting obedience and a change of heart. Deuteronomy 30

---

8. In the qal: 2 Kgs 10:29; Isa 59:15; Prov 13:19; 14:16; 16:6, 17; Job 1:8; 2:3; 28:28; in the hiphil: Gen 35:2; Josh 24:14, 23; Judg 10:16; 1 Sam 7:3; Isa 1:16; Ezek 45:9; Hos 2:2; Prov 3:7; 4:24–27; 13:14; Job 33:17. Boda, 'Return to Me,' 26.

9. Boda, 'Return to Me,' 26. He also includes *pnh* ("turn"; Isa 45:22; Jer 2:27); *sbb* ("turn back"; 1 Kgs 18:37); *śth* ("turn away"; Prov 4:15); *hdl* ("cease"; Isa 1:16); *rûm* (hiphil; "stop"; Ezek 45:9); *'zb* ("forsake"; Isa 55:7; Prov 9:6); *šlk* (hiphil; "cast away"; Ezek 18:31; 20:7); *rhq* ("remove [sin] far away"; Job 11:14; 22:23); *prq* (Aram "break away"; Dan 4:27 [Heb 4:24]); *bdl* (niphal: "separate oneself"; Ezra 6:21; 10:11; Neh 10:28) and *zkr* ("remember"; e.g., Ezek 36:31; Ps 78:35; Eccl 12:1) (27).

10. Boda, 'Return to Me,' 29.

11. Boda, 'Return to Me,' 31.

12. Boda, 'Return to Me,' 31.

anticipates a divine work that will enable the community to fully embrace the obedience that follows repentance.[13]

Boda offers two basic repentance patterns in the Latter Prophets (2 Kgs 17:12-15; 18; Jer 18:7-17; Ezek 3:17-21; Zech 7-8): First, Israel sins. Yahweh responds with a call to repentance through the prophets. Israel responds by not listening, stiffening the neck, not believing, and forsaking the commandments. Yahweh responds.[14] Second, a positive human response to the call to repentance earns a positive divine response of salvation or withholding of judgment. A negative human response to the call to repentance ends with a negative divine response of judgment.[15]

The following OT references, which are from Boda,[16] are significant for understanding OT repentance and Jesus' teaching in the Gospel of Matthew as the repentance message parallels the OT prophets: Isaiah 6:9-10, which Jesus cites, indicates his teaching as a repentance message; Jeremiah 7:5-6 contains a detailed repentance message including a reward. The

---

13. From Boda's references I also chose a few other places from the OT prophets that speak of repentance. First Samuel 7 reports Samuel's first speech after Israel's failure under the leadership of Eli. Samuel calls Israel to return to Yahweh with all their heart, by removing foreign gods and directing their heart to serve Yahweh alone, and so returning with their whole life. And there was a blessing promise later (7:3). Also, 7:4 confirms that they serve God alone with their whole life. First Samuel 12:20-25 is Samuel's last speech emphasizing serving God with the heart and with obedience. Second Samuel 12 tells of David's sin and repentance: David killed Uriah and took his wife. Nathan's parable and its interpretation made David confess his sin. There was judgment, the death of their son. This story is similar to Jesus' parabolic teaching for repentance.

First Kings 8 reports Solomon's prayer designating the temple as a place for prayer. He asks for the forgiveness of the sins of Israel. In his prayer, repentance is returning to God with heart and life. First Kings 8:33-36 defines repentance as turning from their sins to good ways of life. First Kings 8:41 opens repentance to the whole nation. First Kings 8:58-9 includes the Immanuel theme in relation to the repentance theme. Solomon's prayer on the temple is very similar to Matthew's emphasis and the sermon. They are all fulfilled by Jesus, the new temple who restores the temple as a prayer house for all nations for the forgiveness sins, the teacher of new ways of living and prayer for the forgiveness of sins.

Second Kings 23:3 tells of Josiah's repentance with Israel in heart and deed. He destroyed all idols and their temples to confirm what was written in the law, which was found in the temple. So, here we find two things related to repentance: the law and returning to the Lord. These are the same in the Gospel of Matthew, the law of Jesus and its need to return to the Lord Jesus and his teaching. Second Kings 23:25 uniquely praises him: "Before him there was no king like him who turned to the LORD with all his heart and with all his soul and with all his might, according to all the law of Moses; nor did any like him arise after him." Josiah's turning to the Lord (=repentance) involves heart, soul, and might, in other words one's whole being in life.

14. Boda, 'Return to Me,' 62.

15. Boda, 'Return to Me,' 65.

16. Boda, 'Return to Me,' 61-93.

returning (repentance) message of Jeremiah 18 includes changing behavior: "Oh turn back, each of you from his evil way, and reform your ways and your deeds." Jeremiah 24 is also significant because it includes good fruit language with repentance and restoration. It echoes later chapters of the book (32:37–41). Ezekiel 3 and 33 explain that repentance is returning to the Lord from wicked deeds to ensure salvation.

Boda concludes that the biblical understanding of repentance is not a one-time event but rather a lifelong relationship. "Repentance is not just the gateway into relationship with the triune God; it is the pathway for that continuing relationship, as Luther wrote: 'the entire life of believers should be one of repentance.' The Christian life involves a lifelong relationship, and as long as we are in this fallen world repentance will be an enduring part of our lives."[17] "Repentance is thus a way of life."[18] "Repentance is fundamentally a return to intimate fellowship with the triune God."[19]

Many scholars explain μετανοέω and μετάνοια under the influence of the Hebrew counterpart šub. For example, Davies and Allison argue, "The Greek word literally means, 'change of mind'; but it stands for the Hebrew šub, 'turn around,' 'return,' and a complete change in conduct, not just a change of opinion, is involved. . . Israel is called to turn to God and away from sin, to arise in moral earnestness from a sinful slumber and to gain a wakeful heart and sober thought (cf. Isa 55:7; Jub 21:23; and *m.'Abot* 4:11, where repentance is a 'shield against punishment')."[20]

In short, Davies and Allison state that it means "a radical change of heart and mind, a 'rebirth' of sorts."[21] Warren Carter strictly states that μετανοέω means "turn" or "return" to a faithful relationship with God in comparison to the OT prophets' commandments of turning Israel to God, such as Moses (Deut 30:2, 10), Hosea (Hos 2:7; 3:5; 6:1; 11:15), Amos (Amos 4:6, 8–9), Isaiah (Isa 6:10; 9:13; 31:6), Jeremiah (Jer 2:27; 3:10, 12, 14, 22), and Ezekiel (Ezek 14:6; 18:30, 32).[22]

---

17. Boda, *'Return to Me,'* 194.
18. Boda, *'Return to Me,'* 194.
19. Boda, *'Return to Me,'* 198.
20. Davies and Allison, *Matthew 1–7*, 305–6.
21. Davies and Allison, *Matthew 1–7*, 388–89. Davies and Allison, though, think repentance is not a key theme of the Gospel of Matthew since it only appears two times in noun form and four times in verb form. Also, he thinks that Matthew understands repentance as entrance into the Christian community.
22. Carter, *Matthew and the Margins*, 91. He also mentions the prophetic traditions found in John's narrative in the Gospel of Matthew: in those days, preaching, in the desert, fruit, fire, water, winnowing wheat, repentance, prophetic critique of false piety, the Spirit, and some rhetorical techniques. These echoes of the prophetic tradition further support that μετανοέω has its counterpart in the Hebrew term šub that carries the

R. T. France finds John's message in relation to the OT prophets calling God's people to "return" to their true allegiance. The difference between the two is "a new note of urgency," the coming kingdom of heaven.²³

Lexical Methodology and Critical Scholarship

Gerhard Kittel explains μετανοέω and μετάνοια in the NT (except for Luke 17:3; 2 Cor 7:9) as meaning "to change one's mind," "change of mind," or "to convert," "conversion."²⁴ These terms only share religious and ethical OT and Jewish concepts of conversion. These terms are new expression of the NT concept of conversion, in contrast to the ancient concept of religious and moral conversion.²⁵ In the NT, μετανοέω and μετάνοια mean to change one's mind and life (Matt 3:8), that is, to live "a life of love and righteousness in accordance with the will of God" (Luke 3:10-14).²⁶ Jesus "demands radical conversion, a transformation of nature, a definitive turning from evil, a resolute turning to God in total obedience" (Mark 1:15; Matt 4:17; 18:3).²⁷ Jesus' understanding of them is not just a negative break with one's past life, but the positive creation of a new relationship between man and God.²⁸

---

concept of the OT prophets' proclamation, that is, "turning," not "repenting."

23. France, *Gospel of Matthew*, 101.

24. *TDNT* 4:999–1001.

25. Johannes Behm notes that the ancient Greek usage of μετανοέω and μετάνοια means, "to change one's mind," "to adopt another view," "to change one's feeling," and "to regret and to feel remorse." In contrast with biblical usage, they do not suggest "an alteration in the total moral attitude, a profound change in life's direction, a conversion which affects the whole of conduct." In other words, the ancient Greek usage does not influence the origin of the NT μετανοέω and μετάνοια (*TDNT* 4:975–80.)

26. *TDNT* 4:999–1001.

27. *TDNT* 4:1002.

28. *TDNT* 4:1003. Philo and Josephus use the term μετανοέω in the same sense. Philo defines μετανοέω as a full change in being and conduct (Praem. Poen., 15; Abr., 26; Spec. Leg., I, 187), "radical turning to God (Virt., 179; Spec. Leg., I, 309, 51), turning from sin (Virt., 177; Fug., 99 and 158; Leg. All., III, 106), change of nature (Praem. Poen., 15), turning from the many false gods to the one true God (Virt., 176 f.; Spec. Leg., I, 51), and turning from sin to draw a line under past sins (Virt., 176; Fug., 157) and to sin no more (Fug., 160; Deus Imm., 8 f.)." "Conversion affects the whole man (Mut. Nom., 124; Sobr., 62)." Josephus defines repentance as "an alteration of will or purpose which is then translated into action (Vit., 110 and 370), so also the giving up of evil or ungodly plans (Ant., 2, 23)" and "to change one's life from one full of discord to a better one (Cl. Al. Strom., II, 97, 3)." μετάνοια is one mark of the pious life among others (1 Cl., 62, 2). Part of μετάνοια is keeping the commandments (Herm. V., 5, 6; m., 2, 7; s., 6, 1, 3; 7, 6). *TDNT* 4:975–1008.

Louw and Nida define μετανοέω as "to change one's way of life as the result of a complete change of thought and attitude with regard to sin and righteousness—'repent, to change one's way, repentance.'" Also, they add, "the focal semantic feature is clearly behavioral rather than intellectual." In addition, they challenge the English translation "repent" since "its focal component is not the sorrow or contrition that a person experiences because of sin," but they clarify that "μετανοέω and μετάνοια seem to be more specifically the total change, both in thought and behavior, with respect to how one should both think and act."[29] Bauer defines it as to "change one's mind then feel remorse, repent, be converted (in religio-ethical sense)."[30]

Moisés Silva explains that μετανοέω and μετάνοια first convey the idea of thinking differently as μετά indicates "change" and νοέω indicates, "to understand, think." Secondly, after the change of mind or thinking, there is possibly the sense of feeling remorse or regret for the previous false or bad opinion or will. μετανοέω and μετάνοια only appear seven times in the LXX, but they are dominant terms for the conversion of the whole person in later Jewish–Greek writings including Philo (65 occurrences) and Josephus (75 occurrences). In the Synoptics, the idea of μετανοέω and μετάνοια "is viewed in terms of commitment to a person; the call to repentance becomes a call to discipleship. So, repentance, faith, and discipleship are different aspects of the same thing (Mark 1:15, "Repent and believe")."[31] Moisés Silva importantly points out that the theme of repentance appears conceptually in the NT without the terms μετανοέω and μετάνοια (cf. Matt 18:3; Luke 14:33). Pauline writings and the Johannine corpus convey the theme of repentance by highlighting faith, self-dying images, new life, new creation, new birth, and turning from darkness to light and death to life.[32]

David L. Turner explains the aspects of repentance: the emotional sorrow for sin, the etymological–intellectual change of mind, the temporal initial conversion, and the volitional actions of penance. But he also states that repentance is more than those; it is "the turning of the whole person from sin to God in obedience to the message of the kingdom."[33] John Nolland also says, "John's call is for a fundamental change of life direction."[34] Craig Keener explores this argument within John's discourse material and

---

29. Louw and Nida, *Greek-English Lexicon*, Domain 41, 510. They examine στρέφομαι, ἐπιστρέφω, ἐπιστροφή, μετανοέω, and μετάνοια in the category "Change Behavior" with the basic meaning of "to change one's way, to turn to God."

30. BDAG 640.

31. Silva, *New International Dictionary*, 3:290–91.

32. Silva, *New International Dictionary*, 3:292.

33. Turner, *Matthew*, 106–7.

34. Nolland, *Gospel of Matthew*, 143–44.

the Sermon on the Mount well. He especially emphasizes the fruit image that appears in both of them.[35] Lastly, Bruner translates μετανοέω as "Turn your lives around" (3:2; 4:17)[36] and he traces the German translation *umkehren*, "turn around," and the French *retour*.[37] Many scholars all agree with these explanations of the term μετανοέω.[38]

μετάνοια and μετανοέω in the NT

These meanings for μετάνοια and μετανοέω are also found elsewhere in the NT. Within Matthew, John the Baptist proclaimed that μετάνοια includes bearing good fruits, which refers to good conduct (3:2–12). As already mentioned in chapter 2, Luke-Acts also includes deeds in μετάνοια,[39] for example, Acts 26:20 ("They should repent and turn to God, performing deeds appropriate to repentance.") Hebrews 6:1 more directly includes good deeds in μετάνοια by saying "repentance from dead works." The Revelation of John also deals significantly with μετάνοια in its meaning of turning (or changing) one's way of life, with a warning about the judgment of God. Μετανοέω occurs twelve times in Revelation (the most in the NT)

---

35. Keener, *Matthew*, 80.

36. Bruner, *Matthew*, 87; 137–39.

37. Bruner, *Matthew 1–12*, 137–39. Erasmo Leiva-Merikakis says μετανοέω means "Turn your minds away from the attitudes you have defined for yourselves as the goal of your life and come back to the mind of God" (Leiva-Merikakis, *Fire of Mercy*, 109). He states that "Repentance is the heat that melts us so that we can start moving, since if there is no movement there is no life" (114). He then adds, "Repentance means, not only to forsake our old sinful ways, since this would be a merely moral change: repentance means to put on a new attitude because we recognize the compellingly royal presence of God before us. This entails a change of vision, a change of home, a change of lover" (114).

38. See also, Merklein, *Exegetical Dictionary of the New Testament*, 2:417–18. Merklein similarly points out that μετανοέω and μετάνοια in ancient Greek denote a particular change of mind, but in the NT they denote a comprehensive change of attitude affecting one's entire existence. Repentance is a turning away from sin (Mark 1:4) and bearing fruit worthy of repentance (Matt 3:8) for protection from the immediate judgment (Matt 3:10). Repentance is "committing oneself to the words and deeds of Jesus (Luke 10:13; 11:32)," and it is "the beginning of a turning toward Christian faith (Mark 6:12)" or "the change of attitude that leads to conversion, which must be followed by corresponding deeds (Acts 26:20; Luke 3:7)." Also, Cremer, *Biblio-Theological Lexicon*, 792, says "In the NT, with rare exception (Luke 17:3, 4; 2 Cor 12:21), μετανοέω and μετάνοια are used in an ethico–religious sense with reference to the entire conduct, the character, and the tendency of personal life as a whole." See also Mitch and Sri, *Gospel of Matthew*, 62; Dunn, in Marshall, *New Bible Dictionary*, 1007–8. Morris, *Gospel according to Matthew*, 83.

39. See ch. 2 for more discussion of μετανοέω in Luke-Acts.

indicating that μετάνοια is not only a one-time initial event for entering the Christian community but also a lifelong pattern.

For example, Revelation 2:5, "Remember therefore from where you have fallen; repent (μετανοέω) and do the works you did at first. If not, I will come to you and remove your lampstand from its place, unless you repent (μετανοέω)," gives a clear understanding of the biblical idea of μετανοέω, that is, returning to do the works of love they did at first (Rev. 2:4). Revelation 2:16 warns people who follow the teaching of the Nicolaitans, which is the wicked conduct of Balaam (2:14), to change their life (μετανοέω). Revelation 2:21 commands a change of life (μετανοέω) from sexual immorality. Revelation 2:22 also deals with μετανοέω as changing conduct: "I will throw into great tribulation, unless they repent of her works." Revelation 3:3 is significant because μετανοέω appears with τηρέω ("to keep") ("τήρει καὶ μετανόησον what they have received and heard"), which indicates that μετανοέω is changing one's way of life, that is, keeping the commandments of God. Also, it is not a coincidence that μετανοέω and τηρέω appear individually in the first and last words of Jesus in the Gospel of Matthew, together with kingdom language, "the kingdom of heaven" (4:17) and "all authority in heaven and on the earth" (28:20). This appearance indicates that 4:17 and the Great Commission conceptually overlap.[40] In addition, Revelation 9:20–21 and 16:11 list what the wicked must turn (μετανοέω). This μετανοέω theme of Revelation, that is, turning one's life, appears as a significant theme in the new Jerusalem image. Revelation 21:8–9 list what people must not do if they wish to enter the new Jerusalem, that is, what they should change in their life (μετανοέω). Even in "the book of life" is written what people have done and God will judge them accordingly (20:12) to encourage μετάνοια. A final reference in relation to Revelation's emphasis on μετανοέω and corresponding good life appears in the image of the fine linen in 19:8 that is granted to the Bride. This fine linen is significant because it is the righteous deeds of the saints (τὰ δικαιώματα τῶν ἁγίων). These righteous deeds are John's emphasis through the commandment of turning (μετανοέω).

Translation Problem

People today who use English say that they understand "repent" as the idea of "turning." I think it might be the result of these works cited above, which rightly define the meaning of μετανοέω. However, as examined in

---

40. See ch. 5 of this book for more discussion on the conceptual overlap between 4:17 and the Great Commission.

this chapter many scholars, even Tyndale who use "repent/repentance" for the first time, suggest different English translations, which convey the idea of "turning" or "changing." In agreeing with these scholars' explanations and suggestions, I suggest "turn" as a proper English translation of μετανοέω in Matthew 3:2 and 4:17.

Most scholars from the late nineteenth century to early twentieth century agree that μετανοέω as used in the Gospel of Matthew means "change one's mind and conduct," or "change of life." Not a few scholars reflect this meaning in their own translation of Matthew 4:17 and some even criticize "repent" as an improper translation. For example, Eduard Schweizer translates μετανοέω as "Turn away from your sins" (3:2; 4:17).[41] A. T. Robertson suggests "to return" instead, and points out that John and Jesus do not mean "to be sorry, but to change their mental attitudes and conduct."[42] William Hendriksen translates the word as "be converted" or possibly "make a complete turnabout in mind and heart (or will)." Hendriksen himself argues that "repent" only explains the negative aspect of μετανοέω, but ignores the positive aspect, that is, "fruit bearing."[43] Hendriksen declares, "In the original the word used by the Baptist indicates a radical change of mind and heart that leads to a complete turnabout of life."[44] Young's literal translation (1862) uses "reform." The Amplified Bible (1987) uses "repent" but corrected the meaning of repent, defining it as to "think differently; change your mind, regretting your sins and changing your conduct."

John Albert Broadus suggests "reform" as a possible English translation. He states the basic idea of μετανοέω as "to change thought, and so to change the opinion or purpose that include a corresponding change of the outward life." He removes the idea of grief, sorrow, and regret from μετανοέω, saying that μετανοέω was used to signify a mere change of opinion or judgment. But he notes that μετανοέω can cause grief and regret as a result, or grief and regret can cause a change of purpose and conduct. He examines the OT prophets who told Israel to mourn and weep over their sins,

---

41. Schweizer, *Good News according to Matthew,* 45, 74.

42. Robertson, *Word Pictures,* Matt 3:2.

43. Hendriksen, *New Testament Commentary,* 196–97. He cites Warfield's definition of μετάνοια as "the inner change of mind which regret induces and which itself induces a reformed life" (Warfield, *Biblical and Theological Studies,* 366).

44. Hendriksen, *New Testament Commentary,* 197. This definition is from his citation of Chamberlain, *Meaning of Repentance,* 22. Philip A. Micklem defines it as "a change of mind issuing in corresponding conduct, as the essential condition of admission to the kingdom just announced" (Micklem, *St. Matthew,* 14). Hugh J. Schonfield uses šub and translates Matt 3:2 as "Repent ye of your lives," 4:17 as "Turn ye, turn ye, in repentance," 11:20 as "because they turned not from their evil deeds," and 12:41 "they repented" (Schonfield, *Old Hebrew Text).* Also, the Modern Hebrew Bible uses šub.

but never exhorted them to "repent," simply to "turn." Finally, he examines different versions of the translation of the word. For example, Jerome's Vulgate, *paenitentiam agere*, is connected etymologically with pain, signifying grief or distress. It rarely extends to a change of purpose, an error existing within Latin Christianity for a long time. Also, the English term "repent" is derived from Latin term *repaenitere* and it makes grief the prominent element and change of purpose secondary.[45]

William Tyndale

It is a bit of out of scope for this work, but it will be helpful to understand how we get to this English translation and what the translator says about the term μετάνοια in Matthew 3:2 and 4:17. William Tyndale, in his English translation from the original Greek, translates μετανοέω and μετάνοια as "repent" and "repentance." This choice diverges from the previous English translation in the Wycliffe English Bible, "do penance" and "penance," which are from the Latin Vulgate *paenitentiam agite* and *poenitentia*. *Paenitentiam agite*, *poenitentia*, "do penance," and "penance" were the basis of the Catholic sacrament of penance. Tyndale wants to reject the Catholic sacrament of penance; therefore, he used "repent" and "repentance" instead. Specifically, Tyndale wants to remove any form of satisfaction for sin through human works.[46] In his explanation of penance in relation to the Latin term *paenitentiam agite* and *poenitentia*, Tyndale said, "Of repentance [Roman Catholics] have made penance, to blind the people, and to make them think that they must take pains, and do some holy deeds, to make satisfaction for their sins; namely

---

45. Broadus, *Commentary*, 33–35. John J. Owen's commentary on Matthew also emphasizes changing one's life and conduct, referring to the background of John's preaching of μετανοέω: "The nation had become exceedingly wicked, given to traditionary forms and ceremonies, and to a corresponding degree, neglectful of the spirit and requirements of God's moral law." And he explains, "μετανοέω designates a change in one's views and principles and implies a radical reformation of life and conduct." He excludes any emotional aspect of the term by distinguishing it from μεταμέλομαι that is also translated "repent" and means a mere feeling of sorrow or remorse, not accompanied or followed by true reformation (Owen, *Commentary*, 14). Also, Campbell Morgan defines μετανοέω as "Change your mind." He also expresses it in another way: "You are all wrong, wrong at the heart and core of things, wrong in your seeing, and therefore in your doing" (Morgan, *Gospel according to Matthew*, 22).

46. This aim of Tyndale's through his translation was rejected by the Roman Catholic Church along with four other major terms that emphasized works in salvation: "church," "priest," "do penance," and "charity," which Tyndale translated "congregation," "senior" (changed to "elder" in the revised edition of 1534), "repent," and "love."

such as they enjoin them."⁴⁷ Because Tyndale tries to remove any form of works as satisfaction for sin, he translated μετανοέω as "repent."

Tyndale's translation has been used today. The most influential and widely used King James Version takes up Tyndale's translation, along with the Darby Bible, the Webster Bible, and almost all English Bibles today. That is why we need to study how Tyndale understood the terms repent and repentance.⁴⁸

Tyndale first explains μετανοέω (and μετάνοια) as "change one's way of life." He says "μετανοέω is from the Hebrew *šub*, 'turn, or be converted,'" and most often, Jerome's Latin translation of *šub* is *converti*, or sometimes *agre poenintentiam*, which means Tyndale could have used "convert" when translating μετανοέω, instead of "repent." Also, he writes that μετανοέω means "to turn, to be converted, and to come to the right knowledge, and to a man's right wit again" and confirms that "the very sense and significance both *šub* and μετανοέω is, to be converted and to turn to God with all the heart, to know his will, and to live according to his laws; and to be cured of our corrupt nature with the oil of his Spirit, and wine of obedience to his doctrine."⁴⁹ Tyndale states μετανοέω means conversion or turning and μετανοέω contains four elements: (1) confession of sins, sinfulness, and unrighteousness to God in the heart; (2) contrition, sorrowfulness for sin and sinful nature; (3) faith in God's forgiveness through Jesus Christ; (4) satisfaction or amendment to neighbor against whom one sins, not to God with holy works.

Tyndale's main emphasis on the term repent and repentance lies in life changing or turning to God. The closing words of Tyndale's "Repentance" section in his book *Doctrinal Treatises and Introductions to Different Portions of the Holy Scriptures*, are very significant, because he allows for another English translation of μετανοέω and μετάνοια that is different from repent. His other suggestions include amendment, converting, and turning to God. "Wherefore now, whether ye call this (μετάνοια) repentance, conversion, or turning again to God, either amending &c.; or whether ye say, 'Repent, be converted, turn to God, amend your living,' or what ye lust; I am content, so ye understand what is meant thereby, as I have now declared."⁵⁰

---

47. Tyndale, *Doctrinal Treatises*, 260.

48. In contrast to Tyndale's English Bible, there are other translations from the same era: the Geneva Bible (1557–1560) translated "repent" in Matt 3:2, but "Amende your liues" in 4:17; "amendment of life" in 3:8, but "had repented" in 11:21; "repented" in 12:41, but "the baptism of amendment of life" in Mark 1:4; and "repent" in 1:15. In French, Martin (1744) uses "Convertissez-vous," which means "convert" in English.

49. Tyndale, *Doctrinal Treatises*, 477.

50. Tyndale, *Doctrinal Treatises*, 478.

Tyndale confessed that repent (and repentance) is one option for the English translation. Other English terms, such as amend, convert, or turn, can be used for μετανοέω (and μετάνοια), as long as people understand what Tyndale declares.

While Tyndale rejects any satisfaction through human works for the forgiveness of sin and so translates μετανοέω as repent, he also pays attention to human works as the term μετανοέω indicates. He emphasizes human works, doing good, or changing one's life from an earthly perspective to the new life of a believer rather than satisfaction with holy works for sin. Tyndale's understanding of μετανοέω in relation to "changing life" is easily found in his writings. For example, in *Expositions and Notes on Sundry Portions of the Holy Scriptures*, commenting on the Gospel of Matthew chapter five, he emphasizes "a new life" in relation to repentance. "The sin we do before our conversion is forgiven clearly through faith if we repent and submit ourselves to a new life. The sin, after our conversion, is also forgiven us through faith if we repent and submit ourselves to amend."[51] Again he says, "Whatever thou hast done, yet if thou repent and will amend, he promiseth that he will not think on thy sins."[52] This emphasis on amendment and new life after the term "repent" in terms of the forgiveness of sin indicates that μετανοέω and μετάνοια in Tyndale's mind emphasize changing one's life.

Beside this new life and amendment of life, Tyndale's translation of μετανοέω (and μετάνοια) as "repent" (and "repentance") emphasizes emotion, feeling sorry or regret for the past sin.[53] In his dialogue with Thomas More, Tyndale defines μετανοέω and μετάνοια as "repent and repentance, or forethinking and forethink,"[54] while he rejects "penance," which indicates the works of satisfaction for sins. He further explains that μετανοέω means to be sorry, saying, "as we say in English It forethinketh me, or I forethink; and I repent, or It repenteth me, and I am sorry that I did."[55] In other words, he emphasizes emotion in his translation of μετανοέω by using *repent*, a synonym of *forethink* meaning to be sorry. In addition, he explains μετανοέω by using an emphatic demonstrative pronoun "this" to emphasize emotion strongly, "this mourning and sorrow of the heart," and continues that it "lasteth all our lives long: for we find ourselves, all our lives long, too weak for God's law, and therefore sorrow and mourn,

---

51. Tyndale, *Expositions and Notes*, 76.
52. Tyndale, *Expositions and Notes*, 156, 221.
53. Tyndale, *Expositions and Notes*, 118, 156, 221. Tyndale explained that μετανοέω means "to forthink" ("to displease, cause to regret)."
54. Russel, *Works of the English Reformers*, 2:23.
55. Russel, *Works of the English Reformers*, 2:23.

longing for strength. Repentance is no sacrament."[56] He says that μετανοέω is not the work of sacraments but a deep, lifelong sorrow and mourning of the heart because all people are weak.

Conclusion

This chapter examines the meaning of μετανοέω and μετάνοια from the OT, critical dictionaries, and scholars. What is striking is that there is a parallelism between the OT prophets and Jesus. Both command a turning and emphasize the law or the will of God as the contents of μετάνοια (Matt 5:17; 7:12, 21; 22:40). This parallelism shows Jesus' ministry as a μετάνοια ministry similar to the prophets. It also examines the translation problems of the terms. However, we discovered that the OT background, modern scholars, and even Tyndale agree in the meaning of the terms as "turning to God in mind and heart" and suggest different translation options. Tyndale's translation of μετανοέω uses "repent" to emphasize both emotion and a new life. His main emphasis as noted above is on "a new life," that is, "amendment of life" or "changing life." However, Tyndale's English translation eventually lost the emphasis on change of life that the Greek term μετανοέω carries, but means to be sorry, to stop doing sin, and to change one's mind. The English terms "repent" and "repentance" mean feeling sorry or regret. This reductionism creates a difficulty with understanding the first words of Jesus Christ in the Gospel of Matthew 4:17 as the significant theme in Matthew.

---

56. Tyndale, *Doctrinal Treatises*, 260–61.

Chapter 4

John the Baptist's μετάνοια Preaching (Matt 3:1–12)

Introducing the Thematic Significance of μετάνοια in Matthew

Introduction

THIS CHAPTER DEMONSTRATES THE thematic significance of μετάνοια in John the Baptist's μετάνοια preaching (3:1–12), and it serves to introduce the thematic significance of μετάνοια in the whole book of Matthew. As the previous chapter discussed, the OT prophetic repentance tradition continues in John the Baptist's μετάνοια (turning) teaching and ministry.[1] The location of John the Baptist's μετάνοια preaching block (3:1–12) in the early chapters of Matthew likely indicates Matthew's emphasis on μετάνοια and introduces the thematic significance of a message of μετάνοια in Matthew. The significance of μετάνοια in John the Baptist's preaching mirrors Jesus' emphasis because Jesus continues to preach and teach this same message (4:17). This is best seen in the Matthean parallelism between John and Jesus' prophetic μετάνοια ministries and teachings. The commandment of turning (μετανοέω) and its concepts in the beginning of John and Jesus' ministry is echoed in the body of Matthew in a variety of ways. This shows the thematic significance μετάνοια in Matthew.

This chapter first reviews Malachi 4:5–6 as the direct OT background of John the Baptist's μετάνοια preaching, the history of research on John the Baptist, and the parallelism between John and Jesus in Matthew. Secondly, this chapter provides evidence for the significance of μετάνοια in Matthew 3 and examines the introductory function of 3:1–12 as shown by the parallelism between John and Jesus' teaching and ministry in Matthew. It will show how John's prophetic μετάνοια preaching parallels and

1. See ch. 3 for the OT prophets' repentance tradition review section.

continues in Jesus' teaching and ministry. Finally, this chapter will show that both Jesus' baptism for μετάνοια and his temptation are categorized as one unit with chapter 3:1-12, demonstrating Jesus as a model of the fruitful life of repentant people.

The Theme of μετάνοια in Malachi Continued and Fulfilled in John the Baptist and Jesus Christ

As discussed in the previous chapter, μετάνοια in the Gospel of Matthew has a strong OT prophetic background. Specifically, John the Baptist, in the shape of Elijah, and Jesus' continuing μετάνοια ministry recall the very last verses of the OT, Malachi 4:5-6, which prophesied the coming of Elijah, that is John the Baptist (Matt 3:3-4), and his μετάνοια ministry that would turn the hearts of the children to God to avoid judgment. These last verses of the prophet Malachi and their theme of μετάνοια continue to the Gospel of Matthew and are fulfilled through John the Baptist and Jesus' μετάνοια ministry (3:2-12; 4:17). Specifically, the fire judgment image, the law of Moses, and the heart language in Malachi 4 are reemphasized in Matthew (cf. Matt 3:10-12; 5:17-20; 7:12; 13:30, 40, 49, 50, and so on). Matthew begins with the same concept of μετάνοια of the prophet Malachi and this signifies the significance of the theme of μετάνοια in Matthew.

History of Research of John the Baptist and Parallelism between John and Jesus

Scholars who study John the Baptist in Matthew and the other Gospels tend to focus on the historical aspect of his life[2] and on the origin of his water baptism.[3] Some scholars, however, have examined the parallelism

---

2. For the history of research on John the Baptist, see Strecker, *Theology of the New Testament*, 217-18; Meier, "John the Baptist in Matthew's Gospel," 383. For historical study of John the Baptist, see Taylor, *Immerser*; Taylor, "John the Baptist and the Essenes," 256-85; Webb, *John the Baptizer and Prophet*. Webb, "John the Baptist," 179-229.

3. In regard to the origin of John's baptism there are many explanations. First, baptism symbolizes submission to judgment and features eschatological imagery. Kraeling, in *John the Baptist*, 117-18, explains that immersion in running water symbolizes submersion in the river of fire, meaning one who is baptized declares he is a sinner who deserves punishment from God. However, Nolland, in "'In Such a Manner,'" 67, argues it is hard to relate the image of baptism to judgment, because there is no indication in the Bible for judgment being connected to the threat of disaster with a "flood of water" (2 Sam 22:5; Pss 69:2-3, 15; 32:6; 124:4-5). A second approach is Jewish proselyte baptism theory. However, Nolland considers it unlikely that Jewish proselyte baptism was practiced at the time of John the Baptist, or even the time of Matthew. Beasley-Murray,

between John the Baptist and Jesus Christ but focus on the redaction of the parallelism and the theological reasons behind it.[4] The common historical and theological reading of John the Baptist indicates him as Jesus' forerunner.[5] Scholars have not sufficiently recognized that John the Baptist's μετάνοια preaching (3:1–12) and the literary parallelism between John and Jesus both highlight the μετάνοια theme in Matthew. The Matthew 3:1–12 introduction demonstrates μετάνοια as a significant theme of Matthew, and this introductory function is shown by the parallelism between John's and Jesus' ministry and teaching.

Parallelism between John the Baptist and Jesus in Matthew

Now I will review representative works on the parallelism between John the Baptist and Jesus Christ in Matthew. Scholars here do not deal with this parallelism literarily, but rather theologically or historically. In any case, they help to show Matthean parallelism between John the Baptist and Jesus Christ and demonstrate that Matthean John the Baptist is an ally to Jesus. These scholars also explain that Jesus continues John's μετάνοια ministry for the inauguration of the kingdom of heaven.

Walter Wink provides the best representative redaction study of John the Baptist in Matthew. This study also shows the parallelism between John the Baptist and Jesus Christ.[6] Wink first states that his redaction study is

---

in, *Baptism in the New Testament*, 27–29, 41, rightly points out that Jewish proselyte baptism was the baptism of gentile converts to Judaism, but John baptized Jews. For the meaning of baptism, Flemington, in *New Testament Doctrine of Baptism*, 11–12, says that the meaning of the verb *baptize* in John's usage is the literal action, the intensive form of βαπτω, meaning "to dip, to immerse or to plunge." John said "baptize with Holy Spirit and fire" in the same sense in Matthew 3.

The baptism of John probably derived from water-related ceremonies compared to cleansing (Lev 15) and to repentance in the OT (Isa 1:16–17; Jer 4:14; Ps 51:7–9; Isa 4:2–6; Ezek 36:25–26, 33; 37:23; Jer 33:8; Zech 13:1) (Chilton, "John The Purifier," 220). Also, it is related to the image of God washing away sin (Ps 51:7–9; Isa 4:2–6; Ezek 36:25–26, 33; 37:23; Jer 33:8). In Second Temple Judaism, the use of flowing ("living") water was associated with repentance and forgiveness for the most severe uncleanness (Webb, "John the Baptist," 188). However, its form and the way of doing it were unique and new. Therefore, it is likely that this baptism originated from John the Baptist himself for cleansing and repentance as the last prophet of the old era in which he expects eschatological divine judgment and restoration (Matt 3:2) (Webb, "John the Baptist," 187, 189–97).

4. For example, Trilling, *Das wahre Israel*, 271–89; Wink, *John the Baptist*; Meier, "John the Baptist in Matthew's Gospel"; Allison, "Continuity between John and Jesus," 6–27.

5. Strecker, *Theology of the New Testament*, 224. Webb, "John the Baptist."

6. Wink, *John the Baptist in the Gospel Tradition*, 27–41.

based on theologian Wolfgang Trilling's analysis of John the Baptist in Matthew.[7] Wink analyzes the fate of the prophet noting the parallel in John and Jesus' passion and death (13:57; 21:33–43; 23:29–36; 14:3–12). Wink points out that both John and Jesus inaugurate the kingdom of heaven (3:2; 4:17; 11:12–13). Then Wink shows readers how John as the Elijah-like prophet (Mal 3:1) necessarily suffers before Jesus Christ and the inauguration of the kingdom of heaven (11:10; 17:10–12).

Wink insists that John the Baptist and Jesus Christ are united, but Jesus has superiority in both "assimilation and distinction." First, various texts relate to the assimilation of John and Jesus: (1) Both John and Jesus use the statement: "every tree therefore that does not bear good fruit is cut down and thrown into fire" in 3:10b; 7:19; 15:13; (2) both use the term "brood of vipers" in 3:7; 12:34; and 23:33; (3) both include the proclamation of the kingdom in 3:2 and 4:17; and (4) both suffer the same opposition by the Pharisees in 3:7; 21:32; 21:23–46. Second, other texts show the distinction between the two men: (1) Jesus is the Messiah and the light of the world (4:16); (2) Jesus is superior (3:11b; 14); (3) Jesus forgives sins (26:28); (4) Jesus is John's successor (3:11; 4:12, 17); and (5) John is least in the kingdom of heaven (11:12–15) but more than a prophet (11:9). In short, Wink's analysis shows that unlike the other Gospels, in Matthew, John the Baptist and Jesus are united as allies who inaugurate the kingdom of heaven together (3:2; 4:17).[8]

John Meier represents the study of parallelism between John the Baptist and Jesus Christ in Matthew through redaction study.[9] Meier traces John the Baptist and Jesus' parallel proclamations, rebukes, threats, fates, and martyrdoms: the same commandment of μετάνοια in 3:2 and 4:17; their confrontation with Israel (14:1–12; 16:1–12); their use of the epithet "brood of vipers" (3:22; 12:34); their declaration of woes against the scribes and Pharisees (3:7; 23:33); and the judgment language they use (3:10; 7:19; 13:40–42, 50; 25:31–46). Then he traces the appearance of John the Baptist in the body of Matthew, identifying him as the midpoint of time between Jesus' earthly life (after the OT and before the church time), and the Elijah-like prophet subordinate to Jesus. Finally, Meier asks why Matthew creates this parallelism through redaction of his sources. Meier agrees with Trilling's salvation-historical answer[10] that Matthew has an apologetic need to support his claim that the true people of God are not the people of Israel but

---

7. Trilling, *Das wahre Israel*, 271–89.
8. Wink, *John the Baptist in the Gospel Tradition*, 39.
9. Meier, "John the Baptist in Matthew's Gospel."
10. Trilling, *Das wahre Israel*, 271–89.

the church. Matthew emphasizes the necessity of Israel's rejection of both the Elijah-like prophet John the Baptist and Jesus Christ.

Dale C. Allison is another representative dealing with the continuity between John the Baptist and Jesus.[11] Allison states, "Jesus appears to have been fundamentally indebted to John throughout his ministry."[12] Matthew 3:2 and 4:17 show that both have similar goals and proclamations.[13] Allison demonstrates Jesus' dependence on, and so continuity with, John the Baptist through several factors: (1) Both John and Jesus use descent from Abraham and judgment (Matt 3:9; 8:11). (2) Both shared images such as "bearing fruit worthy of μετάνοια" and the according judgment (Matt 3:8, 9; 7:16–21; 12:33–35), as well as "the ax already lies at the root of the trees that every tree not bearing healthy fruit is to be chopped down" (Matt 3:10; 7:19), being "thrown on the fire" (Matt 3:9; 7:19; 13:40), "the winnowing fork," "threshing floor," "wheat into the barn," and "the chaff into unquenchable fire" (Matt 3:12; 13:24–30). (3) Jesus is fulfilling John's proclamation of the coming One (Matt 3:11).[14] Finally, Allison mentions people's reaction to Jesus: regarding him as John the Baptist risen from the dead (Matt 14:1–2; Mark 6:14). Their ends are parallel—arrest, execution, and burial.

Conclusion

The scholars listed above discuss parallelism between Jesus and John. They show that Matthew portrays John the Baptist not just as the forerunner of Jesus Christ, but also as an ally united and continuing with Jesus Christ in many aspects. While the common understanding of John the Baptist as Jesus' forerunner separates John the Baptist and his μετάνοια preaching (3:1–12) from the whole narrative context of Matthew, this parallelism leads to reading John's μετάνοια preaching (3:1–12) in connection with the whole narrative context of Matthew. The previously mentioned scholars do not read John's μετάνοια preaching (3:1–12) literally as an introduction of the μετάνοια theme of Matthew. The continuity of preaching contents between John the Baptist and Jesus in Matthew demonstrates that John the Baptist's ministry and proclamation of μετάνοια (3:2–12) are continued in the rest of the book, especially in Jesus' proclamation and ministry.

11. Allison, "Continuity between John and Jesus," 6–27. Allison mainly deals with the continuity between John the Baptist and Jesus Christ through the Q source.

12. Allison, "Continuity between John and Jesus," 16.

13. Allison, "Continuity between John and Jesus," 27.

14. Allison, "Continuity between John and Jesus," 16–27. Allison uses the Q source in discussing the continuity, but I change the Q source references to the Gospel of Matthew since I am arguing for a Matthean continuity between John and Jesus.

The main topic—μετάνοια—in John the Baptist's ministry and preaching (3:1–12) continues to appear as a significant theme in the body of Matthew. Through this continuity, John the Baptist's preaching functions literarily as an introduction to Matthew and demonstrates that the theme of μετάνοια is a significant theme of the whole book of Matthew.

μετάνοια in the Parallelism Between John the Baptist (3:1–12) and Jesus

Matthew's early reference to John the Baptist's μετάνοια ministry and preaching indicates its likely function as the introduction to the significance of μετάνοια in Matthew and Jesus' ministry and teaching in particular, while acknowledging John's subordinate role to Jesus' power and authority (3:11). The scholars named previously examined the parallelism between John and Jesus in Matthew, but their analyses were not comprehensive, especially the literary function of John's μετάνοια preaching (3:1–12). This section reveals how the μετάνοια introducing the preaching of John the Baptist parallels Jesus' ministry and teaching throughout the body of Matthew through parallel language and images and supports the significance of μετάνοια in 3:1–12 and therefore in the body of Matthew.

Four μετάνοια Thematic Elements in John's Preaching (3:1–12)

John the Baptist's preaching begins with the summary commandment of μετάνοια (3:2). Matthew expands it in the following verses (3:3–10) and introduces Jesus as the baptizer with the Holy Spirit and fire for μετάνοια (3:11–12). John the Baptist's μετάνοια preaching block includes four thematic ideas related to the theme of μετάνοια: the term μετάνοια (3:2, 8); bearing fruits worthy of μετάνοια (3:8, 10); judgment and vindication language corresponding to μετάνοια (3:7, 10, 11, 12); and the reconstitution of the people of God corresponding to μετάνοια (3:9). These μετάνοια preaching elements can be grouped under the theme of μετάνοια. Each of these four μετάνοια thematic elements comprise the essence of the theme of μετάνοια. As we will see in the next section, these four elements continue to appear in Jesus' teaching and ministry. And this widespread parallel μετάνοια theme and language demonstrate that the theme and the essence of μετάνοια introduced in Matthew 3 continues in the body of Matthew and its significance in Matthew. The commandment of turning (μετανοέω) in the beginning of John and Jesus' ministry (3:2; 4:17) is echoed in the body of Matthew in these μετάνοια themes and language.

Analysis of the μετάνοια Parallelism Between John the Baptist and Jesus

Now I will elaborate on how John the Baptist's μετάνοια preaching block functions as the introduction to the whole of Matthew to show that the theme of μετάνοια is a significant theme in Matthew. I will comprehensively analyze the parallelism related to μετάνοια language between 3:2-12 and the rest of the gospel.

First, the strongest case is that John the Baptist and Jesus both begin their ministry and teaching with the same summary phrase: "Repent, for the kingdom of heaven is near" (3:2; 4:17). This parallelism only appears in the Gospel of Matthew. John the Baptist appears as the returning Elijah and begins to preach, "Repent, for the kingdom of heaven is at hand" (3:1-2). John the Baptist's Elijah figure shows that Matthew begins to write his gospel with the prophetic theme of μετάνοια.[15] Jesus retains John the Baptist's μετάνοια ministry and teaching by using the same opening summary phrase for his own ministry and teaching (4:17). The parallelism between 3:2 and 4:17 denotes that Jesus and John the Baptist's ministry and teaching are parallel in their use of the theme of μετάνοια. This continuity shows that 3:1-12 and Jesus' ministry and teaching are united and coherent and that the theme of μετάνοια governs the body of Matthew. This opening commandment of μετάνοια is echoed in the body of Matthew in a variety of ways. The terms μετανοέω and μετάνοια in 3:2, 8, 11 occur in 4:17; 9:13; 11:20, 21; 12:41. Also, synonyms and terms with similar meanings of μετάνοια and μετανοέω occur in the body of Matthew expressing the theme of μετάνοια throughout the text: στρέφω occurs in 18:3, ἐπιστρέφω occurs in 13:15, and μεταμέλομαι occurs in 21:29, 32.

In particular, the unique redaction in Matthew of the first phrase of John the Baptist and Jesus Christ "repent for the kingdom of heaven

---

15. There are some supporting arguments: First, John's appearance (Matt 3:4) recalls Elijah (2 Kgs 1:8), which further enhances his prophetic appearance. Second, Evans, "Baptism of John," 48-50, says both are associated with the Jordan River: Elijah hid east of the Jordan (1 Kgs 17:3, 5; 2 Kgs 2:6); Elijah divided the Jordan River, recalling the Exodus (2 Kgs 2:6-8); Elisha commanded Naaman the Syrian to dip in the river (2 Kgs 5:10, 14). Matthew's intention is related to the traditions concerning Elijah's return to avert the wrath of God and lead Israel to repentance (Mal 3:23-24; Sir 48:9-10). Also, in relationship to the judgment day and to Jesus Christ, John mentions Jesus' baptism to confirm Jesus Christ as the judgment agent. John preaches, "He will baptize you with the Holy Spirit and fire" (Matt 3:11).

is at hand" (Matt 3:2 and 4:17) emphasizes the thematic significance of μετάνοια. Mark records the first phrase of Jesus' ministry as, "The time is fulfilled, and the kingdom of God is at hand; repent and believe in the gospel" (1:15). While Mark adds the time and the command to believe in the gospel, Matthew includes only the command to repent (μετανοέω) in view of the coming kingdom. Matthew's shorter version of John and Jesus' opening summary phrases highlights the theme of μετάνοια in contrast to Mark. Matthew probably wants to emphasize μετάνοια more than believing. Luke and John do not include the opening summary phrase.

More importantly, Matthew's unique parallel redaction of the first phrase of John the Baptist and Jesus Christ (3:2 and 4:17) emphasizes the continuity of μετάνοια as a significant theme. Matthew alone creates this parallelism between John and Jesus by writing the exact same summary opening phrase for both men. Mark and Luke do not create this parallelism between the two. Instead, Mark and Luke introduce John as the baptizer for the forgiveness of sins (Mark 1:4; Luke 3:3). John and Jesus' parallel summary statements in Matthew demonstrate that Matthew insists on μετάνοια as a significant theme for his gospel, and John the Baptist's ministry and teaching parallels Jesus' public ministry and teaching. John the Baptist's preaching block functions as an introduction to Matthew, introducing μετάνοια as a significant theme.[16] Matthew 4:12–13 indicates that Jesus continues John's ministry after the latter's arrest. The images and ideas found in John the Baptist's preaching appear repeatedly throughout the body of Matthew.

Second, the phrases "bearing fruits worthy of μετάνοια" and "good fruits" (3:8, 10), which are consistent with "good" (καλός), "bearing" (ποιέω), "fruit" (καρπός), and "worthy" (ἄξιος), keep appearing in the body of Matthew comprising the commandment of turning (μετανοέω). What is "fruits worthy of μετάνοια"? John the Baptist does not fully explain or give the contents of the fruits, but the expression "bearing fruits worthy of μετάνοια" in 3:8 recalls Matthew's frequent expressions about bearing good fruit, which denotes doing what Jesus commands—good fruits/works. Even John uses "good fruit" and "fruits worthy of μετάνοια" in same meaning in 3:8–10. Jesus continues and expands John the Baptist μετάνοια preaching while giving the contents of the fruits worthy of μετάνοια and hereby expressing the theme of μετάνοια in the body of Matthew.

Overall, these words are widespread in the body of Matthew. The word "good" (καλός) occurs in 3:10; 5:16; 7:17, 18, 19; 12:33; 13:8, 23, and 48, indicating good fruit or good works. With that, the term "fruit" (καρπός) occurs in 7:16–20; 12:33; 13:8, 26; 21:19, 34, 41, and 43. Additionally, the

---

16. See ch. 1, n. 2 for scholars who note Matt 3:2 and 4:17 as a summary statement.

word "bearing" (ποιέω) occurs in 5:19, 32, 46, 47; 6:1, 2, 3; 7:12, 17, 18, 19, 21, 24, 26; 12:12, 33, 50; 13:23, 41; 18:35; 19:16; 21:13, 31, 43; 23:3, 5, 15, 23; 24:46; 25:40, and 45. Worthy (ἄξιος) occurs in 10:11, 13, 37, 38; and 22:8. The commandment of turning (μετανοέω) in the beginning of John and Jesus' ministry (3:2; 4:17) is echoed in the body of Matthew in these images and language.

In detail, the first appearance of the term "good" in 5:16 connects the Beatitudes and the good fruits in 3:10 and the fruits worthy of μετάνοια in 3:8. This close connection denotes that the Beatitudes comprise the good, worthy fruits of μετάνοια. The first appearance of the good fruit imagery in 7:16–21 warns the false prophets and ends with the commandment to do the will of God in order to enter the kingdom of heaven. The good tree and good fruit imagery illustrate μετάνοια as meaning turning to do the will of God as Jesus taught in the sermon. The verb ποιέω translated "bearing" and "doing" frequently occurs in the sermon (5:19, 32, 46, 47; 6:1, 2, 3; 7:12, 17, 18, 19, 21, 24, 26) to express a change of heart and conduct. This repeated phrases indicate that the sermon illuminates the nature of the good fruit of μετάνοια. Verse 12:33 commands hearers to bear good fruit as an expression of μετάνοια (12:41). The contrast between not turning(μετάνοια) Israel and turning(μετάνοια) Nineveh in verse 12:41 indicates that this good tree/fruit and bad fruit/tree image are related to worthy fruit of μετάνοια. The verb ποιέω also occurs in 12:12, 33, 50 to express the theme of μετάνοια in relation to good fruit-bearing language in 12:33. The parables in Matthew 13 are full of similar imagery, which expresses the theme of μετάνοια echoing the commandment of turning (μετανοέω). References in 13:8, 23, 26, 41 use fruit images and the verb ποιέω to express the theme of μετάνοια as meaning to do what Jesus has commanded, not lawlessness. Also, the wheat and chaff image in 3:12, which expresses the fruits worthy of μετάνοια in 3:8 occurs in 13:12, 17, 25, 29, 30. This reoccurrence shows that the parables in Matthew 13 convey the theme and the fruits worthy of μετάνοια. Verse 19:16 uses the verb ποιέω to express turning one's heart from love of money to obedience to Jesus, especially by giving money to the poor (19:21) echoing the fruit of μετάνοια. Fruit-bearing language occurs in 21:13, 19, 31, 34, 41, 43, which include both negative and positive meanings indicating that the fruit of μετάνοια can be good or bad. The verb ποιέω in 21:13 expresses the theme of μετάνοια by indicating what people in the temple turned from. In 21:19 the theme of μετάνοια is visualized through the fruitless fig tree and judgment of the temple. The two parables in Matthew 21 use the verb ποιέω and the fruit image (21:31, 34, 41, 43) to express the theme of μετάνοια. The first son in the parable of the two sons (21:28–32) expresses μετάνοια through changing his mind and actions and obeying the will of his father. The parable of the wicked tenant in the vineyard (21:33–46) also uses the verb ποιέω and a fruit image (21:34, 41, 43). This parable depicts the wickedness of religious leaders of Israel and what they needed to turn away from in order to turn to Jesus—echoing the commandment of turning (μετανοέω). Matthew 24:46 uses the verb ποιέω to signify the fruits worthy of μετάνοια for a follower of Jesus. Finally, 25:40, 45 uses the verb ποιέω to indicate the fruits worthy of μετάνοια for the righteous to enter eternal life.

Two synonyms of the verb ποιέω, ἐργάζομαι (7:23; 21:28; 25:16; 26:10) and ἔργον (5:16), also carry the theme of μετάνοια by indicating the bearing of fruits worthy of μετάνοια, echoing the opening commandment of turning (μετανοέω) in 3:2 and 4:17. Matthew 7:23 uses ἐργάζομαι to convey the theme of μετάνοια, commanding his audience to do the will of God instead of living in lawlessness (7:21). The parable of two sons in Matthew 21:28 also uses ἐργάζομαι to communicate the theme of μετάνοια related to the command to do the will of the father. The parable of the talents in Matthew 25:10 uses ἐργάζομαι to express the theme of μετάνοια as meaning to observe what the master commands. In 5:16, ἔργον repeats the theme of μετάνοια, commanding the disciples to do good work as the truly repentant and the people of God. "Good work" in Matthew expresses the theme of μετάνοια echoing the opening commandment of turning (μετανοέω) in 3:2 and 4:17.

"Worthy" (ἄξιος) language also speaks to the theme of μετάνοια. The term occurs four times in Matthew 10 (10:11, 13, 37, 38, and 22:8) echoing the worthy fruit of μετάνοια. The disciples will find people who are worthy and stay with them (10:11, 13). The character of those who are worthy in 10:37, 38 perhaps indicates the worthy fruit of μετάνοια when they love Jesus more than their family, they take their own cross to follow Jesus, and they lose their life for Jesus. These people show μετάνοια through turning their lives to follow Jesus, leaving everything behind.

The summary phrase in 3:2 and 4:17 and the widespread use of the metaphorical image of bearing fruits worthy of μετάνοια indicates μετάνοια as a significant theme in the body of Matthew. This fruit-bearing image echoes the commandment of turning (μετανοέω) (3:2; 4:17) in the body of Matthew. "Bearing fruits" appears in the body of Matthew as a metaphorical expression for doing good, righteousness, and the will of Father. In other words, Matthew's emphasis on righteousness, doing the will of God, and doing good or good action should be understood under the theme of μετάνοια. As noted in chapter 3, critical dictionaries includes theses Matthean topics as the definition and the contents of μετάνοια.[17] These emphases illustrate

---

17. See ch. 3, especially the first half.

μετάνοια through their meaning: the changing (or turning) of one's mind, heart, will, and conduct, thus one's whole being and life. Doing good, righteousness, and the will of the Father comprise the fruits worthy of μετάνοια. Righteousness occurs in 3:15; 5:6, 10, 20; 6:1, 33, 21:32 and the related idea of doing the will of God in 6:10; 7:21; 12:50; 18:14; 21:31; 26:42.

Third, the judgment and vindication language of μετάνοια in Matthew 3:1–12 appears throughout the body of Matthew, demonstrating the theme of μετάνοια and echoing the commandment of turning (μετανοέω). As the two summary phrases, 3:2 and 4:17, include the commandment of turning (μετανοέω) and references to judgment and vindication, together they demonstrate the theme of μετάνοια in the body of Matthew. Verses 3:2 and 4:17 indicate that μετάνοια determines judgment and vindication, and the latter motivates the former. The judgment and vindication theme of 3:2b, "for the kingdom of heaven is at hand," is expressed with the wrath, the axe, fire, hell, the winnowing fork, the threshing floor, the chaff thrown into unquenchable fire, and the wheat gathered into the barn in 3:3–12. This language and imagery occur throughout the body of Matthew. They typically follow the opening command to turn in meaning to change in heart and deed.

First, wrath, the axe, fire, hell, the winnowing fork, the threshing floor, and throwing the chaff into unquenchable fire (3:7, 10, 11, 12) appear in 5:22, 29, 30; 7:19; 8:12; 13:30, 40, 42, 48, 50; 18:8, 9; 22:13; 24:51; 25:30, 41, 46 demonstrating the judgment corresponding to μετάνοια and echoing the opening commandment of turning (μετανοέω) meaning to change one's heart and conduct. For example, verses 5:22, 29, and 30 demonstrate the theme of μετάνοια when Jesus commands Christians not to be angry or to insult their brothers and not to sin, for they will be thrown into the fire of hell. The fire image appears in 7:19 with the image of bearing fruit, repeating Matthew 3's theme of μετάνοια. The parables in Matthew 13 use judgment and vindication language in 13:30, 40, 42, 48, 50 with a fruit-bearing image to repeat and demonstrate Matthew 3's theme of μετάνοια. Verses 18:8, 9 command μετάνοια: do not sin with hand, foot, or eye so that one will not be thrown into eternal fire or fire of hell. Verse 22:13 uses "outer darkness" to demonstrate Matthew 3's theme of turning to the kingdom of heaven with proper fruits of μετάνοια, which is depicted by the proper wedding garment in the parable of the wedding guests. In 25:41 and 46 the terms "eternal fire" and "eternal punishment" and "eternal life" demonstrate Matthew 3's theme of μετάνοια related to doing good for the hungry, thirsty, naked, sick, stranger, prisoned, and the least. Verses 8:12; 13:42, 50; 22:13; 24:51; 25:30 use "outer darkness" and "gnashing of teeth and weeping," but they still demonstrate the theme of μετάνοια by carrying the same judgment, meaning to motivate μετάνοια to do good things.

Secondly, "gather his wheat into the barn" in 3:12 implies life, eternal life, and entering the kingdom of heaven, themes which occur in 5:20; 7:13, 14, 21; 18:3, 8, 9; 19:16, 17, 29; 23:13; 25:10, 21, 23, 46 demonstrating rewards of μετάνοια and echoing the commandment of turning (μετανοέω). For example, the same wording is found in 13:30 indicating the parallelism between John the Baptist and Jesus Christ in Matthew related to the theme of μετάνοια. Most of the gospel's occurrences of "life," "eternal life," and "entering into the kingdom of heaven" are with the judgment language examined in the previous paragraph. These vindication terms also demonstrate that the theme of μετάνοια in the body of Matthew parallels John the Baptist's μετάνοια preaching, echoing the opening commandment of turning (μετανοέω) in 3:2 and 4:17.

In addition, the leadership of Israel comes under judgment in the term "brood of vipers," a reference to the Pharisee and Sadducees. The expression also appears in 12:34 and 23:33 indicating parallelism between Matthew 3 and the rest of Matthew as it relates to the theme of μετάνοια. Jesus rebukes the unrepentant generation and proclaims woes to the religious leaders of Israel in chapter 23.

Fourth, "God is able from these stones to raise up children for Abraham" (3:9) indicates the reconstitution of the people of God, not according to Israelite ethnicity but by μετάνοια toward Jesus. This reconstitution of the people of God by μετάνοια appears in the gentile μετάνοια (or inclusion) theme in the body of Matthew (1:1, 2, 3, 5, 6; 8:5–13; 15:21–28; 24:14; 28:19–20 and so on). The reconstitution of the people of God includes Israel (10:5–6) and the gentiles (28:19), and all nations (28:19), through μετάνοια toward Jesus with worthy fruits. Verses 8:11–12 and 24:31 even rephrase 3:9. This repeat of Matthew 3's reconstitution of the people of God through μετάνοια in the body of Matthew demonstrates the thematic significance of μετάνοια in Matthew.

In conclusion to this section, above examination of μετάνοια parallelism between John the Baptist and Jesus, especially in terms of the four elements of μετάνοια in John's preaching, shows the thematic significance of μετάνοια in Matthew.

Jesus' Baptism of the Holy Spirit (3:11–12) in Relation to the Theme of μετάνοια

The parallels continue in their baptism ministries. The last part of John the Baptist's μετάνοια preaching block, verses 3:11–12, introduces Jesus Christ as mightier than John and as the baptizer with the Holy Spirit and fire. The obvious difference between their baptisms is that John baptizes with water, but Jesus baptizes with the Holy Spirit and fire as meaning purification[18] or judgment(3:12).[19] Then for what does Jesus baptize with the Holy Spirit and fire? While Matthew writes that John baptizes for μετάνοια, he does not directly state for what Jesus will baptize. The context indicates that as John the Baptist baptizes with water for μετάνοια, Jesus baptizes with the Holy Spirit and fire for μετάνοια. John the Baptist identifies Jesus as one who has authority for salvation and judgment in order to motivate people to turn to Jesus.[20] This introductory identification of Jesus as the

---

18. Marshall, "Meaning of the Verb 'Baptize,'" 13–17. Marshall has pointed out that fire and spirit are also regarded as a liquid, that is, a symbol of judgment. For the spirit as liquid, he presents some OT passages: Isa 32:15; 44:3–5; Zech 12:10; Ezek 36:25–27; 39:29; Joel 2:28–29; 1QS 4:20–21; T. Jud. 24:2–3. See also, Flemington, *New Testament Doctrine of Baptism*, 18–19; Dunn, *Baptism in the Holy Spirit*, 12–14. There are many interpretations of this statement. First, some argue that it indicates inflaming, or the purifying work of the Holy Spirit. However, Nolland, in *Luke 1–9:20*, 152–53, says that this is not connected to verse 17. Some say he will judge the wicked with fire and give the Holy Spirit to those who repent, but Fitzmyer, in *Gospel According to Luke 1–9*, 473, says this is one baptism rather than two. Third, some say it is Pentecostal fulfillment, but Nolland says there was no real fire at Pentecost. Fourth, Fitzmyer says it is a modeling of purification and refinement, but the judgment theme follows in the very next verse (474). In light of these issues, it is difficult to judge which interpretation is correct; however, considering the context, judgment is the most likely explanation. John preached repentance before the coming kingdom (Matt 3:1), and there were those who repented (Matt 3:5, 6), as well as Sadducees and Pharisees who deserved the coming wrath (Matt 3:7–10). Furthermore, this story is located before the coming wrath of God, so it is likely that Jesus' baptism with the Holy Spirit and fire represents judgment. And finally, as I mentioned earlier, Matt 3 has strong similarities to Mal 3 where Jesus is described within the judgment motif.

19. Dunn, "'Baptized' as Metaphor," 302–5. He says, πνεύματι is not spirit but a strong wind of judgment. Also, Mal 3 describes Jesus as a refiner's fire and fuller's soap, thus referencing purification and judgment. Smith, in *Micah-Malachi*, 329, says, "Fire purifies as well as destroys." Meier says that Jesus' baptism is a punitive plunging of men into fire, yet purification by the Holy Spirit, is poured out in the end time (Meier, "John the Baptist in Matthew's Gospel," 390). Clendenen, in *Haggai, Malachi*, 387, considers it more likely that it is about judgment, as indicated by the rhetorical questions "Who can endure?" and "Who can stand?," as well as the statement "So I will come near to you for judgment" (Mal 3:5). He also supports this notion with "Who can stand?," which is both a wrath image of the Lord (Nah 1:6; 130:3; 140:17) and a battle image (Josh 10:8; 2 Kgs 10:4; Jer 46:15), "our God is a consuming fire, a jealous God" (Deut 4:29; 9:3; Isa 30:27; Ps 50:3; Heb 12:29), "smoking fire pot with a blazing torch" (Gen 15:17; Exod 3:2). Also, Dunn, "John the Baptist's Use of Scripture," 47–54, says the image of coming, burning, anger, and fire in Isa 30:27–28 supports judgment meaning of the spirit. Among the restoration themes in Matt 1–3, Matthew writes about John the Baptist within an Elijah motif that speaks of the final judgment. See also 1 Pet 3.

20. John's account in Matt 3:11 corresponds exactly to Malachi's judgment motif, particularly when John describes Jesus' baptism as the Holy Spirit and fire (Matt 3:11),

Holy Spirit and fire baptizer for μετάνοια demonstrates that following Jesus' ministry and teaching is for μετάνοια.

The supporting clues are as follows. First, the context of Matthew 3, which highlights the command to repent and in light of the corresponding judgments, implies that Jesus' identification as the Holy Spirit and fire baptizer commands μετάνοια toward Jesus. Just like John preaches μετάνοια motivated by judgment, the Holy Spirit and fire baptism of Jesus motivated μετάνοια toward Jesus. This causal relationship between the command to repent and Jesus' judgment power and authority parallels 3:2 and 4:17, which command μετάνοια with a warning and the motivation of the coming kingdom.

Second, Matthew 3:11 implies that Jesus baptizes with the Holy Spirit and fire for μετάνοια as John does with water for μετάνοια. Verse 3:11 states that John baptizes for μετάνοια, but it does not repeatedly state that Jesus baptizes for μετάνοια. However, their parallel baptism ministry and teaching of the theme of μετάνοια (3:2–12; 4:17) show that 3:11 does not mention Jesus' baptism for μετάνοια, but it is implied. Jesus and John the Baptist's baptism ministries for μετάνοια have parallels, but the means are different: John with water, Jesus with the Holy Spirit and fire.

Finally, Jesus commands his disciples to baptize all nations in the name of the Father, the Son, and the Holy Spirit, making disciples, teaching them what Jesus has commanded. The trinitarian baptism is for μετάνοια. The trinitarian baptismal formula in the Great Commission indicates that the work of the Holy Spirit is critical for μετάνοια. Also, the Immanuel theme in 1:23 and 28:20 indicates the critical role of Jesus and the Holy Spirit for μετάνοια.

This introductory identification of Jesus, the Holy Spirit, and the fire baptism for μετάνοια demonstrates that Jesus' powerful ministry and teaching with authority (7:28–29) in the body of Matthew are for μετάνοια. Also, the baptism with the Holy Spirit and fire (3:12) reveals Jesus as one who enables μετάνοια through the Holy Spirit and as the one who has authority to punish the unrepentant sinner with fire. The Immanuel idea (1:23; 28:20) and judgment ideas and images of fire in the body of Matthew demonstrate that they enable and motivate μετάνοια. Jesus fulfills the OT

---

which is a symbol of judgment or a judgment metaphor. However, the narrative context of Matt 3:1–12 demonstrates that the Holy Spirit and fire baptism indicate both judgment and vindication, since 3:12 rephrases it with both vindication and judgment images: "... gather his wheat into the barn, but the chaff he will burn with unquenchable fire." The basic meaning of βαπτίζω is to dip. Jesus will dip people into the Holy Spirit or fire. Those who turn to Jesus will be dipped into the Holy Spirit for reward and those who do not receive and do not turn will be dipped into fire for judgment. This baptism indicates Jesus' power and authority for judgment and salvation.

prophetic call of μετάνοια through the baptism with the Holy Spirit and fire. This introduction of Jesus as the eschatological μετάνοια baptizer with the Holy Spirit and fire shows the significance of μετάνοια in Jesus' teaching and ministry in the body of Matthew.

John the Baptist in the Body of Matthew in Relation to the Theme of *μετάνοια*

John the Baptist's appearance in the body of Matthew (chapters 11, 14, 17, 21) demonstrates the continuity of the theme of μετάνοια. John the Baptist's μετάνοια ministry and preaching led to his persecution and death (14:3–5). His persecution and death parallel Jesus' (17:12). This parallelism also indicates that Jesus' μετάνοια ministry and teaching also contribute to his persecution and death. Their parallel suffering and death demonstrate their continual μετάνοια ministry and preaching and the theme of μετάνοια as a significant theme of Jesus' ministry and teaching in the body of Matthew.

μετάνοια in Matthew 3:13–4:16

Here we will stretch our scope to Matt 3:13–4:16 since it is closely tied to John the Baptist's μετάνοια preaching block. We'll discuss Jesus' baptism of μετάνοια, the coming of the Holy Spirit, and temptation narrative in Matthew 4 to show Jesus' life in the body of Matthew as a model of repentant people's righteous or good life.

The sequential narrative context of Matthew 3–4, John the Baptist's μετάνοια baptism and preaching (3:1–10), Jesus' baptism by the Holy Spirit and fire (3:11–12), Jesus baptized for μετάνοια, the endowing of the Holy Spirit (3:13–17), and Jesus' successful response to temptation while led by the Holy Spirit (4:1–11) are related to the theme of μετάνοια. Jesus' baptism of μετάνοια and immediate coming of the Holy Spirit connect the theme of μετάνοια and the Holy Spirit. Then the Holy Spirit and the sonship language connect Jesus' μετάνοια baptism (3:13–17) and his temptation (3:17 and 4:1, 3, 6). Lastly, right after 3:1–4:11 Jesus begins his ministry with the commandment of μετάνοια(4:17). This connection likely indicates that the temptation narrative after Jesus' baptism for μετάνοια and the coming of the Holy Spirit (3:13–17) demonstrates Jesus' success of the temptation in keeping with the Father's will as a model for μετάνοια people of God and for the work of the Holy Spirit in accomplishing it.

Jesus' Water Baptism for μετάνοια

Jesus was baptized by John for μετάνοια (Matt 3:13–17). Most scholars think that Jesus' baptism serves as an announcement that he will be crucified as a sacrifice for the sins of the world. Jesus, who did not need baptism for μετάνοια, was baptized in order to place himself under the burden of sin, showing that he was going to take on the sins of the world.[21] This explanation is likely because in John's Gospel, John the Baptist says "Behold, the Lamb of God, who takes away the sin of the world" (John 1:29). In Matthew this perspective is announced directly, when Jesus says he has come to give his life as a ransom (Matt 16:13–16; 20:28).

However, this reading only reveals the negative side of Jesus' water baptism for μετάνοια. Here I suggest that this baptism scene illustrates Jesus and his life as the model of μετάνοια people. The positive aspect of Jesus' baptism for μετάνοια is that Jesus' life provides a model or fulfillment of the worthy fruit of μετάνοια. This baptism for μετάνοια foreshadows Jesus' μετάνοια ministry.[22] Jesus is not only the incarnation of God but also the one entrusted with what it means to be a person of God. Jesus' temptation and his victory model the life of the true people of God. In the temptation scene, Jesus shows fruits worthy of μετάνοια that people of God must show.

What is striking is that Jesus connects all righteousness and μετάνοια in 3:15. Matthew 3:15 implies that fulfilling all righteousness requires the baptism of turning (μετάνοια) to God. More boldly, this scene shows turning (μετάνοια) is righteousness of God. As mentioned previously, many lexical studies define μετάνοια as turning from sin to righteousness. This also indicates that Matthean righteousness language demonstrates the theme of turning (μετάνοια) in the body of Matthew, which will be fully discussed in chapter 6.

Additionally, scholars have suggested that the coming of the Holy Spirit upon Jesus indicates Jesus as the "Spirit-endowed servant" of Isaiah 11:2; 42:1; 61:1,[23] "the eschatological bearer of God's Spirit," [24] and the "visible equipment and commission for his mission as the spirit giver."[25] Also,

---

21. Yri, "Seek God's Righteousness," 101.

22. Webb, "John the Baptist," 188. Webb includes the following positive functions of water baptism together with the negative function: (1) expression of conversionary repentance, (2) mediation of divine forgiveness in some way, (3) purification from uncleanness, (4) foreshadowing of the ministry of Jesus, (5) the initiatory function into the true Israel, and (6) protest against the temple establishment.

23. Davies and Allison, *Matthew 1–7*, 338. See also Carson, *Matthew*, 109.

24. Davies and Allison, *Matthew 1–7*, 335.

25. France, *Gospel of Matthew*, 121.

according to Matthew 3:17, when the Holy Spirit comes upon Jesus, he becomes convinced more than ever before of his unique messianic (and divine) sonship.[26] However, in the narrative context of Matthew 3–4, I suggest that Jesus' receiving of the Holy Spirit confirms that Jesus will be the Holy Spirit baptizer for μετάνοια (3:11) and that the Holy Spirit will enable Jesus' success within temptation. As mentioned above, Jesus' response to temptation while led by the Holy Spirit demonstrates his life and response to temptation as the model of the life of μετάνοια people, therefore this scene indicates that Jesus is the one who gives people the Holy Spirit to enable μετάνοια and its worthy life.

Jesus' Temptation and μετάνοια

Jesus' temptation is a recapitulation of the temptation in which old Israel failed. Jesus now is victorious over Satan's temptation and offers a model of success. In this respect Jesus overturns Israel's failure to keep the will of God, thus demonstrating μετάνοια of sin to the will of God. Jesus was baptized for μετάνοια for the sins of Israel and now demonstrates himself as a model of μετάνοια in meaning to turn from sin to the will of God and righteousness. Jesus' faith and actions embody the standard of repentance God requires of his children. This is seen most clearly as Jesus does what Israel should have done, but failed to do in their temptations in the wilderness and the test of obedience that Adam and Eve failed in the garden. Jesus models himself as the One who turns away from Satan's temptation and toward God and his will. Jesus does not need μετάνοια, but as the representative of Israel, Jesus models the life of the true people of God who should turn to follow Him. The narrative context of 3:1–4, 17 and 4:17 shows that Jesus commands μετάνοια following his own model.

Conclusion

Chapters 3 and 4 of Matthew feature many references to μετάνοια. John the Baptist's μετάνοια preaching introduce the significance of μετάνοια to Matthew. The unique parallelism between John and Jesus' teaching and ministry in Matthew shows the continuity of the thematic or paradigmatic significance of μετάνοια between them. John's identification of Jesus as the baptizer with Holy Spirit and fire encourages μετάνοια to Jesus. With the Holy Spirit, Jesus enables μετάνοια and with fire he punishes the wicked, fruitless, and

---

26. Flemington, *New Testament Doctrine of Baptism*, 29; Dunn, *Jesus and the Spirit*, 62–67.

unrepentant people. Jesus clearly indicates that μετάνοια is righteousness (3:15). After Jesus baptism of μετάνοια, the Holy Spirit came down on him and led to the temptation. Both Jesus' baptism for μετάνοια and his temptation should be understood as one unit with chapter 3:1–12, demonstrate the significance of μετάνοια. Jesus' victory over Satan's temptation right after his baptism of μετάνοια shows his representative role of the people of God as a model life of μετάνοια that obeys the word of God in heart and act.

Chapter 5

The Thematic Significance of μετάνοια Expressed in Matthew's Discipleship, the Great Commission, and Gentile Inclusion

Introduction

IN PART THIS BOOK argues the thematic significance of μετάνοια in Matthew that ties together and summarizes Jesus' ministry and teaching in Matthew (4:17). This chapter and the next chapter will examine other important Matthean topics to show their conceptual overlaps and close relationship to μετάνοια as different expressions of the nature of μετάνοια, and therefore show the significance of μετάνοια in Matthew. As chapter 3 discussed, critical dictionaries define the nature of μετάνοια and the fruit worthy of μετάνοια as a total change of both mind and behavior from sin to discipleship, righteousness, doing good, and doing the will of God. This definition already shows the organic relationship between μετάνοια and these Matthean topics. This chapter will deal with discipleship, the Great Commission, and related gentile-inclusion μετάνοια. The next chapter will deal with righteousness, doing the will of God, and Matthean soteriology as it relates to the theme of μετάνοια.

The driving idea in this chapter is that despite the rare occurrence of the term μετάνοια, in the beginning of Jesus' ministry, Jesus proclaims μετάνοια (turning) for the coming kingdom of heaven and this proclamation is echoed in the body of Matthew in many ways, showing its significance in Matthew. For example, the discipleship language and images express μετάνοια in its inseparable relationships and conceptual overlaps. Jesus' calling of the disciples, their turning their lives to Jesus, and his teachings and life illustrate the nature of μετάνοια and the fruit worthy of μετάνοια. The (universal) Great Commission has a significant conceptual overlap with the commandment of turning (μετανοέω). Jesus, in the opening of his public ministry, commands people to turn their hearts and corresponding deeds, thus, their whole being and life. In the final words of the Great Commission, Jesus commands people (μετάνοια, to turn,) to become his disciples and to keep what he commands. Therefore, the first and the last words of Jesus Christ in Matthew create a conceptual inclusio of μετάνοια indicating the significance of μετάνοια in Matthew.

The Significance of μετάνοια Expressed in Discipleship

Matthew puts Jesus' commandment of μετάνοια at the outset of Jesus' public ministry (4:17). After the commandment of turning (μετανοέω), Matthew places the calling of the disciples and the disciples' turning to Jesus (4:18–23). Why does Matthew locate Jesus' commandment of μετάνοια and Jesus' calling of the disciples together at the dawn of Jesus' public ministry? First, this proximity indicates that the themes of μετάνοια and discipleship are connected, as scholars also note. For instance, Strecker says that the command to turn (μετανοέω) and be saved implies discipleship.[1] Furthermore, Schnelle comments that μετάνοια, discipleship, and faith are inseparable.[2] Moisés Silva says μετανοέω and μετάνοια "is viewed in terms of commitment to a person; the call to repentance becomes a call to *discipleship*. So, repentance, faith, and *discipleship* are different aspects of the same thing" (Mark 1:15, "Repent and believe").[3]

In agreeing with this insight and building upon it, I contend that Matthew places μετάνοια at the opening of the book as the summary of Jesus' ministry and teaching. Then he begins to unpack the nature of μετάνοια through one of Matthew's major themes and the language of discipleship. In other words, the Matthean discipleship theme and language conceptually express and illustrate the essence of μετάνοια. Also, the connection between μετάνοια in 4:17 and discipleship in 4:18–23 denotes that Matthew defines μετάνοια through Jesus' calling of the disciples and their leaving everything behind to follow him (4:18–25). Thus, in Matthew, discipleship illustrates the meaning of μετάνοια, turning (or amending or changing) one's mind (will or heart) and deeds—one's whole being and way of life—toward Jesus. Thus, Matthean discipleship shows the significance of μετάνοια. This section will continue to show how the discipleship theme and language in the body of Matthew illustrate and express the essence of μετάνοια.

---

1. Strecker, *Theology of the New Testament*, 407.
2. Schnelle, *Theology of the New Testament*, 423.
3. Silva, *New International Dictionary*, 3:290–91. Emphasis is mine.

Matthean Discipleship and its Conceptual Connection to μετάνοια

A review of assorted works on the theme of discipleship in Matthew shows the centrality of this idea in the First Gospel and how it connects strongly with the theme of μετάνοια. This section reviews representative works on the Matthean discipleship theme and discusses how Matthean discipleship expresses the theme of μετάνοια signifying the importance of μετάνοια in Matthew.

Michael J. Wilkins provides a comprehensive background study of the term μαθητεύω. Wilkins includes classical and Hellenistic sources, the LXX, Rabbinic literature, Qumran documents, and the NT.[4] He refutes the traditional understanding of the term μαθητεύω as suggested by Rengstorf.[5] Wilkins contends that the term does not specifically refer to a master-disciple relationship, but to a general learner or adherent relationship. The master determines the type of adherence. He concludes:

> The progression to 'adherent' in Hellenism at the time of Christ and the early church made μαθητής a convenient term to designate the followers of Jesus, because the emphasis in the common use of the term was not upon 'learning,' or upon being a pupil, but upon adherence to a great master. Hence a 'disciple' of Jesus, designated by the Greek term μαθητής, was one who adhered to his master, and the type of adherence was determined by the master himself.[6]

Wilkins says that the early church read this adherent relationship between Jesus and the disciples in Matthew as a role model for their relationship with Jesus.[7]

Wilkins' work contributes to a correct understanding of the relationship between Jesus and the disciples as not limited to a teacher-student or master-learner relationship, but instead as a master-intimate follower or adherent relationship. In fact, Matthew describes that they are united to each other by life (10:38–39; 16:24–25) and that they share a family-like intimate relationship (10:37; 12:49–50). These relationship images express Jesus' calling for a μετάνοια of turning one's mind (heart or will) and conduct, and so one's whole being and life, to Jesus. Also, Jesus teaches the contents of μετάνοια as including both a turning of heart and deeds—one's whole

---

4. Wilkins, *Discipleship in the Ancient World*.
5. *TDNT* 4:394–99.
6. Wilkins and Theological Research Exchange Network, *Greek Disciples*, 22.
7. Wilkins and Theological Research Exchange Network, *Greek Disciples*, 22.

being and life—in a variety of ways, especially in the image and language of discipleship in the body of Matthew.

While Wilkins contributes to an understanding of Matthean discipleship from a lexical study of μαθητεύω, Warren Carter provides insight using the narrative contextual interpretation of 4:18-23.[8] Carter agrees with the common view that 4:18-23 is the center scene of Matthean discipleship because the disciples left everything behind to follow Jesus.[9] He argues for 4:18-22 as key verses that begin the main section of the book. The introduction of Jesus in 1-4:16 and his call to turn (μετανοέω) for the coming kingdom of heaven creates the significance of Jesus' calling in 4:18-22 and the disciples' reaction. This is the salvation call and the rejection of it means judgment. Matthew 4:18-22 insists on two different directions for discipleship: one is leaving everything behind to follow Jesus, and the other is going to other human beings as a fisher of men. Leaving everything behind is not a literal detachment for Jesus says that his disciples are the salt of the earth and the light of the world (5:13-16). In contrast with the common view, Carter emphasizes the dual function of discipleship indicated in 4:18-22, "detachment and participation." This dual function means "the coexistence of both a settled way of life involving participation in social and economic structures and a life of wholehearted commitment to doing and obeying God's will which prevents disciples from being wholehearted participants in societal structures."[10]

Carter's work reveals the importance of 4:18-22 in terms of Matthean discipleship. Moreover, Carter emphasizes the call to the implied readers in 1-4:17 to read 4:18-22 significantly as an invitation to μετάνοια, a turning toward the Jesus who has been introduced in 1-4:17. Carter implies that 4:18-22 expresses Jesus' μετάνοια calling in 4:17. I argue that 4:17 is key to understanding both the introduction section (1-4:17) and Jesus' calling of his disciples (4:18-22). Verse 4:17 functions as a door that closes the previous section and opens a new section on the public ministry and teaching of Jesus. This structural function of 4:17 indicates 4:18-22 unpacks and expresses the theme of μετάνοια.

Ulrich Luz defines a disciple in Matthew as one who understands Jesus' teaching (13:16) and does the will of God (12:50). He thinks that the disciples of Jesus are transparent and models for Christians in every age and that Matthew uses μαθητής as an ecclesiological term referring to Christians

---

8. Carter, "Matthew 4:18-22," 58-75.

9. For this view, see *TDNT* 4:210-15; Wilkins, *Discipleship in the Ancient World*; Strecker, *Theology of the New Testament*, 407; Carter, *Households and Discipleship*, 129-45; Luz, "Disciples in the Gospel," 98-128; Edwards, "Uncertain Faith," 47-61.

10. Carter, "Matthew 4:18-22," 71.

of all ages to assert the connection of the earthly Jesus with Christians in every age. Disciples in Matthew equal Christians in the church.[11] Luz does not mention the theme of μετάνοια in this work. However, Luz's dual explanation of Matthean discipleship as understanding and doing what Jesus commands demonstrates the theme of μετάνοια if, indeed, as I am arguing μετάνοια means changing (or turning) one's mind (heart or will) and conduct is based on understanding Jesus' teaching and following Jesus' commands and life as a model.

Donald A. Hagner defines Matthean discipleship as "a calling to fulfill the righteousness of the Torah, but in a new way,... (which is) upon Jesus and his teaching."[12] The disciples are doers of the twofold love commandment—loving God and loving one's neighbor (22:40)—an idea similar to doing to others as you want them to do to you (7:12). The disciples' priority must be to do righteousness (6:33). Hagner asserts that Matthean discipleship and its accompanying righteousness is neither nomism nor new covenantal nomism but is accomplished by the presence of the Messiah.[13] Like Hagner, George Strecker also connects Matthean righteousness and discipleship by stating that righteousness is a "comprehensive term for the right conduct of disciples in general."[14] Matthew begins his writing about Jesus' ministry with μετάνοια (4:17) and expresses this μετάνοια through the themes of discipleship (4:18–22) and righteousness (5:20). In short, μετάνοια is turning from everything past and turning to follow Jesus with heart and deed, and so with one's whole being and life. The essence of μετάνοια means to turn to be an adherent or disciple (4:18–22) of Jesus.

Significance of μετάνοια Expressed in Discipleship

Now, based on the conceptual connection between the themes of μετάνοια and discipleship in Matthew, I argue that the theme of μετάνοια is illustrated in the book of Matthew through the discipleship theme and language. The opening commandment of turning (μετανοέω) is echoed in the discipleship theme and language in the body of Matthew and shows μετάνοια to be a significant theme of Matthew.

First, as mentioned above, the link between the concept and location of the term in 4:17 and the calling of the disciples and their following Jesus in 4:18–23 demonstrates that Matthew defines μετάνοια through

11. Luz, "Disciples in the Gospel."
12. Hagner, "Law, Righteousness, and Discipleship," 369.
13. Hagner, "Law, Righteousness, and Discipleship," 364–71.
14. Strecker, *Theology of the New Testament*, 382.

discipleship. In addition to the now well-understood sense of to turn or change one's whole being and life, Matthew also includes the concept of following Jesus as an adherent (or disciple) and leaving behind everything belonging to the past. As mentioned above, Silva comments that the idea of μετανοέω and μετάνοια "is viewed in terms of commitment to a person; the call to repentance (μετάνοια) becomes a call to discipleship. So, repentance (μετάνοια), faith, and discipleship are different aspects of the same thing (Mark 1:15, *Repent and believe*)."[15] This shows that the opening commandment of turning (μετανοέω) is echoed in the body of Matthew through the discipleship theme and language.

Second, the discipleship theme and language in the body of Matthew convey the nature of μετάνοια.and the contents of fruits worthy of μετάνοια. Examples include suffering for righteousness (5:10; 8:20); the fulfilling of righteousness according to Jesus' teaching (5:20); being whole (5:48; 19:21); being righteous (10:41; 13:43, 49; 20:4; 23:28–29; 25:37, 46; 27:19); being followers of Jesus and being persecuted/carrying one's own cross (5:10; 10:38; 16:24); being commissioned to preach repentance and turning toward Jesus (10:7, 24–25; 28:19–20); leaving houses and family (10:37; 19:27–30); giving up one's life for Jesus and taking up one's cross (10:38–39; 16:24–25); being the family of Jesus (12:50); doing the will of God (7:21–23; 12:49–50); loving God, one's neighbor (22:34–40), and one's enemies (5:43–46); forgiving (18:21–35); being humble (18:1–8; 20:26–28; 23:11–12); and living in contrast to the Pharisees and Sadducees (23).[16] These thematic teachings and sayings about discipleship illustrate the essence of μετάνοια and its implications, showing what disciples turn from and turn to. Specifically, the discipleship theme of 18:3—"turn and become like children," an expression using a synonym of μετάνοια—expresses the theme and fruit worthy of μετάνοια.

Third, the widespread stories of universal repentance of both Jew and gentile followers, manifest μετάνοια as a significant theme of Matthew (1:3–6; 8:5–13; 15:21–28; 28:18–20). Examples include the turning of the four disciples (4:18–22), the following of the great crowd (4:25; 8:1), the following of a scribe (8:19), and Matthew (9:9). Also, references to the unrepentant generation, indicating those who do not repent and follow Jesus (12:20), demonstrate the theme of μετάνοια. The μετάνοια that makes up this theme in Matthew is universal. The references to the great faith of the centurion (8:5–13), the unrepentant generation in contrast with the μετάνοια people of Nineveh and the Queen of the South (12:41–42), the Canaanite woman

---

15. Silva, *New International Dictionary*, 3:290–91.
16. This list is based on Donaldson, "Guiding Readers-Making Disciples," 41–49.

(15:21–28), and the feeding of four thousand gentiles (15:33–38) all express the universal μετάνοια (returning) theme of Matthew. Jesus' universal μετάνοια discipleship sayings in 8:11–12; 12:17–21; and 24:14 point to the theme of universal μετάνοια in Matthew.

Fourth, the two summary phrases of Jesus' public ministry 4:17–4:22 and 28:19–20 demonstrate μετάνοια as a significant theme of Matthew as illustrated in discipleship language.[17] As mentioned above, the location of 4:17 and 4:18–22 at the inception of Jesus' teaching and ministry indicates the significance of the theme of μετάνοια and its expression in discipleship in Matthew in meaning to turn one's whole being and life to follow Jesus and his instructions. The Great Commission that summarizes Matthew also conceptually commands μετάνοια using discipleship language; it calls for making disciples and teaching them to observe what Jesus has commanded (28:19–20). The Great Commission echoes the commandment of turning (μετανοέω) in the beginning of Jesus' public ministry. (I will elaborate on this in a later section). Thus, the two summary phrases of Jesus' teaching and ministry (4:17; 28:19–20) create a μετάνοια discipleship conceptual inclusio. This μετάνοια discipleship inclusio between the beginning and end of Jesus' ministry indicates μετάνοια as a significant theme of Matthew expressed in the book's discipleship theme and language.

Fifth, Matthew 16:21–28, another major structural division section, conceptually signifies the opening commandment of turning (μετανοέω) in discipleship language, indicating μετάνοια as a theme of Matthew.[18] The phrase Ἀπὸ τότε ἤρξατο Ἰησοῦς Χριστὸς signals a thematic division and the beginning of a new section of the gospel at both 4:17 and 16:21.[19] Verses 4:17 and 16:21 divide the book's sections and remind the readers of a significant theme of Matthew. Verse 16:21 predicts the passion and resurrection of Jesus, but 16:22–28 also expresses the theme of μετάνοια in discipleship language. In 16:22–23, Jesus rebukes Peter for thinking according to the will of man not the will of God. The discipleship language of 16:24–28 conveys the nature of μετάνοια as following Jesus by denying oneself and taking up one's cross to earn eternal life. In all three places where Matthew discipleship language appears, it expresses the theme of

---

17. For more discussion about this conceptual inclusio, see the later section on the Great Commission and μετάνοια.

18. A similar concept of discipleship is found in 11:28–30, expressing the theme of μετάνοια.

19. Kingsbury, *Matthew*, 29–30. His structure is (1) The Person of Jesus Messiah (1:1—4:16); (2) The Public Proclamation of Jesus Messiah (4:17—16:20); and (3) The Suffering, Death, and Resurrection of Jesus Messiah (16:21—28:20). Also, the temporal conjunction *tote* clearly divides the two sections.

μετάνοια as a significant theme in meaning to turn (or change or amend) one's whole being and way of life to Jesus.

To strengthen the case, one can examine all three places where kingdom language implying judgment is found: "for the kingdom of heaven is at hand" (4:17), "for the Son of Man is going to come with his angels in the glory of his Father, and then he will repay each person according to what he has done" (16:27-28), and "all authority in heaven and on earth" (28:18).[20] These three passages all enforce the commandment of turning (μετανοέω) meaning to change one's heart and deeds. Jesus' prediction of the coming kingdom of heaven in 4:17 and his coming with the kingdom in 16:28 are fulfilled in 28:18 where his disciples hear and see Jesus and he states, "All authority in heaven and on the earth has been given to me." These connections indicate that the first word of Jesus Christ is accomplished by being a follower of Jesus Christ and his commandments. Disciples who abandon the old way of life and even life itself, takes up their cross and go to the end of the earth with Immanuel Jesus Christ (Matt 1:18), the Savior, the Lord (King) of heaven and earth, are assured of his promise to be with his people forever (Matt 28:20).

Finally, the five major discourse blocks demonstrate μετάνοια in discipleship theme and language. For example, Matthew 5–7 gives the essence of μετάνοια by instructing the disciples what to turn from and turn to. Matthew 10 calls the disciples to universal proclamation of μετάνοια (10:7). Matthew 18 commands the disciples μετάνοια, meaning to turn and become like a little child. Matthew 23–25 explains the theme of μετάνοια through a negative discipleship model (23) and positive parables about μετάνοια discipleship (24–25).

---

20. More parallel content between these three sections exists. First, the first words of Jesus in both 4:17 and 16:21 each begin with same phrase, Ἀπὸ τότε ἤρξατο Ἰησοῦς Χριστὸς. Second, the prophetic message of Jesus' suffering, death, and resurrection in 16:21–28 is fulfilled in the last section of the Gospel of Matthew. Third, there are disciples in 5:1; 16:21, 24; and 28:16, and discipleship appears in 16:24, "follow me" (ἀκολουθείτω μοι), as in 4:18–25 and 28:19. And "taking up the cross" appears in 16:24 and 27:32. Also, the "losing and finding life" theme appears in 6:25 and 16:25–26. Fourth, all have judgment and reward statements: 4:17, "for the kingdom of heaven is near"; 16:27, "then he will repay according to what he has done"; 28:20, "behold, I am with you always, to the end of the age." Fifth, in addition to the kingdom language that appears in all three places (4:17; 16:28; 28:18), angels also appear in all three places (4:11; 16:27; 28:2, 5).

Conclusion

Matthean scholars agree on the inseparable nature of μετάνοια and discipleship. The nature of Matthean discipleship and the contents of that discipleship equal the nature and contents of μετάνοια. Matthew expresses and comprises μετάνοια by using the discipleship theme and language. The connection between the concept and location of μετάνοια in 4:17 and the calling of disciples in 4:18–23 demonstrates that Matthew identifies being a Christian with μετάνοια discipleship that means turning and adhering to Jesus, leaving behind everything belonging to the past. The μετάνοια discipleship inclusio between the first words (4:17) and the last words (28:19–20) of Jesus' public ministry shows the thematic significance of μετάνοια in Matthew. Another major structural division, verses 16:21–28, also summarizes Matthew's theme of μετάνοια discipleship. The widespread thematic materials on discipleship in the body of Matthew also echo the commandment of turning (μετανοέω) and indicate the paradigmatic importance of μετάνοια in Matthew. Also, this thesis reconsiders the role and function of μετάνοια to show that it is not just an event that initiates being a Christian but is a lifelong process of turning and following.

The Significance of μετάνοια Expressed in the Great Commission

This book has argued first that Matthew locates μετάνοια in the beginning words of Jesus' ministry to indicate the major message of the Gospel of Matthew (cf. 3:2–18). Even though the word μετάνοια occurs in Matthew only seven times (3:2, 8, 11; 4:17; 11:20, 21; 12:41), its location at the onset of Jesus' ministry indicates its major role in the gospel. Μετάνοια means a turn (or change or emendation) of one's mind (and heart and thinking) and one's way of life by following Jesus and his teachings. It includes the positive action of turning one's whole life, for example, as shown by Jesus' disciples turning their lives to follow Jesus and his teachings (Matt 4:18–23). Μετάνοια is constantly taught and illustrated in a variety of ways in the body of Matthew.

The strongest evidence for the significance of μετάνοια in Matthew is the Great Commission. The last words of Jesus, the Great Commission (28:16–20) reflects the same meaning of μετάνοια as Jesus' first words in public ministry (4:17). Both the opening phrase (4:17) and the last phrase of Jesus' ministry command all nations (28:19) to turn and follow Jesus who has all authority in heaven and earth. In this respect, the first and the last summary words of Jesus' ministry in Matthew create a μετάνοια conceptual inclusio. The message of the Great Commission culminates in the commandment of turning (μετανοέω)—turning one's whole being and life toward Jesus by making disciples, baptizing them in the name of the Father, the Son, and the Holy Spirit,[21] and teaching them to observe all Jesus' commandments. This μετάνοια conceptual inclusio between the opening and ending of Jesus' ministry and teaching shows that the book of Matthew speaks of the theme of μετάνοια and worthy fruit of μετάνοια.

In addition, as the first words of Jesus public ministry have been recognized as the summary phrase of his ministry and teaching, the Great Commission has been recognized as the summary of the whole Gospel of Matthew and impacts the structure of the book.[22] Since the Great Commission expresses μετάνοια, the Great Commission-centered reading also demonstrates the thematic significance of μετάνοια in Matthew.

The Strong Conceptual Overlap of 4:17 and 28:19–20

Matthew 28:20 mirrors 4:17 with a strong conceptual overlap. In Jesus' last words, the reference to the need "to make disciples of all nations teaching them to observe all that Jesus has commanded" (28:20) conveys a similar concept to 4:17, that is, "to turn one's will and life toward Jesus and his teaching." Immediately after 4:17, Matthew includes Jesus' calling of his disciples and their turning to follow Jesus in order to illustrate what μετάνοια is. This image of the calling and turning of the disciples parallels the Great Commission, demonstrating further that 4:17 and the Great Commission convey similar meanings. In short, the Great Commission (28:16–20) conceptually commands μετάνοια in its references to becoming a disciple of Jesus, following Jesus, and keeping his teachings.

In addition, "teaching them to observe all that I have commanded you" in 28:20 and "μετανοεῖτε" in 4:17 both command people to do what Jesus taught in the sermon (5–7). The sermon gives the ingredients of μετάνοια, and "what Jesus taught" in 28:20 refers to the sermon. Moreover, both commandments are bolstered by kingdom language: "for the kingdom of heaven is at hand" (4:17) and "all authority in heaven and on earth has been

---

21. This baptismal formula has as its backdrop John the Baptist's μετάνοια preaching and Jesus' μετάνοια baptism with the Holy Spirit. In addition, the Immanuel theme (1:17; 28:20) governs the theme of μετάνοια in that Jesus and the Holy Spirit make possible one's repentance.

22. Brooks, "Matthew 28:16–20," 2–18; Kingsbury, "Composition and Christology," 573–84; Michel, "Conclusion of Matthew's Gospel," 28; Keener, "Matthew's Missiology," 3–20; Strecker, *Theology of the New Testament*, 368–71. For more history of research on Great Commission-centered reading, see Sim, "Is Matthew 28:16–20?"

given to me [Jesus]" (28:18). This kingdom language provides the reason for μετάνοια, and the latter statement the culmination of the former by showing Jesus as the one who has all authority in heaven and earth is the one to whom people should μετανοέω.

μετάνοια Conceptual Inclusio Between 4:17 and 28:19–20

Thus, the first and the last words of Jesus in public ministry create a μετάνοια conceptual inclusio. This framing demonstrates μετάνοια as a governing theme of Matthew. As noted in the preceding section, 4:17 and 28:16–20 share the theme of μετάνοια and the connotation of judgment in the kingdom language.

In addition, there are parallel terms between the first words and the last words of Jesus in ministry that complete the inclusio. Jesus' Great Commission to the disciples is in unity with the "fisher of men" promise of 4:19. Galilee appears in both places (4:12, 15, 18, 23; 28:16). Also, διδάσκω (4:23; 5:2; 28:20), making disciples (4:18–25; 28:19), ὄρος (5:1; 28:16), ἔθνος (4:15; 28:20), "seeing a great light" (4:16) and "seeing Jesus" (28:17) appear in both places. Matthew 4:17 does not include the baptism in the name of the Father, of the Son, and of the Holy Spirit that appears in 28:19. However, this baptismal formula has as its backdrop John the Baptist's μετάνοια preaching and baptism and Jesus' baptism with the Holy Spirit. Matthew 3 as an introduction to Jesus and his ministry summarized in 4:17 includes language of the Holy Spirit, the Spirit of God, and the Son.

Also, both 4:17 and the Great Commission are universal. First, 4:17 is universal in its near context. Satan's temptation of Jesus (4:1–11) shows Jesus' worldwide messiahship and the universal μετάνοια calling of 4:17. The citation of Isaiah 9:1–2 in 4:12–16 highlights 4:17 as a worldwide calling of μετάνοια toward Jesus because the kingdom of heaven has already been inaugurated with Jesus and he has every authority. In addition, the whole context of Isaiah 9 indicates 4:17 as Jesus' judgment call on Israel. Israel failed to act in its Abrahamic covenantal role for the salvation of all nations (Genesis 12:3), but Jesus fulfills the Abrahamic covenant. The Great Commission coheres to this principle of including all the nations, not only Jews but also gentiles (28:19).²³ The Matthean gentile inclusion theme reflects universal μετάνοια from the beginning to the end of the book.²⁴

Therefore, this inclusio verifies that μετάνοια of all nations is an overarching plot of the Gospel of Matthew.²⁵ Jesus' first words in his public ministry serve as a universal μετάνοια call with the dawn of the kingdom of heaven (4:17b), and the last words of his public ministry expand the universal μετάνοια call to the postresurrection church of the apostles (28:19-20). One could think that the theme of discipleship creates inclusion between 4:18-23 and 28:18-20 because the discipleship language appears at both places that Jesus calls disciples in 4:18-23 and Jesus commands to make disciples of all nations in 28:18-20. However, the opening commandment of turning (μετάνοια) comes right before the theme of discipleship as a governing idea in the narrative flow.

This inclusio is not alone in supporting the imperative μετανοεῖτε as a significant theme of the whole Gospel of Matthew. As mentioned above, another major division of the Gospel of Matthew, 16:21-28, shares the same μετάνοια ideas and expresses the theme of μετάνοια.²⁶ Matthew 16:21-28

---

23. πάντα τὰ ἔθνη in the Great Commission can mean "all nations," including both Israel and the gentiles (Meier, "Nations or Gentiles," 94-102), or "all Gentiles," excluding Israel (Hare and Harrington, "Make Disciples of All the Gentiles," 359-69). The gentile inclusion theme and Jesus' reconstitution of the people of God apart from the Jews indicates that πάντα τὰ ἔθνη means "all nations," including Israel. Also, Matthew's universal Christology supports this interpretation. In addition, the four consecutive usages of πᾶς ("all authority," "all nations," "all that I have commanded," and "all the days [always]") indicate the universal character of the Great Commission. Also, the total authority given to Jesus in the Great Commission repeats and reminds the reader of 11:25 (cf. 7:29; 9:6, 8; 10:1; 13:37-43; 21:23-27) and serves as a summary for the Gospel of Matthew as a whole. Even more, Jesus' universal commissioning of his disciples already appeared in 24:14. In conclusion, the salvation historical perspective based on reading πάντα τὰ ἔθνη as "all Gentiles," excluding Israel, is not likely. The other salvation historical perspective that does read πάντα τὰ ἔθνη as "all nations" is also not likely because it downplays the gentile inclusion theme that is widespread and prominent throughout Matthew and creates an illogical succession in which Israel's rejection of Jesus opens salvation to both Israel and the gentiles. Instead, reading the phrase as "all nations" coheres with Jesus' overarching worldwide repentance ministry that extends from the first word of his public ministry to his last command.

24. Schnelle, *Theology of the New Testament*, 456. Schnelle states, "The universal mission to all nations is the theological matrix in which Matthew and his church live." He mentions numerous examples of this widespread universalistic direction (24:9, 14; 25:32; 28:19; 12:21; 13:38a; 24:9-14; 26:13). He also argues that the Matthean community was not within the frame of Judaism but under the universal lordship of Jesus Christ.

25. Luz argues that 28:20 is christological, ecclesiological, and ethical (Luz, *Matthew 21-28*, 633). I think both 4:17 and 28:16-20 are christological, ecclesiological, and ethical, and so parallel.

26. Kingsbury, *Matthew*, 29-30.

has the same ideas as Jesus' first and last words in terms of changing one's life and doing good, "to change one's life" (4:17), "to observe all that Jesus has commended" (28:20), "to repay according to what he has done" (κατὰ τὴν πρᾶξιν αὐτοῦ) (16:27). Also, in all three places the kingdom language is found, "the kingdom of heaven" (4:17), "the son of man coming in his kingdom" (16:28) and "all authority in heaven and on earth" (28:18).[27] In fact, Jesus' prediction of the coming kingdom of heaven in 4:17, and his coming with the kingdom in 16:28 are fulfilled in 28:18 where his disciples hear and see Jesus and he states, "All authority in heaven and on the earth has been given to me." This coherent emphasis in the major dividing sections of the Gospel of Matthew supports the thematic significance of μετάνοια in the whole book of Matthew.

μετάνοια–Centered Reading Through the Great Commission–Centered Reading

As noted above, the Great Commission has been recognized as a summary of the Gospel of Matthew.[28] This Great Commission-centered reading of Matthew demonstrates the theme of μετάνοια as an important theme because the Great Commission echoes the commandment of turning (μετανοέω) in the beginning of Jesus' ministry (4:17). I will review the representative works on the Great Commission-centered reading through the lens of the theme of μετάνοια.

Oscar S. Brooks Sr. suggests that the Great Commission provides the structure for the whole Gospel of Matthew. He argues that all the material before the Great Commission serves to persuade people to believe and obey the Great Commission's two-fold idea: "all authority in heaven and on earth has been given to me" and "teaching them to observe all that I have commanded you"—in short, "authority" and "teaching."[29] Brooks analyzes every chapter of Matthew in relation to the Great Commission to argue for 28:16–20 as the main thesis of the Gospel of Matthew.

Brooks sees neither that the Great Commission coheres with the first words of Jesus in his public ministry (4:17), creating a large inclusio between 4:17b and 28:16–20, nor that 28:16–20 serves as the expanded definition and repetition of 4:17b, saying "Repent to Jesus, for Jesus has all authority in heaven and earth." One disagreement is with Brooks' title "teaching." "Teaching" is not the exact sum of the Great Commission, but

---

27. There are parallel contents between those three sections. See note 20.
28. See note 22.
29. Brooks, "Matthew 28:16–20," 2.

rather "teaching and making to follow" which has an equal meaning with repentance.³⁰ Therefore, it is likely that 4:17 indicates that Jesus is the One who has all authority on heaven and earth and thus that he is the One to whom people must turn. In other words, turning to follow Jesus and his teaching and Jesus' total authority of judgment (4:17 and 28:16–20) are the main themes of the Gospel of Matthew.

Davies and Allison are representatives of the Great Commission-centered reading of Matthew who include a detailed analysis of the passage. They provide eleven pieces of evidence for the Great Commission-centered reading of Matthew. Sim summarizes Davies and Allison's argument as follows:

> (1) the motif of Galilee fulfills the prophecies in 26:32 and 28:7 and creates a bracket with 4:12. (2) The mountain setting recalls other mountain scenes in the Gospel, especially 4:8 and 5:1. (3) The reference to worshipping Jesus but some doubting refers back to 14:31–33. (4) Jesus being given all authority in heaven and on earth echoes 11:27 and also the prophecy of Daniel 7:13–14 that Jesus had previously applied to himself in 24:30; 26:64. (5) The mention of making disciples is reminiscent of 13:52. (6) The reference to 'all the nations' overrides the earlier prohibition in 10:5–6 and realizes the promise made to Abraham in Genesis 12; 18:18 and 22:18. (7) The baptismal formula of the Father, the Son and the Holy Spirit recalls the baptism of Jesus, where all three figures are mentioned. (8) The command to teach mentions a central theme and gives the disciples a task previously attached to Jesus alone. (9) In referring to 'all that I have commanded you', there is a general summary of all Jesus has taught and done in the Gospel. (10) The final 'I am with you always' forms an *inclusio* with 1:23 (cf. too 18:20). (11) The mention of the end of the age recalls 13:39, 40, 49; 24:3 and brings to mind Jesus' teaching about the end.³¹

The Great Commission-centered reading requires a reconsideration of the conceptual inclusio between the Great Commission and the first words of Jesus in public ministry (4:17b) to demonstrate the theme of μετάνοια in Matthew. Both summary statements command μετάνοια as expressed in a

---

30. Matt 28:16–20, "Go; make disciples; baptize; teach whatever Jesus taught; make them keep," includes all the contents of μετάνοια that appear fully in the Gospel of Matthew. Specifically, it is not impossible that the main verb of Matt 28:16–20, μαθητεύσατε, equals the main verb of Matt 4:17, μετανοεῖτε, as it is immediately followed by Jesus' calling of the disciples and their following Jesus (Matt 4:18–22).

31. Sim, "Is Matthew 28:16–20?," 2.

variety of ways in the body of Matthew to mean "a change (or emendation) of one's mind (or thinking) and one's way of life by following Jesus and his teachings." These include: becoming a disciple of Jesus and following Jesus (4:20, 22, 25; 8:19, 22, 23; 9:9, 27; 10:37–38; 16:24; 19:21, 27; 20:34; 21:9) by keeping his teachings (4:18–23; 11:28–30; 16:24–27; 28:16–20), pursuing righteousness (5:17–20), doing good works (5:16), doing the will of God (6:10; 7:21; 12:50; 18:14; 21:31; 26:42), being whole before God (5:48), and bearing fruits worthy of repentance (3:8; 5:16, 17–20; 7:21; 10:37, 38; 12:48). Images and language related to entering the kingdom of heaven and to eternal life and judgment, which motivate to repentance (4:17; 7:19–23; 13:30, 40–43), express Jesus' total authority in heaven and earth (28:19).

Neither Brooks and Davies nor Allison reference a universal μετάνοια conceptual inclusio between the first and last words of Jesus' public ministry. Almost all of Davies and Allison's eleven evidences support the inclusio between 4:17 and 28:16–20, with both passages providing a summary of Matthew. This demonstrates the theme of μετάνοια as a governing theme in Matthew. First, the Galilee motif and the mountain setting are found in both the Great Commission and 4:17 (4:14–16, 18, 23, 25 and 5:1). The language of "all authority on heaven and earth" also refers to Jesus' μετάνοια message, with the declaration of the present kingdom of heaven in 4:17. The mention of making disciples refers back to Jesus' first calling of his disciples in 4:17–22. The baptism of Jesus in Matthew 3 is close to both 28:16–20 and 4:17 as an introduction to Jesus' ministry. The command to teach "all that I commanded you" alludes to Jesus' teaching and commandment of μετάνοια. The mention of the end of the age also connects to 4:17, which commands μετάνοια based on the inaugurated kingdom of heaven in the end time, which has come with the force of judgment. All the language of eschatological judgment in Matthew bolsters μετάνοια by providing a motivation. However, Davies and Allison's understanding of a contradiction between the reference to "all the nations" in the Great Commission and 10:5–6 is less likely because if the two passages contradict, the Great Commission cannot be a summary of Matthew. Rather, Matthew 10 as well as the universal μετάνοια conceptual inclusio between 4:17 and the Great Commission refer to a universal mission, in that 10:5–6 designates the prior concern of Jesus for the lost Israel in the universal mission.

Conclusion

Some scholars object to citing the Great Commission as the main summary of Matthew since it is at the end of the book[32] and the body of Matthew does not insist on gentile inclusion.[33] However, the conceptual inclusio between

---

32. Powell, "Plot and Subplots," 187–204. Powell criticizes the Great Commission-centered reading of Matthew because "the most significant elements of the story find their resolution earlier and the 'very end' of the narrative deals with lesser concerns." Therefore, the Great Commission cannot be involved in the core theme of the narrative of the Gospel of Matthew but is more likely a new beginning than an ending.

33. Sim, "Is Matthew 28:16–20?," 1–7. Sim disagrees with the Great Commission-centered reading of Matthew for two reasons. First, the Great Commission includes new themes and motifs, and second, the Great Commission does not summarize all the major themes of the Gospel of Matthew. Rather, the Great Commission introduces the new historical stage of the church and their mission for all the nations.

However, Sim's two objections are not convincing. First, he argues that the Great Commission has two new elements not mentioned before, the triadic baptism formula and the evangelism of "all the nations." Firstly, he says that even though the baptismal scene of Jesus (3:13–17) includes the Father, the Son, and the Holy Spirit, the triadic formula of the baptism in the Great Commission is totally new and Matthew's readers are hardly prepared to accept the new formula. However, Matthew's readers already know the triadic formula and have practiced it before the composition of the Gospel of Matthew. In other words, the reader does not need to be prepared for it. When the reader reads 3:13–17 they must recognize the triadic formula for baptism. As Davies and Allison have said, 3:13–17 indicates the triadic baptism when Jesus received the Holy Spirit, and the Great Commission commands baptism in the name of Father, the Holy Spirit, and Jesus. In addition, all the materials before it prepares the reader to understand Jesus' authority as Christ for the triadic baptism formula.

Secondly, Sim argues that evangelizing all nations, gentile inclusion in other words, is a new element in the Great Commission. He says that 10:5–6 and 15:24 restrict gentile inclusion but the Great Commission opens it. He sees the centurion and the Canaanite women as exceptions and states that no one can be sure that they followed Jesus afterward. However, as I explained in earlier sections, the restriction of 15:24 is immediately resolved since Jesus heals her daughter, so the Canaanite woman actually indicates Jesus' gentile inclusion. Also, 10:5–6 is not a restriction but indicates Jesus' prior call to failing Israel, to his calling to the gentiles. Moreover, as many scholars argue, Matthew 10 is full of gentile mission instruction, including words of comfort from Jesus, just as the Great Commission includes the Immanuel concept. As far as the uncertainty of the centurion's and the Canaanite woman's following Jesus, of course nobody can say with certainty whether they followed Jesus or not since the text is quiet, but it is more likely that they followed Jesus. Even more, Jesus' universal commissioning of his disciples has already appeared in 24:9, 14. As this book argues, the last words of Jesus in the Great Commission parallels the first words of Jesus (4:17b). Matt 4:17b is a worldwide call of Jesus, as 4:12–16 indicates. The idea of a worldwide call to repentance (4:17b) is also further supported by the worldwide Christ and worldwide salvation expectation of the Gospel of Matthew. Also, Sim never shows interest in the first words of Jesus in his public ministry.

The second objection Sim offers is that the Great Commission omits dominant Matthean themes: firstly, the eschatological judgment and its aftermath, and secondly,

4:17 and 28:18–20 solves the first objection. The Great Commission forms an inclusio with the first words of Jesus in his public ministry (4:17), so it effectively appears from the beginning of the book, making it a core theme of the discourses of Matthew. This universal μετάνοια inclusio and gentile inclusion materials in the body of Matthew also solve the second objection.

The Significance of μετάνοια Expressed in Gentile Inclusion Theme and Universal μετάνοια

In addition to the previous section on the Great Commission and μετάνοια, which plays a key role in Matthew, this section shows the universal range of μετάνοια in Matthew through examining the gentile inclusion theme[34]—bolstering the significance of μετάνοια of all nations in the Gospel of Matthew. Specifically, three occurrences of the term μετανοέω (Matt 11:20, 21; 12:41) out of seven signify the repentant gentiles in contrast to unrepentant people of Israel.[35] Jesus' emphasis on the repentant gentile demonstrates the significance of μετάνοια in Matthew. And the summary of these verses—that the story of gentile believers or followers of Jesus, gentile inclusion theme in Matthew—shows μετάνοια. The widespread gentile μετάνοια and thus gentile inclusion theme show the significance of μετάνοια in Matthew. This section first briefly introduces the theme of gentile inclusion (and by extension universal μετάνοια) from the beginning chapters, which appear not symbolically or implicitly but directly and explicitly. And it gathers thematic materials from the Gospel of Matthew related to gentile inclusion

---

the conflict with Formative Judaism, and thirdly, the issue of the Mosaic Law. However, Sim's reading of Jesus' judgmental and authoritative saying, "all authority in heaven and on earth has given to me," and his command to make all nations observe all that he has commanded clearly indicates Jesus' judgment according to one's works. Also, the things "that Jesus has commanded" includes all the judgment language of Jesus. Sim does not read the text thematically but only terminologically. Also, as Sim agrees, Davies and Allison suggest that the "end of the age" includes a judgment theme.

The second missing element, the conflict with Formative Judaism, is indicated in that Jesus, after his resurrection, does not meet and command the Jewish leadership but the eleven with whom he establishes his church and to whom he gives his authority (10:7). This confirms Jesus' abandonment of Israel's leadership and replacement of them with the eleven apostles.

34. For more information see Brown, "Matthean Community and the Gentile Mission," 193–221; Byrne, "Messiah," 55–73; Carter, "Matthew and the Gentiles," 259–82; Clark, "Gentile Bias in Matthew," 165–72; Hare and Harrington, "Make Disciples of All the Gentiles," 359–69; Meier, "Nations or Gentiles," 94–102; Meier, "Two Disputed Questions," 407–24.

35. Ch. 9 will deal more on these passages as the backdrop of Matthew 13.

Universal Commandment of μετάνοια and Gentile Inclusion in Matthew

Jesus' commandment of μετάνοια in the beginning of his public ministry (4:17) is universal (cf. 4:12–16) and the widespread gentile inclusion theme in the Gospel of Matthew proves it, including the Great Commission. Matthew 4:12–16 denotes Jesus as the shining light for the world in the darkness and death, and 4:17 begins Jesus' μετάνοια ministry. In other words, the Gospel of Matthew from the beginning to the end focuses on a worldwide Messiah, worldwide μετάνοια, and worldwide salvation. In this respect, it is not likely that the Gospel of Matthew begins by speaking of a Jewish Messiah and salvation limited to Israel only, then suddenly at the end widens this Jewish Messiah to be worldwide and suddenly introduces the salvation of all nations (28:18–20).

The theme of gentile inclusion (and so universal μετάνοια) appears from the beginning chapters not symbolically or implicitly but directly and explicitly. For instance, from the beginning Matthew speaks of the worldwide Messiah Jesus using γένεσις (1:1) in relation to the creation of Genesis 1:1 and to worldwide salvation including both Jews and gentiles including Abraham (1:1). Davies and Allison's comment connecting Abraham in 1:1 and "all nations" in 28:19 as fulfilling the Abrahamic covenant through the church [36] strongly shows gentile inclusion in the Gospel of Matthew. Moreover, Matthew begins Jesus' public ministry with a μετάνοια call for all the nations in the dawn of the kingdom of heaven (4:17b; also the last words of the book, 28:18–20).

The Abrahamic genealogy supports this theme as seen in the inclusion of four gentile women, the magi, John the Baptist's judgment language on ethnic Israel and the new definition of the true seed of Abraham (3:2–12), the reference to world authority in Satan's temptation of Jesus (4:8–9), Jesus' worldwide μετάνοια call with the Isaiah citation (4:12–17), the great faith of the centurion (8:9), and so on. The four gentile women in the Abrahamic genealogy indicate a redefinition of the children of Abraham, along with the great faith of the centurion (and the Canaanite woman).[37] They are models of repentance among the nations, i.e., turning

---

36. Davies and Allison, *Matthew 19–28*, 683.
37. Krentz, "Missionary Matthew," 29.

away from the nation's idols to God and pursuing righteousness.[38] Since Abraham was recognized as the father of faith, Matthew's praising the faith of the centurion and the Canaanite woman is a significant indication of the redefinition of the children of Abraham.

In addition, the gentile inclusion theme appears with the fulfilled judgment of Israel in the dawn of the kingdom of heaven with Jesus Christ. gentile inclusion and the fulfillment of judgment against Israel especially appears in the introductory section, Matthew 3:1–12, the first Matthean discourse of John the Baptist which introduces the major ideas of the Gospel of Matthew and the five discourse blocks.[39] In particular, "from these stones to raise up children for Abraham" indicates demolition of the physical nation Israel as the people of God, and on the other hand gentile inclusion, or reconstitution of the people of God only through true repentance and the bearing of worthy fruits (3:11). Also, the explicit language of 3:10, 12, "Even now the axe is laid to the root of the trees," indicates judgment and destruction of the old, failing Israel. Theses languages and themes appear throughout the book.

Kenneth W. Clark argues that Matthew wrote with an intentional gentile bias theme, not as an afterthought. He cites the traditional arguments of a Jewish gospel: the genealogy from Abraham, the blocks of teaching material, the quotations from Jewish scripture, the eschatological passages, the Jewish particularism, Semitic words and idioms, particularly the use of "kingdom of heaven" avoiding "kingdom of God."[40] Therefore, "Gentile bias becomes necessary to explain as a secondary trait, which crops forth in the story of the virgin birth, the heightening of miracle, the rejection of Israel (e.g., 21:43), the denunciation of Pharisees (chapter 13) and Sadducees (e.g., 16:6), and the Great Commission."[41] He concludes, "Gentile bias is the primary theme in the Gospel of Matthew."[42] He refutes this traditional view that "Luke, a gentile writer, also used a genealogy; Luke also interested in the type of teaching materials employed in Matthew

---

38. This idea is from Jason B. Hood's review on this book. See Hood, *The Messiah, His Brothers, and the Nations*. He argues for Jesus' royal role from Gen 49:8–10 allusion in the genealogy. Matthew includes Judah and his brothers to indicate Judah's and Jechoniah's self-sacrifice image in the Second Temple literature. Four Gentile returners in the genealogy indicates Jesus' royal role for the all nations in its close relation to the Great Commission. Therefore, the beginning and the ending of the Gospel of Matthew parallel by the theme of Jesus' messianic royal role and signify the restoration of all nations.

39. See ch. 4.

40. Clark, "Gentile Bias in Matthew," 165.

41. Clark, "Gentile Bias in Matthew," 165.

42. Clark, "Gentile Bias in Matthew," 166–67.

that all Christians had long since become accustomed to scriptural proof texts and prophecies as also to the eschatological background of Christian belief; Jewish particularism in the earlier part of Matthew is overshadowed by the main theme of the gospel which is better presented in the Great Commission; Semitic terms and rabbinic avoidance of the divine name are subjected to refutation by detailed analysis."[43]

In fact, the overtone of the Gospel of Matthew presupposed that Israel had already been judged and its era ended. Clark further says that gentile-dominant Christianity is the true people of God replacing Judaism and Jewish people, indicated with Matthew's Israel judgmental language: "The children of the kingdom will be cast out" (8:12); "in his name will the Gentiles trust" (12:21); "The kingdom of God will be taken away from you, and given to a people producing the fruits of the kingdom" (21:43); "Go and make disciples of all the gentile people teaching them to obey all the commands I have laid on you" (28:19–20); Jews rejected and killed God's son (21:39); Messiah cannot be a descendent of David (22:41–46; 23:37–39), the destruction of the temple of Judaism" (24).[44] Parables contain a similar message: "God has rejected them and shut them out of the kingdom, transferring his favor to Christian believers as the true Israel," as seen in the following passages: the Two Sons (21:28–32); the Vineyard Tenants (21:33–43); the Wedding Feast (22:1–14); the Ten Virgins (25:1–13); the Talents (25:14–30); the Judgment by the Son of Man (25:31–46); the faithful slave of 24:45 representing the gentile Christian; the wicked slave representing the Jewish hypocrites in 24:51 in a reflection of chapter 23.[45]

The parables cited above relocate the boundary of and redefine the true people of God. However, it is not necessarily the case that Matthew insists on the replacement of Israel as the people of God by gentile believers, rather he sees a reconstitution of or gentile inclusion in the people of God. Matthew envisions a worldwide, ethnically diverse church not only a gentile Christian church. The gentile inclusion theme of Matthew does not mean the replacement or abandonment of Israel but a redefinition or reconstitution of the people of God through Jesus. All nations, including Israel and gentiles in 28:19–20, are clearly stated in this theme. This is clearly indicated in the very first discourse block of John the Baptist saying, "for I tell you, God is able from these stones to raise up children for Abraham" (3:9).

In addition, the Canaanite woman, who Jesus rebuked once but then offered salvation, emphasizes Israel's status as a nation under judgment and

---

43. Clark, "Gentile Bias in Matthew," 165–66.
44. Clark, "Gentile Bias in Matthew," 166.
45. Clark, "Gentile Bias in Matthew," 166–67.

points to the dawn of gentile inclusion as Jesus ushers in the kingdom of heaven. Similar language appears in 15:24, the parable of the lost sheep, again indicating the destroyed Israel and Jesus' compassionate concern for gentiles. His first priority is always to rescue and save the injured one. Jesus' concern for this gentile woman indicates Matthew's interest in gentile inclusion from the beginning rather than Jewish particularism. Before this event, Jesus judged the leadership of Israel as wicked and dirty. After this incident, Jesus fed four thousand gentile people with a holy meal.

David C. Sim disagrees with Clark on the theme of gentile inclusion in Matthew. Sim acknowledges that Clark's thesis has generally been accepted, but he objectively argues that "the Jewish Matthaean community largely avoided contact with the surrounding Gentile society and had good reason for doing so."[46] Sim's overall argument is based on his historical presupposition that the Matthean community was a strict law-keeping and anti-gentile community. He refutes Clark's argument as follows: first, the three women in Matthew's genealogy (Ruth, Rahab, and Tamar) were not considered as gentile but proselyte in Matthew's day and their gentile background should not be considered and femaleness must be understood as the pre-role of Mary.[47] However, proselyte women were converters from gentile. They are examples of the Abrahamic covenant and were saved through their faith with good deeds. Also, their inclusion in genealogy critiques and rejects Jewish pride in the pure bloodline of Abraham and David. If femaleness was for foreshadowing Mary, then why should not Sara, Rebecca, or Rachel be included?[48] Rather these four women speak not only to four persons' stories, but also four familiar OT stories that contrast the great faith of gentile believers and wicked Israel.[49]

Sim also argues that wicked gentile characters such as the Gadarenes (8:28–34), Pontius Pilate (27:2–65), and the Roman soldiers executing Jesus (27:27–37) counterbalance good gentile characters and the gentile inclusion theme.[50] In addition, Sim analyzes "anti-Gentile statements" found in 5:46–47; 6:7–8, 31–32, and 18:15–17 arguing that "Gentiles are outsiders

---

46. Sim, "Gospel of Matthew and the Gentiles," 21.

47. Sim, "Gospel of Matthew and the Gentiles," 22–23.

48. Hakh, "Women in the Genealogy of Matthew," 116–18.

49. Hutchison, "Women, Gentiles, and the Messianic Mission," 152–64. Hutchison says, "The faith of Tamar versus that of Judah, of Rahab versus that of the Israelites in the wilderness, and of Ruth versus that of the judges generation illustrates that at crucial times in Israel's history Gentiles demonstrated more faith than Jews in response to God. Bathsheba is probably cited by Matthew as 'the wife of Uriah' in order focus attention on Uriah's faith in contrast to that of David."

50. Sim, "Gospel of Matthew and the Gentiles," 23–25.

DISCIPLESHIP, THE GREAT COMMISSION, AND GENTILE INCLUSION

and contact with them is to be discouraged rather than encouraged."[51] Moreover, gentile persecution (10:17–22; 24:4–14) hindered the Matthean community's approach to gentiles.[52] However, counterbalancing good gentile characters with wicked gentile characters to get rid of the gentile inclusion theme is a false dichotomy, because the gentile inclusion theme does not refer to any or every gentile, but a reconstitution of the people of God only through faith in Jesus and the bearing of good fruit. In the same sense, anti-gentile statements cannot remove the gentile inclusion theme. Lastly, gentile persecution and negative statements do not necessarily rule out the gentile inclusion theme, rather Jesus instructs his followers to go to gentile nations and endure persecution for the gospel.

Brendan Byrne, responding to Sim, identifies Sim's views as the most extreme representative of Jewishness in the Gospel of Matthew and the Matthean community remaining in Judaism and regarding themselves Jews.[53] Byrne does not object to Sim historically but Christologically saying, "whatever the external evidence, the downplaying of Gentile inclusion is not compatible with what emerges from a reading of the gospel as a whole. . . . from the very beginning, right through to the end, the narrative of Matthew's Gospel is designed to present Jesus of Nazareth not only as Messiah but as a Messiah having essential reference to the Gentiles—the one in whose name 'the Gentiles will hope'" (12:21, quoting LXX Isa 42:4).[54]

Byrne focuses on five major landmarks: opening (1:1—2:23), summary of Jesus inaugural preaching (4:12–17), further summary (12:15–21), encounter with a Canaanite woman (15:21–28), conclusion (28:16–20). In these sections he analyzes the gentile inclusion theme. First, the opening of the gospel, Jesus' infancy, and the arrival of the magi in 1:1–23, includes the most important direction and tone of the Gospel of Matthew. Matthew titling Jesus as "Son of Abraham" (1:1) in relation to John the Baptist's rebuke of the Pharisees and Sadducees seeking to be baptized ["And do not presume to say to yourselves, 'We have Abraham as our father,' for I tell you, God is able from these stones to raise up children for Abraham" (3:9)] indicates Jesus as creator of a new people of God from all nations. Also, the four gentile women named in the genealogy "already betrays an openness to the non-Israelite, Gentile world conventionally considered unclean."[55] The magi's identification of Jesus

---

51. Sim, "Gospel of Matthew and the Gentiles," 28.
52. Sim, "Gospel of Matthew and the Gentiles," 30–35.
53. Byrne, "Messiah in Whose Name."
54. Byrne, "Messiah in Whose Name," 57–58.
55. Byrne, "Messiah in Whose Name," 60.

as "king of the Jews," which was also written on Jesus' cross, indicates their gentileness and expectation of gentile inclusion.

Second, God's direct reference to Jesus, "in whom I am well pleased" in 3:17 and 17:5, cites Isaiah 42:1 which includes the gentile inclusion theme, "he will bring forth justice to the nations." In the temptation narrative (4:1–11) and 28:19 appears "all the kingdoms of the world. . . (Satan) will give to Jesus" (4:8–9) and "all power on heaven and earth has been given to Jesus" (28:18) refers to Jesus as Christ of all the world. Also, the Isaiah 9:1–2 citation in 4:12–16 laying out Jesus' geographical movement toward gentile territory prior to his public ministry and preaching summary in 4:17 indicates Matthew's gentile inclusion theme. In addition, two major section headings of the Sermon on the Mount, "salt of the earth" (5:13) and "light of the world," clearly show Jesus' intent is for the world. Byrne does not forget to mention the great faith of the centurion (8:5–13) in contrast to Jesus' judgment on faithless Israel (8:11).

Third, another Isaiah 61:1 citation in Matthew 12:18–21 anticipates gentile inclusion. Fourth, the Canaanite woman in 15:21–28 and the feeding of four thousand gentiles function as representatives of the gentile world. The parable of the laborers in the vineyard (20:1–16) and the wicked tenants (21:33–46), especially "a nation" in 21:43 "the kingdom of God will be taken away from you and given to a people producing its fruits" is reminiscent of the centurion and points to the gentile inclusion theme. The Olivet discourse includes worldwide persecution (24:9b, 14; 25:31–46) indicating gentile inclusion theme. Finally, the Great Commission 28:16–20 clearly indicates gentile inclusion theme.

I agree with Byrne with one exception. He regards gentile inclusion thematic materials before the Great Commission only as anticipation or a foreshadow of the gentile inclusion theme throughout Matthew. In contrast, I think they directly and explicitly indicate Matthew's gentile inclusion or reconstitution of the people of God through Jesus Christ from the very beginning to the end of the Gospel of Matthew.

Donald Senior sustains Matthew's historical relationship to Judaism and gentiles in balance.[56] Senior seems to try to balance Davies and Allison's view of the Matthean relationship to Judaism, that is, the anti-Pharisaic reformation movement after AD 70 still remaining in Judaism but mixed with Jewish and gentile Christians and Jewish Christians defending their Jewish roots against gentile Christians. In Luz's view, the community has broken from Judaism yet continues dialoguing and wrestling with Israel's rejection of the gospel. Luz further examines Davies and Allison's argument on Matthew's

---

56. Senior, "Between Two Worlds," 1–23.

polemic relationship to the gentile world "to be relatively homogeneous and untroubled."[57] Also, Senior argues that the Great Commission does not indicate the end of Israel's mission but extends it to gentiles, denying the polemic relationship of Jew and gentile saying, "The purpose of Matthew's Gospel was ultimately not to defend the legitimacy of his Jewish heritage over against Pharisaic Judaism but to deliver it to a new generation of Christians who would determine the future of his community."[58]

He further bolsters the argument that "Matthew's consistent emphasis on good deeds rather than status or ethnic identity as the criteria for righteousness also paves the way for acceptance of gentiles who exhibit faith and good works" (7:21–23; 12:46–50; 21:28–32; 22:45; 25:31–46).[59] In addition, Matthew's emphasis on forgiveness, loving one's enemy, seeking reconciliation (5:21–26; 6:14–15; 18:21–35), avoiding retaliation (5:38–42), praying for and loving one's enemy (5:43–48) largely signal gentile inclusion. Senior points out that Matthew's gentile mission does not supersede or invalidate Israel's mission, rather Matthew respects the Jewish character of Jesus and the Law (5:17).[60]

Senior also thinks that gentile inclusion materials before the Great Commission only signal future gentile inclusion. And he explains Jesus'

---

57. Senior, "Between Two Worlds," 6.
58. Senior, "Between Two Worlds," 21. Senior himself found eighteen lists of gentile inclusion materials in the Gospel of Matthew (few are parallel to the other scholars). 1) 1:1, "Son of Abraham," 2) 1:2–16, four gentiles and "outsiders," women, 3) 2:1–12, the magi, Jesus' flight to Egypt of gentile contrasting Israel's rejection, 4) 4:12–16, "Galilee of the Gentiles" and "sat in darkness" indicating gentile, 5) 4:23–26, "all Syria" and the "Decapolis" indicates Jesus healing and teaching of both gentiles and Jews, 6) 8:5–13, the centurion's exemplary gentile faith, 7) 11:20–24, Tyre, Sidon, and Sodom's probable positive reaction to Jesus contrasting to Galilean towns, 8) 12:18–21, fulfillment citation of Isaiah 42:1–4 "proclaiming justice to Gentiles" and "in his name the Gentiles will hope," 9) 12:38–41, positive response of people of Nineveh to Jonah and the queen of the South to Solomon in contrast to rejection of Israel, 10) 15:21–28, Canaanite woman's faith and breaking Jesus' mission statement on Israel, 11) 20:1–16, the parable of the laborers alluding to marginal Jews and gentiles, 12) 21:43, the parable of the vineyard "people who will produce the fruit" referencing both Jew and gentile in contrast with Jewish leadership, 13) 22:1–14, the parable of the wedding banquet, the rejection of Jesus' invitation hinting at "a wider mission in the wake of the destruction of Jerusalem and the rejection of Jesus' invitation, a mission including both Jews and Gentiles," 14) 24:14, "through the world" as a testimony "to all nations," 15) 25:31–46, the parable of the sheep and the goats from "all the nation," 16) 27:19, Pilate's wife, a gentile woman, attempting to rescue Jesus contrasting to Jewish leaders, 17) 27:54, climax of the Gospel of Matthew the centurion and soldiers' confession of faith in Jesus as "Son of God," 18) 28:16–20, commandment to proclaim the gospel to "all nations."
59. Senior, "Between Two Worlds," 16.
60. Senior, "Between Two Worlds," 20.

contradictory mission charge between Israel and gentile (10:5-6; 15:16 28:19-20) is meant to persuade Jewish Christians in the community who object to the gentile mission. However, the gentile inclusion theme appears directly and explicitly from the beginning chapter and Jesus' commission of Israel and gentile do not contradict each other but only indicate Jesus' earlier concern over Israel's failure as well as the natural and geographic mission sequence when the eschatological kingdom of heaven and its judgment is inaugurated.

Warren Carter is representative of scholars who argue for the widespread gentile inclusion theme in Matthew. Carter discusses seven aspects of this theme in Matthew: Matt. 1:1, the allusions to Isaiah in 1:23 and 4:15, Satan's role, representative gentiles, Pilate, the parousia, and discipleship in the meantime. He argues, "Matthew engages the Gentile world (dominated by Roman imperial control) systemically with a much broader focus on God's just and transforming reign."[61] Carter agrees with previous works on the Matthean gentile inclusion theme by Byrne and Senior and suggests that the Matthean gentile inclusion materials indicate "the Gospel's much larger systematic concern with God's purposes to establish God's just reign or empire that will transform the whole world."[62] I briefly summarize Carter's analysis of gentile inclusion in Matthew: First, Carter argues that Βίβλος γενέσεως in Matthew 1:1, used in Genesis 2:4 and 5:1, evokes the whole creation, the fall, the judgment of God and God's restoration plan in Genesis and indicates that the Gospel of Matthew is a new book of Genesis for the whole world, against the Roman Empire. In the Matthean genealogy, Abraham recalls the Abrahamic worldwide covenant of God in Genesis 12:1-3.[63] Second, Isaiah 7-9 in Matthew 1:23 ("Immanuel") and 4:15-16 ("Galilee of the Gentiles") indicate Matthew's theme of God's judgment and the hope of the salvation of the whole world from the Roman Empire.[64] Third, Satan's test, with "all the kingdoms/empires of the world and their glory" (4:8), a phrase which parallels 28:18, indicates Matthew's emphasis on Jesus' victory against Satan's control of the world, especially Rome. Jesus' healing, exorcisms, and raising of the dead (4:17-23; 8-9; 10:7-8; 11:2-6; 12:22-32; 15:29-39) demonstrate his overturning of Satan's control of the

---

61. Carter, "Matthew and the Gentiles," 259, 261. For the gentile inclusion theme of Matthew, see also Brown, "Matthean Community and the Gentile Mission"; Byrne, "Messiah in Whose Name"; Clark, "Gentile Bias in Matthew"; Senior, "Between Two Worlds"; contra Sim, "Gospel of Matthew and the Gentiles"; Sim, "Matthew and the Gentiles," 74-79.

62. Carter, "Matthew and the Gentiles," 260.

63. Carter, "Matthew and the Gentiles," 261-64.

64. Carter, "Matthew and the Gentiles," 264-66.

harassed and helpless world. Specifically, the phrase "like sheep without a shepherd" in 9:36 rebukes Israel's rulers and the Roman emperor, indicating Matthew's concern for worldwide salvation through the true leader Jesus Christ (266–72). Fourth, gentiles such as the magi, the centurion, and the Canaanite woman function as representatives of the gentile world, indicating Matthew's systematic worldwide engagement.[65] Fifth, the confrontation between Jesus and the Roman governor Pilate depicts a collision of claims of sovereignty, Rome versus God, and Jesus' death and resurrection defeats the Roman Empire.[66] Sixth, Jesus' parousia (24:17–31) will accomplish the judgment of all earthly dominions (25:32) and bring about the gentiles' hope of salvation. This worldwide judgment indicates Jesus' worldwide authority and points to gentile inclusion.[67] Seventh, in the meantime, before Jesus' return, the church has been commanded to evangelize all nations, indicating Matthew's systematic worldwide transformation.[68] Matthew 10 also coheres with this worldwide gentile inclusion theme as instruction to the postresurrection church for its mission to all the nations. The universal Christology and gentile inclusion theme that is widespread in Matthew expresses the theme of universal μετάνοια.

Conclusion for Universality of Matthean μετάνοια

The gentile inclusion theme or gentile μετάνοια has a close relationship to the theme of μετάνοια in Matthew (cf. Matt 3:9) in that the gentile inclusion theme shows the significance of universal μετάνοια in Matthew. Jesus begins his public preaching ministry with the words, "Repent for the kingdom of heaven is at hand" (4:17b). In this summary proclamation of Jesus' public ministry (4:17), μετανοέω means to change (or amend) one's way of life to God. This commandment of μετάνοια is universal (4:12–16). This universal μετάνοια call coheres the whole of Matthew around the gentile inclusion theme since this theme appears explicitly from the beginning chapter of the Gospel of Matthew to the end. Three occurrences of the term μετανοέω out of seven in Matthew 11:20, 21; 12:41 signify the μετάνοια of gentiles in Matthew in contrast to the unrepentant people of Israel. Specifically, in his last words, the reference to the need to become a disciple of Jesus and observe all that Jesus has commanded (28:20), that is, to turn or change (μετανοέω) one's mind, conduct, and entire life to Jesus and his teachings, conveys the

65. Carter, "Matthew and the Gentiles," 273–74.
66. Carter, "Matthew and the Gentiles," 275–77.
67. Carter, "Matthew and the Gentiles," 277–79.
68. Carter, "Matthew and the Gentiles," 279–81.

same idea and so the Great Commission echoes the commandment of turning (μετανοέω) in the beginning of Jesus' ministry (4:17). As the Great Commission is universal, which means for all nations (28:19), the commandment of turning (μετανοέω) in Matthew 4:17 is also universal from the near context (4:12–17). This conceptual inclusio indicates μετάνοια is a universal, framing idea in the gentile inclusion theme in Matthew.

Chapter 6

The Thematic Significance of μετάνοια Expressed in Matthew's Righteousness and Soteriology

IN A CONTINUATION OF the previous chapter, this chapter will discuss the significance of μετάνοια in relation to Matthew's important topics. The opening phrase of Jesus ministry (4:17) proclaims the commandment of turning (μετανοέω), meaning to turn (or change) one's whole life and being toward Jesus and the kingdom of heaven. Jesus commands μετάνοια in order to enter the kingdom of heaven and to avoid the judgment (3:2; 4:17). This soteriological theme of a whole change of being, including both mind (heart and will) and conduct, opens Jesus' teaching and suggests the significance of μετάνοια in the body of Matthew. How does Matthew express this beginning commandment in the body of his gospel? What does Jesus command people to turn from and turn to? What is the essence or the contents of μετάνοια (3:8)?

As noted in the previous chapter, μετάνοια does not occur many times in the body of Matthew. However, the significance of μετάνοια appears in various ways, from John the Baptist's μετάνοια preaching in 3:2–12 to Jesus' teaching and ministry. For instance, as noted in chapter 3, critical dictionaries say that the essence of μετάνοια conveys Matthew's emphasis on righteousness, doing good, and doing the will of the Father.[1] In particular, righteousness, doing the will of the Father, and doing good all are the contents of μετάνοια and express the worthy fruit of μετάνοια(3:8) in the body of Matthew. The Matthean Jesus comprises μετάνοια in keeping with his instruction to do the will of God (7:21; 12:50), good works or bear good fruits (5:16–19; 12:33; 13:8, 23, 48), and to live righteously (3:15; 5:6, 10, 20; 6:1, 33; 21:32). Righteousness and doing good works (or fruits) and the will of God are the essence of the commandment of turning (μετανοέω) and fruit worthy

---

1. See pages 39–41 of this book.

of μετάνοια in that they instruct what people turn from and turn to. These μετάνοια expressions and examples in the body of Matthew echo the opening commandment of turning (μετανοέω) in 3:2, 3:8, and 4:17, and show the thematic significance of μετάνοια in Matthew.

μετάνοια is also significant for the Matthean soteriological category, as 4:17 commands μετάνοια as a requirement for entering the coming kingdom of heaven. Also, μετάνοια's contents—righteousness and doing good works (or fruits) and the will of God—are important Matthean soteriological themes. This chapter first discusses righteousness and doing good works (or fruits) and the will of God as the contents and essence of μετάνοια and their significance in Matthean salvation structure.

The Significance of μετάνοια Expressed in Righteousness, Doing the Will of Father, and Doing Good

Louw and Nida define μετανοέω and μετάνοια as "to change one's way of life as the result of a complete change of thought and attitude with regard to sin and *righteousness* . . . the focal semantic feature is clearly behavioral rather than intellectual. . . . μετανοέω and μετάνοια seems to be more specifically the total change, *both in thought and behavior*, with respect to how one should *both think and act*."[2]

Louw and Nida emphasize that μετανοέω regards righteousness and good behavior. This definition shows that Matthean righteousness, doing the will of God, and doing good, which follows the opening commandment of turning (μετανοέω), comprise the fruit worthy of μετάνοια. They show the thematic significance of μετάνοια in Matthew.

Robert Gundry notes that the worthy fruit of μετάνοια is genuine righteousness (cf. 21:32).[3] Ulrich Luz notes that this turning (μετανοέω) message is "the entry gate" to the greater righteousness of the sermon and *dominates* it.[4] Again, if it is not the case this opening commandment will remain empty and lose its emphasis after all. Therefore, righteous living, obeying the will of God, and outward expressions of goodness illustrate what μετάνοια looks like.

This section will review representative works on Matthean righteousness with its related ideas of doing good and doing the will of God. Then,

---

2. Louw and Nida, *Greek-English Lexicon*, Domain 41, 510. Emphasis is mine. See ch. 3 for more critical dictionaries' definitions of the term in close relationship with righteousness and doing the will of God and good.

3. Gundry, *Matthew*, 46–47.

4. Luz, *Matthew 1–7*, 198.

it will examine how the passages on righteousness, doing good, and doing the will of God express the theme of μετάνοια and its contents and thus how these passages show the thematic significance of μετάνοια in Matthew.

Righteousness in Matthew

Current Matthean scholarship has discussed the law and righteousness as main themes in the Gospel of Matthew.[5] For instance, George Strecker titles the Gospel of Matthew "the way of righteousness"[6] and Udo Schnelle "the new and better righteousness."[7] Strecker points to righteousness as a summary of Jesus' teachings in Matthew.[8] Roland Deines also argues for righteousness as the main theme and 5:17-20 as the center of Matthew.[9] In particular, righteousness in Matthew has been discussed in contrast to Pauline righteousness as to whether it is an imputed gift of God or God's demand of humans.[10] Recently the latter has been accepted in much Matthean scholarship. But many scholars have argued for reading Paul and Matthew separately rather than in contrast.[11] Some scholars argue that Matthean righteousness does not refer to a legalistic demand for human righteousness that contradicts Paul, but

---

5. For a history of research of the law and righteousness in Matthew, see Deines, "Not the Law but the Messiah," 53–84, Irons, *Righteousness of God,* 263–67. Przybylski, *Righteousness in Matthew.*

6. Strecker, *Theology of the New Testament,* 364.

7. Schnelle, *Theology of the New Testament,* 429.

8. Strecker, *Theology of the New Testament,* 382.

9. Deines, *Die Gerechtigkeit,* 95–101.

10. Some scholars even argue that Matthew insists on the whole Torah-keeping righteousness as a way of entering the kingdom of heaven. For a history of research for this approach, see Sim, "Rise and Fall," 478–85. Sim uses "works righteousness" as a summary of this understanding. This article tries to show the current movement of Matthean scholars toward an anti-Pauline works righteousness understanding that causes the fall of Matthew. They argue that Matthew is written for the law-keeping Jewish Christian community and emphasizes works of the law in contrast to Pauline law-free faith or grace righteousness. This works righteousness reads Matthew as a legalistic and anti-Pauline gospel. However, as clearly indicated, Matthew's foe is contemporary religious leaders of Israel, not Paul. For more discussion on the difference between Matthean and Pauline righteousness, see Mohrlang, *Matthew and Paul.*

11. Hagner, "Righteousness in Matthew's Theology," 108. Hagner reports George Strecker, David Hill, and Jacques Dupont as forerunners of this view and representatives of Matthean scholarship on righteousness. Benno Przybylski and Roger Mohrlang, as well as the two monumental commentaries of Ulrich Luz and William David Davies and Dale Allison have accepted this view.

instead Matthean righteousness is based on the grace of God for salvation along with being something God demands of humans.[12]

Strecker defines Matthean righteousness (3:15; 5:6, 10, 20; 6:1, 33; 21:32) as "the comprehensive term for the right conduct of the disciples in general, and thus for the whole Christian community, that must be different from that of the Pharisees and scribes (5:20)."[13] Strecker argues that Matthean righteousness is "the human answer to the redemptive act of God;" it is a demand and not a gift obtained for human beings by Jesus' substitutionary death.[14] Strecker does not deny divine power or help for this human answer.

Benno Przybylski also concludes that Matthean righteousness consistently means "the conduct demanded of the disciples, a conduct characterized by the meticulous observance of the law,"[15] or God's will, which pleases to God.[16] He argues that this righteousness is demanded according to Jesus' new interpretation of the law (5:20–48). And this newly interpreted law creates a quantitative and qualitative difference between Christian righteousness and the Pharisees' and the scribes' righteousness. He denies that any idea of Matthean righteousness as God's gift is what creates the qualitative difference between Christian righteousness and the Pharisees' righteousness.[17] In terms of the relationship to Pauline righteousness Przybylski notes that both Matthew and Paul demonstrate that salvation is God's gift but that Matthean righteousness does not attach to the salvation structure. He rather argues that Matthew uses ἐλεέω (5:7; 9:27; 15:22; 17:15; 18:33; 20:30, 31) to designate God's saving grace upon people. He argues Matthean righteousness designates proper religious people but not disciples of Jesus. Rather the "doers of the will of God" designate the disciples of Jesus.[18] However, Matthean righteousness designates the disciples of Jesus. Jesus instructs his disciples to hunger and thirst for righteousness (5:6) and to suffer for righteousness for the sake of the kingdom of heaven (5:10), and even commands them to seek first the kingdom of heaven and righteousness (6:33). Also, Matthean righteousness attaches to the

---

12. For a representative work on this view, see Hagner, "Righteousness in Matthew's Theology," 108.
13. Strecker, *Theology of the New Testament*, 364.
14. Strecker, *Theology of the New Testament*, 364.
15. Przybylski, *Righteousness in Matthew*, 84.
16. Przybylski, *Righteousness in Matthew*, 94.
17. Przybylski, *Righteousness in Matthew*, 85.
18. Przybylski, *Righteousness in Matthew*, 107–8.

salvation structure, because the greater righteousness is necessary to enter into the kingdom of heaven (5:20).[19]

W. D. Davies and Dale C. Allison distinguish Matthean and Pauline righteousness and define Matthean righteousness as follows:

> "Righteousness" is therefore Christian character and conduct in accordance with the demands of Jesus—right intention, right word, right deed. Hence "righteousness" does not refer, even implicitly, to God's gift. The Pauline (forensic, eschatological) connotation is absent. This conclusion is confirmed by the mention of the scribes and Pharisees. For they too have a righteousness, but it is of a sort insufficient to enable them to enter the kingdom of heaven. So what they are is clearly not the gift of God; instead their want of righteousness is a failure in their conduct. . . The greater righteousness is a doing more (5:47). It is therefore a quantitative advance. Yet this is not to deny that, in Matthew's eyes, there is also a qualitative advance. After all, love cannot be quantified. Further, in following Jesus' example and obeying his commandments, the disciples are to obtain "perfection."[20]

Davies and Allison note that there is no indication in Matthew of righteousness as God's gift. Matthean righteousness has its own emphasis on deeds. However, this emphasis does not mean there is no divine empowerment for righteous deeds and that Matthean righteousness and Pauline righteousness are in conflict. Davies and Allison's definition of Matthean righteousness can be summarized as quantitative and qualitative development of Christian character and conduct following Jesus' example and obeying his commandments for "perfection."

Donald A. Hagner argues for reading Matthew's ethical demand for righteousness "in proper perspective by seeing the lager framework of grace present in the Gospel."[21] He says as follows: Matthew's righteousness is grounded in the salvation of God, so it is a gift rather than demand. It is true that Matthew emphasizes human works, but he puts more emphasis on the concept of gift, and the idea of gift always precedes human demand in Matthew. Examples include the arrival of the kingdom of heaven, and so the announcement of good news, before the call to righteousness (4:23; 9:35; 24:14); a statement of grace in the Beatitudes before references to righteousness (5:3, 10); the acceptance of the unworthy (9:10–13; 11:9; 18:10–14; 21:31; 22:1–10); the humble childlikeness of the disciples indicating total

---

19. Pennington, *Sermon on the Mount and Human Flourishing*, 91.
20. Davies and Allison, *Matthew 1–7*, 499–500.
21. Hagner, "Righteousness in Matthew's Theology," 101–20.

dependence on God and his favor (18:1–4; 10:42; 18:6, 10, 14, 23–35; 20:1–16); and Jesus' ministry of forgiving sins (1:21; 6:12, 14; 9:2, 6; 12:31; 20:28). Hagner examines all occurrences of righteousness in Matthew and concludes that the righteousness in 5:20 and 6:1 refers to an ethical demand but that other references to righteousness refer to God's saving grace. Reviewing Hagner, Irons argues that only 3:15 and 5:6 are plausible in reference to saving righteousness and that the other references (5:10, 20; 6:1, 33; 21:32) are to an ethical demand.[22]

Roland Deines argues that righteousness in Matthew should be reconsidered as referring to "Jesus-righteousness," which denotes that "righteousness is not possible without Jesus" and that disciples "get a share of this righteousness and thus can be addressed concerning their righteousness, as in 5:20 and 6:1."[23] He argues that Matthew instructs "the practice of eschatological righteousness" (5:16–48) as fulfilled and made possible by Jesus (and so by grace).[24] Righteousness in Matthew is "actual obedience to God's will as revealed by Jesus."[25] Therefore, Roland Deines argues that the law is not the central demand in Matthew, but discipleship.[26] He further argues that the sermon is not about the disciples' ethics (*Jüngerethik*) but the disciples' commissioning (*Jüngerbeauftragung*).[27] In terms of the law, Deines says that Matthew neither insists on whole-law-keeping righteousness nor stands against Judaism and the law. For instance, 5:21–48 does not stand against the law but makes the law superfluous. Verse 7:12 follows the love commandment in Leviticus 19:18. Verse 8:3 does not mean to abolish the law because ordinary people can be unclean (8:22; 9:10; 11:11–15, 28–30; 12:1–8, 9–14; 15:1–11,

---

22. Irons, *Righteousness of God*, 264–66. Irons argues that every ethical demand in Matthew "is always grounded in the gift of the saving grace brought by the coming of the kingdom in the person of Jesus."

23. Deines, "Not the Law but the Messiah," 81.

24. Deines, "Not the Law but the Messiah," 83. Deines, *Die Gerechtigkeit*, 122.

25. Deines, quoted in Irons, *Righteousness of God*, 266.

26. Deines, "Not the Law but the Messiah," 70. Roland Deines disagrees with the idea of a law-keeping, Matthean Jesus because "many references in the description of Jesus' life and teaching show him exactly as what the he was: a Jew." Matthean Jesus' keeping the law should be understood within history in that Jesus was a Jew who kept the ritual law. Jesus' keeping the law does not indicate that Matthew insists on law-keeping works righteousness. In addition, Roland states that the use of *anomia* (7:23; 13:41; 23:28; 24:13) does not make Matthew an anti-Pauline, law-keeping book, because *anomia* is also used as an accusation against the Pharisees (23:28). Roland argues for distinguishing the ethical demand of the law-keeping materials (5:21–48; 7:12 and 22:36–40) from a whole-law-keeping demand (5:18; 23:2, 23). Also, gentile inclusion materials indicate a transition "from an inner Jewish messianic movement to a new people with a vision for the whole world" (62–63).

27. Deines, *Die Gerechtigkeit*, 157–81.

32–39; 16:19; 17:24; 18:3; 19:3–9; 21:12; 21:31).[28] Similarly to Hagner, Deines takes the middle way that Matthean righteousness is a demand of humans but that it is only made possible by Jesus.

Jonathan T. Pennington in his book on the sermon, notes that Matthean righteousness should be understood in its "natural ethical sense of what is expected of Jesus' disciples," rather than as God's imputed righteousness for salvation.[29] Pennington says that righteousness in Matthew is "doing the will of God" (7:21, 24; 12:50; cf. 6:10; 7:12; 18:14; 26:39, 42), that which is required to enter the kingdom of heaven (5:19–20; 7:21).[30] He defines righteousness in Matthew as "whole person behavior that accords with God's nature, will, and coming kingdom." And the righteous person is "the one who follows Jesus in this way of being in the world. . . the *whole/teleios* person (5:48) who does not just do the will of God externally but from the heart" (in contrast to the Pharisees).[31] Pennington's view is similar to Mohrlang, who concludes, "Righteousness to Matthew, then embraces both being and doing; it refers both to a mode of behavior and to the fundamental inner disposition from which that behavior derives."[32]

What is important in Pennington's work is that Matthean righteousness involves not only deeds but also the heart. In particular, Matthew's ideas of righteousness, doing good, and doing the will of God involve changing both one's mind, heart, and will and one's conduct.[33] This involvement of mind and conduct equals the lexical and biblical meaning of μετάνοια, which also involves changing mind and deed. Jesus does not mean that Christians need to do more works of righteousness than the Pharisees. Jesus rebukes sinners like the Pharisees as hypocrites because their hearts are lacking while they keep the law. Matthean righteousness is not just a matter of the number of deeds, but righteousness must involve both one's heart and one's deeds. Jesus commands righteousness from a right heart to right deeds. Matthean righteousness involves both the heart and deeds, so it is not legalism. The perfect example is the love commandment that involves the heart and deeds together. In this sense, higher righteousness refers both to heart and deed righteousness, to having a right heart toward God and corresponding right deeds toward others.

---

28. Deines, "Not the Law but the Messiah," 70–83.

29. Pennington, *Sermon on the Mount and Human Flourishing*, 90.

30. Pennington, *Sermon on the Mount and Human Flourishing*, 90. Also, Hagner, "Righteousness in Matthew's Theology," 118.

31. Pennington, *Sermon on the Mount and Human Flourishing*, 91.

32. Mohrlang, *Matthew and Paul*, 114.

33. Pennington, *Sermon on the Mount and Human Flourishing*, 87–91.

In light of the preceding discussion, I suggest that Matthean righteousness involves one's heart and deeds, not deeds alone. This righteousness of both heart and deeds expresses the theme of μετάνοια corresponding to and echoing the summary phrase in 4:17, a commandment to change one's heart and deeds. Righteousness in Matthew is also μετάνοια—righteousness. The demand of righteousness in Matthew expresses the demand of μετάνοια and instructs regarding the contents of μετάνοια. Matthean righteousness expresses a way of being and the life of the followers of Jesus, who turn to him (μετάνοια) with their heart, mind, will, and conduct—their whole life. In particular, "all righteousness"(3:15) and "higher righteousness"(5:20) show what μετάνοια (= returner, and so disciple) looks like in heart and deed.

Deines notes five framing ideas of righteousness in Matthew, but he does not emphasize the role and the definition of μετάνοια in the first words of Jesus' public ministry (4:17).[34] Roland's framing ideas for righteousness are (1) Davidic Messiahship;[35] (2) the forgiveness motif;[36] (3) the fulfillment of Scripture;[37] (4) the universal perspective of the gospel;[38] and (5) entrance into the kingdom of God, salvation, and eternal life through eschatological righteousness[39] that Jesus imputes (3:15; 5:20).[40] Roland's framing ideas are helpful. However, as I have argued above, the first summary word of Jesus' Matthean ministry of μετάνοια is also an important framing concept that righteousness, doing good, and doing the will of God.

Recognized Matthean themes of righteousness, doing good, and doing the will of God express the essence of μετάνοια. They unpack the nature of μετάνοια by following the summary phrase of Jesus' teaching and ministry (4:17): "Repent, for the kingdom of heaven is at hand." The idea of a change (or turn) of both heart and conduct governs Matthean righteousness, as well as the ideas of doing good and doing the will of God. In Matthew μετάνοια is depicted through the language of righteousness and doing the will of God. These concepts are also elaborated expressions of the fruit worthy of μετάνοια.

---

34. Deines briefly mentions repentance in John the Baptist's messages as a prerequisite to enter the kingdom of heaven (3:2; 4:17; 10:7) (Deines, "Not the Law but the Messiah," 72). Roland represents current Matthean scholarship's ignorance of repentance in Matthew.

35. Matt 1:1–17, 20, 23; 2:2–6; 9:27; 11:2; 12:3, 23; 15:22; 16:16–20; 20:30; 21:9; 22:42; 26:63.

36. Matt 1:21; 3:6; 9:2–6, 10, 13; 11:19; 12:31; 20:28; 26:28.

37. Matt 1:22; 27:9.

38. Matt 1:1; 28:19.

39. Matt 5:20; 7:13, 21; 18:3, 8; 19:17, 23, 25; 25:10, 21, 23, 46.

40. Deines, "Not the Law but the Messiah," 71–72.

Righteousness as an Expression and Essence of μετάνοια

As the previous definition of μετάνοια indicates, righteousness (3:15; 5:6, 10, 20; 6:1, 33; 21:32) and the related idea of doing the will of God (6:10; 7:21; 12:50; 18:14; 21:31; 26:42) express the theme of μετάνοια as its contents or examples. When Jesus teaches and commands righteousness (5:6, 10, 20; 6:1, 33; 21:32), all righteousness (3:15), higher righteousness (5:20), and doing the will of God, he means to turn (μετανοέω) to what is right according to the will of God revealed in his instruction. The first summary commandment 4:17 is echoed in the major Matthean theme of righteousness and doing the will of God, that is, changing (or turning) one's heart (will or mind) and deeds. Several arguments can be made for this conceptual relationship between the themes of μετάνοια and righteousness and doing the will of God.

First, Jesus' command to seek all righteousness (3:15) and to seek higher righteousness (5:20) illustrates the theme of μετάνοια in its meaning to change (turn) both mind and deed to what is right. What does "all righteousness" mean? What is "higher righteousness"? Is it to do more good works than the Pharisees and scribes? How is Jesus' righteousness different from that of the Pharisees and scribes, and what exactly does this superfluous righteousness mean? According to Strecker's interpretation, the "all righteousness" of Jesus' baptism (3:15) means "righteousness in attitude and deed."[41] "Higher righteousness" refers not only to doing more works but to a righteousness of mind (heart, will) and deed being proclaimed by Jesus. The Pharisees and scribes' righteousness involves only outer conduct so Jesus rebukes them as hypocrites, but Jesus' righteousness involves both inner and outer righteousness. In other words, Matthean righteousness involves not only doing more visible acts of righteousness but also having a right inner mind, heart, or will. Therefore, this concept of righteousness is not legalistic or one that emphasizes behavior only. The Matthean demand for all righteousness and a higher righteousness expresses the theme of μετάνοια that means to change one's mind and deed toward Jesus, his teachings of the law, and his life. "All righteousness" and "higher righteousness" express μετάνοια in mind and deed, in contrast to the hypocritical righteousness of the Pharisees and scribes (23:28). "All righteousness" and "higher righteousness" are the summit of μετάνοια, and these concepts instruct people what to turn (μετανοέω) to.

---

41. Strecker, *Theology of the New Testament*, 388. Strecker goes on to say, "By being baptized by John the Baptist, Jesus fulfills the requirement of righteousness in attitude and deed."

Second, δικαιοσύνη in 3:15 demonstrates that "fulfilling all righteousness" expresses μετάνοια. In this passage, John the Baptist preaches μετάνοια (3:2-12) and baptizes for μετάνοια (3:11). Jesus, who does not need to be baptized for μετάνοια (3:14), says that he wants a baptism of μετάνοια and that this reception of the baptism of μετάνοια fulfills all righteousness (3:15). Matthew's connection between Jesus' receiving the baptism of μετάνοια and fulfilling all righteousness denotes the idea of μετάνοια through the term "fulfilling all righteousness," which means returning to the righteousness of God. In short, "fulfilling all righteousness" is μετάνοια. In addition, δικαιοσύνη in 21:32 describes John the Baptist's μετάνοια ministry as the way of righteousness. This usage also indicates that μετάνοια and fulfilling righteousness point to the same meaning. Matthean righteousness language signifies μετάνοια.

Third, the Sermon on the Mount especially conveys the theme of μετάνοια and does so through the main idea of the sermon, δικαιοσύνη. As many scholars argue, the sermon gives the content or essence of μετάνοια, instructing how people turn and what people turn from and turn to.[42] Another major theme of the sermon, δικαιοσύνη displays the content of μετάνοια, instructing from what and to what people must turn. Almost all occurrences of δικαιοσύνη in Matthew are in the sermon (5:6, 10, 20; 6:1, 33 except 3:15 and 21:32). Jesus advocates μετάνοια by instructing his followers on the correct way to have and pursue righteousness (5:6, 10; 6:33) and "higher" righteousness (5:20), rather doing so hypocritically and in a self-honoring way (6:1). The proximity of 4:17 to Jesus' sayings about righteousness in 5:17-20 implies that, as Nave says, "the demand for repentance (μετάνοια) is a demand for righteousness. Righteousness in Matthew is about how one lives in relationship to God in terms of God's will for what is right."[43] In fact, 4:17 is rephrased in 5:20. Both phrases command μετάνοια and righteousness in order to enter the kingdom of heaven. Righteousness in Matthew is μετάνοια-righteousness, turning from sin to the righteousness in heart and action taught by Jesus Christ.

Fourth, those who are righteous in Matthew illustrate the truly μετάνοια ones who follow Jesus with their whole heart and conduct (5:45; 13:43, 49; 25:37, 46). Followers or disciples of Jesus who appear after Jesus' μετάνοια call in 4:17 are those who hear this calling and turn(μετάνοια) to follow Jesus in the narrative context. Therefore, these texts, which describe these people as righteous, necessarily describe them as true μετάνοια ones. In particular,

---

42. See ch. 1 overview of the arguments section and ch. 6 on the sermon and μετάνοια.

43. Nave, *Role and Function of Repentance*, 92.

27:4, 19 call Jesus the righteous one who follows the will of God and fulfills it on the cross (26:39, 42). Being righteous in Matthew involves not only doing good but also having the mind, will, and heart of God.

In addition to righteousness, Jesus' instruction about "doing the will of God (or Father in heaven)" (6:10; 7:21; 12:50; 18:14; 21:31; 26:42) communicates and exemplifies the fruit worthy of μετάνοια as both content and consequences for entrance into the kingdom of heaven (or for eschatological judgment), relating back to the first words of Jesus in 4:17 (cf. 3:2, 8). As chapter 4 shows, doing the will of God and doing good are parallel expressions to doing/bearing the fruit worthy of μετάνοια.

The first appearance of "doing the will of the Father in heaven" is in 6:10, in which Jesus asks for the coming of the kingdom of God and that the will of God will be done on earth. Verse 6:10 expresses 4:17, in which Jesus commands people to change their heart and deeds, showing that command to mean for God's will to be done on earth and for the kingdom of heaven to come.

The second occurrence of "doing the will of the Father in heaven" is in the concluding remarks of the sermon in 7:21. Jesus states that only those who do the will of the Father in heaven will enter the kingdom of heaven. In other words, 7:21 denotes a change of both will and deeds according to God. The meaning of verse 7:21 and 4:17 are not conceptually different because "doing the will of the Father in heaven" points to doing Jesus' teachings in the sermon, and the sermon is the contents of the commandment of μετάνοια in 4:17. In this way, 7:21 and 4:17 command the same sermon, which is the contents of μετάνοια (returning). Also, both verses command the same sermon for the sake of the kingdom of heaven. In this sense, 7:21 express the essence of μετάνοια as changing both one's heart (will or mind) and accordingly, one's deeds. Verses 4:17 and 7:21 point to the same meaning using different language. Also, 5:20 equals 7:21 (and 4:17) in terms of righteousness and eschatological judgment. As mentioned above, "doing the will of God" is righteousness that allows entry to the kingdom of heaven. Verses 5:20 and 7:21 create an inclusio and indicate the thematic significance of μετάνοια in the sermon.

The third occurrence of "doing the will of the Father in heaven" is in 12:50, where Jesus insists that the one who does the will of the Father in heaven is Jesus' family, and thus a person who can enter into the kingdom of heaven. Jesus stretches his hand to his disciples who turn to Jesus from 4:17 and depicts them as the doers of the will of the Father in heaven. This indicates that "the doers of the will of the Father in heaven" refers to μετάνοια disciples who are called and turn to follow Jesus from 4:17. As noted above, doing the will of God depicts μετάνοια and the will of God is the contents of fruits worthy of μετάνοια.

The location of 12:50 indicates that it is the opening focal point or governing idea of the parables of the kingdom of heaven in Matthew 13 and that the parables illustrate the theme of μετάνοια. As the same phrase in 7:21 refers to the sermon as the contents of μετάνοια and its worthy fruit, this phrase in 12:50 also indicates that the parables, specifically their fruit and judgment language depict μετάνοια and its worthy fruit. In 18:14, the fourth reference to "doing the will of the Father in heaven," also expresses the essence of μετάνοια. The child in Matthew 18:14 is the child 18:3 illustrates who turns and becomes like a child and who will enter the kingdom of heaven (18:3). Verse 18:3 uses στρέφω(μετάνοια), the synonym of μετάνοια and illustrates μετάνοια with the child image. And 18:14 denotes that the will of Father in heaven vindicates the μετάνοια ones who turn and become like children by humbling themselves (18:4).

Matthew 21:31–32, a fifth reference, demonstrates that the doers of the Father's will are the righteous and they are the μετάνοια ones who change their mind according to the μετάνοια ministry of John the Baptist. The parable of the two sons in Matthew 21:31-32 depicts the commandment of turning (μετανοέω) that the second son turns (μετάνοια), changing his mind, and does the will of God, but the first does not do the will of the Father. The tax collectors and the prostitutes demonstrate the theme of μετάνοια when they change their minds and believe the μετάνοια preaching of John the Baptist, who came in the way of righteousness (21:31-32). Changing their minds and deeds ensures their entrance into the kingdom of heaven (21:31). Finally, 26:42 points to the theme of μετάνοια through Jesus' prayer in which he seeks the will of God, not his own will.

Finally, "doing good" language illustrates the nature of the worthy fruit of μετάνοια. This section will not examine all "doing good" language, because chapter 4 already fully shows "doing good" related to the image of "bearing fruit worthy of μετάνοια" (Matt 3:8).[44]

Conclusion

The Matthean Gospel recognizes the major theme of righteousness together with the related ideas of doing the will of God and doing good. All portray the essence of Jesus' first summary phrase of his ministry and teaching (μετάνοια) and parallel language of doing good, and fruits show that they are examples of the fruit worthy of μετάνοια in Matthew

---

44. See ch. 4.

3:8. Matthean righteousness is not just a problem related to whether it is something demanded of human beings or God's gift, but it is part of Jesus' commandment of μετάνοια, that is, turning one's whole life to Jesus and keeping his teachings. The truly μετάνοια person seeks the righteousness of God, "higher righteousness," which involves one's heart and deeds in contrast to the legalistic Pharisees and scribes, and results in doing the will of God. The truly μετάνοια one is part of the family of Jesus and he/she is the one who enters the kingdom of heaven.

The Significance of μετάνοια as a Soteriological Category in Matthew

Jesus' summary proclamation in 4:17, "repent, for the kingdom of heaven is at hand," states that those who μετανοέω will enter the kingdom of heaven (or eternal life) but those who do not μετανοέω will not. This summary phrase, which initiates Jesus' teaching and ministry, also demonstrates the significance of μετάνοια as a Matthean soteriological category. It is also shown in John the Baptist's μετάνοια preaching (3:2–12). The Baptist employs soteriological words such as of the wrath of God, the axe, cutting down fruitless tree, gathering the wheat into barn, and throwing the chaff into the fire of hell that call for μετάνοια and worthy fruit of μετάνοια. These examples of soteriological language also occur in the body of Matthew echoing 3:2–12 and 4:17. After a brief history of research of Matthean soteriology, I examine several texts that mirror 3:2–12 and 4:17 in the body of Matthew.

Ignoring μετάνοια as a Soteriological Theme in the History of Research

Even though Matthew puts μετάνοια in a soteriological context at the beginning of his gospel, Matthean scholarship has not sufficiently developed μετάνοια as an important idea for Matthean soteriology. Misunderstandings about the biblical and lexical meaning of μετάνοια, the infrequent use and insufficient emphasis on the location of the term contribute to this oversight. As a matter of fact, scholarly discussion on Matthean soteriology tends to focus on the Matthean righteousness discussion concerning whether Matthew views righteousness as something demanded from humans or as God's gift. Most scholarly arguments about Matthean soteriology see it in three ways: as a legalistic human demand,[45] as God's gift,[46] or based on the perspective of covenantal nomism.[47] Some argue that both the indicative and the imperative are present in Matthew.[48]

It is not my focus here to review all scholarly works on Matthean soteriology,[49] but I will briefly review the third view: covenantal nomism. A representative of this view is Petri Luomanen who argues that the Matthean salvation structure has been influenced by the covenantal nomism of Judaism. Petri argues that the Matthean Jewish community developed their salvation theory based on the ideas of "getting in" and "staying in." One enters the community through repentance (meaning acceptance of Jesus' message) and stays in the community by keeping Jesus' ethical teaching, such as loving one's neighbor. Petri mainly examines Matthean texts in two categories: how one enters into salvation (5:17–20; 7:15–23; 13:24–30, 36–43; 19:16–20; 16; 21:28–22; 14; 25:31–46) and how one maintains it (18; 26:26–30; 28:16–20). In particular, Petri argues that Matthew 18 explains how a Christian can stay in the community and how the community should expel one who does not follow its regulations.

However, I suggest that μετάνοια does not indicate only a one-time event of entering the community. Μετάνοια is a lifelong event of turning one's heart, mind, will, and conduct, and so one's whole being and life toward Jesus and his teaching. Matthew puts μετάνοια at the genesis of Jesus' ministry not because it means entrance into the Christian community but because it summarizes Jesus' ministry and teaching. According to Petri, Matthew's redaction of "for the forgiveness of sins" from the baptism of John indicates that baptism and repentance denote not salvation but only entrance into the community. However, 3:2–12 and 4:17 indicate μετάνοια as a way for salvation, for entering the kingdom of heaven, for receiving

---

45. For a legalistic reading of Matthew, see Marxsen, *New Testament Foundations*, 231–48.

46. For some scholars who argue for divine grace based on human works, see Kupp, *Matthew's Emmanuel*. See also Talbert, *Matthew*, 13–27.

47. For a covenantal nomism understanding of the Matthean community, see Luomanen, *Entering the Kingdom of Heaven*; Mohrlang, *Matthew and Paul*. The first and the second options are already mentioned in the previous section dealing with whether one should read Matthean righteousness as God's gift or as something demanded of humans.

48. Luz, *Matthew 1–7*, 201–2.

49. For a history of research on Matthean soteriology, see Luomanen, *Entering the Kingdom of Heaven*. Since Matthean soteriology and righteousness are closely related, see the research on righteousness in the previous section for additional information.

eternal life, and for avoiding judgment.⁵⁰ Verses 11:20–24 note that judgment follows a lack of μετάνοια.

Concerning this theme of μετάνοια, Matthew 18 instructs Jesus' followers to turn and become like a child by being humble (18:3–4) and forgiving each other unceasingly (18:21–22, 35). In Matthew 18 Jesus repeats the command to μετάνοια to Jesus' disciples who already turn to follow him (4:17). This repetition of μετάνοια indicates that μετάνοια is not only a one-time, initial event but also a lifelong event. Matthew does not give instructions here about how one stays in the community and avoids being expelled but about how one continues in lifelong μετάνοια, turning to Christ in community, through humility and servanthood in order not to be a false turner (μετάνοια) but a true turner and follower of Jesus. The judgment language in Matthew 18 motivates this μετάνοια (18:6–9, 17, 34–35) and distinguishes true and false μετάνοια. Matthew 18's commandment for unbounded forgiveness indicates an embrace of sinners and an effort to turn them from their sin to the community rather than to expel them. The Immanuel theme in Matthew 1:17 and 28:20 frames the entire gospel and insists on God's initiating grace of salvation and the assurance of salvation.

Matthew 4:17 as Summary of Matthean Salvation Language

Matthew puts μετάνοια at the opening of Jesus' public ministry, as well as John the Baptist's, along with a judgment and reward connotation: "Turn, for the kingdom of heaven is at hand (3:2; 4:17)." This summary phrase subsumes Matthean soteriological themes such as righteousness, doing the will of God. As mentioned above, these are the expressions and contents of μετάνοια. Also, this summary phrase subsumes soteriological reward and judgment language such as on the one hand, "entering the kingdom of heaven," "receiving eternal life" (5:20; 7:13, 21; 18:3, 8, 9; 19:17, 23, 24; 23:13; 25:10, 21, 23), family language of Jesus (12:50) and on the other hand, being thrown into hell, eternal fire or darkness (3:10, 11, 12; 5:22, 29, 30; 7:19; 8:12, 29; 10:28; 13:40, 42, 50; 17:15; 18:8, 9, 34; 22:13; 23:15, 33; 24:51; 25:30, 41). This language and these images are the explanation or elaboration of 4:17's soteriological reward and judgment connotation: "for the kingdom of heaven is at hand (3:2; 4:17)." In particular, this soteriological reward and judgment language follows soteriological themes such as righteousness and doing the will of God in the body of Matthew as in 4:17 the soteriological connotation follows the commandment of turning (μετανοέω).

50. See Runesson, *Divine Wrath and Salvation in Matthew*, 119–36.

In other words, the commandment of turning (μετανοέω) for the coming of the kingdom of heaven in the beginning of Jesus' ministry in 4:17 meaning to turn one's whole being and life toward Jesus and his teaching is echoed in these various soteriological expressions. Matthew 3:2-12 already proclaims μετάνοια and the accompanying judgment and reward as an important soteriological category in the Gospel of Matthew. As chapter 4 showed, these various soteriological languages and images repeat and expand the soteriological theme of μετάνοια and its related language and images in 3:2-12 and 4:17. This repetition and expansion show the theme of μετάνοια as an important soteriological theme of Matthew.

This μετάνοια for salvation is based on the work of the Holy Spirit as indicated by John's identification of Jesus as the baptizer with the Holy Spirit and fire for μετάνοια (3:11-12). This Holy Spirit baptism for μετάνοια denotes a divine, grace-based μετάνοια of both mind and works. Jesus' baptism with the Holy Spirit and fire assures entrance into and living in covenant and community. Although references to the work of the Holy Spirit occur infrequently in the Gospel of Matthew, 3:12 indicates the presence of the Holy Spirit in the believers and his help for lifelong μετάνοια. Verse 10:20 indicates the presence of the Holy Spirit in Jesus' disciples while verse 28:19 denotes the work of the Holy Spirit in making disciples and keeping Jesus' commandments—an illustration of μετάνοια.

Matthean Soteriology Texts as Expressions of 4:17

Here I examine several Matthean texts based on Petri Luomanen's book (5:17-20; 7:15-23; 13:24-30; 36-43; 18; 19:16-20:16; 21:28-22:14; 25:31-46; 28:16-20; 26:26-30) to express and demonstrate the significance of the opening soteriological summary commandment of μετάνοια in 4:17. These passages include the Matthean soteriological themes of righteousness, doing the will of God, and doing good, which convey the essence of μετάνοια and its worthy fruit (3:8). They also include Matthean judgment language related to entering the kingdom of heaven, receiving eternal life, being thrown into the fire of hell, and similar expressions to motivate μετάνοια (cf. 3:7-12). In this respect, they all parallel the summary of Jesus' teaching, "Turn, for the kingdom of heaven is at hand" (4:17; cf. 3:2, 7-12) in the body of Matthew[51] and show the soteriological thematic significance of μετάνοια in Matthew.

---

51. See ch. 4 for judgment and reward language, images in John the Baptist's μετάνοια preaching, and their parallelism in the body of Matthew.

First, Matthew 5:20 mandates righteousness surpassing that of the scribes and Pharisees for entering into the kingdom of heaven. This verse mirrors 3:2-12 and 4:17's commandment of μετάνοια for entering into the kingdom of heaven. As mentioned above, righteousness is the contents of μετάνοια and 5:20 says that entering into the kingdom of heaven depends on righteousness, the contents of μετάνοια. In addition, 5:20 is the opening and thus governing passage of the antitheses (5:20-48) and of the sermon. Therefore, the antitheses and the sermon explain the contents of μετάνοια what people must turn (μετανοέω) from and must turn (μετανοέω) to enter into the kingdom of heaven and avoid judgment. These verses direct people what they must turn (μετανοέω) from and to with judgment language (5:22, 26, 29, 30).

Second, the concluding remark of the sermon, 7:15-23, states that those who are good trees bear good fruit and they are doers of the will of the Father in heaven who will enter the kingdom of heaven. These verses also illustrate 3:2-12 and 4:17. In particular, the good tree and fruit image parallels John the Baptist's μετάνοια preaching that emphasized fruit worthy of μετάνοια in 3:8, as well as that the bad tree would be cut down and thrown into the fire. In 7:15-23, Jesus also warns people who do lawlessness to turn (μετανοέω), which also parallels John the Baptist's μετάνοια preaching. These parallelisms of salvation and judgment images indicate that 7:15-23 expresses μετάνοια in 3:2-12 and 4:17, or that 7:15-23 elaborates on μετάνοια in 3:2-12 and 4:17 as an important Matthean salvation theme.

Third, Matthew 8:11-12 denotes in the narrative context that the centurion of great faith accepts Jesus' call for μετάνοια (4:17) and he will sit in the kingdom of heaven but those who do not turn (μετανοέω) to Jesus but reject him will be cast out into outer darkness. Therefore, 8:11-12 demonstrates 3:2, 9 and 4:17 and indicates their salvation thematic importance. Specifically, the great faith of the gentile centurion is an example of Matthew 3:9—raising up children from the stone not from ethnic Israel.

Fourth, Matthew 12:50 expresses the theme of μετάνοια when Jesus defines his family, which indicates salvation, by saying that whoever does the will of the Father in heaven is Jesus' brother, sister, and mother. As mentioned before, doing the will of the Father in heaven refers to μετάνοια and its worthy fruit and this statement reveals μετάνοια as an important salvation theme in Matthew. Through this soteriological saying Jesus defines the true people of God as those who to turn (μετανοέω) to him by doing the will of his Father who is in heaven in order to be in the family of Jesus—to be saved.

Fifth, Matthew 13:24-30, 36-43 illustrate two kinds of people in the world—wheat and tares and soteriological future reward and judgment. This parable describes 3:2–12 and 4:17. In the narrative context of Matthew 3–12 this parable explains Jesus' μετάνοια (4:17) ministry and its mixed earthly reception (ch. 11–12).[52] The wheat illustrates those who μετανοέω to Jesus and so who will enter their Father's kingdom, while the tares illustrate those who do not μετανοέω to Jesus and so will be thrown into the furnace of fire. Additionally, 13:50 commands people to be the righteous and not the wicked expressing 3:2–12 and 4:17.[53] This parable shows that μετάνοια is an important soteriological theme in Matthew and even governs it.

Sixth, Matthew 18:3–9 echoes 3:2–12 and 4:17 and show μετάνοια as an important soteriological theme in Matthew. In 18:3 Jesus commands to turn and become like a child to enter into the kingdom of heaven. Specifically, 18:3 uses στρέφω, a synonym of μετανοέω echoing 3:2 and 4:17 to show μετάνοια as an important soteriological theme. Verses 18:8–9 command leaders not to make these little ones whose angels see Jesus' Father in heaven stumble because one who makes them stumble will be cast into the eternal fire or the fiery hell. These passages thus show how much Jesus values the one who μετανοέω and becomes like a child.[54]

Seventh, Matthew 19:16–20:16 demonstrates 3:2–12 and 4:17, showing μετάνοια as the significant soteriological theme. "Little one" in 19:13–14, which serves as the opening point of 19:16–19:30, recalls the μετάνοια commandment in 18:3. The emphasis on turning and becoming like a child and so turning to humble himself for entering into the kingdom of heaven opens and governs the story that follows of the rich young man. This parallel child image indicates that 19:16–30 demonstrates the soteriological theme of μετάνοια. This young man asks how he can earn the eternal life and replies that he keeps everything that the law says, but Jesus disagrees. Jesus asks the rich young man to follow him by selling everything he has to have eternal life. But he rejects. After this young man's rejection, Jesus teaches his disciples that a rich man can hardly enter the kingdom of heaven. This scene recalls 4:17–23 when Jesus calls his disciples to turn (μετανοέω) and they follow leaving everything behind. This rich young man should turn (μετανοέω) to Jesus and follow him by selling everything he has to be saved. This contrasted parallelism between the disciples and rich young man reveals the soteriological theme of μετάνοια implied in 19:16–30. Also, the concluding remark in 19:30 and 20:16, "the last shall be first, and the last first," indicates that 19:16–20:16 demonstrates the theme of μετάνοια by

---

52. For more discussion on the backdrop of Matt 13, see ch. 9.

53. For this passage and more detailed discussion, see ch. 9, which deals with Matt 13 and the parables of the kingdom of heaven.

54. Ch. 10 elaborates more on this passage.

showing that the world must turn (μετανοέω) upside down. In addition, the parable of the vineyard (20:1-16) reveals that salvation is based only upon the will of God and is freely given to whom God wishes.

Eighth, Matthew 21:28-22:14 illustrates 3:2-12 and 4:17 and builds up Matthean salvation structure with the theme of μετάνοια. The parable of the two sons (21:28-32) illustrates the theme of μετάνοια as the second son repents (μεταμέλομαι) in heart and deed and does the will of the father. A similar term to μετάνοια, μεταμέλομαι is used to show that this parable is about μετάνοια. The second son shows what μετάνοια is when he not only changes his mind (μεταμέλομαι) but also does the will of his father by going to vineyard. The μετάνοια second son refers to the tax collectors and prostitutes who μεταμέλομαι and believe in Jesus (21:31-32). They will enter the kingdom of God. Verse 21:43 indicates μετάνοια as bearing fruit of the kingdom of God and shows that the one who μετανοέω will enter the kingdom. The parable of the wedding feast that follows (22:1-14) illustrates this theme of μετάνοια and the corresponding judgment. The people who were invited declined to participate in the wedding feast, which means rejection of Jesus and his call for μετάνοια since this parable illustrates the whole Matthean context from the beginning of Jesus' ministry, 4:17 the calling of μετάνοια. The ones who accept the invitation but don't wear wedding garments illustrates those who accept Jesus and his call of μετάνοια but do not have the proper or worthy fruit of μετάνοια. Neither will enter the kingdom of heaven. (This parable will be discussed in ch. 11.) In this respect, Matthew 21:28-22:14 shows μετάνοια and its worthy fruit as important Matthean salvation structure.

Ninth, Matthew 25:31-46 expounds on 3:2-12 and 4:17. The parable of the sheep and goats includes "the least" twice in 25:40 and 45 in relation to the child image of 18:3 and 19:16. This parallel image depicts the theme of μετάνοια through humility and servanthood and provides the contents of μετάνοια through which people attain eternal life. The sheep and goats are divided according to what they do to "the least;" the former will enter eternal life but the latter the eternal fire.

Finally, Matthew 28:16-20 parallels 3:2-12 and 4:17 in their salvation structure. As mentioned in the previous chapter, they share the same meaning but 28:16-20 consummates 3:2-17 and 4:17. "Go therefore and make disciples of all the nations, baptizing them in the name of the Father and the Son and the Holy Spirit, teaching them to observe all that I commanded you" consummates the opening commandment of turning (μετανοέω) in 4:17. Raising up children out of the stone, not ethnic Israel in 3:9 is realized through the universal μετάνοια mission 28:16-20. "All authority has been given to Me in heaven and on earth" consummates "for the kingdom of heaven is at hand," which indicates Jesus' authority and the reason to turn (μετανοέω) to Jesus. The baptism formula and Immanuel language "I am with you always, even to the end of the age" parallel 1:18 and 3:12–17. They are closely related to 4:17, the opening summary of Jesus' ministry. The first and the last words of Jesus' public ministry show the thematic importance of μετάνοια in terms of Matthean salvation structure.

Conclusion

The commandment of turning (μετανοέω) for the coming of the kingdom of heaven in the beginning of Jesus' ministry in 4:17 (cf. 3:2, 7–12) demonstrates its significance as Matthean soteriological structure in its meaning of turning one's whole being and life toward Jesus and his teaching. The soteriological commandment of μετάνοια is also seen in a variety of expressions such as righteousness, doing the will of God and discipleship. These terms are followed by soteriological language of reward and judgment: entering the kingdom of heaven, eternal life, the fire of hell and so on (cf. 3:7–12). These show the soteriological importance of μετάνοια and its various expressions in Matthew.

Conclusion

Chapters 5 and 6 show that selective Matthean important topics unpack the theme of μετάνοια in the summary phrase of John the Baptist and Jesus' ministry and teaching in 3:2–12 and 4:17. They possibly demonstrate the thematic or paradigmatic significance of μετάνοια in Matthew, echoing Jesus' first commandment of μετάνοια. They also provide the contents of μετάνοια and fruit worthy of μετάνοια. If it is not the case this opening commandment of turning (μετάνοια) remains empty without its contents and essence. The concepts of becoming a disciple of Jesus and following Jesus (4:20, 22, 25; 8:19, 22, 23; 9:9, 27; 10:37–38; 16:24; 19:21, 27; 20:34; 21:9) by keeping his teachings (4:18–23; 11:28–30; 16:24–27; 28:16–20) and of being whole before God (5:48) illustrate the nature of μετάνοια. The Great Commission imparts the μετάνοια theme in the language of discipleship and obedience to Jesus' teachings. The theme of μετάνοια in 3:2–12; 4:17 is universal. The widespread gentile inclusion theme and gentile μετάνοια show the significance of universal μετάνοια theme in Matthew. In Matthew, righteousness (5:17–20), doing good works (5:16), and doing the will of God (6:10; 7:21; 12:50; 18:14; 21:31; 26:42) outwardly display the essence and the contents of the fruit worthy of μετάνοια (3:8; 5:16, 17–20; 7:21; 10:37, 38; 12:48).

These expressions of the theme of μετάνοια consist of Matthean soteriology. Verses 3:2–12 and 4:17 proclaim μετάνοια for entering into the kingdom of heaven or salvation. Soteriological images and language related to entering the kingdom of heaven and to eternal life and judgment give motivation for μετάνοια (3:2, 7–12; 4:17; 7:19–23; 13:30, 40–43) and demonstrate the significance of μετάνοια as a soteriological category in Matthew. These various related and important ideas in Matthew are all best understood as a fleshing out of the commandment of μετάνοια in the beginning of Jesus' ministry, even though the word itself rarely appears in the gospel.

Chapter 7

The Thematic Significance of μετάνοια in the Sermon on the Mount

The Contents of μετάνοια

Introduction

THIS BOOK ARGUES FOR the thematic and paradigmatic significance of μετάνοια ("turning," "amendment," "change") in Matthew. From this chapter it will focus on Jesus' five major teaching blocks (Matt 5–7, 10, 13, 18, and 23–25) to show the significance of μετάνοια in Jesus' teachings in Matthew.

To indicate μετάνοια as a significant theme of his book, Matthew begins Jesus' public ministry with a key phrase: "Μετανοεῖτε (Turn), for the kingdom of heaven is at hand" (4:17). What does Jesus command to turn from and turn to? Or what is the essence and contents of the turning? If there is no further explanation or elaboration of the commandment, it will remain an empty commandment and lose its meaning and significance. Some critical scholars note that this opening statement (4:17) especially governs the discourse block closest to it, the Sermon on the Mount (4:17—8:1) and the sermon gives the contents of μετάνοια.[1] This chapter suggests that the sermon expands or elaborates on Jesus' opening summary commandment of

---

1. See Talbert, *Reading the Sermon on the Mount*, 143–44; Keener, *Gospel of Matthew*, 149; Luz, *Matthew 1–7*, 198; Scaer, *Sermon on the Mount*, 49, 64; Kintu, "Repentance in the Sermon on the Mount"; France, *Gospel of Matthew*, 143; Allison, "Structure of the Sermon on the Mount," 423–45. In addition it is well known that the sermon is Jesus' public teachings selected by Matthew, so that it is quite sure that Jesus preaches his message of μετάνοια and the sermon in the all regions of Israel in the synagogues (4:23) during his public ministry. Luke's version of the Sermon on the Plain does not have clear connection with the calling of repentance. However, Luke 5:32 points out that Jesus' ministry is to call sinners to repentance. And after the calling of the disciples, 6:17–19 reports Jesus' healing of the people whom Jesus calls, thus the sinners. Then Jesus teaches them the Sermon on the Plain. This narrative sequence likely shows that the Sermon on the Plain also teaches the essence of repentance.

turning (μετανοέω) by showing μετάνοια's essence, contents, necessity, and corresponding reward and judgment. This relationship shows the thematic significance of μετάνοια in the sermon.

The first section of this chapter will briefly survey scholarship on the sermon and the theme of μετάνοια in the sermon. The rest of the chapter will argue for the significance of the theme of μετάνοια in the sermon using the following arguments: (1) The sermon reveals the essence and the contents of μετάνοια according to the lexical meaning of μετάνοια in 4:17, which means to turn, change, or amend both one's heart and conduct away from sin and to a right mind and behavior, such as righteousness and doing the will of the Father in heaven. (2) The literary structure of the sermon shows that 4:17 begins the sermon, indicating the importance of the theme of μετάνοια. (3) The parallelism between John the Baptist's μετάνοια preaching (3:2–12) and the sermon also demonstrates that the sermon is a message of μετάνοια. (4) Major themes and contents of the sermon provide the essence of the directive of μετάνοια (4:17).

A Survey of Scholarship on Repentance (μετάνοια) and the Sermon

This survey is to see various readings of the sermon and suggest the significance of μετάνοια in the sermon as a way of understanding the sermon. How to understand the sermon has been a long-debated question among many scholars. Throughout the centuries, scholars have suggested many views and driving ideas for the sermon.[2] For example, Clarence Bauman provides thirty different views on the sermon.[3] Harvey McArthur offers twelve—six minor and six primary.[4] His six primary views represent noticeable historical readings of the sermon: the absolutist view, the hyperbole view, the general principal view, the "attitudes-not-acts" view, the repentance view, and the unconditioned divine will view.

---

2. See McArthur, *Understanding the Sermon on the Mount*, 105–27. He gives twelve views on the reading of the sermon. See also Davies and Allison, "Reflections on the Sermon on the Mount," 283–309; Guelich, "Interpreting the Sermon on the Mount," 117–30; Guelich, *Sermon on the Mount*, 14–24; Talbert, *Reading the Sermon on the Mount*, 29–31. For a comprehensive review of the history of modern scholarship on the Sermon on the Mount up to 1991, see Bauman, *Sermon on the Mount*.

3. Bauman, *Sermon on the Mount*, 3–4.

4. McArthur, *Understanding the Sermon on the Mount*, 105–27.

Practicability of the Sermon

Robert A. Guelich claims that the practicability of the sermon has been a major question that has divided different readings. According to Guelich, the early church did not question the practicability of the sermon but simply read it as "the perfect measure of Christian life."[5] The Reformers began to raise the question of practicability and emphasized the sermon's impracticability. Luther's repentance view is representative; he argues that the sermon makes people realize the impracticability of the sermon and leads them to repentance. John Calvin takes a middle way. He criticizes the literalism of the sermon because of its impracticability. But he argues for the practicability of the sermon based on reading the commandments of the sermon in the broader context of the Bible.[6]

Ethical and/or Eschatological Readings of the Sermon

Recent trends have focused on ethical and (or) eschatological readings of the sermon rather than the question of its practicability. The ethical reading validates the sermon for human life. The eschatological reading commands practicing the sermon, not in the literal sense, but rather based on the context of Matthew. For example, George Strecker reads the sermon as "the radical, eschatologically based call to repentance and the practicable, ethically obligatory instruction as it is presented by the sermon in the context of the Gospel of Matthew."[7] The sermon exhorts a new, different, and better righteousness as a requirement for entrance into the kingdom of heaven.[8] William D. Davies defines the sermon as "Messianic Torah," in that Jesus reinterpreted the Torah with his own divine authority.[9] Hans Dieter Betz says that the sermon is not law to obey but more likely theological philosophical work in connection to the contemporary "philosophical epitome" for human life.[10] Jack D. Kingsbury designates the sermon as an ethic for disciples. The disciples are called by Jesus to enter the sphere of the kingdom of heaven and summoned to lead a life of greater righteousness, which means "to love God with heart, soul, and mind and to love the neighbors

---

5. McArthur, *Understanding the Sermon on the Mount*, 118.

6. Guelich, "Interpreting the Sermon on the Mount," 118–20. This is the so-called third use of the law.

7. Strecker, *Sermon on the Mount*, 184.

8. Strecker, *Sermon on the Mount*, 61.

9. Davies, *Setting of the Sermon on the Mount*, 107. Also, Allison, *Sermon on the Mount*, 25.

10. Betz, *Essays on the Sermon on the Mount*, 11–16.

as the self."[11] In terms of the practicability of the sermon, Kingsbury notes that Matthew is aware of the disciples' failure through sin and little faith and their need for continual forgiveness (6:12–13). However, "bound to him [Jesus] and assured of his forgiveness, disciples 'follow after him' as they hear his call and lead the life of the greater righteousness."[12] Charles Talbert argues that the sermon aims for character formation and decision-making.[13] Scot McKnight defines the sermon as a combination of divinely revealed law, prophetic teaching, and wisdom. The sermon is an invitation to a messianic ethical vision for church that can be lived by the power of the Spirit.[14] Jonathan Pennington argues that the sermon gives a Second Temple Judaism and Greco-Roman epitome of wisdom and virtue. Pennington defines the sermon as "a Christocentric, flourishing-oriented, kingdom-awaiting, eschatological wisdom exhortation."[15] He argues that the sermon aims to form character or virtue. Pennington suggests that the main themes of the sermon for human flourishing are

> the combined themes of *makairos*-ness, *teleios*-ity, wholeness, singularity, righteousness, and others that together create a vision ('a moral imagination') for a way of being in the world that promises true human flourishing, now partially and eschatologically fully, through believing in and aligning oneself with Jesus Christ, God's authoritative Son. Jesus is embodiment—even incarnation—of the ideal Philosopher-King, inviting people into flourishing in God's coming kingdom.[16]

My view is similar to Strecker's and to Luther's repentance view. The sermon commands turning (μετάνοια), which is turning one's heart, conduct, and whole life toward Jesus and the kingdom of heaven according to Jesus' reinterpretation of the law presented in the sermon. The sermon teaches lifelong μετάνοια. But my view differs from Luther's "repentance view (or impossible ideal view)," which argues that the sermon brings people to turn (μετανοέω) because of the human impossibility of following the sermon perfectly. The sermon directly commands μετάνοια. It declares what people, especially Israel, must turn from and turn to in order to follow Jesus Christ according to his reinterpretation of the law and the prophets. In addition, I agree with Kingsbury's approach to the question

11. Kingsbury, "Place, Structure, and Meaning," 143.
12. Kingsbury, "Place, Structure, and Meaning," 143.
13. Talbert, *Reading the Sermon on the Mount*.
14. McKnight, *Sermon on the Mount*.
15. Pennington, *Sermon on the Mount and Human Flourishing*, 15.
16. Pennington, *Sermon on the Mount and Human Flourishing*, 290.

of the practicability of the sermon, i.e., Jesus commands his followers to turn to follow him and his teaching, but he also understands their failure due to human weakness and teaches them to ask for continual forgiveness. Also, while Betz argues that the sermon is only a Hellenistic philosophical epitome, I agree with Pennington who approaches the sermon through its dual settings of Greco-Roman and Jewish background. The sermon is the ideal Philosopher-king Jesus' teaching. I agree with Pennington's human flourishing view in the sense that Jesus commands μετάνοια for true human flourishing as revealed in Jesus Christ the Son of God.

A Scholarly Survey on μετάνοια Reading of the Sermon

Most scholars fail to connect μετάνοια (4:17) to the sermon for several reasons. First, the term μετάνοια does not occur in the sermon.[17] Second, it is easy to see that μετάνοια message belongs only to John the Baptist. Third, the structures for the Gospel of Matthew that scholars have suggested divide the key phrase (4:17) from the sermon, making it more difficult to see the close relationship between the two.[18] Fourth, the tendency for many to think of μετάνοια as just turning the heart, including confessing sins[19] and feeling remorse, obscures the close relationship between 4:17 and the heart and behavioral change of life instructed in the sermon.[20]

Some scholars do note the importance of μετάνοια in the sermon. For example, Charles H. Talbert explains the role of Jesus in the sermon as eschatological judge (7:13–27) who demands μετάνοια (4:17). He states that the sermon gives the contents of μετάνοια.[21] Also Craig Keener mentions that the sermon is connected to 4:17 as "the repentant lifestyle," or "the nature of the ethic of repentance."[22] He rightly captures their close

---

17. "The kingdom of heaven" appears many times in the Gospel of Matthew. Meanwhile "repent" appears seven times in the Gospel of Matthew: five times in verb form (3:2; 4:17; 11:20, 21; 12:41) and two times in feminine noun form (3:8, 11).

18. Most scholars structure the introduction section of the Gospel of Matthew from chapter 1 to 4:23 or 25, titling it "Jesus' early history" or "preparation for public ministry," and the sermon begins at 5:1. As a result, 4:17 and the sermon are separated, and their close connection is obscured.

19. We need to distinguish between ἐξομολογέω and μετανοέω. Matthew does not use the two terms with the same meaning. He reports the people of Israel confessing (ἐξομολογέω) their sins at 3:6, but this is not exactly what μετανοέω is all about. Μετανοέω is not confessing one's sins but turning one's heart and deeds.

20. BDAG 640 defines μετανοέω "to change one's mind, feel remorse, repent, be converted."

21. Talbert, *Reading the Sermon on the Mount*, 143–44.

22. Keener, *Gospel of Matthew*, 149.

relationship. Ulrich Luz argues that the μετάνοια message is "the entry gate" to the greater righteousness of the sermon and *dominates* it [italics mine].²³ David P. Scaer also argues that 4:17, which marks the beginning of Jesus' public ministry, is a characteristic summary of Jesus' common message, especially the sermon. One of his supporting ideas is the appearance of agricultural parables in both John and Jesus' preaching (3:12; 5:26; 6:16–18; 13:24–30).²⁴ Despite the way these scholars observe the importance of μετάνοια, none of them read the sermon through μετάνοια or elaborate μετάνοια as a significant theme in it.

Moses Kintu examines the theme of μετάνοια in the sermon conceptually.²⁵ Kintu argues that the sermon is a commentary on 4:17. Kintu notes that μετάνοια in the sermon means "(1) the original once-for-all turning away from sin and to Jesus and all that he stands for; (2) the small turns otherwise known as 'penance,' a description of the change in thinking and behavior in response to failure by those who are already Jesus' disciples; (3) an expectation for the disciples of Jesus that they 'bear fruit worthy of repentance' (Matt 7:15–20)."²⁶

Kintu examines μετάνοια in the DSS as a forerunner of μετάνοια in the sermon with μετάνοια in Qumran designating two things: (1) "entry" and (2) "continuing membership" in the community.²⁷ "Repentance encompassed both the initial change in thinking and behavior and an ongoing mechanism to live out the initial act of repentance."²⁸ Kintu emphasizes that the Qumran sect's purpose was a life of μετάνοια (1QS V, 1–VI, 23; 1QS V, 1–6:23).²⁹ Qumran's μετάνοια parallels μετάνοια in the sermon because both call people to turn (μετανοέω), turning toward the coming kingdom of heaven (Matt 4:17), and to bear fruit worthy of μετάνοια (Matt 3:8).³⁰ Also,

23. Luz, *Matthew 1–7*, 198.
24. Scaer, *Sermon on the Mount*, 49, 64.
25. Kintu, "Repentance in the Sermon the Mount."
26. Kintu, "Repentance in the Sermon the Mount," 7.
27. Kintu, "Repentance in the Sermon the Mount," 343.
28. Kintu, "Repentance in the Sermon the Mount," 119. "Repentance was comprehensive in scope, beginning with one's entry into the community and going on throughout one's membership, and covering one's thinking, attitude (1QS V, 4–5) and behavior (1QS VII, 1–25). It involved confession of sin (1QS I, 24–II, 1) and commitment to obey the Law (1QS I, 6–18)" (Kintu, "Repentance in the Sermon the Mount," 129). It is "incorporated into the community's liturgical prayers (4 Q504 II, 1–10) (130) related to OT penitential prayer in Dan 9; Ezra 9; and Neh 9." And "the judicial aspect (1QS V, 25–VI, 1; CD IX, 2–8, 16–22) looks back to the OT (Lev 19:17; Deut 19:15) and forward to the NT (Matt 18:15–17)" (130).
29. Kintu, "Repentance in the Sermon the Mount," 115.
30. Kintu, "Repentance in the Sermon the Mount," 131.

the DSS's concept that μετάνοια demands a change of the whole person in thinking and behavior (1QS I, 1–3) is similar to the sermon.[31] The sermon is a commentary of the opening commandment of turning (μετανοέω) in view of the coming kingdom (Matt 4:17). The sermon expands the commandment of turning (μετανοέω) by teaching what people must turn from and turn to as they live out μετάνοια in their whole lives.

The Meaning of μετάνοια

Understanding μετάνοια is important for reading the sermon correctly, because it begins Jesus' ministry and the sermon forms the focal point of its entire message.[32] As this book has argued, the meaning of μετάνοια is not just turning the heart—or confessing sins or feeling remorse for past sin and stopping it—but it is a radical turn (or change) of one's whole being and life from bad to good or righteousness, which includes not only the heart but also deeds (1 Kgs 8:47; Isa 55:7–8; Ezek 33:11; Matt 3:8; Acts 26:20; Heb 6:1).[33] Chapter 3 already includes a full discussion of the meaning of μετάνοια; therefore I do not need to repeat every detail here. Almost all Matthew commentaries agree that the meaning of μετάνοια (repentance) is a significant turn of one's heart and deeds from evil to God, "walking perfectly in all God's ways."[34] Two synonyms of μετανοέω, στρέφω and ἐπιστρέφω clearly carry the same returning idea, which means "to cause a person to change belief or course of conduct, with focus on the thing to which one turns, turn"; "to change one's mind or course of action, for better or worse."[35] As I have noted in chapter 3, the central concept of μετάνοια is turning one's whole being and life from evil to God, following Jesus' teachings about the law as righteousness and the will of God. The sermon spells out these contents of μετάνοια, showing what people turn from and turn to.

In conclusion, Jesus' commandment of μετανοέω in the opening focal point of the sermon (4:17) means to turn (or amend or change) one's heart and deeds, and so one's whole being and life. This commandment opens the sermon and the sermon reveals the essence and the contents of μετανοέω, showing what people should turn from and turn to in terms of heart and

---

31. Kintu, "Repentance in the Sermon the Mount," 115.

32. A more detailed argument on this structural issue follows in the next section.

33. For example, Ezek 33:11 ("Turn back, turn back from your evil ways!") also includes heart and deeds by using the symbolic expression "ways."

34. Kintu, "Repentance in the Sermon on the Mount," 118.

35. BDAG 382.

deeds. In other words, the sermon expands the commandment of turning (μετανοέω) given in 4:17.

The Commandment of Turning (μετανοέω) in Matthew 4:17 as Opening Focal Point of the Sermon

Μετάνοια (4:17) begins Jesus' public ministry and teachings and this beginning summary phrase suggests that the theme of μετάνοια dominates in Jesus' first discourse block, the sermon. This key phrase is critical to understanding the sermon as well as Jesus' other five discourse blocks in Matthew,[36] since the phrase begins Jesus' ministry and teaching in Matthew. Specifically, 4:17a "Jesus begins to preach and say," (ἤρξατο ὁ Ἰησοῦς κηρύσσειν καὶ λέγειν) implies not only that Jesus begins μετάνοια teaching but also that μετάνοια teaching will be continuous as the significant theme in Jesus' teaching and ministry in Matthew.

Scholars hold slightly different views about where the introduction of the Gospel of Matthew ends and the main body, especially the first discourse block (the sermon), begins. Many scholars argue for 5:1 as the starting point of the sermon, emphasizing the geographical setting, "the mount." This structural anaysis separates the sermon (5:1—8:1) and the summary statement (4:17) and obscures the connection between the sermon and μετάνοια. Meanwhile, some scholars argue that 4:17 begins the sermon. For example, Kingsbury suggests 4:17 as the beginning of a new section.[37] Talbert argues that the sermon begins at 4:18.[38] Also, Carter argues that 4:16 ends Jesus' origin and identification section and 4:17 begins Jesus' public ministry.[39] These scholars all see the close connection between the sermon and the theme of μετάνοια (4:17).

Among various sturctural analyses of the sermon, Allison offers a representative and widely accepted structure. I will examine Allison's structure of the sermon to argue that the sermon begins at 4:17 with the commandment of turning (μετανοέω). Allison sets 4:23—5:2 as the beginning of the sermon by finding an inclusio based on corresponding materials in

---

36. The five discourse blocks are chapters 5–7, 10, 13, 18, and 23–25. This five-discourses-centered structure of Matthew's Gospel is well known and supported by many scholars. This discourse-centered structure implies Matthew's emphasis on Jesus teaching materials, and therefore the importance of the catchphrase.

37. Kingsbury, *Matthew*, 29–30.

38. Talbert, *Reading the Sermon on the Mount*, 11.

39. Carter, *Matthew*, 141–43.

7:28–8:1: "great crowds followed him," "the crowds," "the mountain," "going up," "teaching." His structure is as below:

> I. Early history (1:18—4:22)
>> 1. The conception and infancy of Jesus (1:18—2:23)
>> 2. John the Baptist and Jesus (3:1-17)
>> 3. The beginning of Jesus' ministry (4:1-22)
>>> A. The temptation (4:1-11)
>>> B. The return to Galilee (4:12-17)
>>> C. The calling of four disciples (4:18-22)[40]
>
> II. The Sermon (4:23—7:29)
>
>> Introduction: the crowds on the mountain 4:23—5:2
>>
>> Discourse: 5:3—7:27
>>
>> Conclusion: the crowds and the mountain 7:28—8:1[41]

Allison's inclusio seems very plausible and would advance the beginning point of the sermon to 4:23 rather than 5:1. However, while the argument for his structure is helpful, the beginning of the sermon should be moved even further back to 4:17. The reasons are as follow.

First, in Allison's structure, the division of the two story blocks, 4:18–22 and 4:23-25, does not seem obvious, because categories like "early history" and "the beginning of Jesus' ministry" do not clearly divide the two. Both could likely be considered either "early history" or "the beginning of Jesus' ministry." Also, it seems more probable that Matthew 1–4:16 is the identification section of Jesus Christ while 4:17 begins Jesus' public ministry and the sermon by calling his disciples.[42] Also, many scholars argue that 4:17 opens the main body of the Gospel of Matthew.[43] Talbert argues

---

40. Davies and Allison, *Matthew 1–7*, 68–69.

41. Allison, "Structure of the Sermon on the Mount," 429.

42. Some argue that the calling of the disciples is preparation for Jesus' public ministry. However, the division of the calling of the disciples implies 4:18-22 is not preparation for public ministry. If Matthew wanted to report the calling of the disciples as part of Jesus' preparation for ministry, the Twelve would need to be shown in ch. 4 as consisting of the inner circle before ministry, but the full members of the disciples are shown at 10:2-3. This implies that there is another reason for the calling of the four disciples. Moreover, I do not find convincing reasons from scholars for why the calling and following of the four disciples are in ch. 4.

43. France, *Gospel of Matthew*, 3, 139, 144; Hagner, *Matthew 1–13*, 74, points to the same argument. Also, from 16:21, Jesus' teachings change to focus on his Jerusalem ministry: His death in Jerusalem, the resurrection, and eschatological sayings. Also, τότε and its explicit temporal development makes a distinct step. Contrast Carson, *Matthew*, 146, where Carson argues that the identical preaching of John and Jesus

well that Matthew 1:18–2:23 and 3–4:16 have similar endings, 2:22–23 and 4:12–16, imply that one section ends and a new section begins;[44] including political history, the settlement of Jesus, and the OT prophecy fulfillment formula. Especially, according to Kingsbury "Ἀπὸ τότε ἤρξατο ὁ Ἰησοῦς" (4:17), which signals thematic division in the Gospel of Matthew and appears at 4:17 and 16:21,[45] notifies the reader that a new section begins at 4:17. While some scholars disagree with Kingsbury's structure for the Gospel of Matthew, strong evidence supports 4:17 as the division point for the sections. And ἤρξατο κηρύσσειν καὶ λέγειν ("began to preach and say" (4:17) would then signal the beginning of the teaching section of the Gospel of Matthew, especially the sermon.

Second, Allison's inclusio seems to miss a clear bond between 4:18–22 and 4:23–25 formed by the parallel use of ἀκολουθέω (to follow). Verses 4:23–25 report that the crowd was following Jesus (ἠκολούθησαν 4:25); 4:18–22 also introduces the four disciples as following Jesus (ἠκολούθησαν 4:20, 22). Moreover, even the crowd in 8:1, which forms an inclusio with 4:23–25, is paralleled by ἀκολουθέω (ἠκολούθησαν).[46] This strong unity expands Allison's inclusio to 4:18.

Third, the parallelism between the first (4:17—8:1) and the second discourse block (9:35—11:1) supports the beginning of the sermon as 4:17.[47] The catch phrase "Repent for the kingdom of heaven is near" is found in both discourse blocks (4:17 and 10:7), implying that 4:17 can be included in the sermon.[48] Also, the appearance of the disciples, named

---

binds this section together. However, he does not regard a clear division between John and Jesus.

44. Talbert, *Reading the Sermon on the Mount*, 11.

45. Kingsbury, *Matthew*, 29–30. His structure is: (1) The Person of Jesus Messiah (1:1—4:16); (2) the Public proclamation of Jesus Messiah (4:17—16:20); and (3) The Suffering, Death, and Resurrection of Jesus Messiah (16:21—28:20). Also, the temporal conjunction τότε clearly divides the two sections.

46. One might argue that the disciples are not found in 7:28—8:1, but the crowd in 8:1 implicitly includes the disciples, and Matthew might not want to replicate his mention of them.

47. The two teaching units are paralleled by many points: (1) the summary phrase of Jesus' preaching and healing in the Synagogue (4:23; 9:35); (2) the judgment motif (10:14–15); (3) persecution of the disciples (10:16–18, 21–22; (4) trusting God (10:29–31); and (5) reward (10:41–42).

48. Matthew omits "repent" in 10:7 since the second discourse block focuses more on the disciples' code of conduct for their trip (16–42), and the nearness of the kingdom of heaven, which indicates future rewards (10:8–13) and judgment (10:14–15, 28). Comparatively, the repetition of the summary statement in 10:7 without "repent" might imply that μετάνοια is one of the driving ideas of the sermon. Since the first and the second blocks differ in content, the existence or nonexistence of "repent" is natural, and

as sub-characters in front of the second teaching block (10:2-4), implies that 4:18-22 can be included in the sermon. Finally, Jesus' preaching commandment to the disciples (10:7) repeats 4:17 and implies that 4:17—8:1 as one unit is what the disciples will preach, since 4:17—8:1 is the only thing the disciples have heard so far. This argument supports the idea that 4:17 begins the sermon and it contains the whole idea of the sermon, functioning as a summary statement. Therefore, it is likely that the sermon carries the idea of μετάνοια at the beginning.

Then, why does Matthew include the disciples at the outset in both the discourse blocks? Matthew unpacks the theme of μετάνοια (amendment, turning, changing) through the theme of discipleship.[49] Also, Matthew shows them as sub-characters before Jesus' discourse. In the case of chapter 10, it is obvious that Matthew needs to mention the disciples because they will be the ones to hear Jesus' commandment and preach. This hints that Matthew begins the sermon by introducing two groups of sub-characters, the disciples and the crowd who will listen.[50] It is not unjustifiable that the Gospel of Matthew, which is very thoughtfully designed literature, conveys character traits before the main body of the story unit.

Therefore, I suggest that Allison's inclusio can be extended to 4:17, which begins Jesus' first teaching block and functions as a summary phrase alluding to the μετάνοια idea of the sermon. Matthew 4:18-25 shows the two sub-character listener groups of the sermon, the disciples and the crowds, and illustrates the theme of μετάνοια by the theme of discipleship.[51] This

---

the presence of μετάνοια in 4:17 refers to μετάνοια as the theme of the sermon.

One might say it is a small difference and not very significant, but Matthew is a careful writer, and probably he intended it for some reason. For example, the same case is found in 3:17 and 17:5. Matt 3:17: οὗτός ἐστιν ὁ υἱός μου ὁ ἀγαπητός, ἐν ᾧ εὐδόκησα. Matt 17:5: οὗτός ἐστιν ὁ υἱός μου ὁ ἀγαπητός, ἐν ᾧ εὐδόκησα· ἀκούετε αὐτοῦ. Matthew intentionally adds ἀκούετε αὐτοῦ in 17:5 concerning Jesus' Mosaic prophet identity (Deut 18:15-18) where Moses and Elijah (the law and the prophet) appear (Carson, *Matthew*, 438-39). Therefore, it is not wise to ignore the small change between 4:17 and 10:7.

49. For more discussion, see ch. 5.

50. See also Davies and Allison, *Matthew 1-7*, 393. Davies and Allison also suggest that Matthew intentionally puts the two stories before the sermon since the sermon is for the two groups. Also, Hagner, in *Matthew 1-13*, 76, comes to the same conclusion that Jesus calls the disciples who are the hearers prior to the sermon. Carter, *Matthew*, 141-43, suggests that 4:17-25 begins Jesus public ministry section and functions as a "kernel" or "hinge" that introduces a new section.

51. Also, notice that the appearing of the disciples both in the sermon and in the last commandment forms another large inclusio. The contents of "what he has taught" in the last commandment clearly includes the sermon, and this inclusio binds together the sermon and the calling of the disciples. In addition, it is interesting that the same μετάνοια message is proclaimed subsequently by John, Jesus, and the disciples in 3:2,

expansion indicates that Jesus' commandment of μετάνοια is closely related to the sermon and could possibly be one of the driving ideas of the sermon as revealing the contents of the commandment of turning (μετανοέω).[52] My structural analysis of the sermon is as following,

> Μετάνοια proclamation in the Summary Statement 4:17
> "Following" of the listeners to the mount 4:18–5:2
> Discourse 5:3—7:27
> "Following" of the listeners from the mount 7:28–8:1

Parallelism Between the μετάνοια Preaching of John the Baptist (3:2–12) and the Sermon

Matthew's parallelism between his collections of John's messages (3:2–12) and Jesus' message, the sermon (4:17—8:1), evidences the sermon to be a message of μετάνοια as John's message (3:2–12) is a μετάνοια message (3:2). Matthew's two teaching units parallel each other within one theme, μετάνοια. It is interesting to raise the question of why Herod and the people of Israel thought that Jesus was John the Baptist in Matthew (14:2; 16:14). The similarity between the content of their preaching is one possible answer. The ministerial continuity between the two is already well known,[53] while the continuity between the preaching material of the two is especially noticeable in the Gospel of Matthew. Matthew forms a parallelism between

---

4:17, and 10:7.

52. The story of the crowd (4:23–25) also implies that the sermon is a μετάνοια message. Jesus might expect the crowd to repent as a result of his sermon, for they have gathered because of Jesus' miracles (4:23–25) that are intended to encourage people to repent (Matt 11:20–21). In Matt 11:20–21, Jesus denounces cities because they did not repent despite the many miracles Jesus had performed. This also likely supports μετάνοια theme of the sermon.

53. See Allison, "Continuity between John and Jesus," 6–27. Allison also argues for the continuity between John and Jesus in preaching content. For example, John's call to μετάνοια, breaking the confidence of Abrahamic descent (3:9) and referencing imminent eschatological judgment (3:10), parallels Jesus' call to μετάνοια and for his converts to be like a reborn baby (18:3). John warns Israel, "Do not suppose that you can say to yourselves, 'We have Abraham for our father'; for I say to you that from these stones God is able to raise up children to Abraham" (3:9). And Jesus, in Matt 18:2–3, says, "Truly I say to you, unless you are converted and become like children, you will not enter the kingdom of heaven." Also, Allison includes many parallel images: "true Israelite" (Matt 3:9; 7:16–21), "bear fruit worthy of μετάνοια" and "good fruit" (Matt 3:9; 12:33–35), "thrown into the fire" (Matt 3:9; 7:19), and "the ax already lies" (Luke 13:6–9).

John's μετάνοια message (3:2–12) and the sermon that indicates μετάνοια as a cohesive theme of the two.[54]

First, as already mentioned, Matthew uses the same summary statement in 3:2 and 4:17, and it opens both preaching blocks. Moreover, Matthew intentionally introduces the two catch phrases with the same word κηρύσσω (3:1; 4:17), also signaling the parallelism between the two. The two summary statements indicate that both teaching blocks mainly preach μετάνοια, strengthened by future rewards and final judgment.[55]

A second similarity is that John includes the final judgment for μετάνοια and Jesus also includes the same final judgment, which signifies the sermon as μετάνοια message. Specifically, they both use "fire of hell" images to illustrate the opposite of entering the kingdom of heaven (3:7, 9, 10, 12; 5:13, 20, 22, 29; 7:19; 27): "The axe is already laid at the root of the trees; therefore every tree that does not bear good fruit is cut down and thrown into the fire" (3:10); "He will burn up the chaff with unquenchable fire" (3:12); "You will not enter the kingdom of heaven" (5:20); "You will be in danger of the fire of hell" (5:22); "Your whole body thrown into hell" (5:29); "Every tree that does not bear good fruit is cut down and thrown into the fire" (7:19).

Third, John emphasizes people's need to bear worthy fruit of μετάνοια and good fruit in same meaning. Jesus also emphasizes the same fruit image indicating the sermon as μετάνοια message. In particular, John and Jesus' messages cohere in their use of the image of "the tree and fruit" (3:8, 10, 12; 7:16–20). In fact, both message units' main theme is to do righteousness, the will of the Father in heaven, and good deeds. John uses warnings to emphasize good deeds, while Jesus explains in the sermon what the good deeds are.

---

54. For detailed arguments and discussions, see ch. 4. Matt 3:1–12 and the sermon are Matthew's collections of John's and Jesus' everyday message, characterizing the similarity of their preaching ministries. It is clear that neither John's μετάνοια message (3:2–12) nor the sermon is one-time preaching, but their content must have been repeated during their ministries (4:23). For this reason, Herod and people thought Jesus was John in terms of their preaching similar μετάνοια messages.

55. As I demonstrated in the previous chapter that the summary statement matches the sermon, another instance of the same summary statement (3:2) also matches to μετάνοια message of John the Baptizer (3:2–12). John proclaimed μετάνοια using the same catch phrase (3:2), and it governs his following message (3:3–12). First, John calls for μετάνοια by rebuking the Pharisees and Sadducees and demanding good conduct (3:8). Second, he warns of the final judgment (3:7, 9–12) to encourage people to turn. Also, according to John's case we can characterize a general form of the μετάνοια message as including changing one's heart and deeds from evil to good and proclaiming rewards and judgment. This is also a typical μετάνοια message structure in the OT prophets, and it is also found in the sermon.

Fourth, Matthew also closes the two message units with the exact same phrase (3:10 and 7:19) that encourages people to turn (μετανοέω): "Every tree that does not bear good fruit is cut down and thrown into the fire." This phrase closes John's preaching section, emphasizing the bearing of good fruits of μετάνοια and the final judgment (3:10–12), and this phrase also closes the sermon in the same meaning of the bearing of good fruits of μετάνοια encouraged by the final judgment. These fruit images manifest the outward expression of μετάνοια.[56] Matthew locates it right after the main part of the sermon, that is, the inclusio section formed by "the law and the prophets" (5:17–21; 7:12). This location indicates that what Jesus teaches in the main part of the sermon is the contents of good fruit of μετάνοια, things people of Israel should turn from and turn to. Consequently, we observe that the two message units open with the same phrase (3:2; 4:17) and close with another instance of the same phrase (3:10; 7:19). This structural parallelism demonstrates the centrality of μετάνοια in both preaching units. Less significantly, Matthew begins both story units with the gathering of the crowd from all areas (3:5–6 and 4:18–25), and John and Jesus both rebuke the Pharisees, the Sadducees, the scribes, and the false prophets (3:7 and 5:20; 7:15).

In addition, Matthew's identification of Jesus as the prophet-like Messiah who parallels the prophet John the Baptist likely supports the μετάνοια theme of the sermon. The people of Israel understand John the Baptist as a prophet of God (Matt 21:25–26), and they also think of Jesus as Jeremiah or one of the OT prophets (Matt 16:14). In fact, Matthew portrays Jesus as the new Moses (ch. 2; 5:1) and thus clearly as a new prophet (Deut 18:15–18).[57] In general, Mosaic typology reveals Jesus as the new lawgiver, but Moses also preached a μετάνοια message (e.g., Deut 30:2, 8, 10).[58] Therefore, it is likely that John and Jesus both proclaim a μετάνοια message just like OT prophets such as Moses, Isaiah, Jeremiah, and Hosea, for in general these prophets proclaimed a μετάνοια message.

Why did Herod and the people of Israel think Jesus was John the Baptist? Was it not because their messages were similar in terms of prophetic

---

56. Donahue, *Gospel in Parable*, 90–91.

57. See Allison, *New Moses*. Also, it is quite interesting that Moses and Jesus proclaim the exact same phrase—"be perfect (τέλειος)"—in Deut 18:13 and Matt 5:48.

58 In fact, Deut 30 and the sermon parallel each other in many ways: ἐπιστρέφω (30:2, 8, 10); the heart (30:2, 6, 10); mercy (30:3); inherit the land (30:5, 16, 20); love and live (30:6); enemies, hate, and persecution (30:7); to do all God's commandments and righteousness (δικαιώματα) in the law (3:10, 16); blessing (land, life) and curse (death) (30:1, 16, 19, 20); do not serve other gods (30:17); heaven and earth (30:19); the voice of God (30:20). The parallelism of the Mosaic μετάνοια message and the sermon might imply that Jesus as the new Moses preaches a μετάνοια message and that the sermon is this μετάνοια message.

μετάνοια? This explanation suggests that the sermon teaches μετάνοια, especially given its nature and contents.[59] Moreover, it seems likely that the sermon elaborates John's brief μετάνοια message, giving more explanation as to why the people of Israel needed μετάνοια, what their problem was, and what was the bad fruit they must eliminate and the good fruit worthy of μετάνοια they must bear. Specifically, John's phrase καρπὸν ἄξιον τῆς μετανοίας (3:8), which demands more explanation, is fully explained as good works through the sermon. In sum, I suggest that the sermon as a continuation of John's message unit proclaims μετάνοια and reveals the contents of μετάνοια by showing what people should turn from and turn to.

Contents of the Sermon as Contents of the Commandment of Turning (μετανοέω) in 4:17

In General

As the previous section tries to show μετανοέω in the catch phrase (4:17) opens the sermon and it becomes the expanded μετάνοια message unit, the sermon. After this opening commandment of μετανοέω, it is likely that the sermon naturally gives further explanation or contents of μετάνοια. It is natural narrative flow that Jesus commands μετάνοια at front and gives the contents both negative and positive, in other words things to turn from and turn to. Just like John the Baptist commands μετάνοια and further gives the contents preaching (3:2–12), the sermon gives the content of μετάνοια, that is, the things people must turn from and turn to in terms of the heart and deeds (because the biblical idea of μετάνοια is not only changing one's heart but also one's deeds). This close relationship between 4:17 and the sermon shows the significance of μετάνοια in the sermon and Matthew.

Jesus proclaims μετάνοια in the sermon by rebuking the wicked heart and deeds of Israel and demanding a righteous heart and deeds. His rebuking and demanding elaborate the commandment of turning (μετανοέω) from the summary statement (4:17). These contents of μετάνοια in the sermon parallel the contents of the OT and the NT μετάνοια. The use of the Hebrew term *šub* ("to go back again" "to return" in a religious and moral sense), which is the counterpart of μετανοέω,[60] gives information about things people should

---

59. The final judgment motif in this section and the command to bear good fruit do not imply "covenantal nomism," or an "entrance requirement" to the kingdom of heaven, but a pure warning and calling to repent. Salvation theory materials do not appear here but only pure warnings to return to God. Also, this content does not mean people can repent by themselves and be saved.

60. In the LXX μετανοέω occurs fourteen times for *nhm*, "to change one's mind or

turn from that parallel the sermon: evil conduct, previous conduct, wicked acts, violence, idols, abomination, sin, ingratitude, unfaithfulness, and disobedience (Jer 1:16; 2:13, 17, 19; 3:22–4:2; 5:7, 19 etc.).[61] Jesus in the sermon first rebukes the wickedness of Israel, and the contents of his rebuke do not deviate from the contents above.

As chapter 3 shows, the background of the opening commandment of turning (μετανοέω) (4:17) is found in the OT. Specifically, OT prophets' turning ministry always commanded Israel to turn to the law of God (Deut 4, 30; 1 Sam 7; 12:20–25; 1 Kgs 8; 2 Kgs 23; Jer 7, 24, and so on). Jesus also commands his listeners to turn in Matthew 4:17 and refers to the law and the prophets in the sermon (Matt 5:17; 7:12). Jesus reinterprets the law and the prophets, thus revealing their true meaning so that people can turn to the true will of God. This parallelism between the OT's turning theme found in the law and Jesus' turning theme in the law and the prophets show that the sermon expands on the opening commandment of turning (μετανοέω) (4:17).

As μετάνοια demands "the worthy fruit of a changed life" (Matt 3:8; Luke 3:7–14; Eph 4:17–32; Col 1:10), the sermon fully reveals the contents of the "good fruit and good tree" (3:10; 5:16; 7:16–20). Specifically, the "fruit in keeping with μετάνοια" (3:8) that John the Baptist calls for is fully revealed in the sermon. While the people of Israel have thought of themselves as righteous, Jesus reveals their wicked heart and hypocritical behavior and commands them to change their heart and deeds and pursue greater righteousness (5:17–48; 6:1–8; 16–24; 7:1–5).[62] Again, this shows the significance of μετάνοια in the sermon and thus in Matthew.

---

intention" or "to repent" (Jer 8:6; 31:19). And ἐπιστρέφω occurs many times for *šub*: they can be almost synonymous (Jer 8:6; Isa 46:8) for religious and ethical conversion.

61. *TDNT* 4:975–1008.

62. In particular, one of the opening phrases of the Antithesis (5:17–48), "not to abolish but to fulfill the law" (answering a possible objection to Jesus' authority as Christ), assures that Jesus does not teach a new thing but teaches a deeper or more genuine meaning of the law that Israel does not follow, thus revealing the wickedness of Israel. And based on this point it must be clear that Mosaic typology indicates Jesus as the one who has the divine authority that allows for the trustworthiness of his teachings, revealing the divine intention of the law. Therefore, it is more likely to understand the sermon not as a new law but as a μετάνοια message responding to the false interpretation of the law and the external, heartless, false use of the law. Also, "unless your righteousness surpasses that of the scribes and Pharisees, you will not enter the kingdom of heaven" (5:20) warns Israel to turn from the wicked way of the Pharisees and the Sadducees, that is, their hypocritical behavior.

Righteousness (5:20) and τέλειος (5:48) as the Contents of μετάνοια

The theme of righteousness in the sermon gives the contents of the opening commandment of turning (μετανοέω) (4:17). First, the focal point of the body of the sermon (5:17–20), which commands higher righteousness (5:6, 10, 20; 6:1, 33), a major theme in the sermon,[63] denotes the contents of μετάνοια. As mentioned in the previous chapter the definition of μετάνοια is to turn from sin to righteousness. As Ulrich Luz notes, the repentance is "the entry gate" to the greater righteousness of the sermon.[64] And as Robert H. Gundry argues, the worthy fruit of μετάνοια is genuine righteousness.[65] In other words, it shows μετάνοια as to turn to have greater righteousness. In addition, since Matthew 5:17–20 shows that the demand for μετάνοια is a demand both for righteousness and for higher righteousness, the fulfillment of all the law and the prophets through higher righteousness for entering the kingdom of heaven also denotes the demand for μετάνοια and corresponding reward and judgment (4:17). Finally, Matthew 5:17–20 in the opening focal point of the body of the sermon indicates that the body of the sermon provides the contents of μετάνοια.

Closely related idea to righteousness is "doing good" and "doing the will of Father" in the sermon. They also give the contents of μετάνοια in its proximity and conceptual connection to 4:17's μετάνοια commandment. For example, Matthew 5:16 commands to do good works referred to as "good fruits" and "worthy fruits of μετάνοια" in 3:8, 10. These repeated and conceptually parallel terms and images indicate that good works in the sermon are the contents of good fruits worthy of μετάνοια. Specifically, "good works" in 5:16 refer to the nine characters of the Beatitudes and indicate the contents and outward expression of μετάνοια.

Also, in the final remark of the sermon (7:21) about entering the kingdom of heaven (6:10; 7:21), "doing the will of Father in heaven" is the same concept of good works and shows the contents and so the outward expression of the commandment of turning (μετανοέω). Like 5:17–20, 7:21 mirrors the opening commandment of turning (μετανοέω) (4:17). Verses 5:17–20 and 7:21 are two different conceptual expressions of the

---

63. Strecker, *Theology of the New Testament*, 364. Strecker titles the Gospel of Matthew the book of "the way of righteousness." Strecker defines righteousness (3:15; 5:6, 10, 20; 6:1, 33; 21:32) as "the comprehensive term for the right conduct of the disciples in general, and thus for the whole Christian community, that must be different from that of the Pharisees and scribes (5:20)."

64. Luz, *Matthew 1–7*, 198.

65. Gundry, *Matthew*, 46–47. For more discussion see ch. 6.

one meaning of μετάνοια (4:17). "Doing the will of God," worthy fruit of μετάνοια(3:8), good fruit(3:10), good deeds(5:16), and Matthean righteousness (5:17–20) are not different concepts.⁶⁶ The opening and the ending of the body of the sermon include languages such as "the law and the prophets" (5:17; 7:12), "righteousness" (5:20), "doing the will of father in heaven" (7:21), and "entering into the kingdom of heaven" (5:20; 7:21), which all conceptually convey 4:17's commandment of μετάνοια.

Another important idea of the sermon is τέλειος (5:48). It means "singleness" or "singular devotion" or personal "wholeness," and this concept deals with the problem of one's being before addressing one's doing.⁶⁷ For example, Jesus in the Antitheses rebukes the Israelites as double-minded, which means they externally followed God but internally did not (James 4:8), and calls them to turn to singleness of heart and life (τέλειος), a change of both heart and deeds. As noted above μετάνοια means turning one's heart as well as one's deeds from bad to good. This definition corresponds with the commandment of τέλειος (5:48), a word that rebukes the wicked heart and deeds of the people of Israel and demands a single or whole Godward heart with corresponding deeds.

The Nine Beatitudes: The Nine Contents of Good Fruits Worthy of μετάνοια

The Beatitudes, by teaching true happiness or flourishing (μακάριος), show that disciples bear good worthy fruits (or works in 5:16). "Good works" in 5:16 refers to the nine characters of the Beatitudes. As discussed above, 3:8, 10, and 5:16 use the same terms—"good works," "good fruits," and "worthy fruits of μετάνοια" that denote the nine characters of the Beatitudes as the contents of good worthy fruits of μετάνοια. Why does Jesus give nine illustrations of μακάριος ("happy," "well-being" or "flourishing")?⁶⁸ I suggest,

---

66. Pennington, *Sermon on the Mount and Human Flourishing*, 91. Pennington defines righteousness in Matthew as "whole person behavior that accords with God's nature, will, and coming kingdom" (91). And the righteous person is "the one who follows Jesus in this way of being in the world... the *whole/teleios* person (5:48) who does not just do the will of God externally but from the heart" (in contrast to the Pharisees) (91, emphasis his).

67. Pennington, "Be Ye Virtuous," 6–9. This, Pennington calls, "Godward virtue," which means that "one must also not even lust or covet at the level of the heart. Constantly Jesus is pushing us to think in terms of internal wholeness and purity rather than external duty and piety."

68. France, *Gospel of Matthew*, 160–61. France translates μακάριος to "Happy" in the sense of a happy situation, not feeling itself. For more information about the meaning and translating μακάριος into "flourishing," see Pennington's helpful discussion in

based on the commandment of turning, (μετανοέω) the idea of the sermon that Jesus implicitly rebukes Israel's secularized false concept of happiness or well-being by proclaiming the true characteristics of happiness or flourishing with God, and he demands Israel turn to true happiness from false happiness. The Beatitudes show the content of good fruit worthy of μετάνοια (3:8, 10; 5:16), and all their reward language parallels the reward of the coming kingdom of heaven (4:17b).

In the Psalms, the μακάριος describes one who turns to God from evil, is forgiven, takes refuge in God, and follows the way of the Lord (1:1–2; 2:12; 4:8, 22; 32:1–2; 33:12; 84:12; 112:1; 119:1; 128:1; 144:15), but the sermon rebukes Israel because they failed to do such. Also, Isaiah 61, which forms part of the OT background for the Beatitudes, implies that those who possess true happiness are the poor, the brokenhearted, the captives, and the mourning, while Israel is laughing and rich with money (Matt 6:24), and earthly rewards (Matt 6:2, 5, 16, 19). James 4:8–10 demands a turn to the true happiness by instructing the same characteristics as the Beatitudes: "Cleanse your hands, you sinners; and purify your hearts, you double-minded. Be miserable and mourn and weep; let your laughter be turned into mourning and your joy to gloom. Humble yourselves in the presence of the Lord." Also, the following warning of judgment for the tasteless salt (Matt 5:13) implies that Israel has lost true happiness and its characteristics, so that Jesus demands them to return to the truth to avoid judgment. In addition, the light image (5:14–16) encourages the crowd to turn to the Beatitudes' nine characteristics and shine in the world.[69]

Interestingly, some of the Beatitudes are characteristics of μετάνοια. For example, to mourn, to weep, and to be meek are external expressions of μετάνοια in the OT (Joel 1; 2:12, 13; Is. 22:12).[70] Also, the first Beatitude, "poor in spirit," is not different, because it is a form of confession,[71] a "full sense of need for God,"[72] and a sign of "spiritual bankruptcy"[73] (Ps 69:29; 70:55; 86:1), all of which are signs of μετάνοια. In another place Jesus commands forms of

---

Sermon on the Mount and Human Flourishing, 41–67.

69. Moreover, interestingly enough, the Greek use of μετανοέω also means to turn from the false μακάριος to the true, "to come out of the misery by freeing him from false thoughts, passions and joys (μακάριος, *eudaimon*) and by showing him the way to true, rational and ethical development (Ceb., Ceb. Tab., 10, 11,1. 11,2)" (*TDNT* 4:975–1008).

70. Davies and Allison, *Matthew 1–7,* 449. He says poor and humble are same.

71. Carson, *Sermon on the Mount,* 17–18.

72. Davies and Allison, *Matthew 1–7,* 444.

73. Carson, *Matthew,* 162.

confession when he asks people to repent (Matt. 11:21): "Sackcloth and ashes" demonstrate the deep grief or sorrow[74] when people repent well.

Also, "meek," "merciful," "hunger and thirst for righteousness," "pure in heart," and "the peacemaker" also implicitly invoke people to turn, for those characteristics are lacking in Israel, and Jesus demands people to have these characteristics. In addition, the meek inheriting the land signifies μετάνοια theme. The land in the OT, especially the prophets, is related to the reward God promised Israel when they repent and return to God (Jer 31:1–14). Mercy is related to forgiveness (Joel 1). Jesus being merciful to the sinners and tax collectors refers to him forgiving them (Matt 9:13; 9:27; 15:22; 17:15; 18:33–35; 20:30, 31; Rom 11:30–33; 1 Tim 1:13, 16; 1 Pet 2:10). Those who are not merciful shall even receive judgment (23:23). Those who are sick ask Jesus to have mercy on them, which might refer to asking forgiveness. Jesus is merciful (Heb 2:17). One who is pure in heart is one whose heart is free from greed and self-indulgence. Also, that person is not a hypocrite like the scribes and Pharisees (Matt 23:25–26). Psalm 51:9–10, "Hide your face from my sins and blot out all my iniquity. Create in me a pure heart, O God, and renew a steadfast spirit within me," asks for a pure heart, which refers to μετάνοια here.

Furthermore, all the future rewards in the Beatitudes are nothing other than the rewards of μετάνοια, for 4:17 proclaims that only through μετάνοια can people inherit the kingdom of heaven. The promise of the future rewards in the Beatitudes (4:17; 5:3–12) encourages Israel to turn so that they will enter the kingdom of heaven. Specifically, "Poor in spirit" and "be persecuted" form an inclusio by referring to the same reward of the kingdom of heaven. This *inclusio* parallels the catch phrase "Turn for the kingdom of heaven" (4:17).[75] Jesus proclaims μετάνοια before the kingdom of heaven, so that people who turn will enter the kingdom of heaven, and he promises the kingdom of heaven as a reward to those who are poor in spirit and persecuted for righteousness. What does this parallelism of the kingdom of heaven reward imply? It implies that those who are poor in spirit and persecuted are those who turn. Jesus who calls for people to turn reveals the characteristics of the returner in the Beatitude. Furthermore, all the promised rewards in the Beatitude are futuristic heavenly rewards, and they encourage people to turn, for they will be given to people only through μετάνοια.

74. Carson, *Matthew*, 316.
75. 4:17, μετανοεῖτε· γὰρ ἤγγικεν ἡ βασιλεία τῶν οὐρανῶν.
5:4, μακάριοι οἱ πτωχοὶ τῷ πνεύματι, ὅτι αὐτῶν ἐστιν ἡ βασιλεία τῶν οὐρανῶν.
5:10, μακάριοι οἱ δεδιωγμένοι ἕνεκεν δικαιοσύνης, ὅτι αὐτῶν ἐστιν ἡ βασιλεία τῶν οὐρανῶν.

The Antitheses Proclaim μετάνοια from the False Interpretation of the Law to the True

The Antitheses rebuke Israel for false interpretations of righteousness and the OT and call them to turn to the true meaning of the law and the prophets (5:17-20).[76] The Antitheses are essentially Jesus' reinterpretation of the law and the prophets. This reinterpretation of the Torah goes to the heart of the commandment of turning (μετανοέω) (4:17) by teaching that people should turn from sin and turn to genuine righteousness. The Antitheses expands its opening in 5:17-20, which deals with righteousness, doing good, and doing the will of God as the contents of μετάνοια. The Antitheses reveals the true and deep meaning of the law and demands hearers to turn (μετανοέω) to true righteousness, good works, and the will of the Father in heaven.

This reinterpretation of the law related to the theme of μετάνοια is also found in Qumran μετάνοια. Qumran repentance tried to return to the Torah according to the reinterpretation of the Torah by the sons of Zadok (1QS V, 8-9), echoing OT repentance (Deut 9:29-31; 30:2-3; 1 Sam 7:3; 1 Kgs 8:47-50; 2 Kgs 23:25; 1 Chr 22:29; Jer 29:13-14; and Joel 2:12).[77] The Qumran community set itself apart from the authority of Jerusalem and its teaching of the Torah but followed their own reinterpretation of the Torah. Bilha Nitzan says this Zadokian interpretation was "the hidden matters in which all Israel had gone astray (CD 3:13-16, cf. 1QS 1:13-15)" and only allowed for sectarian members.[78] The Qumran community considered themselves "the men that have entered the new covenant," as promised in Jeremiah 31:30-32 (CD 6:19; 8:21).[79]

The Antitheses parallel the Zadokian interpretation of the Law by which the teachers of righteousness led the μετάνοια of the Qumran sect.[80] Through the Antitheses, Jesus plays the same role, "reinterpreting the law

---

76. See Luz, *Studies in Matthew*, 185-214, for the interpretation of Matt 5:17-20, especially fulfilling the law. I think fulfilling the law here means to make and reinterpret the law whole τέλειος (5:48) as the heavenly father is whole. See above for the discussion of the τέλειος (5:48).

77. Kintu, "Repentance in the Sermon on the Mount," 120.

78. Nitzan, "Repentance in the Dead Sea Scrolls," 150-51.

79. Nitzan, "Repentance in the Dead Sea Scrolls," 150-51.

80. For the full argument on the parallelism between 4QMMT and Matt 5:21-48, see Foster, *Community, Law, and Mission*, 80-93. Foster argues that "both documents contain a series of antithetical halakah and they understand the performance of the legal rulings, as interpreted by respective groups, as pertaining to righteousness" (83). Foster distinguishes between Qumran antithetical halakah and Matt 5:21-48 in that while "4QMMT invites the opposing group to their practices, Matthew dismisses the opposing group as the "hypocrites and unrighteous" (Matt 6:1) (86).

and the prophets" for μετάνοια. The Antitheses according to Jesus the Son of God's reinterpretation of the law and the prophets (5:17; 7:12) command a turn (μετάνοια) to it by giving the substance of μετάνοια, which designates what people should turn from and turn to. In the Antitheses, Jesus through his interpretation of the law and the prophets reveals Israel's sin and the need of μετάνοια. Israel thought themselves righteous following their own interpretation of the OT law, but Jesus reveals them as sinners through his new and correct interpretation and this interpretation teaches them where they turn(μετανοέω) to.

Matthew 6 and 7 as the Contents of the Commandment of Turning (μετάνοια)

Matthew 6 rebukes people for doing what they should not do. This rebuke implies the contents of μετάνοια indicating what they must turn from and to. Verses 6:1–7 bid μετάνοια by telling the hearers "not to do acts of righteousness before men, but to seek first the kingdom of heaven and God's righteousness" echoing the commandment of turning (μετανοέω) to genuine righteousness (4:17). The Lord's Prayer also turns people's way of praying. Jesus rebukes wrong prayer (6:5–8) and then teaches the right way.

In addition, the Lord's Prayer expresses μετάνοια based on the biblical idea of μετάνοια, which includes confession and renunciation of sin, and prayer for God's forgiveness (Lev 5:5; Prov 28:13; 1 John 1:9). For instance, people called on Yahweh (prayer) for the forgiveness of sins with the confession of sin on the day of penitence (Neh 9; Dan 9:4–19; Bar 1:15–3:8; 2 Chr 20:3ff.). It is not coincidental that the people of Israel confess their sins in response to John's μετάνοια message (Matt 3:6), and at the center of the sermon Jesus teaches prayer to ask God for forgiveness of their sins (6:12, 14–15).

In 6:16–18 Jesus calls for turning when he tells his hearers to fast before God, not to be seen before people. In 6:19–24 Jesus requires turning through serving God only, not wealth. Verses 6:25–34 and 7:7–11 proclaim turning as trusting and pursuing the heavenly Father rather than earthly goods.[81] The biblical idea of μετάνοια directs one to trust God for one's life and to renounce the help of other humans and of false gods and idols (Hos 14:1–3; Isa 10:20; 30:15; Jer 3:22, 23; 25:5).[82] In 6:25–34 and 7:7–11 Jesus rebukes faithless disciples (ὀλιγόπιστοι) and commands turning through trusting God, not mammon (6:24).

---

81. France, *Gospel of Matthew*, 263.
82. *TDNT* 4:975–1008.

Jesus summons the contents of μετάνοια when he calls on his hearers not to judge others but to take the log out of their own eye. In 7:12 μετάνοια demands people treat others as they want to be treated. The following verses, 7:13-14, command hearers to turn to enter the narrow gate of life, not the wide road and gate of destruction. Verses 7:15-22 picture μετάνοια by referring to the image of good and bad fruit to indicate the worthy fruit of μετάνοια (3:8). This fruit image indicates that doing the will of God (7:21) is the fruit of μετάνοια. The parable of the rock and sand in 7:23-27 is yet another illustration of turning (μετανοέω) and of the corresponding reward and judgment according to one's μετάνοια.

The Logic of 4:17, the Command–Enforcement (or Reason), Match the Sermon

While the sermon expands on the opening summary proclamation of Jesus' ministry, "Turn (Μετανοεῖτε), for (γὰρ) the kingdom of heaven is near," the logic of the phrase between the two ideas, "Turn (Μετανοεῖτε)" and "for (γὰρ) the kingdom of heaven is near," is also elaborated in the sermon. The conjunction γὰρ indicates the explanatory relationship between the two ideas of 4:17 and functions so that the latter strengthens the former.[83] The sermon demonstrates the contents of μετάνοια and unpacks the nearness of the kingdom of heaven through the words of future rewards and judgment to enforce the charge. Since the coming of the kingdom of heaven refers to "God's eschatological activity as ruler,"[84] it indicates the time when God will judge people: the good one enters the kingdom of heaven and gets rewards, and the evil one suffers judgment.[85] In the sermon Jesus promises future rewards, which include the entrance to the kingdom of heaven (5:3-12; 6:1, 4, 6, 18), and warns of the final judgment (5:20, 29, 30; 6:1-5, 16, 14-15; 7:19, 21-28). As the catch phrase strengthens μετάνοια through the nearness of the

---

83. Runge, *Discourse Grammar*, 51-54. According to Runge, the conjunction γὰρ introduces background information explanation or expositions of the previous assertion, strengthening it rather than providing distinctive information. It does not introduce development but rather offline material.

84. Davies and Allison, *Matthew 1-7*, 389.

85. See Osborne, *Matthew*, 110-11. He gives five ideas of the prophetic and intertestamental concepts of "the day of the Lord," connected especially with final judgment (Isa 13:6, 9; Joel 1:15; 2:31; Zech 14:1-21; cf. Ezek 7:7; Obad 15; Mal 3:2; 4:1, 5): the regathering of Israel (4 Ezra 13:39-41), the destruction of the nations (Dan 2:44; 7:26; 2 Bar. 36-40), the reign of God's people (Dan 7:27; Wis 3:8; T. Jud. 25:1-2; Matt 19:28; 1 Cor 6:2; Rev 20:4), the harvest of judgment (Dan 12:2; 4 Ezra 4:30; 2 Bar. 72-74; Matt 3:12; 13:30, 40), and the transformation of this world into new earth (Isa 65:17; 66:22; 1 En. 45:3-5; 2 Bar. 32:1-7; Matt 19:28; Rev 21:1).

kingdom of heaven that refers to future rewards and judgment, Jesus rebukes the wickedness of Israel and demands that people change their heart and deeds, and then reinforces his commandments with reward and judgment (5:13, 19, 20, 22, 29; 6:1, 2, 4, 5, 6, 16, 18, 19–21; 7:19, 21, 24–27). In many cases, reward and judgment immediately follow a rebuke and demand unity, so we can also easily find γὰρ between the two. Moreover, the sermon opens with rewards (5:3–12) and closes with judgment[86] to strengthen μετάνοια. Therefore, it is likely that the summary statement governs the sermon, and it indicates that μετάνοια is an important driving idea in the sermon revealing the contents of the opening commandment of turning (μετανοέω) (4:17) that the explanatory rewards and judgment strengthen.

Conclusion

In this chapter I suggest that in the sermon Jesus continues the μετάνοια message of John the Baptist. The summary statement of John and Jesus' teachings, "Turn (Μετανοεῖτε), for the kingdom of heaven is near" (3:2; 4:17), demonstrates the significance of μετάνοια in the two preaching units. Matthew forms a structural parallelism between John's message and the sermon to indicate the continuation and development of the same message, indicating the thematic and paradigmatic significance of μετάνοια in the sermon and in Matthew.

The sermon reveals the nature and the contents of μετάνοια by rebuking the wicked heart and behavior of the people of Israel and demanding the law and the prophets (5:17; 7:12), the will of Father in heaven (7:21), true righteousness (5:20), doing the will of God, and wholeness (or singleness) of heart and deed in view of the imminent coming kingdom of heaven, so that one can enter the kingdom of heaven and not judgment. The Beatitudes, by teaching true happiness (or flourishing), proclaim the contents of turning for the hearers to reject false happiness and find true joy. By rebuking the false interpretation of the law, the Antitheses proclaims turning of heart and deeds leading to the higher righteousness and single-hearted devotion (τέλειος). In Matthew 6, Jesus directs how his hearers should turn, that is, "not to do acts of righteousness before men, but to seek first the kingdom of heaven and God's righteousness." Jesus instructs people to pray for the forgiveness of sins in the Lord's Prayer and to trust God. In chapter 7, Jesus preaches what his hearers should not do, that

---

86. Allison, "Structure of the Sermon on the Mount," 429–31. Allison suggests the sermon's pair of opening and closing subjects encourages people to act on what Jesus teaches in the sermon. Rather, it encourages people to repent.

is, what they must turn from. Finally, the two-fold idea of the phrase, "turn (Μετανοεῖτε)" and "the nearness of the kingdom of heaven," and the logic between the two indicated by the explanatory conjunction γὰρ strengthening Jesus' μετάνοια message coheres with the sermon. The warnings of the last judgment and reward in 7:13–27 forms an inclusio with the promise of the future rewards in 5:3–12 and enforces the opening commandment of turning (μετανοέω) and its full contents in the sermon.

Chapter 8

The Thematic Significance of μετάνοια in Matthew 10

Universal μετάνοια Commission for the Church

Introduction

THIS BOOK ARGUES FOR the thematic and even paradigmatic significance of μετάνοια in the Gospel of Matthew. Matthew begins his gospel with John the Baptist's μετάνοια preaching and even begins Jesus' teaching and ministry with the summary statement of μετάνοια (4:17). Despite the rare occurrence of the term μετάνοια, its meaning of "turning (or changing) one's heart and conduct, and so one's life, to Jesus and his teaching," is echoed in a variety of ways in the body of Matthew. Matthew's important themes (discipleship, righteousness, soteriology, the Great Commission, and gentile inclusion) communicate the essence and contents of μετάνοια. As seen in the previous chapter, the Sermon on the Mount both advances and illustrates by various examples of μετάνοια (4:17).

This chapter examines the significance of μετάνοια in Matthew's missionary discourse (9:36—11:1). The typical understanding of Matthew 10 is as Jesus' historical commissioning and instruction of the twelve disciples for the Galilean commission during Jesus' lifetime. However, a close reading of Matthew 10 reveals it to be Jesus' commissioning of the postresurrection church of the twelve apostles (10:2) for a universal μετάνοια call to the kingdom of heaven (10:7) that includes both the lost Israelites (10:6; cf. 9:17; 10:28; 15:24; 21:41; 22:7; 26:52) and gentiles (10:18). Scholars have noted that Matthew redacts the commissioning story of the twelve disciples using postresurrection language to instruct the postresurrection church for its universal mission and life in a hostile world.[1] Matthew 10

---

1. See Luz, *Studies in Matthew*, 144–47. Brown, "Mission to Israel," 73–90. Brown

explicitly instructs the church about how to call the whole world to turn (μετανοέω) (10:7), with specific teaching about the μετάνοια life, eschatological judgment, and comforting language. These teachings parallel the μετάνοια language and images in John the Baptist's preaching and in the sermon. Furthermore, Matthew 10, as the universal μετάνοια commissioning of the apostles (10:2), shares the same idea of the universal μετάνοια in the Great Commission of 28:18-20.

This chapter first analyzes the theme of μετάνοια in Matthew 10 to indicate its significance in it. Second, it offers a redaction-critical study of Matthew 10, defining Matthew 10 as Jesus' universal μετάνοια commission for the postresurrection church of the apostles. Third, it examines Matthew 10 as a direct and explicit universal μετάνοια commissioning of the church of the apostles (10:2), serving as an expansion of the universal μετάνοια Great Commission (28:19-20). These discussions will eventually demonstrate the significance of μετάνοια in Matthew 10.

Matthew 10 as μετάνοια Commissioning Discourse

Matthew 10 has been read as a missionary discourse.[2] Its main theme is still μετάνοια because the disciples are commanded to call μετάνοια for the kingdom of heaven is at hand in 10:7, which parallels Jesus in 4:17.[3] The "worthy" (ἄξιος) language in Matthew 10:10-13 and 37-38 creates an inclusio framing Matthew 10 and echoes the worthy fruit of μετάνοια from previous chapters (cf. 3:8). Μετάνοια language and images in John the Baptist's μετάνοια preaching and the sermon occur in Matthew 10, showing that the theme of μετάνοια is also significantly present in Matthew 10.

---

basically argues that the postresurrection church transparently read the twelve disciples' mission in Matt 10, applying it to their situation. See also, France, *Gospel of Matthew*, 380; Luz, *Matthew 8-20*, 120. France and Luz do not agree that the whole of Matthew 10 explicitly and transparently instructs the postresurrection church of apostles, but only that the latter part of Matt 10:17-42 does so. However, the historical setting of Matt 10 as a whole, from the beginning to the end of the chapter, is the twelve disciples' Galilean mission, and also Matt 10 transparently instructs the postresurrection church of apostles for the universal μετάνοια mission in all of the hostile world.

2. See footnote #1.

3. See Luz, *Studies in Matthew*, 147, for this same summary statement and the close connection between the sermon and Matt 10.

Parallelism between 10:7 and Matthew 4:17

Jesus commissions the apostles (10:2) to preach μετάνοια in Matthew 10:7: "And as you go, preach, saying, 'The kingdom of heaven is at hand.'" This repeats 4:17 and shows μετάνοια as a key idea of Matthew 10. This summary statement shows that Matthew 10 is Jesus' commissioning instruction for the twelve apostles in continuation of his μετάνοια mission. Although Matthew omits μετάνοια in 10:7, this statement repeats Jesus' own summary proclamation of his teaching and ministry in 4:17. This μετάνοια parallelism in sequence from Jesus to the disciples and from the sermon to Matthew 10 demonstrates the thematic and even paradigmatic significance of μετάνοια in Matthew 10.

The structure of the text between the sermon and Matthew 10 supports this sequential parallelism. Jesus' second discourse begins at Matthew 9:36 after the first bookends at 9:35, which creates an inclusio from 4:23—9:35 surrounding the first discourse and narrative section. The summary proclamation of μετάνοια (4:17) in view of the coming kingdom of heaven is Jesus' first teaching statement in the sermon and the narrative section, and it demonstrates the significance of μετάνοια. Following the first section, the second discourse (9:36—11:1) demonstrates that Jesus' μετάνοια teaching and miracle ministry passes on to the twelve disciples (or apostles) and the significance of μετάνοια continues in Matthew 10. Jesus' ministry of wonderworks is for the purpose of μετάνοια (11:20–21), and this μετάνοια miracle ministry is passed on to the apostles in Matthew 10.

Just as 4:17 reappears in 10:7, the "disciples" in 4:18–22 reappear in 10:1–4, indicating the close connection between the first and second discourse blocks. In short, Matthew 10 replaces Jesus with the apostles as the proclaimer of μετάνοια call of the kingdom of heaven. In addition to 10:7, which repeats the sum of the sermon, 4:17 assumes that the content of the disciples' proclamation comes from the sermon (chs. 5–7). The apostles will preach and teach μετάνοια and its essence and contents—the sermon.

"Worthy" (ἄξιος) Language in Matthew 10:10–13, 37–38

The "worthy" (ἄξιος) language in Matthew 10:10–13 and 37–38 form an inclusio in the missionary discourse and demonstrate the worthy one as an important idea of the whole instruction between them. In particular, this worthy language in Matthew 10 parallels the worthy language in John the Baptist's μετάνοια call to bear fruit worthy of μετάνοια (3:8). The worthy one in Matthew 10:11–13 and 10:37–38 possibly demonstrates one who accepts μετάνοια and the apostles and bears the fruit of μετάνοια. Also, 10:10–13 and 37–38 express the idea of reward and judgment of the apostles' peace according to the worthy fruit of μετάνοια.

First, 10:10–13 shows that the acceptance of the apostles, their μετάνοια message, and carrying one's own cross can be identified as a worthy fruit of μετάνοια, which reveals one's true μετάνοια to Jesus in mind and conduct (cf. 10:40–42). Matthew 10:10–13 instructs the twelve apostles to judge people according to their "worthiness" as to whether the apostolic peace will remain on the house or not (10:11–13). These verses show that the apostles will stay with those who do μετάνοια and provide a place to stay. Also, 10:13 instructs the apostles to punish the unworthy one who does not accept μετάνοια calling by shaking off their dust. This judgment theme also parallels John the Baptist's judgment and reward language according to fruits worthy of μετάνοια (3:10, 11). Specifically, the judgment on the apostles' message rejecting towns in 10:15—"it will be more bearable on the day of judgment for the land of Sodom and Gomorrah than for that town"—is repeated in 11:24 and proclaimed as judgment on not-turning (μετάνοια) cities (11:20–24). This repeated judgment language clearly shows that the apostles' proclamation in 10:7 is μετάνοια calling and its corresponding judgment in 10:15 is also for not-turning (μετάνοια) cities as it is in 11:20–24.

Second, the worthy language in Matthew 10:37–38 refers to the fruit worthy of μετάνοια as it relates to its universal mission and the corresponding suffering of the followers of Jesus. Jesus' followers, who are sent to preach μετάνοια for entry to the kingdom of heaven, are expected to produce the fruit worthy of μετάνοια (10:37–38). Matthew 10:37–38 describes the fruit worthy of μετάνοια as loving Jesus more than one's family, taking one's own cross to follow Jesus, and losing one's life for Jesus. This is a call of μετάνοια in pair with soteriological judgment in 10:39.

This worthiness of one's μετάνοια toward Jesus determines who is part of the people of God. The one who turns one's mind, heart, and life toward Jesus will enter the kingdom of heaven. In Matthew 3 this worthiness determines who is the seed of Abraham, and the worthiness of one's μετάνοια indicates the reconstitution of the people of God as coming only through returning to (or receiving) Jesus and producing fruits worthy of μετάνοια (3:8). The peace of God would be given not according to Jewish ethnicity but according to the reaction to the apostles' (and Jesus') eschatological calling of μετάνοια. The dawn of the new era and its proclamation of μετάνοια indicate, on the one hand, the accomplishment of judgment on Israel and the end of the old era when ethnic Israel was the people of God. On the other hand, they also indicate the inclusion of the gentiles and the salvation of Israel only through μετάνοια to Jesus Christ.

In conclusion, this parallel language of worthiness between Matthew 3 and 10 shows that Matthew 10 brings together John and Jesus' eschatological judgment μετάνοια call. These parallels indicate Matthew 10 as μετάνοια commission.

μετάνοια Parallelism Between Matthew 10 and the Sermon

The same and similar μετάνοια language and images appear in both the sermon and Matthew 10, borrowing also from the same language in Matthew 3. This parallel language demonstrates the significance of μετάνοια in both Matthew 10 and the sermon. First, for example, the language of confession in 10:32-33 and the reward language in 10:41-42 cohere with the judgment theme of μετάνοια in 3:2; 4:17; 5:12, 46; 6:1-5; 7:23. Judgment language in 10:33 strongly pushes hearers to turn to Jesus and not deny him. In 10:38, following Jesus with each one's own cross is worthy of Jesus, like the fruit worthy of μετάνοια in 3:8. Enduring suffering in 10:17-28 parallels one of the characteristics of true μετάνοια in 5:12. The assurance language in 10:29-31 also parallels the way 6:26 enforces μετάνοια.

Second, it must be noted that Matthew 10 not only includes the μετάνοια commissioning of the apostles but also illustrates their life worthy of μετάνοια. Some scholars identify Matthew 10 as a discipleship discourse rather than a commissioning discourse. For example, Luz calls Matthew 10 a disciple discourse rather than a sending discourse because Matthew 10 is more about discipleship than commissioning.[4] Both descriptions could be valid in that the narrative setting of Matthew 10 is the universal μετάνοια commissioning, and Matthew 10 is a disciple discourse in the form of a commission. However, the commissioning of μετάνοια governs the true discipleship discussed in the body of Matthew 10. As I argued above, the discipleship language in Matthew 10 refers to fruit worthy of the μετάνοια Jesus calls for in his universal mission. As mentioned in the previous section, the body of Jesus' commissioning discourse in Matthew 10 is sandwiched by "worthy" (ἄξιος) language (10:10-13, 37-38) referring to fruit worthy of μετάνοια. The body of Matthew 10 calls for worthy (ἄξιος) fruit from the μετάνοια life of the disciples. Matthew 10 follows Matthew's interest in μετάνοια and includes μετάνοια discipleship in terms of mission.

Third, this μετάνοια life instruction in Matthew 10 parallels the sermon's because in both the true μετάνοια and worthy life endure persecutions with the comfort of the promise of God. Luz explains the parallel materials in the sermon and Matthew 10 as follows: "The disciples' behavior and fate

---

4. Luz, *Matthew 8-20*, 63.

correspond to the commands of the Sermon on the Mount. The disciples are defenseless (10:10, 16, cf. 5:38–42), poor (10:9–14; cf. 6:19–34), and persecuted (10:16–23, 38–39, cf. 5:10–12). They are under God's care (10:28–31, cf. 6:25, 31) and do not need to worry (10:19, cf. 6:25–34). . . . The content of their proclamation corresponds to their lifestyle."[5]

Even though Luz's argument for this parallelism falls within the discipleship theme, these parallel materials between the sermon and Matthew 10 indicate that as the sermon gives the contents of μετάνοια, Matthew 10 also shows the contents of μετάνοια. Specifically, Matthew 10 is a topical μετάνοια discourse relative to the μετάνοια mission of the disciples and their life in a hostile context, which corresponds to the mission and life of Jesus.

Matthew 9:36–38: The Two Opening Images of Matthew 10

Many scholars agree that the structural analysis of 9:36–38 contains two images that function as the heading for Matthew 10. Nolland says, "4:23 and 9:35 serve as an inclusio, bookends that bracket the two books of Jesus' words and deeds within a missional perspective."[6] In other words, the first discourse and narrative block, which is the sermon and Jesus' ministry, ends at 9:35 and it begins the new discourse and narrative block. Allison says, "4:23—5:2 and 9:35–10:4 set the narrative contexts for the discourse 5–7 and 10."[7] Verses 4:23—5:2 and 9:35–10:4 not only set the narrative contexts, but they also head the two discourse blocks thematically. Also, 4:23—5:2 and 9:35–10:4 contain parallel language. They foresee main themes of each discourse block. The first discourse and narrative block and the second discourse and narrative block parallel the μετάνοια ministry of Jesus and the disciples. Specifically, 9:35 and 11:1 create an inclusio, and 9:36–10:4 is the opening of chapter 10 and governs the whole theme of the chapter.

Matthew 9:36–38 gives two opening focal images that parallel John the Baptist's μετάνοια preaching in Matthew 3:1–12, indicating that Matthew 10 is instruction about the eschatological μετάνοια call of the apostles. First, the "plentiful harvest" image appears in John the Baptist's judgmental harvest prophecy of Jesus in 3:12, which enforces the μετάνοια call. Second, πρόβατα μὴ ἔχοντα ποιμένα, the "sheep without a shepherd" image correlates with John the Baptist's words of judgment toward Israel's leadership ("many Pharisees and Sadducees" in 3:7) and his call of μετάνοια for the people of Israel. Thus, the harvest image and the sheep without a shepherd

---

5. Luz, *Matthew 8–20*, 59. See also Luz, *Studies in Matthew*, 147–49.
6. Nolland, *Gospel of Matthew*, 406.
7. Davies and Allison, *Matthew 8–18*, 143.

image demonstrate the theme of μετάνοια and the worthy fruit of μετάνοια. In Matthew 10, Jesus and the apostles replace the leadership of Israel by calling people to μετάνοια.

Matthias Konradt argues that the twelve disciples only replace the authority of Israel, but that does not mean the replacement of Israel by the church. He interprets the three parables in Matthew 21:28–22:14 as showing the replacement of the leadership of Israel only, continuing to chapter 23 and Jesus' rebuke of Israel's leadership there.[8] In contrast to Konradt, Luz says, "the singular 'shepherd' (Matt 9:36) does not suggest a direct polemic against the Jewish leaders," since the OT background (Zech 11:16–17) and even Matthew 9:36 do not refer to bad shepherds. Rather, this image emphasizes the need for Jesus as a shepherd.[9] Luz also argues that the lost sheep of Israel image refers to all Israel and the issue is not the shepherd of Israel, but the sheep.[10] The apostles are commissioned to preach μετάνοια and teach the worthy fruit of μετάνοια as good shepherds who incorporate warnings of judgment along with the charge to turn and bear good fruit.

Specifically, the second image, the plentiful harvest and the need for laborers, indicates the dawn of the eschatological worldwide judgment[11] and the need for the postresurrection church's mission to gather people.[12] These two focal images show and expand the thematic significance of μετάνοια in Matthew 10, in which Jesus commissions the twelve apostles to proclaim μετάνοια to the lost (ἀπολωλότα, which also possibly means destroyed) sheep of Israel (10:6)[13] and to the gentiles because as the judgmental harvest image indicates both groups are under the eschatological judgment of the coming kingdom of heaven. As John the Baptist proclaimed in 3:12, it also points to the destruction of the old Israel with the coming of the new king Jesus and to their absolute need to turn (μετανοέω) to Jesus the new king.

---

8. Konradt, *Israel, Church, and the Gentiles*, 263.

9. Luz, *Matthew 8–20*, 64–65.

10. Luz, *Matthew 8–20*, 71.

11. LeGrand "Harvest is Plentiful," 9. He argues that the two images of the harvest and of the lost sheep in 9:35 "were not meant originally to follow each other." The sheep images of 9:36 and 10:6 govern the Galilean mission and the harvest image governs the worldwide gentile mission in 10:2–3. This interpretation is not likely; instead, the sheep image refers to the prior gathering of failing Israel and the harvest image refers to worldwide judgment.

12. Charette, "Harvest for the People," 29–35. Hagner, *Matthew 1–13*, 260. Beare, "Mission of the Disciples," 7.

13. Almost all English Bibles translate ἀπολωλότα in Matt 10:6 into "the lost," figuratively, with the "sheep" image. However, the basic meaning of ἀπολωλότα is "destroyed," which perhaps refers the postresurrection destruction of Israel as the true people of God and possibly the destruction of Israel after the Jewish War in AD 70.

The workers in the harvest indicate that Matthew 10 is about the end time calling of μετάνοια (turning to Jesus and following him) for Israel and the gentiles. "He had compassion for them" also indicates Jesus' concern for failing Israel and its status of being under judgment.

As Anders Runesson argues, judgment is a prominent theme in Matthew. He also contends that repentance is a key motif and that Matthew has different categories of judgment for each ethnic group. Specifically, Runesson submits that the temple destruction is not the recompense of Israel's rejection of Jesus but the temple was already defiled and its destruction was inevitable.[14] As discussed above about the judgment and destroyed Israel image, I rather say this harvest image and the temple destruction indicates the end of the old era and the beginning of the new era of the church (16:18). Also, Matthew 10 is eschatological and universal μετάνοια commissioning of the postresurrection church of the apostles, which is governed by the harvest image. (We will discuss it more in the next section.) Furthermore, 11:25–27 says that one aspect of Jesus' judgment is to prohibit wicked Israel from recognizing him as the Messiah and thus ensure they will not be saved. In addition, the fact that the veil in the temple was torn when Jesus died indicates the reason the temple was destroyed was not only its defilement by Israel's sin but also their ultimate sin of killing Jesus Christ.

Matthew 10 as Universal μετάνοια Commissioning for the Post-Resurrection Church

The previous section looked at Matthew 10 as μετάνοια commission. This section examines the commissioning of μετάνοια in Matthew 10 as a universal charge for the postresurrection church. Scholars say that Matthew 10 transparently commissions the postresurrection church of the apostles for their universal μετάνοια mission and life based on Jesus' historical commission of the disciples.[15] While Matthew 10 has as its narrative setting Jesus' commissioning of the twelve disciples during his lifetime, the chapter also includes extensive use of eschatological language, a universal range for its commissioning, and postresurrection sayings of Jesus. This postresurrection setting shows that Matthew 10 instructs the postresurrection church about the twelve apostles' (10:2) μετάνοια mission for all nations, including both the lost (ἀπολωλότα) sheep of Israel (10:6) and the gentiles at the same time. The

---

14. Runesson, *Divine Wrath and Salvation*, 119, 126–30. Specifically, he notes repentance as a key motif in Matthew.

15. See n. 1 of this chapter.

church is called to continue Jesus' μετάνοια ministry of proclaiming the dawn of the kingdom of heaven and the end time judgment (4:17; 10:7).

Source and Redaction-Critical Studies of Matthew 10 for Universalism of μετάνοια Commission

Because of their universal and postresurrection setting, Jesus' sayings in Matthew 10, indicate that Matthew 10 as a whole instructs and commissions the church of apostles for μετάνοια. Source criticism shows that Jesus' sayings in Matthew 10 are paralleled in Mark 6, Luke 9 and 10, and John 15-16's postresurrection eschatological sayings. This indicates that Matthew 10 is not only part of Matthew's Galilean mission narrative,[16] but also the universal mission of the postresurrection church. Redaction-critical studies in Matthew 10 also show that the whole of chapter 10 is Matthew's redaction work collecting his sources for the mission of the postresurrection church.[17]

These postresurrection and universal eschatological materials occur from the beginning to the end of Matthew 10. They include the following terms: "apostles" (10:2), reference to raising the dead (10:8), the day of judgment (10:15), persecution and being delivered over to the court and flogged (10:17), being dragged before governors and kings and witnessing to them and the gentiles (10:18), the Spirit of their Father speaking (10:20), family being killed (10:21), enduring to the end (10:22), the Son of Man's coming (10:23), and taking one's own cross (10:38). The way these materials are all found in the apostles' mission in the book of Acts demonstrates that Matthew 10 is the postresurrection church of the apostle's universal μετάνοια commission.

Concerning the redaction work of Matthew 10, B. W. Beare says, "It is the gospel writer who has arranged them as seemed good to him, fitting them into a pattern of his own designing, like an artist setting the tesserae into a mosaic."[18] Regarding the main theme of chapter 10, Beare says the questions

---

16. Allison, "Matthew 10:26-31," 293-94. Davies and Allison, *Matthew 8-18*, 179-80.

17. Morosco, "Redaction Criticism and the Evangelical," 323-31. Pappas, "'Exhortation to Fearless Confession,'" 239-48. He says, "Matthew adapted some original sayings of Jesus and revised them to fit into his missionary discourse in chapter 10. . . . Through commands, injunctions, analogies, and even encouraging and threatening examples Matthew seeks to exhort and embolden his fellow Christians to proclaim the good news to all, though word and deed and in spite of persecution, that God has come in the last times through the person of Jesus Christ, His Son and the Messiah of Israel, to dwell among His people" (247).

18. Beare, "Mission of the Disciples," 4.

to be asked are, what are the evangelist's motives, and both his and the church's circumstances. "Matthew brings together a variety of sayings which deal more broadly with the dangers that beset the followers of Jesus—not the twelve alone, not at all in the circumstances of a mission undertaken at this period—but all who are called to bear testimony to Jesus and the gospel within a community and a world that they will find hostile."[19]

Robert E. Morosco, agreeing with Stendahl's view of the original role of the Gospel of Matthew as a handbook for church leaders and teachers, effectively examines Matthew 10 using redaction criticism. He concludes that Matthew 10 is "a carefully constructed didache on the topic of missions by the evangelist"[20] "to systematically organize important teaching for the church that lifts his readers beyond the context of the days of Jesus."[21] Morosco analyzes difficult materials in Matthew 10, concluding that they do not follow the historical narrative context of the Galilean mission during Jesus' lifetime and rather indicate a universal mission for the postresurrection church. First, he points to the contradictory range of mission: not going to the gentiles (10:5-6) but bearing testimony to the gentiles (10:18). Second, a contrast exists between the lush and ready harvest (9:37-38) and the terrible resistance (10:16-22). Third, the text is silent on the actual mission of the twelve to Israel. Fourth, Jesus' commission seems to be for a short mission trip, but drastic consequences appear within the chapter, such as court trials, floggings, and political actions before governors and gentile kings, families turning against the disciples, the disciples being betrayed to hostile authorities and executed, and Beelzebul. Morosco's fifth example is the coming of the Son of Man (10:23). Therefore, he concludes, "Matthew gives to chapter 10 a wider significance than just the story of the mission of the twelve. The evangelist used the mission of the twelve as a lens with which to focus on the mission of his contemporary community and the future church. Some in the commissioning story belong to the commissioning of the twelve to go to Israel with others seemingly looking to the later mission in the world (10:16-23)."[22]

---

19. Beare, "Mission of the Disciples," 4.

20. Morosco, "Redaction Criticism and the Evangelical," 330.

21. Morosco, "Redaction Criticism and the Evangelical," 330. Morosco, "Matthew's Formation of a Commissioning," 539-56, suggests that the commissioning stories of Moses had been patterned along with prophets in the OT and Jesus' commissioning his disciples in Matthew 9:35—11:1 and 28:16-20. Matthew has redacted his materials a special kind of biblical genre, called "type-scene" (539). Matthew used this as a device for the well-known commissioning type-scene of Moses (Exod 3-4) in Matthew 10 (542-43).

22. Morosco, "Redaction Criticism and the Evangelical," 326.

He supports his conclusion by dealing with the most difficult passage (10:16–23) as a later mission in the world, which must be recognized as so by church:

> 10:16–23 does agree easily with the frame-story of the sending of the twelve. it has been edited in largely from a different context, namely that of Jesus' eschatological discourse in Mark 13. which focus is not on the local Palestinian mission of the twelve but on the eschatological mission of the church that was to be terminated with the parousia. of the son of man. This redaction does not mean to fool his readers; because it is so obvious that 10:16–23 is from Mark's eschatological context. Matthew redacted his discourse for church's mission, that the commission origins from Jesus and the disciples.[23]

Schuyler Brown also helps us understand Matthew 10 as redacted toward the postresurrection church of apostles, proving Matthew's alteration of sources. Brown says Matthew intentionally designed chapter 10 to be "open-ended." Matthew, in contrast with Mark, does not include materials that hinder the application of chapter 10 to the church, such as the sending out two by two (Mk 6:7), the departure of the Twelve (Mk 6:12), or their return and their report (v. 30). Also, Matthew includes Mark's apocalyptic discourse (Mk 13:9–13) for the church.[24] In Matthew, this section does not have a definite beginning or a definite end as in Mark (Mk 6:12, 30); therefore, it applies not as a one-time event related to the twelve in Galilee but as a continuing event for the church.[25] The term "disciple" applies not only to Jesus' earthly followers but also to any Christian, and here "the twelve disciples" transparently refers to the postresurrection church members. "Everything addressed to the twelve disciples is intended for all Jesus' future disciples."[26]

While Brown convincingly shows that Matthew 10 was written not only for the twelve disciples but for a wider community, he excludes the gentile mission theme in Matthew 10 by limiting its range to Israel so that the persecution in chapter 10 comes from the Jews, not gentiles. Rather, he argues that the Great Commission attaches the gentile inclusion theme by reflecting on the converted situation of the Matthean community in which they were persecuted and separated from the Jewish people and physically moved toward the gentile world after the Jewish war (AD 70),

---

23. Morosco, "Redaction Criticism and the Evangelical," 328–29.
24. Brown, "Mission to Israel," 75.
25. Brown, "Mission to Israel," 79–80.
26. Brown, "Mission to Israel," 74–75.

the destruction of the temple, and the departure of the Christians from Jerusalem.[27] However, Matthew 10 is intended to be read by the whole church about the gentile mission. The worldwide gentile territory of the persecution indicates Jesus' commissioning of the later church to the gentile world. Matthew 10 deals with the worldwide mission of μετάνοια and so with the gentile μετάνοια mission theme for the church.

10:1–15 Galilean and 10:16–42 Universal?

Some scholars argue that Matthew 10 includes mission instruction with a twofold historical context, one part for the twelve disciples of Galilee (10:1–15) and the other for the postresurrection church of the gentiles (10:16–42).[28] However, this division of the discourse is not persuasive.

First, the universal and postresurrection language occurs in 10:1–15. The clear postresurrection terminology and events of 10:1–15, such as the term "apostles" (10:2), the raising of the dead (10:8), and the day of judgment (10:15), indicate that Matthew 10:1–15 is instruction to the postresurrection church of the apostles.

Second, Matthew does not give any clear indication to separate the two different ranges of mission between 10:1–15 and 10:16–42. There is no clear indication that Matthew shifts the mission instruction from the twelve disciples' Galilean mission to the postresurrection church's worldwide mission in the later verses of chapter 10.

Third, 10:16–40 is also situated in the disciples' Galilean mission and includes the mission instruction for both Israel (cf. 10:17, 23) and the gentiles (10:17, 18, 34, 38). Therefore, it is hard to limit 10:16–40's mission for the postresurrection church to gentiles alone; instead it includes both the destroyed (ἀπολωλότα) sheep of Israel and the gentiles.

---

27. Brown, "Matthean Community and the Gentile Mission," 193–221.

28. Carson, *Matthew*, 146. Davies and Allison, *Matthew 8–18*, 179–80, explains that Matthew, without explicit notice, changes the historical situation from the twelve disciples to Matthew's own day. Hagner, *Matthew 1–13*, 262, also says that Matt 10:5–6's restriction to Israel is temporary since "28:19 clearly countermands the present restriction." Matthew specifically includes this anachronistic material for Jewish-Christian readers that they should know God's faithfulness to his covenant to Israel and that the church is the true Israel. Similar arguments appear in Byrne, "Messiah in Whose Name," 66. Nolland, *Gospel of Matthew*, 415, says, "The role of the negative statements can only be apologetic. . . . Matthew will reach to a universalism, but for the moment we have not only Paul's 'Jew first' (Rom. 1:16) but the stronger 'Jew only'. Jesus comes as, in the first instance, a thoroughly Jewish and restrictedly Jewish messiah. Through and beyond that, Matthew is here preparing, from the perspective of Jewish concerns, for the affirmation of Gentile mission to which he will reach in 28:19."

Lastly, it seems like 10:5–6 leads to reading Matthew 10:1–15 as a restricted commission for Israel. However, as the previous section has shown, the whole of Matthew 10 clearly instructs the postresurrection universal μετάνοια mission of church and 10:5–6 hardly restricts the mission to only gentiles. Rather it is more natural that 10:5–6 indicates Jesus' prior concern for the lost Israel left out of the coming kingdom of Jesus in the postresurrection church's universal μετάνοια mission. Specifically, ἀπολωλότα in 10:6 presupposes the destroyed status of Israel, which likely refers to the destruction of Israel as the true people of God (9:17; 10:28; 15:24; 21:41; 22:7; 26:52). It also possibly indicates the destruction of Israel after the Jewish war in AD 70 because the missionary discourse of Matthew 10 instructs the postresurrection church around or after AD 70. (This point will be elaborated on in the next section.) Brown argues that the Great Commission indicates the Matthean community's gentile mission after AD 70. However, as I have argued, the Great Commission functions as a summary of Matthew, especially the widespread gentile inclusion theme of Matthew. This also demonstrates that Matthew 10 as a whole is a universal commissioning and 10:5–6 indicates the twelve apostles' prior mission for the scattered Israel to call them to turn (μετανοέω) to Jesus (10:5–7). (10:5–6 will be discussed more in later section of this chapter.)

In short, both 10:1–15 and 10:16–40 transparently deal with the universal μετάνοια mission of the postresurrection church, so 10:1–15 can hardly be a mission only for Israel and 10:16–40 a gentile or universal mission; rather Matthew 10 as a whole should be understood as transparent universal mission instruction for the original readers of the Gospel of Matthew, the postresurrection church of the apostles. Matthew redacts the commissioning story of the twelve apostles to explicitly instruct the postresurrection church about its μετάνοια mission for the whole world. So, Matthew 10 is instruction for the church incorporated into the story of Jesus sending the twelve. This universal μετάνοια commissioning of Matthew 10 coheres with Matthew's widespread gentile inclusion theme for his whole gospel and supports Matthew 10 as the commission of the postresurrection church of the apostles for the worldwide μετάνοια mission including both the lost (destroyed) Israel and the gentiles at the same time.

Matthew 10 as Expansion of the Great Commission (Matthew 28:18–20)

This chapter argues that Matthew 10 is the direct message of Jesus about the church's universal μετάνοια mission. In this respect, it is found that

Matthew 10 as the universal μετάνοια commission of the postresurrection church of the apostles parallels the Great Commission (28:18–20).²⁹ Matthew 10 and 28:18–20 are closely connected in that both are Jesus' explicit μετάνοια commission for the postresurrection church of the apostles for all the nations, including both the lost (destroyed) Israel and the gentiles. As chapter 5 suggested, the last words of Jesus, the Great Commission (28:18–20), and the first words, the commandment of turning (μετανοέω) in 4:17, are conceptually parallel in the theme of μετάνοια and together summarize the Gospel of Matthew with the theme of universal μετάνοια. In this Matthean theme of universal μετάνοια, Matthew 10 develops the theme of universal μετάνοια commissioning of the apostles and the church, expanding or elaborating on the Great Commission (28:18–20). This eventually demonstrates the thematic and even paradigmatic significance of the universal μετάνοια in Matthew.

Matthew 10 and 28:18–20 Contradictory?

The universal commission of Matthew 10 and its close relationship to the Great Commission have not been read appropriately and the significance of Matthew 10 for universal μετάνοια mission of the postresurrection church has been somewhat ignored. One reason is that the salvation-historical plot reads 10:5–6 and 28:18–20 as contrasting passages. The salvation-historical plot reading of Matthew reads Matthew 10 as commissioning the twelve disciples for a Galilean mission during Jesus' lifetime, a mission that Jesus restricts to "the lost sheep of Israel" (10:5–6; cf. 15:24). However, Israel rejects Jesus. And then Jesus in the Great Commission (28:18–20) releases this restriction and sends the disciples to all the nations. This salvation-historical plot reading of Matthew 10 and the Great Commission has been a common view in Matthean scholarship.³⁰

---

29. See ch. 5 for more discussion on the Great Commission as the universal μετάνοια Great Commission.

30. Matera, "Plot of Matthew's Gospel," 253–54; Hooker, "Uncomfortable Words X," 361–65. Hooker says, "salvation did indeed come to the Gentiles through Israel – but it was not through her witness, but through her rejection of the Messiah" (365). Therefore, 10:5–6 was temporal before the crucifixion and resurrection of Jesus. For more discussion on the development of a salvation historical reading of the Gospel of Matthew, see Meier, "Salvation History in Matthew," 203–15. Davies and Allison, *Matthew 8–18*, 179–80, explains that Matthew, without explicit notice, changed the historical situation from the twelve disciples to Matthew's own day. Similar sources are Byrne, "Messiah in Whose Name," 66; Nolland, *Gospel of Matthew,* 415. See also Eloff, "Ἀπό. . . ἕως and Salvation History," 85–107. For a contrasting argument, see Kingsbury, "Structure of Matthew's Gospel," 451–74; Kingsbury, "Plot of Matthew's Story," 347–56; Konradt,

However, as the previous section has demonstrated, Matthew 10 instructs the postresurrection church about the apostles' universal μετάνοια commission including both the lost (destroyed) sheep of Israel and the gentiles. Matthew 10 and the Great Commission (28:18–20) do not contradict but cohere so that the Great Commission summarizes the book of Matthew, including Matthew 10, in terms of commissioning instruction. I will examine the problem of the contradictory reading between Matthew 10 and 28:18–20 and then suggest the coherent reading to show Matthew 10 as universal commissioning of μετάνοια that expands or elaborates on 28:18–20.

The contradictory reading of the salvation-historical plot reading of Matthew 10 and the Great Commission has critical problems. First, the salvation-historical plot reading downplays Matthew's widespread gentile inclusion theme. The salvation-historical plot argues that 10:5–6 restricts the mission from the gentiles and that after Israel's rejection of Jesus, the Great Commission declares gentile inclusion at the end of the book. However, as discussed in chapter 5, the Matthean gentile inclusion theme and materials are widespread. Matthew proclaims the gentile inclusion theme from the beginning of his gospel (for example, the Abrahamic genealogy) to the end, and the gentile-inclusive Great Commission summarizes the whole book of Matthew. Even more, Jesus' universal commissioning of his disciples occurred in 24:14 before the Great Commission.

Strecker also argues that the Great Commission is a summary of the Gospel of Matthew. The Great Commission indicates that Matthew is a universal gospel that includes both Jews and gentiles as the people of God, in other words, the church. This universality rejects the common understanding of Matthew as a Jew-centric gospel, in other words, the idea that Matthew does not include gentile Christians but only Jews. Secondly, Strecker argues for reading 10:5–6 and 15:6 historically with the concept that Matthew redacted those two passages to indicate the Jewish rejection of Jesus during Jesus' lifetime and so the replacement of the Jews as the people of God by the universal church. Thus, Matthew's Gospel is for the universal church.[31] While Strecker argues the replacement of the people of God by the universal church, he does not argue the salvation-historical plot reading, which rejects the gentile inclusion theme before the Great Commission.

The way this gentile inclusion appears from Matthew's beginning chapters to the end does not support the salvation-historical plot. The widespread gentile inclusion context of Matthew and the two universal μετάνοια summary

---

Israel, Church, and the Gentiles.
31. See Strecker, *Theology of the New Testament*, 368–71.

statements at the beginning (4:17)[32] and the end (28:18-20) of Jesus' ministry rather support the theory that the main plot of Matthew is Jesus' universal μετάνοια call in view of the coming kingdom of heaven,[33] precisely Jews first and gentiles at the same time, universal μετάνοια.

Second, since the gentile inclusion theme has already occurred from the beginning chapter of the Gospel of Matthew, Matthew 10:5-6 cannot be a mission charge restricted to Israel. It is nonsensical that after healing the centurion's servant, praising the centurion's great faith, rebuking Israel, and declaring the opening of salvation to the gentiles in 8:11-12, the Matthean Jesus would suddenly overturn this gentile inclusion and limit salvation only to Israel in 10:5-6. In addition, 10:5-6 does not indicate that chapter 10 is a commission only for Israel, excluding the gentiles; rather it is a mission to Israel first and to the gentiles at the same time. (This point will be discussed more in the next section). In addition, "all nations" πάντα τὰ ἔθνη in 28:19 refers to both the lost (destroyed) sheep of Israel and gentile. The Great Commission summarizes this twofold mission charge of the Gospel of Matthew rather than serving as a climax or culmination of the opening of gentile salvation.

Third, while the salvation-historical plot reads Matthew 10 as the commission for the twelve disciples' Galilean mission, Matthew 10, as already discussed above, includes postresurrection eschatological sayings of Jesus paralleled in Mark 6, Luke 9 and 10, and John 15-16, indicating that Matthew 10 is not part of Matthew's Galilean mission narrative but of the universal mission of the postresurrection church of apostles. Also, the salvation-historical understanding of Matthew 10 ignores that Matthew 10 includes eschatological language and postresurrection sayings of Jesus from the beginning to the end of the chapter. As noted above, some salvation-historical readers argue that Matthew 10 includes a twofold historical mission instruction, with one part for the twelve disciples of Galilee (10:1-15) and the other for the postresurrection church of all nations (10:16-42). However, as I have argued, a redaction study of Matthew 10 clearly shows that Matthew 10 is the commissioning of the postresurrection church of the apostles for a worldwide mission and for their hostile life in the world.

Fourth, while the salvation-historical plot reading insists that Matthew intentionally placed 10:5-6 to make it clear that Israel's rejection of Jesus is the reason for Israel's loss of salvation and the shift of the gospel to the gentiles as a judgment, Matthew explains that this rejection is the judgment

32. The universal nature of 4:17 is discussed in ch. 5. The near context of Matt 4 supports the idea that Matthew introduces Jesus as the universal Savior (4:12-16).

33. Supporting ideas are from Kingsbury, "Structure of Matthew's Gospel"; Kingsbury, "Composition and Christology," 573-84; Kingsbury, "Plot of Matthew's Story."

of God according to God's will (11:25–27). Jesus interprets this rejection as a theodicy (11:25–27) that God judges wicked Israel not to believe Jesus so that they will not enter into the kingdom of heaven. Jesus does not say Israel's rejection is a cause of the salvation of the gentiles, but the faith of gentiles is the cause their salvation(cf. 8:10–12). In addition, the Matthean story of the rejection of Jesus is universal, not only applying to Israel; eventually it was the Roman authorities who killed Jesus. Matthew 10:17, 18, 22 indicate that Jesus was rejected not only by Israel but also by the nations.

Matthew 10 Coherent Expansion of 28:18–20

Matthew 10 and 28:18–20, which I call the universal μετάνοια in the Great Commission, both instruct the postresurrection church of the twelve apostles' (10:2) about the μετάνοια mission (10:7) to all nations, including both the lost (destroyed) sheep of Israel (10:6) and the gentiles. Their mission is to continue Jesus' ministry of proclaiming μετάνοια in view of the dawn of the kingdom of heaven and of the end time judgment (4:17b; 10:7); this same goal is rephrased in the universal μετάνοια Great Commission of the twelve apostles to go to all nations, making disciples by teaching what Jesus taught and by following his teaching and warning of his judgment authority over all heaven and earth (28:19–20). Matthew 10 and the Great Commission do not contradict but cohere in that Matthew 10 amplifies the Great Commission.

Oscar Brooks is representative of dealing with Matthew 10 along with the Great Commission. Brooks argues that 9:35–10:42 is "Jesus' direction for conducting to mission having the same components in expanded form that are found in 28:16–20."[34] Brooks argues that first, 10:1 includes a declaration of Jesus' authority as in 28:16. Second, Matthew 10 has a two-stage mission charge: 10:5–15 instructs the apostles not to take provisions and go to the house of Israel to heal, to preach, and to hear, and 10:16–23 instructs them about what to do before accusers. Third, 10:24–47 assures "the abiding presence or reassurance for the mission" as 28:20 does.[35] In regard to sending the disciples, that Matthew 10 is an expanded version of 28:16–20 should not be in doubt. Brooks also points out that chapter 10 and the Great Commission are "the disciples' prominent and applicable teaching of Jesus to the postresurrection community."[36] "Apostle" as a title for the disciples (10:2) is a redaction from the postresurrection community;

---

34. Brooks, "Matthew 28:16–20," 9.
35. Brooks, "Matthew 28:16–20," 9.
36. Brooks, "Matthew 28:16–20," 9.

the warning of bearing testimony before governors, kings, and Gentiles (10:18)"[37] prove that chapter 10 is an expanded version of 28:16–20, the worldwide mission. Verses 25:31–46 clearly connect to chapter 10, indicating chapter 10 as describing the end time worldwide persecution and the end time world mission charge of the postresurrection church of the apostles. Also, "going" in the Great Commission is especially expanded in chapter 10 to include other matters in mission.

The eschatological universal mission theme of Matthew 10 and 28:18–20 shows a cohere, not a contradictory relationship, between them. The former expands the latter in terms of universal mission. As I have shown, Matthew 10 is the eschatological universal commissioning of the postresurrection church of apostles and 28:18–20 coheres with the theme of the universal μετάνοια commission. I will highlight four things that show Matthew 10 and 28:18–20 cohere in terms of the postresurrection eschatological and universal μετάνοια commission. Here, I will examine few more things related to this.

First, πάντα τὰ ἔθνη in the Great Commission means "all nations,"[38] including both Israel and the gentiles, not "all Gentiles,"[39] excluding Israel. In this point, Matthew 10 and the Great Commission cohere in their universal range of commissioning.[40] Matthew 10 is an expansion of the Great Commission, Jesus Christ's commandment for the church to go to preach μετάνοια (10:7) and the gospel to the world—both the lost Israel and the gentiles.

Second, as discussed above, three major focal images, "sheep without a shepherd" (9:36)," "the harvest" (9:37), and the "need for laborers" (9:37)" show that Matthew 10 is the end time universal μετάνοια commission in coherence with the Great Commission. Seeing the implied readers of Matthew 10 as the postresurrection church of the apostles matches the image of the need for laborers. The old era has ended, and the new era has already come with Jesus Christ (3:2; 4:17; 10:7; 28:19–20). Moreover, 10:7–15 indicates that the apostles of the church were sent to proclaim the already-fulfilled dawn of the kingdom of heaven through Jesus Christ and the accompanying judgment

---

37. Brooks, "Matthew 28:16–20," 9.
38. Meier, "Nations or Gentiles in Matthew 28:19," 94–102.
39. Hare and Harrington, "Make Disciples of All the Gentiles," 359–69.

40. Also, Matthew's universal Christology supports this interpretation. The four consecutive usages of πᾶς ("all authority," "all nations," "all that I have commanded," and "all the days [always]") indicate the universal character of the Great Commission. Also, the total authority given to Jesus in the Great Commission repeats and reminds the reader of 11:25 (cf. 7:29; 9:6, 8; 10:1; 13:37–43; 21:23–27) and serves as a summary for the Gospel of Matthew as a whole. "All nations" coheres with Jesus' overarching worldwide μετάνοια ministry that extends from the first word of his public ministry to his last command.

on Israel. Therefore, we should read Matthew 10 and 10:5–6 not as the mission of the twelve, restricted only to the people of Israel, but as the first call to the lost Israel into the new kingdom of Jesus in coherence with 28:18–20. Matthew 10:5–6 does not indicate a prerequisite for gentile inclusion but a mission taking place at the same time. (Coherent relationship between 10:5–6 and 28:18–20 will be discussed more in the next section.)

Third, Matthew's distinct use of the term ἀπόστολος in Matthew 10:2, appearing only this one time in his gospel as the title of the twelve disciples, indicates that all of Matthew 10 is addressed to the postresurrection church of the apostles. This term emphasizes that Matthew 10 deals with the worldwide mission of reconstituting the people of God from the lost (destroyed) Israel and from the gentiles at the same time. Using ἀπόστολος also parallels Matthew's distinct use of the term ἐκκλησία in 16:18 to refer to the new people of God in the new era, showing that Matthew presupposes the end of Israel in the narrative context of the Gospel of Matthew and directly aims his gospel book to be read by the church of the apostles. The actual mission journeys of the first-century missionaries, including the twelve apostles, exactly match Matthew10, especially 10:5–6, in that they first went to Jewish synagogues to proclaim the gospel of Jesus and the judgment at the end of the old Israel and then went into gentile territories to make disciples of Jesus, proclaiming μετάνοια. Also, it is significant that Matthew uses ἀπέστειλεν in 10:5 and ἀποστέλλω in 10:16, which have the same root as ἀπόστολος in 10:2. This word choice possibly indicates that 10:5 and 10:16 are Jesus' sending of the twelve apostles. Specifically, the references to powerful ministry in 10:8 and to the Holy Spirit's leading of preaching in 10:19–20 strongly indicate that Matthew 10 as a whole describes the postresurrection apostles' missionary journey in coherence with the Great Universal Μετάνοια Commission (28:18–20).

Fourth, arraying the twelve apostles' names and the number of the apostles, which parallels the twelve tribes of the old Israel, symbolizes that Matthew 10 is the eschatological commission of μετάνοια for all the nations and the establishment of the new people of God, with the new eschatological twelve tribes including both Israel and the gentiles. In contrast, Luz argues that the twelve indicate the twelve tribes of Israel, meaning that Matthew 10 is about the Israel mission of the disciples as a prototype of the church's mission. [41] He does not deny that Matthew 10 indicates the beginnings of the church but focuses more on it as a prototype of the church's mission. I agree that Matthew 10 is a prototype of the church's mission, but it is clear that in Matthew 10 Jesus does not instruct the twelve apostles for

---

41. Luz, *Matthew 8–20*, 66–67.

Israel only mission; rather, Jesus instructs them for the whole world mission. This universal mission occurs in the situation of the Matthean audience, the postresurrection church of the apostles. Three things about the context for which Matthew was written have to be recognized in order to read Matthew 10 correctly: the judgment on ethnic Israel with the dawn of the kingdom of heaven has already been fulfilled by the destruction of the temple; the people of God are now included only through Jesus Christ, not through ethnic Jewishness; and so gentile inclusion is taking place with the inauguration of the kingdom of heaven.

Coherence Between Matthew 10:5–6 and 28:16–20

In particular, Matthew 10:5–6 and 28:16–20 are coherent, not contradictory. As mentioned above, both 10:5–6 and 28:18–20 indicate the postresurrection universal μετάνοια mission of the church for the Jews first and the gentiles at the same time. Specifically, as noted above, gentile inclusion theme begins from Matthew 1. Also, ἀπολωλότα in 10:6, which is translated "the lost," possibly refers to the lost Israel as the true people of God and possibly the destruction of Israel after the Jewish war in AD 70 (cf. 9:17; 10:28; 15:24; 21:41; 22:7; 26:52). Matthew inserts 10:5–6 to show Jesus' concern for the first son Israel, which is destroyed (ἀπολωλότα) (10:6), and Israel's priority in the church's mission. This interpretation indicates that 10:5–6 does not contradict the Great Commission nor does the Great Commission revoke 10:5–6.

Matthew 10:5–6 does not refer to a restricted commissioning of the twelve disciples for a mission to Israel alone. Jesus commissions the apostles to go to Israel rather (μᾶλλον) than Samaritan and gentile. Matthew 10:5–6 does not restrict the apostles from encountering gentiles and Samaritans on their mission journey but emphasizes the priority of meeting the lost (ἀπολωλότα) sheep of Israel in all the towns of Israel.

France's interpretation of 10:5–6 is likely accurate. He claims that 10:5–6 does not mean Jesus' ban on Samaria and the gentiles, since the gentiles have already appeared in other chapters (2:2–12; 4:15, 24–25; 8:5–13, 28–34; 28:19). He argues that 10:5–6 is a geographical symbol of Jesus as Messiah for Israel and that the gentile mission reaches its culmination after Jesus' death and resurrection in the Great Commission. "The geographical terms used in 10:5–6 ('*way* of the Gentiles,' '*town* of the Samaritans'; cf. '*towns* of Israel,' v. 23) indicate a restriction on the area to be visited rather than a total ban on contact with Gentiles and Samaritans as such."[42] I agree with his argument. It

---

42. France, *Matthew*, 382. Emphasis is France's.

is hard to say that 10:5–6 restricts the apostles from meeting gentiles and Samaritans since it uses the words "way" and "town." As repeatedly mentioned, Matthew 10 instructs gentile mission.

In addition, prohibition of the way of the gentiles and the town of the Samaritans in 10:5–6 should be read with "going all the towns of Israel" in 10:23. They mean the same. Specifically, 10:23 says the Son of Man will come before they go to all the towns of Israel. This indicates that their mission not going the way of the gentiles and the town of the Samaritans in 10:5–6 but going to all the towns of Israel in 10:23 indicate universal mission before the coming of the Son of Man. Because it is nonsensical to prohibit gentile mission before the coming of the Son of Man. And Matthew already instructs gentile mission. Therefore, both verses command church's "Israel first but Gentile at the same time" universal mission before the coming of the son of man. In doing so they would go to the whole world, meeting Israel first and the gentiles at the same time, rather than going to the way of the gentiles and the towns of the Samaritans. Scholars differ in their understanding of 10:23.[43] However, the coming of the son of man clearly indicates the final judgment day, that is, the parousia.

Furthermore, the prohibition of the way of the gentiles and the town of the Samaritans in 10:5–6 and "all the towns of Israel" in 10:23 likely indicates diaspora Israel, which indicates the whole world. It is also nonsensical that the apostles cannot go to all the land of Israel before the Son of Man coming. Therefore, 10:23 makes clear that the mission for the towns of Israel in 10:5–6 is universal μετάνοια mission before the coming of the Son of Man, that is, the parousia. In other words, 10:23 shows that 10:5–7 commands going into the whole world to preach μετάνοια in the towns of Israel before the Son of Man coming.

Also, 10:5–7 and 10:22–23 are clearly connected to 24:13–14 so that they should be read in relation to 24:14. Since they are coherent and do not contradict literarily, 10:5–7; 10:23; 24:14 emphasize the urgency of the universal mission and the immediacy of the coming of the Son of Man.[44] In

---

43. I tend to understand the Son of Man's coming in 10:23 as France reads it. France says 10:23 indicates Jesus' enthronement as one who has all authority through his resurrection and the temple destruction. While I think the Son of Man's coming eventually indicates Jesus' second coming, it has to be understood in terms of already-not-yet eschatology. Therefore, in terms of the judgmental nuance of the language of the Son of Man's coming, that temple destruction is the beginning of the end time judgment that will be fully fulfilled with the parousia. Matt 10:23, therefore, indicates the urgency or priority of the mission to the lost sheep of Israel.

44. Additionally, "the Son of Man coming" theme coheres with the judgment idea of the coming of the kingdom of heaven in 10:7. The idea of judgment appears in 10:11–15 and 28–42, and this judgment is the "already-not-yet" eschatological judgment that

short, 10:5–7; 10:23; 24:14 point to the urgent need for a universal call to turn (μετανοέω) to the kingdom of heaven (10:7), first to the lost sheep of Israel and to the gentiles at the same time, before the imminent parousia.

It is not a coincidence that 10:5–7, the preaching commanded by Jesus for the twelve apostles, becomes the actual preaching of the apostles in Acts that they go to diaspora Israel first and gentiles at the same time. This match indicates that Matthew 10:5–6 is Jesus' commission for the postresurrection church of the apostles in coherence to the universal Great μετάνοια Commission.

Conclusively, Matthew 10 is the eschatological commissioning of the postresurrection church of the apostles (10:2) for a worldwide mission, including both the lost Israel and the gentiles as an expansion of the universal μετάνοια Great Commission. We should read 10:5–6 within Matthew's overall context of the dawning of the kingdom of heaven, indicating the end of the old era, and of judgment on failing Israel that is currently being fulfilled, as shown in phrases like "the sons of the kingdom who will be thrown into the outer darkness" (8:12). The idea of Jews first and then gentiles invalidates that Israel's rejection opens the way for gentile salvation.[45]

Conclusion

The Gospel of Matthew effectively explains Jesus' concerns for all nations. Jesus' first and last words in his public ministry in the Gospel of Matthew call the whole world to turn (μετανοέω) to Jesus the king of the heavenly kingdom and to change their whole life, including their heart and conduct by following Jesus' teaching and life. Matthew refers to the μετάνοια of all nations from the beginning of the book to the end (4:17 and 28:18–20). The universal μετάνοια call is present in the whole of Matthew around the gentile inclusion theme since this theme appears explicitly from the beginning chapter of the Gospel of Matthew to the end. Matthew 10 shows that Jesus' first word (4:17) in his ministry continues to the apostles and the church and is expanding to the whole world through the apostles and the church. Matthew 10 instructs the apostles and the church about how to call the whole world to turn (μετανοέω) with specific teaching about μετάνοια lifestyle, eschatological judgment sayings, and comfort language.

---

accompanies the dawn of the kingdom of heaven in Jesus Christ. In another respect, 10:23 also promises the imminent cessation of persecution.

45. Eloff, "Ἀπό. . . ἕως and Salvation History," 101. Marvin does not say Jewish rejection of Jesus opens the way for salvation of the gentiles.

While the salvation-historical plot of the Gospel of Matthew somewhat forbids the reading of Matthew 10 from the beginning to the end as the explicit commissioning of the postresurrection church's universal μετάνοια mission, Matthew 10 is universal μετάνοια commissioning instruction for the postresurrection church. In this respect, Matthew 10 coherently and not contradictorily expands the Great μετάνοια Commission (28:18–20) by giving explicit instruction to send the postresurrection church of the twelve apostles on an eschatological μετάνοια mission to all nations, including Jews first and gentiles at the same time.

In this way the modern church should hear Matthew 10 as a direct and explicit commission, serving as the expansion of the universal μετάνοια call of Jesus' ministry and of the Great μετάνοια Commission. Jesus' worldwide μετάνοια call in 4:17 is handed over to the church in Matthew 10, and this idea is summarized in the gospel's last summary statement, the Great μετάνοια Commission. This shows the thematic and even paradigmatic significance of the universal μετάνοια in the Gospel of Matthew.

Chapter 9

The Thematic Significance of μετάνοια in Matthew 13

Explanation of Mixed Reception and Exhortation to μετάνοια

Introduction

MATTHEW, A SKILLFUL WRITER, structures his gospel with five discourse blocks by gathering eight parables¹ at the center as the third block.² What do the parables of this central discourse block illustrate? What is the function and meaning of the eight parables? A common view of Matthew 13 in Matthean scholarship is that the eight parables explain previous contexts of Jesus' mixed reception and the presence and the present progression of the

---

1. How many parables are in Matt 13? All agree the first seven stories are parables, as Matthew indicates with the term παραβολή, but the last story about the scribes of the kingdom of heaven is disputed. Jesus does not introduce the last story with the term "parable," παραβολή, in 13:52, but with ὅμοιός. However, right after 13:52, in 13:53, Matthew reports that "Jesus had finished these parables," ἐτέλεσεν ὁ Ἰησοῦς τὰς παραβολὰς ταύτας, which strongly indicates that the last story is also a parable. David Wenham adds that ὅμοιός is used in Jesus' parables (13:31, 33, 44, 45, 47). See Wenham, "Structure of Matthew 13," 516. Also, Matthew 13:24 uses ὁμοιόω to compare the kingdom of heaven to a man who sows good seed.

2. Lohr, "Oral Techniques in the Gospel of Matthew," 427. There is also elevation of the discourse setting that highlights ch. 13 as the center of Matthew: while the first discourse block (5–7) and the last block (23–25) are set on the mountain, the third and so the center of the five discourse blocks, Matt 13, is set on the sea. This setting also indicates that the parables are the center of the Gospel of Matthew.

Mountain				Mountain
5–7				24–25
	10		18	
		Sea		
		13		

kingdom of heaven and that they function to hide Jesus and his message from the rejecters in order that they will not turn to the kingdom of heaven and be healed (13:15).³

In this chapter, however, I will examine the function and meaning of the eight parables in Matthew 13. Specifically, I will examine them in light of the previous context of Jesus' and the disciples' μετάνοια ministry, mission, and mixed reception. I will suggest, firstly, that the eight parables illustrate the previous narrative context of Jesus' (and disciples') μετάνοια teachings and ministry from the beginning of his ministry with the commandment of turning (μετάνοια) for the coming of the kingdom of heaven (4:17; 10:7). Secondly, they illustrate the mixed reception of Jesus' (and disciples') ministry of μετάνοια (11:20–21; 12:41; 13:16). And thirdly, while these parables hide Jesus and his μετάνοια message (11:10–15), they still figuratively exhort the previous context of μετάνοια echoing Matthew 4:17's commandment of μετάνοια as exhortation through illustration, which is a common function of biblical parables. μετάνοια, here and elsewhere in Matthew, means to turn (or change) oneself and one's life from sin toward Jesus and righteousness, or from this world to the kingdom of heaven so as to bear fruit worthy of turning (μετάνοια). That Jesus' (and the disciples') μετάνοια ministry and essence is portrayed with these parables indicates the significance of μετάνοια in Matthew as a whole, and chapter 13 specifically.

To argue for this idea, this chapter will first briefly review a representative survey of scholarship on the function and meaning of Matthew 13. It will then examine the wider and narrower contexts of Matthew 13 and the two OT citations in Matthew 13 in relation to μετάνοια. Then it suggests the meanings of the parables as descriptions of Jesus' μετάνοια ministry and of people's mixed reaction, and as exhortations of μετάνοια. This function and meaning of Matthew 13 indicate the thematic and paradigmatic significance of μετάνοια in Matthew.

Common Understanding of Function and Meaning of the Parables in Matthew 13

Before diving into the text, it is necessary to examine the general function of parables and representative readings of Matthew 13. Davies and Allison note that the usual sense of παραβολή in Greek literature is "comparison."

---

3. See France, *Gospel of Matthew*, 499–50; Davies and Allison, *Matthew 8–18*, 374; Allison, "Matthew," 1203–21; Konradt, *Israel, Church, and the Gentiles*, 244–59; Turner, *Matthew*, 334; Pennington, "Matthew 13," 12–20; Snodgrass, *Stories with Intent*, 145, 169–71, 174. See also Luz, *Matthew 8–20*, 244, who focuses on an eschatological harvest.

The comparison almost always aims to exhort someone to something or persuade someone to do something.[4] Snodgrass defines parable as "an expanded analogy used to convince and persuade,"[5] in most cases by indicating that it is explanation for exhortation. Snodgrass uses the terms "convince" and "persuade," which are close to "exhort." He notes the OT prophets' parables as an important backdrop for Jesus' parables and their importance for understanding Jesus' parables.[6] In Matthew 13:57, Jesus identifies himself as a prophet and hints at the eight parables' prophetic exhortation functions. It shows that the eight parables of Jesus are not mere explanation but aims for exhortation through comparative explanation. Robert Stein also explains the twofold nature of parables in the Bible: they have an informative dimension and an affective dimension. While the first dimension explains some literal facts, the latter serves to "disarm and persuade (cf. Matt 20:1–16; Luke 7:41–43; 10:30–35; 15:11–32)."[7] The words "convince," "persuade," and "exhort" explain the connotation of the parable since parables aim for the listener to do something or to take some action.

Parables also function to hide one's message because one cannot understand the meaning of a parable without interpretation by the author.[8] A parable is a figurative speech containing the author's plain argument in a different form. A parable needs the author to explain its meaning. For example, in Matthew 13 Jesus only preaches in parables to hide his message of the kingdom of heaven. According to Isaiah, this hiding of the mystery of the kingdom of heaven is because of judgment on the wicked people of Israel (13:14–16). Jesus preaches in parables so that the rejecters of μετάνοια (turning) (11:20) never turn (ἐπιστρέφω) to God (13:16). However, Jesus distinguishes his disciples as those who have eyes to see and ears to hear (13:16). Jesus' disciples learn the meaning of the parable from Jesus himself, and they thus receive the fearful, critical ideas about the kingdom of heaven in terms of μετάνοια. Robert Gundry similarly notes the function of the parables in Matthew 13: "the true had understanding prior to the parables and gain more of it through the parables, the false lacked it prior to the parables and lose it in the parables."[9]

Are the parables in Matthew 13 mere explanation or do they aim to exhort? Davies and Allison note that the parable of the sower explains Israel's

---

4. Davies and Allison, *Matthew 8–18*, 378.
5. Snodgrass, *Stories with Intent*, 9.
6. Snodgrass, *Stories with Intent*, 38–42.
7. Stein, "Genre of the Parables," 48.
8. See Pennington, "Matthew 13," 12–20.
9. Gundry, *Matthew*, 251.

rejection of repentance within wider context of Matthew 11–12.[10] However, the parable of the sower not only describes Matthew 11–12, but also Jesus' repentance (μετάνοια) preaching ministry from the beginning chapters, especially since the parable begins with the sower went out to sow the word of the kingdom (13:19). Also, the parable explains not only Israel's rejection of repentance (μετάνοια) but also describes people's acceptance of repentance (μετάνοια) with the fruitful tree image. Likewise, the parable describes the whole previous context of Jesus' μετάνοια ministry from the beginning commandment of repentance (μετάνοια) and its mixed reception.

Also, Jonathan T. Pennington suggests that the main argument of the parables is "revelation and separation" in relation to 11:25–30 and that Matthew 13 explains the rejection of Jesus by Israel narrated in chapters 11 and 12. God reveals Jesus as Christ only to his elect and hides him from his rejecters, and thereby come two separated groups of people, the so-called insiders and outsiders not based on ethnicity but on their faith in Jesus. The parables are primarily explanations of this "mixed reception to Jesus' kingdom message," not exhortation.[11] Pennington does not deny the exhortative nature of the parables but indicates it as a secondary function. According to Pennington, the Isaiah 6:10 citation indicates that this one-sided revelation is punishment on the wicked Israel. Pennington's thesis about what is explained in the parables states, "Jesus' parabolic teaching is a sowing of the Word in the world. This Word from God is simultaneously a message of judgment on the unbelieving and a word of hope and blessing for the believing. The Word both reveals and conceals and in the process it performs a great separation of all people (cf. Heb 4:12), based on their response to the Son, the Incarnate Word."[12] Pennington correctly notes that the function of the eight parables is to explain the mixed reception of Jesus and they thus aim to punish the rejecters of Jesus.

However, some think that explanation and exhortation carry equal importance in the parables. Snodgrass argues that the parables warn readers, which obviously involves exhortation through explanation. "Matthew intends the parables to warn readers not to repeat Israel's failure to respond to the kingdom message and also to help people understand why Israel rejected Jesus' message: hardness of heart, the effort of evil one, the world's cares and money, and the seeming insignificance of the kingdom."[13]

---

10. Davies and Allison, *Matthew 8–18*, 402–3.
11. Pennington, "Matthew 13," 12–20.
12. Pennington, "Matthew 13," 12.
13. Snodgrass, *Stories with Intent*, 174.

Snodgrass' comment indicates that Jesus' parables warn readers not to repeat Israel's failure of turning (μετάνοια), but to turn (μετάνοια) to Jesus and follow his μετάνοια preaching.

John R. Donahue argues that the parables in Matthew 13 not only deal with the rejection of Israel but also the responsibility of Christian ethics of discipleship.[14] The parables explain the rejection of Israel to warn the disciples not to reject Jesus[15] and exhort them to live their present life in the hope of a future with God.[16] D. A. Carson argues that the first parable in chapter 13 not only explains but also "implicitly challenges hearers to ask themselves what kinds of soil they are."[17] Hearers are those who have ears to hear, like the disciples. Carson's wording here means that the first parable exhorts the hearers to do the will of the Father in heaven through comparing the four kinds of soil with oneself. Craig Evans and Craig Blomberg connect the parables in chapter 13 to the parable Nathan told King David about the rich man and the poor man's sheep in 2 Samuel 12.[18] Nathan's aim with the parable is that David repent, and after Nathan's explanation of the parable King David does repent. This scene is the same as in Matthew 13; after an explanation of the parables the disciples are exhorted to turn (μετανοέω) to have and do the will of the Father in heaven.

What these scholars note is that the parables exhort the disciples to follow Jesus' teachings, while in this chapter I argue that they essentially teach and exhort the previous context of Jesus' μετάνοια message, or in other words, what evil people should turn from and what good they should turn to. While Donahue notes that the parables exhort the ethics of discipleship, I rather say it is μετάνοια discipleship when it considers the broader context of Matthew. The nature of ethics instructs people to do good things without legal binding powers, but the parables have legal binding powers whether one will enter into the kingdom of heaven or the fire of hell as illustrations of Jesus' commandment of μετάνοια with the legal binding power. In addition, Isaiah 6:10 cited in Matthew 13:14–15 indicates that the parabolic teaching works to conceal the secret of the kingdom of heaven from rejecters so that they cannot turn (ἐπιστρέφω, synonym of μετανοέω) to God and be healed (13:16)—to bear fruit worthy of μετάνοια (the deeds of the will of Father in heaven 12:50). In other words, this citation implies that the concealed message of the parables is Jesus' μετάνοια message.

14. Donahue, *Gospel in Parable*, 66.
15. Donahue, *Gospel in Parable*, 66.
16. Donahue, *Gospel in Parable*, 70.
17. Carson, *Matthew*, 356.
18. Evans, *Commentary on the New Testament*, 46. Also, Blomberg, *Matthew*, 225.

In addition, since the basic nature of a parable is to depict in order to exhort or persuade, this chapter suggests that "the hot spot" of the parables is not only explanation of the mixed reception of μετάνοια toward Jesus but also exhortation for μετάνοια, corresponding to the near and wider context of Matthew 13. In fact, since the nature of the parables includes both explanation and exhortation, it is not helpful to distinguish explanation from exhortation, identifying the former as being primary and the latter secondary. In other words, by nature the primary function of a parable is twofold: both to explain and exhort. Parallels with OT prophetic parables probably mean that NT parables also have imperatival and exhortative force. One must consider Jesus' prophetic role in the parables, which is also clearly mentioned in 13:57 (cf. 10:41; 12:39; 14:5; 16:14; 21:11, 46). Jesus defines himself as a prophet and thus asks the readers to read the eight parables as a prophetic exhortation. In the wider context of the Gospel of Matthew, Jesus parallels the prophet John the Baptist who exhorted the people of Israel to turn (μετανοέω) (3:2) and to bear fruit worthy of μετάνοια (3:1–12). Also, the appearance in the parables of parallel fruit-bearing image, with its overall imperatival force in Matthew, illustrates the μετάνοια exhortation of the parables and within their interpretation by Jesus. Images in the parables of judgment (both vindication and punishment) accompany Jesus' previous teachings of judgment corresponding to μετάνοια (cf. 3:10–12; 4:17; 7:21; 12:50 and so on). This shows the thematic or even paradigmatic significance of μετάνοια in Matthew 13.

The following sections elaborate on this thesis and its arguments by considering the overall context of Matthew 13 and then examining the meanings of the parables.

The Context of Matthew 13: Exhortation of μετάνοια and Mixed Reception of μετάνοια

The wider context of Matthew 13, from its beginning chapters, has critical importance for understanding the parables' intended authorial meaning. This section will examine the narrative context of Matthew 13. I will suggest that as the third discourse block, which is located at the center of Matthew, the parables in Matthew 13 illustrate the previous context of Jesus' ministry of μετάνοια in Matthew 3–12 and exhort μετάνοια.

The μετάνοια Context from Matthew 3 to Matthew 13

As noted above, scholars focus on Israel's rejection or opposition to Jesus in these chapters and argue that the parables are an explanation of this mixed reception or separation[19] and of the presence and "the present progression of the kingdom of heaven."[20] However, it is important to realize that in the previous context Matthew reports Jesus' μετάνοια ministry and not only the rejection of Jesus but also the rejection of μετάνοια.

The narrative context of Matthew 3–12 is as follows. Following John the Baptist's μετάνοια preaching (Matt 3), Jesus opens his public ministry with the same prophetic exhortation: "Turn (μετανοέω), for the kingdom of heaven is near" (4:17b). Jesus expands this exhortation through the sermon (4:17—8:1), giving the contents of μετάνοια. Jesus sends his apostles to preach μετάνοια in Matthew 10. Then Matthew 11 and 12 report people's reaction: Israel rejects Jesus and also μετάνοια (11:20–22; 12:41). Jesus rebukes Israel for not having μετάνοια in contrast with the μετάνοια of the gentiles. In addition, Jesus calls people to turn again in a different form in 11:28–30 and 12:45–50. Matthew 11:25–30, the important backdrop for the eight parables, explains the reason for the mixed reception as the Father's will and exhorts hearers to turn and follow Jesus by taking on his yoke (11:30).

The parables illustrate these previous exhortations of μετάνοια (3:2; 4:17, 10:7), the contents of μετάνοια in the sermon and in Matthew 10, and the mixed reception and exhortation of μετάνοια (11:2–12:50). As we will see in the following sections the parables also use and illustrate parallel μετάνοια language, images, and μετάνοια thematic materials from chapters 3–12. This previous contextual backdrop is what I suggest the parables illustrate and exhort.

Jesus' public ministry critically changes in Matthew 13 through his use of parables as he confronts the opposition of Israel. The parables hide Jesus and his μετάνοια message as judgment in order that the rejecters will no longer be able to turn to him (ἐπιστρέφω, a synonym of μετανοέω) (13:16), but they figuratively describe and exhort μετάνοια, especially for those who have the interpretation of the parables. (13:16). This shows the significance of μετάνοια in Matthew 13.

---

19. France, *Matthew*, 499–500; Allison, "Matthew," 1203–21. Davies and Allison also state that this separation is a sort of theodicy. Davies and Allison, *Matthew 8–18*, 375, 402–3; Pennington, "Matthew 13," 12–20.

20. See Turner, *Matthew*, 334. Snodgrass, *Stories with Intent*, 145, 169–71.

Matthew 11–12: Rejection of μετάνοια
and Recalling of μετάνοια

As noted above, commentators emphasize Matthew 11 and 12 as the parables near context. While they focus on the mixed reception of Jesus, the actual wording of Matthew 11 and 12 focuses on Israel's rejection of μετάνοια(11:20, 21; 12:41). While Matthew 11 and 12 report many encounters between Jesus and Israel, these stories are summarized at the end of each chapter in terms of Israel's rejection of μετάνοια (11:20, 21; 12:41) in contrast with the μετάνοια of the gentiles (11:20-24; 12:40-42). The near context of Matthew 13 reports not only the mixed reception of Jesus but also the mixed reception of Jesus' and the disciples' μετάνοια call (11:20-22; 12:41). Also, these two chapters end with Jesus' recalling μετάνοια both directly (11:28-30) and indirectly by comparing not μετάνοια Israel and μετάνοια gentile and proclaiming judgment (11:20-24; 12:17-21, 33-37, 41-45, 46-50).

In this sense, Matthew 11 and 12 follow the book of Matthew's emphasis on the theme of μετάνοια (as this book has argued from previous chapters) as they keep demonstrating μετάνοια as their own significant theme. This μετάνοια-focused story line from Matthew 3-12 is illustrated by the eight parables in Matthew 13. The eight parables, therefore, explain the present progress of μετάνοια commandment and ministry and renews Jesus' exhortation of μετάνοια through the eight parables. Jesus teaches in parables to lead people to turn (μετανοέω) to God, just like the OT prophets did (cf. 13:57). Jesus interprets the parables to his followers, with the result that he renews the exhortation of μετάνοια only to his disciples.

In detail, the overall contents of Matthew 11 and 12 are as follows. Matthew 11 reports Israel's rejection of μετάνοια (11:1-19). Jesus rebukes Israel for their lack of μετάνοια in contrast with the μετάνοια of the gentiles (11:20-24). Jesus proclaims consequent judgment (11:22-24). Specifically, in Matthew 11 the appearance of John the Baptist specifically reminds the readers of the μετάνοια ministry of John and Jesus. John's disciples ask if Jesus is the one to whom John exhorted people to turn (μετανοέω). Jesus answers that he is the one to whom people need to turn (μετανοέω). Then it reports the reactions of people after hearing the μετάνοια message proclaimed by Jesus and the twelve apostles. While it includes some positive reaction it mainly shows the lack of μετάνοια among the people of Israel. Matthew 11:18-19 shows that both John and Jesus' message of μετάνοια is denied. Matthew 11:20 uses the term μετάνοια as Jesus reports the lack of μετάνοια in many cities and curses them, contrasting them with the gentile cities Tyre and Sidon that might turn (μετανοέω) if the same miracles had been performed in them as in Israel (11:20-24). Verses 11:25-27 explain this rejection of μετάνοια as a theodicy judgment.

Finally, Jesus conceptually calls people to turn (μετανοέω) again, saying to come to him (11:28-30). This is another conceptual μετάνοια expression and calling that echoes 4:17's μετάνοια commandment. Matthew uses Jesus' calling language, but its meaning expresses μετάνοια (4:17-23). It is natural to read 11:28-30 as another μετάνοια calling because it immediately follows Jesus' rebuke of cities for their lack of μετάνοια cities and his judgment on them in 11:20-27. Jesus rebukes cities that do not μετανοέω, then calls for μετάνοια again inviting others to come to him with persuasive words. However, the μετάνοια calling at this time is limited to those who labor and are heavy laden. This theodicy regarding the un-μετάνοια of Israel contrasts with the gentile μετάνοια, and together with the new μετάνοια calling of Matthew 11, demonstrates that the theme of μετάνοια in Jesus' teaching and miracle ministry continues. Then, through the parables, such as fruitful and fruitless soil, the weed and the wheat, and so on, Matthew 13 describes this contrast between the un-μετάνοια of Israel and the μετάνοια of the gentiles and the continued μετάνοια calling.

Matthew 12 also continues narrating the thematic significance of μετάνοια by reporting the opposition to Israel (12:1-45). The main story line of Matthew 12 is twofold: the opposition of Israel and Jesus' rebuke of Israel for their un-μετάνοια using language that parallels John the Baptist's μετάνοια preaching (3:2-12; 12:33-37). Jesus rebukes Israel for their refusal of μετάνοια, and proclaims consequent judgment (12:33-42). Matthew 11 focuses on Israel's rejection of μετάνοια and of Jesus, and Matthew 12 begins to report the opposition of Israel against Jesus such that they now want to kill him (12:14). This opposition further indicates the un-μετάνοια status of Israel.

This opposition begins with the dispute about the Sabbath between Jesus and the Pharisees (12:1-14) and the dispute about Beelzebul (12:22-32). Jesus' rebuke of the un-μετάνοια Pharisees in Matthew 12:33-45 parallels John the Baptist's μετάνοια preaching (3:2-12): "a good tree is known only by good fruit" (12:33, 35), "brood of vipers" (12:34), and "righteous" (12:37). This good tree-good fruit metaphor for μετάνοια in 12:33-35 is fully developed in the parables, through the image of good soil that bears fruit 100-, 60-, and 30-fold (13). Because of their bad fruit, Jesus denies that the Pharisees are the people of God, and he condemns Israel as "wicked generation" (12:45).

Matthew12 also contrasts the coming of μετάνοια among the gentiles (12:17-21, 38-42). The highlight of Matthew 12 is Jesus' rebuke of Israel for their lack of μετάνοια at his preaching, which is greater than Jonah's, in contrast to the μετάνοια of the people of Nineveh at Jonah's preaching (12:41). This rebuke is followed by a reproach for not listening to Jesus, who is greater than Solomon, in contrast with the Queen of the South who did listen to King Solomon.

Finally, 12:46–50 defines Jesus' family as the doers of the will of God (12:50). This phrase is another conceptual definition of μετάνοια (12:46–50) that parallels the summary exhortation of μετάνοια in the sermon (7:21). Jesus redefines the true people of God as those who turn (μετανοέω) to Jesus and do the will of Father in heaven using family language. Bearing fruits worthy of μετάνοια in 3:8 reappears in 12:33, and the idea is also rephrased as doing the will of the Father in heaven in 12:50. Overall, Matthew 12 explains μετάνοια ministry and reports Israel's opposition to turning (μετάνοια), in contrast with the μετάνοια of the gentiles, and rebukes them by repeating imagery from John the Baptist's μετάνοια preaching.

Aside from the above, the parables in Matthew 13 illustrate Matthew 12 by using the same themes, images and language. For example, "the good tree-good fruit" saying of Jesus in 12:33–35 exhorts people to do good deeds and is fully developed in the parables of Matthew 13, such as in the image of bearing good fruit (13)—indicating that the only criteria for the people of God is not ethical or hypocritical law keeping but μετάνοια to Jesus and bearing good fruit of μετάνοια according to Jesus' reinterpretation of the law, the sermon, which contains the contents of μετάνοια. Also, the turning (μετάνοια) of the people of Nineveh and the Queen of the South (12:41–42) is illustrated in the parables of fruitful good soil, wheat, and so on (13:8, 23, 30). Specifically, in 12:28, "the kingdom of heaven come upon you" parallels the secret of the kingdom of heaven (13:11) and the treasure and the pearl, which indicate the kingdom of heaven, found in front of the landlord and merchant (13:44–46). Also, these two images affirm 4:17b, "the kingdom of heaven is near," as being accomplished and found in Jesus. Also, the parables related to judgment in Matthew 13 illustrate the judgment language of the coming of the kingdom of heaven in Matthew 12 (12:31–32, 34–37, 41–45). In conclusion, the μετάνοια context of the previous chapter of Matthew 13 shows the commandment of turning (μετανοέω) and the mixed reception of μετάνοια are the main illustrations of the parables in Matthew 13.

Universal μετάνοια Theme in Matthew 11 and 12

While Matthew 11 and 12 report Israel's refusal of μετάνοια, they show a universal μετάνοια, that is the μετάνοια of the gentiles. Matthew 11:20–24 alludes to gentile μετάνοια, and 12:39–42 tells stories of faithful gentiles, praising them because of their good fruit—Jonah and the μετάνοια of the people of Nineveh,[21] and the coming of the Queen of the South (12:39–42). Also, through another Isaiah citation in 12:17–21 Matthew identifies Jesus as the light of the gentiles. Jesus proclaims that wicked Israel is not the people of God, but the gentiles, who through μετάνοια do the will of the Father, are instead God's true people. This comparison of the two groups of people implicitly exhorts μετάνοια to do the will of the Father in heaven. This comparison and exhortation are the main purpose of the parables and this universal μετάνοια context continues in Matthew 13. The parables illustrate the theme of gentile inclusion through marking the identity of the people of God only by their μετάνοια and good deeds of μετάνοια, thus rebuking the hypocritical law-keeping ethnic Jews.

μετάνοια Thematic Parallelism Among Matthew 3, the sermon, and Matthew 13

Matthew 13 uses the same and similar μετάνοια language and images as found in Matthew 3 and the sermon. All three discourse blocks include the term μετάνοια, synonyms, conceptual μετάνοια phrases, μετάνοια images, judgment metaphors corresponding to μετάνοια, and so on. This parallelism between Matthew 3, the sermon, and Matthew 13 suggests that the parables illustrate Jesus' theme of μετάνοια and demonstrates the significance of the theme of μετάνοια in Matthew 13.

Parallelism Between John the Baptist's μετάνοια Preaching (Matt 3) and Matthew 13

As chapter 4 argues, Matthew 3 introduces the significance of this theme of μετάνοια in the entire book through John's opening μετάνοια preaching and the parallels between the prophet John the Baptist and the prophet-like Messiah Jesus Christ.[22] While Matthew develops Jesus' birth narrative and identity in chapter 1 and 2,[23] in chapter 3, he moves to his emphasis

---

21. Jesus is like the prophet Jonah, who was raised from the dark and preached repentance in the gentile world. Jonah in Matthew indicates Jesus' ministry to the gentiles.

22. For more discussion on the parallelism between John the Baptist and Jesus in the Gospel of Matthew, see ch. 4.

23. These two chapters also include Matthew's emphasis on good deeds and gentile inclusion; Abraham, the four women, and Mary in the genealogy; Joseph the righteous; and the magi from the east.

of μετάνοια and the good fruits of μετάνοια through the prophet John the Baptist's exhortation. This discourse block shows that the Gospel of Matthew emphasizes the good works or righteous deeds of μετάνοια from 3:2 on.[24] This first discourse block about John the Baptist thus alludes to a clear driving theme of Matthew—the exhortation of μετάνοια.

The main ideas of Matthew 4 discussed in chapter 4 are as follows. First, the imperative μετανοεῖτε in 3:2 asks people to turn or change their whole being and life through the actions of μετάνοια. This μετάνοια exhortation governs John's preaching block as the major theme. Second, this μετάνοια imperative is further developed with the exhortation to bear fruit worthy of μετάνοια, ποιήσατε οὖν καρπὸν ἄξιον τῆς μετανοίας (3:8). Third, this exhortation and fruit-bearing image are enforced by judgment language: ἤγγικεν γὰρ ἡ βασιλεία τῶν οὐρανῶν (3:2b); images of the axe and the fire (3:10); gathering wheat into the barn (3:12). Finally, Matthew relates this exhortation of μετάνοια and the good deeds of μετάνοια to the language of the new identity of the sons of Abraham, through whom Matthew shows his critical interest in gentile inclusion (3:9), or in other words, universal μετάνοια.

This exhortation of μετάνοια (3:2; 4:17) finds parallels in Matthew 13. This parallelism is accompanied by μετάνοια fruit (3:8), enforced by judgment metaphors (3:10), and marks the true people of God that includes gentiles (3:9). The parables in Matthew 13 are full of similar language that illustrates μετάνοια. The phrase "bearing fruit of μετάνοια" (3:8, 10), which consists of "bearing" (ποιέω) and "fruit" (καρπός), keeps appearing in Matthew 13 and illustrates the theme and exhortation of μετάνοια. The fruit (καρπός) images occur in Matthew 13:8, 23, 26, and 41 and the verb ποιέω ("bearing") illustrates the theme of μετάνοια, meaning to do what Jesus has commanded, rejecting lawlessness. Also, the parables in Matthew 13 use metaphors of judgment and vindication parallel to those in Matthew 3 in 13:30, 40, 42, 48, 50, together with a fruit-bearing image to illustrate the theme of μετάνοια and to enforce the exhortation of μετάνοια. In particular, 13:30 shows the μετάνοια parallelism between Matthew 3 and 13 and demonstrates the exhortation of μετάνοια in Matthew 13.

---

24. Morris, *Gospel according to Matthew*, 83. Morris points out Matthew's emphasis on good deeds and the importance of 3:2 and 4:17b for a leading idea of the Gospel of Matthew and its relationship to the grace of God in Matthew: "Such preaching (4:17b) is a clarion call to action, not a recipe for slothful complacency. We should not overlook that importance of this call to repentance at the very beginning of Jesus' ministry; everything else follows from that. Matthew has often been seen as one who stresses the importance of good works, and of course he does. But this must not be held in such a form that his emphasis on grace is missed."

In conclusion, this parallelism between Matthew 3 and 13 points to the significance of the exhortation of μετάνοια and of the fruit of μετάνοια in the parables in Matthew 13. The parables in Matthew 13 illustrate Jesus' ministry and exhortation of μετάνοια.

Parallelism Between Matthew 4:17, the sermon, and Matthew 13

As previously discussed, in the Gospel of Matthew, Jesus takes over John's ministry. The opening words of Jesus in his public ministry (4:17) is exactly the same as that of John the Baptist (3:2). While John the Baptist's small exhortation preaching block (3:2–12) parallels Jesus' Sermon on the Mount (4:17—8:1), more than likely most of the material of the sermon expands John's preaching unit. Here I will show that Matthew 3, 4:17, and the sermon all cohere in their theme and materials with the parabolic discourse block of 12:46–13:58, and the central parabolic discourse block continues and illustrates this theme of μετάνοια. This coherence indicates that the parables have a prophetic exhortation force of μετάνοια as do the sermon and John's preaching block. In short, the third discourse block uses the descriptive manner of the parables to illustrate the opening imperative of Jesus' public ministry (4:17), the contents of the sermon (4:17—8:1), and its mixed reception (11–12).

These different sections include many parallels in terms of language, images, and concepts of μετάνοια showing its significance in the parables. First, Matthew 3, the sermon and the parables share in their parallel materials and images of μετάνοια, especially the fruit-bearing images and consequent judgment concept (3:8, 10; 7:16–20; 12:33; 13:8, 26). Hagner states that the abundant fruit in the parable of the sower is probably the conduct exhorted in the sermon; thus this parable not only includes "the problem of unbelief (cf. 13:10–15), but also a strong element of ethical exhortation."[25] Specifically, the righteousness language is repeated to exhort the good deeds of μετάνοια in both the sermon and Matthew 13 (5:20, 45, 6:1, 33 and 13:43, 49).[26] Also, "wheat and chaff" appears in 3:12 and 13:29–30. The judgment

---

25. Hagner, "Matthew's Parables of the Kingdom," 107–8.

26. Also, righteousness creates an inclusio between 5:20 and 5:45, and 6:1 and 6:33 in the sermon. Matthew 5:20–45 is the so-called antithesis that exhorts the followers of Jesus to do good deeds. Ch. 6 is all about doing good in secret, so doing righteousness in secret, and having faith in God only and not in money. The righteousness language in 3:15 (the first occurrence) may be related to this theme. Jesus being baptized means his death and doing the will of Father in heaven. This idea in relation to Immanuel shows the grace of God in the Gospel of Matthew. Also, it creates another inclusio

concept and language in the parables parallel the sermon and John the Baptist's discourse in chapter 3, referencing punishment with fire (3:10, 11, 12, 5:22; 7:19; 13:40, 42, 50).

Second, the heading of the eight parables in 12:45–50 repeats a conceptual expression of the fruit worthy of μετάνοια, "do the will of the Father in heaven," which also summarizes the sermon in 7:21, thus showing the coherence of the theme of μετάνοια from Matthew 3 to Matthew 13. Both the heading of the parables (12:50) and the summary of the sermon (7:21) conceptually express and echo the exhortation of μετάνοια and its fruit in 3:2, 8 and 4:17. This repeated phrase indicates the interconnectedness and the same μετάνοια exhortation force of those two discourse blocks. In fact, 3:2; 4:17, 7:21, 12:50 all share the same ideas: turning to God, judgment (vindication and punishment), and the kingdom of heaven. These three elements occur in all the parables of Matthew 13. Matthew 3:2; 4:17, 7:21, 12:50 fits well with the overall idea of Matthew 13, as will be discussed later. The concept in the same opening phrase of Matthew 3, the sermon, and the parables (3:2, 4:17, 12:50) governs all three discourse blocks and indicates their interconnectedness with μετάνοια.[27] In other words, Matthew 13 commands μετάνοια through the parables in order for Jesus' disciples to do the will of the Father as expressed in full in the contents of the sermon.

Moreover, the sermon's climatic messages in 7:21 and 24, "doers of the will of Father in heaven," "Everyone then who hears these words of mine and does them," are repeated in 12:50, which is the heading and focal message of the parable in Matthew 13. This repetition in 7:21, 24, 12:50 perfectly connects the sermon to the parables in Matthew 13. In addition, this repetition connects the climatic parable of the builder of the house (7:24–27), which begins with 7:21, 24, and the parables in Matthew13, which begins with the same phrase in 12:50. This connection shows that Matthew 13 is an extension of the sermon and of Jesus' first imperative, μετανοεῖτε (to turn one's whole life to God to do the will of God).

---

with the ideas of Jesus' death and of the Holy Spirit between ch. 3 and Jesus' death and resurrection narrative in chs. 27–28. Also, the statement in 21:32 that John came "in the way of righteousness" indicates John's way of life, including his good deeds and his whole life-giving ministry.

27. "The will of the Father" is even found in the fourth discourse block (18:14). It seems like "the will of the Father" is very important in the Gospel of Matthew (6:10, 7:21, 12:50, 18:14; 21:31; 26:42). In fact, in Matthew, Jesus is depicted as the one who does the will of God through his death. Jesus' sacrificial death is also illustrated with the images of the parables in ch. 13: the mustard seed, the leaven, the treasure buyer, and the merchant of the pearl. Jesus also teaches his disciples to do the same as he did on the cross (10:38–39; 11:29–30; 16:24–27).

Third, not only the openings of the two blocks but also some structural settings of the sermon and the parables connect them. The locations of "mountain" (5–7) and "sea" (13) interestingly connect the two discourse blocks. Matthew 13 follows the theme of gentile inclusion from chapter 12, especially through Matthew's Isaiah citation of gentile inclusion in 12:17–21. The sermon also follows Matthew's Isaiah citation of gentile inclusion in 4:12–16. Interestingly, both narrative sections follow John the Baptist (3:1–12; 11:1–15) and μετανοέω and μετάνοια (4:17; 11:20; 12:41).

In conclusion, the μετάνοια contexts and parallelism of the parables in Matthew 13 suggest that the parables illustrate Jesus' commandments of μετάνοια in 3:2; 4:17 and 7:21 and the mixed reception of μετάνοια. Jesus' parables illustrate this exhortation with abundant fruit-bearing soil, self-sacrificing mustard seed and leaven, a landowner and a merchant who sell everything they have, and judgment metaphors of the wheat and weeds and good fish and bad fish in the same net. These visual images of the parables mark the identity of the true people of God, which includes gentiles. They are titled the mother, sister, and brother of Jesus in 12:50 and 13:55–56. The parables are about fulfillment of the family of God that includes both Jews and gentiles who have a fruitful identity of μετάνοια, that is, faith in Jesus and faithfulness to Jesus' commandments of μετάνοια and the sermon as its contents.

The Meanings of the Parables of Matthew 13: Explanation of Mixed Reception and Exhortation of μετάνοια

This section examines the meanings of the parables. It will try to show that the parables not only explain the mixed reception of Jesus and his μετάνοια calling but also exhort μετάνοια and its fruits/contents from Matthew 3 and the sermon. Before interpreting each parable, this section looks at two key points that demonstrate the thematic significance of μετάνοια in the parables and the μετάνοια exhortation of the parables. The two keys are the inclusio between 12:45–50 and 13:53–58 and two OT citations in Matthew 13.

The μετάνοια Conceptual Inclusio Between 12:46–50 and 13:53–58

As mentioned previously, Matthew 12:45–50 is the heading of the eight parables and demonstrates the exhortation of μετάνοια as a significant theme of 13. Matthew 12:45–50 repeats the summary of the sermon, a conceptual expression of μετάνοια, "do the will of the Father in heaven" (7:21).[28] This repetition indicates that the parables explain and exhort what has been commanded in the sermon as the contents/fruits of μετάνοια. Also, the scene where Jesus stretches out his hand toward his disciples and designates them as his family who are the doers of the will of the Father in heaven(12:49) indicates that the essence of μετάνοια and its worthy fruit of the disciples' μετάνοια are doing the will of the Father in heaven. The disciples represent μετάνοια because they have left everything behind and turned to follow Jesus in 4:17-23. In other words, this scene shows that doing the will of Father in heaven refers to and conceptually expresses μετάνοια and its worthy fruit. This scene also shows that the family of Jesus consists of those who follow Jesus through μετάνοια by keeping the will of Father in heaven. This reference to μετάνοια in the heading of Matthew 13, pointing to the μετάνοια of the disciples, shows that the eight parables exhort μετάνοια by showing what μετάνοια looks like, namely doing the will of the Father in heaven and thus taking on the identity of the family of Jesus.[29]

In addition, 12:46-50 and 13:53-58 sandwich the parables in Matthew 13.[30] This inclusio hints at μετάνοια as an important argument of the parables,[31] just as 4:17-25 and 7:31-8:2 create an inclusio that frames the sermon and hints at the significance of μετάνοια.[32] Both places refer

---

28. For more discussion of this phrase as a conceptual expression of μετάνοια, see chs. 5 and 6.

29. Luz, *Matthew 8-20*, 225 notes this phrase indicates the church.

30. Lohr, "Oral Techniques." Lohr argues that the inclusio is a technique of oral communication that limits a discourse block. He finds an inclusio between 12:46-50 and 13:53-58 but does not expand the inclusio into the main argument of the eight parables.

31. Also, the Markan parallel hints that the parables are about the family of Jesus. Mark 3:31-35 deals with the same story as Matthew 12:46-50, and 4:1 begins with Καὶ πάλιν ἤρξατο, which appears several times as a connecting phrase of the stories and their themes in the gospel of Mark.

32. This inclusio is further supported by other teaching blocks that all have inclusios that hint at their main arguments. For example, ch. 10 is located right after Jesus' words about the workers of the harvest (οἱ δὲ ἐργάται ὀλίγοι). Matt 9:35-38 and 11:1 create an inclusio hinting at the main argument of chapter 10, that is, the harvest laborers and their form of life. The Sermon on the Mount (5-7) and ch. 18 are also so. The beginning of the teaching blocks especially provides the main arguments of the blocks: 5-7, following Jesus leads to a different life; 10, the work of the laborer in the time of harvest; 13, doing the will of God; 18, not to give offense but to forgive one's brothers. Matt 17:24-27 and 18 share the same language: 17:27, μὴ σκανδαλίσωμεν; 18:6, 7, 8, σκανδαλίσῃ; 18:15-35, forgiving one's brother (σκανδαλίσῃ and ἐκέρδησας in 15 appear to have synonym usage, so the same theme follows after 17:27). Also, the same wording—"the will of my Father who is in heaven" in 18:14 and "my heavenly Father" in 18:35—indicates that the two story blocks in ch. 18 (1-14 and 15-35) have the same

to "mother" (12:46, 47, 48, 49, 50; 13:55), "brother" (12:46, 47, 48, 49, 50; 13:55), and "sister" (12:50; 13:56) and similarly to the familiar but unbelieving people in Jesus' hometown. In 12:46–50 and 13:53–58 Jesus denies his blood relatives but defines his family as including only the doers of the will of the Father in heaven (12:50). He does so in two ways: 12:46–50 limits the true people of God to the doers of the will of the Father in heaven; 13:54–58 widens the true family of God to include gentiles through denying Jesus' hometown and Israel as the true people of God.[33] Also, 13:59 at the end of the parables posits Jesus as a prophet (13:59), and this indicates that the parables are a prophetic exhortation of μετάνοια, similar to Nathan's in 2 Samuel 12.[34]

This inclusio alludes to the significance of μετάνοια of all the parables of Matthew 13 as one unit, pointing to the identity of the family of Jesus, namely, those who do the will of the Father in heaven. Specifically, the statement that conceptual expression of μετάνοια, "whoever does the will of the Father in heaven is my brother and sister and mother," clarifies that the true family of Jesus is neither physical family members nor ethnic Israelites from his hometown but only those who do the will of the Father in heaven. Consistently, the parables emphasize μετάνοια and the fruit of μετάνοια, that is, the deeds according to the will of the Father in heaven, as the new identity of the true people of God that now includes gentiles.

At the same time, both 12:46–50 and 13:53–58 include a judgment and reward theme related to μετάνοια as do the parables. Jesus denies his blood relatives and hometown relationships but fills his family only with disciples who in μετάνοια do the deeds according to the will of Father in heaven. This inclusion is a judgment on fruitless Israel. The fact that Jesus does not perform many mighty works in his hometown (13:58) is another form of judgment so that they will not μετανοέω and be saved. The reward of μετάνοια and the good deeds of μετάνοια are also found in that the doers of the will of the Father in heaven are saved or are called the family of Jesus. This judgment and reward are found within the significant

---

theme, that is, doing the will of the Father in heaven.

33. Family imagery actually creates a perfect analogy of God's election of his people based on grace alone, since no one becomes a family member from one's own wishes or out of one's own authority but only by God. Only by God is his family created.

34. Snodgrass distinguishes the parable of Nathan in 2 Sam 12 as a juridicial parable, which can "elicit a self-condemnation from the hearer through the aid of image" (Snodgrass, *Stories with Intent*, 13). However, he does not distinguish the eight parables as juridicial parables because the eight parables of Jesus in Matt 13 have more "self-condemnation" through negative images exhorting good deeds.

argument of the parables through the weeds thrown into the fiery furnace and the bad fish thrown away.

The Significance of μετάνοια in Isaiah 6:10 and Psalm 78:2

The theme of μετάνοια of Matthew 13 is demonstrated in two OT citations. They also explain the near context of Matthew 11 and 12. Beginning in chapter 11, Jesus' confrontation with the rejecters of μετάνοια changes his ministry style, so that in Matthew 13 Jesus begins to teach in parables to hide his message, excluding the rejecters from his teaching ministry.[35]

Isaiah 6:10. The Isaiah 6:10 citation in Matthew 13:15 demonstrates that the theme of μετάνοια continues in Matthew 13. Matthew 13:15 explains this situation in which Jesus teaches in parables so that the rejecters of μετάνοια will not understand his teaching and turn (ἐπιστρέφω, synonym of μετανοέω) to him. Isaiah 6:10 explains this situation as judgment of Israel: Jesus hides his message of the secret of the kingdom of heaven(3:11) through the parables in such a way that they cannot understand and cannot turn (ἐπιστρέφω) to God.[36] Specifically, the Greek term ἐπιστρέφω used in Isaiah 6:10, which is the synonym of μετανοέω and a counterpart of μετανοέω in the LXX,[37] shows that the parables illustrate but hide the

---

35. This judgmental parabolic teaching reflects the Mosaic typology of Exod 34. Moses hides his face with a veil so that the people of Israel might not see the glory, and Jesus hides the secret of the kingdom of heaven from the rejecters through parables. Second Corinthians 3 also uses this same typological idea. Specifically, Moses' veiling himself after giving the law parallels Jesus' parabolic teaching after giving the sermon, the new law.

36. Matt 13 makes clear that the parables are judgment. First, Jesus' saying in 13:11, "To you it has been given to know the secrets of the kingdom of heaven, but to them it has not been given," means that Jesus judges those hearers as not having the truth. Then, 13:12, "but from the one who has not, even what he has will be taken away," clarifies the parables' judgment motif. Also, 13:13, "This is why I speak to them in parables, because seeing they do not see, and hearing they do not hear, nor do they understand," confirms the reason for their judgment in parabolic teaching, that is, their wicked heart that does not hear or see. Second, the Isaiah citation in 13:14–15 confirms that Jesus meant to teach in parables so that the hearers will not understand and will not return to God. This is a clear judgment motif. "The one who has, more will be given, and he will have an abundance" (13:12) might mean that it is the insiders who have Jesus and also the words of Jesus, and so have an abundance of Jesus and his words. In contrast, "but from the one who has not, even what he has will be taken away" (13:12) indicates wicked Israel, because they do not have Jesus and their privilege of having the law will be taken away.

37. Isa 6:10 uses ἐπιστρέφω, "return," instead of μετανοέω, "return," but the words are used with same meaning and both are counterparts of the Hebrew term *šub* in the

message of μετάνοια within them, so that the rejectors of μετάνοια cannot hear the secret of the kingdom of heaven and Jesus' μετάνοια message and turn (ἐπιστρέφω/μετανοέω) to Jesus and be saved. This phrase shows that the parables illustrate and hide the call of μετάνοια, so that they cannot turn to the kingdom of heaven and Jesus. As a matter of fact, Jesus' parables in Matthew 13 and their interpretation carry the same theme of μετάνοια from previous chapters, but only Jesus changes his teaching style to hide his message of μετάνοια.

Jesus only reveals the μετάνοια message in the parables by giving an interpretation for his followers (13:16–18).[38] Therefore, the parables still exhort to turn and to be healed for the people who hear Jesus' parables and his interpretations that they must bear good fruit of μετάνοια, the will of the Father in heaven, as a mark of his true followers. This point is the heart of Matthew 13. As Nathan exhorted David toward μετάνοια through his parable and its interpretation, Jesus exhorts his followers toward μετάνοια to God through his parables and their interpretations. The parables are judgment for the wicked, but at the same time the parables are a μετάνοια message in a different form from earlier in Matthew.

Psalm 78:2. Psalm 78:2 in Matthew 13:35 indicates that the parables aim for the people to turn and place their trust in God and keep the law. Psalm 78:7–8 as the larger unit of Psalm 78:2 discusses not only the things hidden since creation but also the turning (μετάνοια) of God's people: "Then they would put their trust in God and would not forget his deeds but would keep

---

OT. See also Konradt, *Israel, Church, and the Gentiles*, 250.

38. See also Konradt, *Israel, Church, and the Gentiles*, 250–64. Konradt argues the judgment through parables is not for the whole of Israel. Therefore, it is not the judgment of Israel which affects the salvation of gentiles. However, as noted above, Matt 11–12 clearly contrast that Israel (=crowd in Matt 13:10) rejects Jesus, especially the religious leaders, but gentiles turn (μετανοέω) to Jesus as the backdrop of the parables. The appearance of the followers of Jesus through turning (μετανοέω), including the disciples and gentiles, rather indicates the reconstitution of the new people of God through turning (μετανοέω) to Jesus Christ (16:18). The church replaces the old Israel, but the church includes the lost sheep of Israel (12:45–50) and gentiles (11–12). Also, judgment statements on the faithless Israel as a whole and the replacement of the people of God by all nations (8:12) and by those who do the will of Father (12:50) show the judgment status of Israel. Phrases like "lost sheep of Israel" in 10:6 and "sheep without a shepherd" in 9:36 also show the judgment status of Israel. Also, Jesus judges those rejecting Israel through the parables and gives the revelation of the secret of the kingdom of heaven for those who accept Jesus (13:11). However, this new people of God, the church (16:18), does not exclude the ethnic Israel if they believe in Jesus Christ and do the will of the Father in heaven (12:50; 28:18–20), but excludes the faithless, Jesus-rejecting people of Israel. For the contrast reading on Matt 8:12, see Konradt, *Israel, Church, and the Gentiles*, 202–8.

his commands. They would not be like their forefathers a stubborn and rebellious generation, whose hearts were not loyal to God, whose spirits were not faithful to him" (Ps 78:7, 8 niv). These verses demonstrate the theme of μετάνοια in the parables and reflect the way the parables aim to exhort μετάνοια. In addition, "the creation of the world" hints at the universal μετάνοια theme of the parables.

In conclusion, the μετάνοια idea of Isaiah 6:10 and the μετάνοια concepts of "trusting in God" and "keeping the commands of God" in Psalm 78:1–8 are fully revealed in the parables: the abundant fruit-bearing soil of doing the will of the Father, the self-dying mustard seed and self-sacrificing leaven for the benefit of many, selling everything a landowner and a merchant have for the kingdom of heaven, and bringing everything the master of the house has. Also, all the negative images in the parables, such as the fruitless soil, the weeds, or the bad fish, warn the disciples to consider whether they are like them or not and thus exhort μετάνοια. In addition, the judgment metaphors of the parables, especially in the second and seventh, strengthen those good deeds of μετάνοια.

μετάνοια in Each Parable

As noted previously, the main point of the parables in Matthew 13 depicts the wider narrative context, which includes the ministry and exhortation of μετάνοια and the mixed reception of μετάνοια. The heading exhortation of "doing the will of the Father in heaven" in 12:50 is an argument that expands on the first imperative of Jesus Christ, μετανοεῖτε·ἤγγικεν γὰρ ἡ βασιλεία τῶν οὐρανῶν (4:17). Each parable has this imperatival force enforced by judgment metaphors and emphasis on the fruits of μετάνοια,[39] together with an explanation of the present progress of the kingdom of heaven. This section will examine the meaning and the theme of μετάνοια in the parables in Matthew 13.

The following is my structure for the eight parables.

>   Heading (12:46–50) *the family of Jesus are the doers of the will of the Father, that is, μετάνοια*
>
>   **a** the sower (*interpretation*)
>
>   (*OT citation*)
>
>   **b** the wheat and the weeds (*interpretation*)
>
>   **c** the mustard seed
>
>   **d** the leaven

---

39. Donahue, *Gospel in Parable*, 90–91.

(*OT citation*)
d' the hidden treasure
c' the pearl of great value
b' the net (*interpretation*)
a' the old and new treasure

Ending (13:53–58) *the family of Jesus is not ethnic Israel, but* μετάνοια *disciples*

The parable of the sower. Despite Jesus' naming it "the parable of the sower" (13:18), the main message focuses not only on the sower,[40] but also the different actions of different groups of people, the four kinds of soils.[41] In fact, it is obvious that the sower illustrates Jesus' μετάνοια ministry and his teaching of μετάνοια in the sermon(4:17—8:1) and Matthew 10 and the four kinds of soils depict the mixed reception of Jesus and his μετάνοια message.[42]

First, sowing the seed indicates Jesus' calling of μετάνοια and the four kinds of soil illustrate reactions of people about Jesus' calling and teachings of μετάνοια and his μετάνοια calling reported in previous chapters of Matthew. They also exhort μετάνοια by contrasting the fruitless and fruitful soils. Snodgrass also sees that this parable exhorts the fruitful life of conversion (=μετάνοια).[43] The interpretation of the first three kind of soils explains

---

40. It must be noted that the formula of each parable that likens the kingdom of heaven through some figures does not always indicate that the main argument of the parables stays on that figure, but instead it may point to the deeds in the parables. For example, the first parable, titled the parable of the sower (13:18), is not about the sower, but the four kinds of soils, and thus their deeds of the will of the Father in heaven. Also, while the fifth and sixth parables carry the exact same meaning of the value of the kingdom of heaven and the actions of the two men are the same, one introduces the kingdom of heaven as a figure, "the kingdom of heaven is like a hidden treasure," (13:44) but the other introduces the kingdom of heaven as a man, "the kingdom of heaven is like a merchant" (13:45).

41. Davies and Allison, *Matthew 8–18*, 378. Snodgrass, *Stories with Intent*, 169. Luz notes that the four kinds of soils reflect the situation of the entire church and their life and to see them self-critically (Luz, *Matthew 8–20*, 250).

42. See the first section of this chapter where I discuss this parable's main argument with Davies and Allison's view.

43. Snodgrass, *Stories with Intent*, 176. He also sees this parable as an exhortation of fruitful life of conversion (μετάνοια) citing Craig Keener. He says that the conversion (=repentance) is only confirmed by true fruitful discipleship and that "the parable emphasizes both receptivity and bearing fruit. . . . Receiving the kingdom with joy is not enough – a message the modern church desperately needs to hear" (176). Davies and Allison argue that the explanation of mixed reception is the main theme of the parable (Davies and Allison, *Matthew 8–18*, 402–3).

the rejection of μετάνοια reported in Matthew 11-12. They do not turn to Jesus because they do not endure suffering and persecution (Matt 5:10-12; 10:16-28, 36, 39) and care about the world or worry about riches (Matt 6:19-34; 10:29-31). These negative reactions contrast and exhort positive reaction of μετάνοια and its worthy fruit. The fourth soil illustrates and exhorts the positive reception of Jesus and his μετάνοια message also reported in Matthew 8-9 and 11-12. Also, the image of fruit bearing 100-, 60-, and 30-fold illustrate fruit worthy of μετάνοια as exhorted in Matthew 3, the sermon, and Matthew 10.[44]

Second, the μακάριος language in 13:16 right before Jesus' interpretation of the parable of the sower shows that the parable of the sower connects with the idea of μακάριος in the sermon. The disciples are μακάριος because they hear and see Jesus and his μετάνοια calling and react positively by turning (μετάνοια) to follow him (4:17-23).[45] Jesus' designation of his disciples as μακάριος in 13:16 notes that the μετάνοια disciples are the μακάριος who have the kingdom of heaven and suffer for righteousness as the sermon teaches (5:3-12). Thus, the parable of the sower illustrates the mixed reception of μετάνοια and the exhortation of μετάνοια to have a fruitful life of μετάνοια in suffering, of "the evil one," "trouble or persecution," and "the worries of this life and the deceitfulness of wealth" (v. 19-22).[46]

The parable of the weeds. The second parable, typically known as an explanation of the "delayed Parousia,"[47] enforces the first parable through "en-

44. The parable in 22:1-14 coheres to this parable in Matt 13. "But when the king came in to look at the guests, he saw there a man who had no wedding garment" (21:11). "For many are called, but few are chosen" (22:14). Those many who were called are Jesus' followers, and those few who were chosen are Jesus' true believers who prove their identity by bearing good fruit, that is, good deeds. The garment refers to the good works of true believers. First of all, the whole Gospel of Matthew commands and emphasizes the fruit-bearing people of God and the judgment on those who are fruitless. Second, ch. 21 clearly reveals this interpretation. Third, Rev 19:8 shares the same garment image and its explanation. John explains that the garment of Jesus is the good works of the saints. As in Matt 22:1-14, these clothes appear as a visible boundary or identity marker; good fruits in ch. 13 visually reveal the identity or mark of the church.

45. Also, μακάριος in 13:16 connects back to the μακάριος language in 11:6, which corresponds to the parable of the sower by showing that μετάνοια disciples should not be offended by Jesus.

46. Craig Blomberg similarly states that this parable indicates, "the true believers' perseverance in faith." He states that this parable gives an important reminder from Jesus on his continued blessings on his disciples' work in a hostile situation (Blomberg, *Matthew*, 214-15).

47. Carson, *Matthew*, 363. See Luz, *Matthew 8-20*, 271-74, for the history of interpretation of this parable. We have to realize that this parable describes the previous context of Matt 1-12. The image of the weeds describes the mixed reception of Jesus'

couragement and warning."⁴⁸ The wheat and the weeds mainly illustrate the mixed reception of Jesus whether people do μετάνοια and bear fruit worthy of μετάνοια (cf. 3:12),⁴⁹ which are likened to the good, fruit-bearing wheat and to the weeds. The parable of the weeds strengthens the first parable, and so the ideas of μετάνοια and its worthy fruit, through the judgment images of the harvest: the wheat in Jesus' barn and the burning of the weeds in the fiery furnace. And the parable illustrates the delayed judgment of God corresponding to one's μετάνοια and worthy fruit of μετάνοια. The landowner says that he will gather the fruitless weed in the time of the harvest and burn them up. Thus this parable aims to explain and exhort people toward μετάνοια, meaning to turn to do the will of the Father in heaven.

In fact, the harvest image repeats John the Baptist's judgment saying about the harvest (Matt 3:12) that exhorts people to do μετάνοια and bear its worthy fruit (Matt 3:8-11). As the harvest image in Matthew 3:12 exhorts μετάνοια and its worthy fruit, the parable of the weeds with its harvest image further describes and exhorts μετάνοια and the fruit worthy of μετάνοια that the parable of the soils describes.

Also, Jesus' interpretation of the second parable using the language of righteousness (v. 43) has a clear connection to "suffering for righteousness" in 5:6, 10-12 in relation to the three suffering images of the first parable. In addition, the parable of the weeds illustrates Matthew 10 in that both use the harvest language (9:37-38 and 13:30, 39). The sower of good seed describes Jesus and his disciples' universal μετάνοια mission in the world from Matthew 10. The weed and the wheat describe the worthy and unworthy ones from Matthew 10:13-15, 37-38, where the worthy accepts the disciples and their μετάνοια message (10:6) with fruit worthy of μετάνοια, but the unworthy does not. The apostolic peace will stay with the worthy, which is illustrated in the wheat going into the barn, but the peace will not stay with the unworthy, which is illustrated in the weed burned with fire. Therefore, this parable of the weeds explains Jesus and his disciples' μετάνοια ministry, its mixed reception, and the delayed reward and judgment to exhort μετάνοια. The parable of the weeds and the parable of the soils as a pair explain the mixed reception of μετάνοια and exhort μετάνοια by proclaiming consequent delayed judgment.⁵⁰

μετάνοια ministry and their delayed judgment.

48. Hagner, "Matthew's Parables of the Kingdom," 113.

49. Davies and Allison, *Matthew 8–18*, 408.

50. See also Snodgrass, *Stories with Intent*, 174. Specifically, Matt 24 elaborates the final judgment theme in this parable. As this parable is in the central discourse, this parable depicts the later part of Matthew.

The parables of the mustard seed and the leaven in the flour. Scholars explain that the parable of the mustard seed and the parable of the leaven in the flour explain the small or humble presence of the kingdom of heaven and a great future.[51] Hagner who represents the typical understanding of the third and fourth parables notes that these two parables indicate the already–not yet presence of the kingdom of heaven, emphasizing its presence and its future success. Also, he notes the gentile inclusion image of the birds and the future growth and effect of the kingdom of heaven indicated by the yeast image.[52]

On the other hand, the self-sacrifice of the mustard seed to bear abundant fruits and the self-sacrificial active working of yeast to leaven bread illustrate a self-sacrificing, fruitful life for the benefit of many.[53] This concept basically coheres with the fruitful good soil and wheat images of μετάνοια in the first and second parables. As previous context noted in Matthew 10:38–39 and 11:28–30, the third and the fourth parables coherently explain the significance of μετάνοια and its worthy fruit to turn to follow Jesus with suffering and bearing one's own cross for others. The line in John 12:24, "unless a kernel of wheat falls to the ground and dies, it remains only a single seed. But if it dies, it produces many seeds" (niv), means exactly the same thing. Both places use κόκκος "grain." The interpretation of 12:24 in John 12:25, 26 hints at the meaning of the parables, namely suffering: "The man who loves his life will lose it, while the man who hates his life in this world will keep it for eternal life. Whoever serves me must follow me; and where I am, my servant also will be. My Father will honor the one who serves me" (niv). These verses match Matthew 10:38–39 and 11:28–30.

In conclusion, the main arguments are still about the good actions of μετάνοια according to the will of the Father in heaven as in the other parables. There are also different forms of the worthy fruit of μετάνοια in serving and humbling for the benefit of many. This theme of μετάνοια in humility and servanthood are elaborated in the latter part of Matthew, such as 16:21–28; 18:1–6; 19:13–15; 19:30; 20:16; 20:26–28; 23:11–12; 25:31–46. Specifically, Jesus as a model of fruitful life demonstrates these

---

51. Davies and Allison, *Matthew 8-18*, 415; Luz, *Matthew 8-20*, 263. However, it is not sure if this parable signifies the future greatness of the kingdom of heaven. This parable can describe the present great value of the hidden kingdom of heaven. The kingdom of heaven in the present time of Jesus appears as the smallest seed, but its present value or power is still great and life-giving. This explanation of the parable is just like Jesus who appears as a small and humble king, but his value or power is great and life-giving (cf. 11:1–6, 12, 25–30).

52. Hagner, "Matthew's Parables of the Kingdom," 113–16.

53. Snodgrass, *Stories with Intent*, 227–28, 235.

two parables of self-sacrificing fruitful life for the benefit of many in his own death on the cross. In short, the third and fourth parables describe exhort μετάνοια and the worthy fruit of μετάνοια in terms of serving and suffering for the benefit of many.

The parables of the hidden treasure and the pearl of great value. These parables refer to the hidden value of the kingdom of heaven and our lives toward Jesus and the kingdom of heaven.[54] Although Jesus likens the kingdom of heaven to the hidden treasure and the pearl of great value, the main message of these parables focuses on the actions of the landowner and the merchant who sell everything to buy the land and the pearl. This action also involves the suffering of selling everything they have. These two parables likely describe the four disciples in Matthew 4:17-22 who heard Jesus' μετάνοια calling and left everything behind and turned to follow Jesus. Thus, these two parables likely illustrate the nature of μετάνοια in meaning to turn oneself and one's life away from the past to Jesus. They explain and exhort μετάνοια in its meaning of turning one's life to Jesus, leaving everything behind to enter the kingdom of heaven.[55]

Specifically, these parables illustrate Jesus' exhortation of μετάνοια in 4:17 for the coming of the kingdom of heaven.[56] First, the nearness of the kingdom of heaven in 4:17b is perfectly illustrated by the images of the hidden treasure found close to a man and the pearl of great value found in front of a merchant. Second, the turning image in imperative μετανοεῖτε is perfectly described in the image of the man and the merchant selling all they have to buy the treasure and the pearl, which refers to turning one's whole being and life to Jesus by believing in him and following his commandments. As mentioned above, these two parables perfectly describe Jesus and the four disciples in Matthew 4:17-22. Jesus calls for μετάνοια and the four left everything behind and turned to follow Jesus.

---

54. Snodgrass, *Stories with Intent*, 247; Davies and Allison, *Matthew 8-18*, 435.

55. Hagner also agrees with the point that while these two metaphors of hidden treasure and the pearl indicate the worth-everything reality of the kingdom of heaven, the reactions of the finders of the two treasures indicate "a rigorous, self-denying and costly discipleship" (Hagner, "Matthew's Parables of the Kingdom," 116-18). While Hagner insists that the reactions of the two men are merely supportive details, I think they are the hot spot of the two parables based on the worth-everything reality of the kingdom of heaven. These reactions are encouraged by the following parable of the net.

56. See Luz, *Matthew 8-20*, 279-80. Luz shows the classical church interpretation of these two parables with the exhortation of selling of everything. This history of interpretation helps us to see the parable's exhortation of turning to the kingdom of heaven by selling everything what one has.

The parable of the net. The parable of the net illustrates the judgment imagery of good and bad fish. Good fish will be kept, and bad fish will be thrown away. From the previous parables, this judgment is likely corresponding to μετάνοια in its meaning of turning to do the will of God. Just like the parable of weeds, this parable enforces the exhortation or encouragement of μετάνοια similar to the earlier parables through delayed judgment.[57] Luz notes that this parable teaches "the future and the purchase price of the kingdom of God" with "a warning: Praxis will show where true church has existed."[58] Blomberg interestingly argues that "all kinds of fish" indicates all ethnic races, thus emphasizing "the universality of God's judgment of people."[59] "All kinds of fish" thus indicates Matthew's gentile inclusion theme, in other words, universal μετάνοια. Conclusively, this parable illustrates that every nation, every people, and every tribe who do μετάνοια and the good deeds of μετάνοια will enter the kingdom of heaven.

The parable of the old and new treasure. The last parable—of the old and the new treasure—describes the kingdom of heaven as a scribe who provides everything he has, both the old and the new out of his treasure. "The old and the new things" probably refer to the commandment of Jesus, specifically the sermon, the new teaching, which fulfills the OT.[60] Jesus through this parable commands his disciples to teach and keep his commandments, the sermon, the content of μετάνοια. In addition, this parable likely reflects one of the contents of μετάνοια, the higher righteousness of the disciples who are designated as scribes in the kingdom of heaven compared with the scribes of Israel (5:20). Thus, the reference to both the old and the new treasures of the disciples indicates the self-sacrificing μετάνοια righteous life of the Twelve, giving everything they have including heart and deed. In this sense, this parable coheres to the abundant fruit provided by the soil of the first parable. In these ways this parable illustrates and exhorts μετάνοια and its worthy fruit.

---

57. Snodgrass, *Stories with Intent*, 215, 492. Snodgrass says that the eschatological judgment nature differentiates this parable from the parable of the wheat and weed. Davies and Allison, *Matthew 8–18*, 440, sees the similarity between this parable and the parable of weeds.

58. Luz, *Matthew 8–20*, 284.

59. Blomberg, *Matthew*, 224.

60. Hagner, "New Things," 333–34, states that the new and the old treasures indicate the OT law and its fulfillment in Jesus, the gospel. He specifically includes the church and gentile inclusion in the new treasure. See, also Davies and Allison, *Matthew 8–18*, 447–48, for different options.

Finally, the appearance of the disciples in 13:51, which refers to the scribe of the kingdom of heaven since this parable is directly given to them (13:51),[61] parallels the appearance of the disciples in 12:49 where Jesus states that the twelve disciples are his family. Therefore, they create another inclusio of the eight parables. This inclusio indicates that the eight parables are about the μετάνοια life of Jesus' followers who turn to him and keep his teaching of the will of the Father in heaven (12:50).

Conclusion

This chapter discussed what the eight parables in Matthew 13 describe and what is their function in the narrative context of the Gospel of Matthew. As Snodgrass notes, the eight parables in Matthew 13 explain the presence of the kingdom of heaven, the mixed reception of Jesus, and delayed judgment.[62] In addition, as we discussed above, Matthew 13 as one unit describes what has happened to Jesus and his disciples from the beginning of their μετάνοια ministry (3:2; 4:17;10:7). Specifically, the parables focus on two things: Jesus and his disciples' exhortation/ministry of μετάνοια and its worthy fruits with judgment metaphors and the mixed reception of μετάνοια, namely the progression of the kingdom of heaven through μετάνοια.

The two OT citations in Matthew 13 explain the function of the parables. Isaiah 6:10 explains that Jesus hides what he has proclaimed in parables, so that the rejecters might not turn to God and be healed (13:14-16). Psalm 78:1-8 also explains that the parables aim for people to trust in God and keep his commands, that is μετάνοια.

In the wider context, the third discourse block (Matthew 13) renews the exhortation of John the Baptist's preaching (3:2-12) and Jesus' sermon (4:17—8:1) in parables. Parallel language also appears in the three blocks, such as references to fruit-bearing and judgment. John's preaching, the sermon, and the parables cohere in their μετάνοια themes. The heading of the parables (12:50) and the summary of the sermon (7:21) are exactly the same and conceptually express and exhort John's and Jesus' opening commandment

---

61. Carson, *Matthew*, 380-82. Carson argues that the scribe refers to the twelve disciples and their mission to teach.

62. Snodgrass, *Stories with Intent*, 174. Snodgrass summarizes Matt 13 as follows, "The kingdom involves a proclamation that must be received and lived out. The proclamation is an assertion about reality that is to be believed and allowed to have defining force. . . . the kingdom's coming does not now obliterate evil but one day will involve separation of the just and the unjust, that the kingdom appears discouragingly small and unseen but will have overwhelming impact, and that the kingdom is valuable beyond all else and incorporates both the new and what is good from the old."

of turning (μετανοέω) in 3:2 and 4:17. The eight parables visualize the true identity of the family of Jesus (12:48–50), that is, turning (μετάνοια) to Jesus and bearing the fruit worthy of μετάνοια revealed in Jesus' new teachings on the law and the prophets in the sermon. These functions of the parables demonstrate the thematic and even paradigmatic significance of μετάνοια in Matthew 13 and the exhortative force of the parables. Specifically, Matthew 13:57 indicates that the parables should be read in line with prophetic μετάνοια messages of John the Baptist and the OT prophets.

The 100-, 60-, and 30-fold fruit of the good soil, the mustard seed becoming a large tree, the leaven leavening three measures of flour, a man selling everything to buy the hidden treasure, a merchant selling everything to buy the pearl of the great value, and a master of a house bringing everything out of his treasure, both new and old describe Jesus and the disciples' turning (μετάνοια) commandment/ministry(3:2, 8; 4:17; 10:7) in its meaning of turning (or changing) one's being and whole life to Jesus and the kingdom of heaven while bearing fruit worthy of μετάνοια, that is, doing the will of the Father in heaven (7:21; 12:50). On the other hand, the three fruitless kinds of soils, the weed, and bad fish indicate the rejectors of Jesus and the disciples' turning (μετάνοια) exhortation/ministry.

Also, the wheat that goes into the barn, referring to the righteous shining like the sun in the kingdom of the Father, the weeds that are thrown into the fiery furnace, referring to the fruitless wicked weeping and gnashing their teeth, the good fish that go into a container, referring to the vindication of the righteous, and the bad fish that go into the fiery furnace, referring to the punishment of evil ones portray the idea of vindication and punishment corresponding to μετάνοια (cf. 3:2; 4:17; 7:21; 12:50).[63]

---

63. The parables' imagery of fruit-bearing, self-denial, and sacrifice exhort μετάνοια, meaning to do the will of the Father, namely suffer, which has its model in Jesus' life and death on the cross. Jesus fulfills what he teaches about μετάνοια through the eight parables. He prays, "The will of the Father who is in heaven be done on earth" (6:9–10), and "the Father's will be done through my suffering" (26:39, 42), and he dies on the cross. He is good, soil-bearing, abundant fruit, a mustard seed and leaven dying and suffering for the universe, the hidden treasure and pearl of great value only revealed for his people, and the model of the scribe of the kingdom of heaven giving everything he has for others. And now Jesus says to his hearers, "turn" (μετανοέω) yourself and your life to Jesus and embrace the life of μετάνοια that suffers and serves for the will of the Father in heaven.

Chapter 10

The Thematic Significance of μετάνοια in Matthew 18

The Community Discourse of μετάνοια through Humility and Servanthood

Introduction

THIS BOOK ARGUES THE thematic significance of μετάνοια in the Gospel of Matthew. μετάνοια means not only to change one's mind or to stop past sins and feel regret, but also to turn one's whole being and life toward Jesus Christ, following his teachings and life. The term μετάνοια does not occur many times, but its essence and contents echo in many corners of the Gospel of Matthew. The three previous chapters examined the first three major discourse blocks of Matthew: the Sermon on the Mount teaches the nature and the contents of μετάνοια and the fruit worthy of μετάνοια; the missionary discourse commissions the apostles to preach μετάνοια and teaches the life of μετάνοια; and the parables depict Jesus and the disciples' μετάνοια teaching and ministry, the mixed reception of μετάνοια, and figuratively exhorts μετάνοια, its fruits, and its consequent rewards and judgments.

This chapter focuses on the fourth discourse block of Matthew, Matthew 18, "the community discourse."[1] The overall arguments of this chapter are as follows. Matthew 18 begins with a commandment, "turn (στρέφω) and become like little children" (18:3–4). This commandment rephrases 4:17's μετάνοια commandment by using στρέφω, "to turn," a synonym for μετανοέω. The community discourse begins with this exhortation of μετάνοια and the life of μετάνοια in humility and servanthood and thus also suggests the thematic significance of μετάνοια in Matthew 18, echoing 4:17's commandment of μετάνοια. Little children serve as a perfect image of μετάνοια, turning the definition of the greatest to humility and

---

1. This title is from Luz, *Matthew 8–20*, 423.

servanthood in the kingdom (18:1-14). Jesus commands the protection of the little ones of μετάνοια (18:5-10). This command shows how important the little ones of μετάνοια are to God (18:11-14). Jesus also instructs the church in μετάνοια to lead the sinner back, to turn (μετανοέω) (18:15-20), and promises unlimited forgiveness for those who once sinned but turn (μετανοέω) again (18:21-35).

The following sections discuss a survey on the discourse, especially the theme of μετάνοια. Then I examine each unit of the discourse in relation to the opening focal commandment of turning, suggesting it as a significant theme of the discourse.

A Survey of Scholarship on Matthew 18 and Repentance (μετάνοια) in Matthew 18

Scholars generally identify Matthew 18 as "the community discourse," which includes the instituted church.[2] In particular, the opening of the discourse, Jesus' commandment to turn and become like little children (18:3), signifies humility as one unifying theme of the community discourse.[3] Don Garlington similarly says that one unifying theme of the community discourse is personal and social humility in the church.[4] Donald A. Hagner states, "Jesus reverses the perspective of the world by his statement of a fundamental paradox: greatness in the kingdom is a matter of humility, not power or position."[5] This image of little children designates the status of the disciples of Jesus, focusing on their servanthood.[6] The theme of humility, which appears

---

2. Thompson, *Matthew's Advice to a Divided Community*, 44. He notes that Matt 18 is proverbial wisdom literature to help Christian members who are struggling with the problem of internal strife and discord. Carter, *Matthew*, 148. See also Carter, "Resisting and Imitating the Empire," 260-72. Carter argues that the two imperial parables of Matthew (18:23-25; 22:1-14) criticize the kingdoms of the world (Herod) and contrast them to the kingdom of Jesus. Carter emphasizes the social virtues of humility, mutual consideration, and forgiveness as unifying themes of the discourse, which follows Jesus' death and resurrection.

3. Davies and Allison, *Matthew 8-18*, 753. For various interpretations of the meaning of the "little child," see Luz, *Matthew 8-20*, 427-29. Luz notes that ταπεινόω oneself like a child (Matt 18:4) primarily means to become "low" and "humble" and signifies Matthew's reversal of one's previous and secular standards about the values marking the greatest. Luz says that the visual aid of the "child" does not refer to "good and well-behaved children," but instead that the child here is synonymous with a "slave." See also Patte, "Jesus' Pronouncement," 3-42.

4. Garlington, "'Who is the Greatest?,'" 290.

5. Hagner, *Matthew 14-28*, 518.

6. France, *Matthew*, 264-65; Carson, *Matthew*, 451. Davies and Allison, *Matthew 8-18*, 754. While it is true that this image of the little child indicates believers, Matt 18:3

in the heading of the community discourse, becomes the governing idea for the following instructions to the church and about forgiveness, showing that church powers must be humble like little children.[7]

At the same time, in the study of μετάνοια, Matthew 18, especially 18:3, has been a hot spot. Matthew 18:3 commands to turn (στρέφω) and become like a child (18:3), echoing 4:17's μετάνοια commandment. Matthew 18:3 uses στρέφω, which is the synonym for μετανοέω. στρέφω also means to turn. στρέφω illustrates μετάνοια as turning to become like a child with emphasis on humility and servanthood. While studies on the Matthean μετάνοια theme have not earned much interest, almost all scholars who do examine it deal mainly with two passages: Matthew 4:17 and 18:1-14.[8] They emphasize the location of 4:17. The position of the commandment of turning (μετάνοια) ahead of Jesus' public ministry shows the importance of the theme of μετάνοια in Jesus' ministry throughout Matthew (Matt 3:2; 4:17; 10:7; also Mark 1:4, 15; 6:12). In addition, they mention 18:1-4 because a synonym of μετανοέω, στρέφω, occurs. Robert Nicholas Wilkin, whose study is mainly focused on the occurrences of the terms μετανοέω and μετάνοια in Matthew (3:2-15; 4:17; 12:41), widens his study to include conceptual repentance: (1) Matthew 9:13 and 11:20-21, where Jesus declares that he came to call sinners, not the righteous; (2) Matthew 18:1-4, where στρέφω occurs; and (3) 21:28-32, in which the parable of the two sons represents conceptual repentance.[9] Wilkin exegetes 18:1-4 as an additional example of Matthean repentance in that a person must realize one's smallness in front of God and so change one's attitude.[10] Mark Boda also extends his discussion of repentance to Matthew 18:1-4 and to carrying the yoke and dying to oneself (Matt 11:28-30; 16:24-25; 18:4).[11] In discussing Matthew 18:1-4, Joachim Jeremias says that turning and becoming like a child is the

---

shows that this image also designates the repentant people.

7. Ramshaw, "Power and Forgiveness in Matthew 18," 397-404. See also Carmody, "Matt 18:15-17," 141-58.

8. See Nave, "Repent," 87. See also Chamberlain, *Meaning of Repentance*; Carlston, "Metanoia and Church Discipline"; Wilkin, "Repentance as a Condition for Salvation"; Boda, '*Return to Me*'; Boda and Smith, *Repentance in Christian Theology*; Dupont, "Repentir et Conversion," 137-73; Michiels, "Conception Lucanienne de La Conversion," 42-78; Merklein, "Die Umkehrpredigt," 29-46; Bailey, "Repentance in Luke-Acts"; Nave, *Role and Function of Repentance*; Kintu, "Repentance in the Sermon on the Mount." See also, Croteau, "Repentance Found?," 97-123; Hägerland, "Jesus and the Rites of Repentance," 166-87.

9. Wilkin, "Repentance as a Condition for Salvation," 95-117.

10. I think rather that to be a child means to be the least in the world as a worthy fruit of turning.

11. Boda, '*Return to Me*,' 164-66.

heart of repentance.¹² Bruner notes that turning and becoming like a child in Matthew 18:3 is a call to turn (μετανοέω) (the repentance of conversion), which means "to be born again (John 3:3) and again and again." Bruner explains μετάνοια in Matthew is both once for all (Matt 3:2, 8, 11; 4:17; 11:20; 12:41, etc.), and "an event constantly repeated in the Christian's life (Matt 18:3)."¹³ Luz also emphasizes 18:3-4 for Matthew's metaphorical expression for conversion through lowliness.¹⁴ Luomanen also notes that στρέφω in Matthew 18:1-4 conveys the theme of μετάνοια in that 18:1-4 does not indicate initial μετάνοια but the μετάνοια of straying disciples, who are described as the lost sheep in the parable of wandering sheep (18:12-14).¹⁵ Jesus' commandment to turn and become like a child commands both initial and continuous μετάνοια. Community members need μετάνοια every day since they will sin again and again.

Garlington says "turning" (στρέφω) in Matthew 18:3 does not refer to conversion or to repentance because the disciples are already called and invited as insiders of Jesus (13:10-17; 16:15-18).¹⁶ However, the biblical meaning of μετάνοια (repentance or conversion) not only refers to a one-time event, but it also means a lifelong turning of one's whole being and life. Also, it is not necessary that Jesus calls his disciples to and teaches them about μετάνοια only once. Jesus actually calls his disciples to turn again and again (4:17; 11:20; 12:20; 13). The Matthean Jesus also keeps teaching μετάνοια using different terms and images. These repeated μετάνοια callings of Matthew 18:3 do not indicate that the disciples' initial μετάνοια was not genuine. The term στρέφω and little one image in 18:3 emphasize the positive aspect of μετάνοια through humility and servanthood. Matthew 18 also coheres with teaching about μετάνοια in other parts of Matthew, where it not only means a one-time event but a lifelong event. It is more likely within Matthew's literary style that Matthew repeats the theme of μετάνοια in each of the five major discourse blocks as a significant theme. As previously discussed, Jesus teaches about μετάνοια throughout his discourses in Matthew, from the sermon, the missionary discourse, and the parables, to

12. Jeremias, *New Testament Theology*, 155-56.

13. Bruner, *Matthew 13-28*, 209. I do not agree that Matt 18:3 alone indicates lifelong repeated μετάνοια, since Matt 3:2, 8, 11; 4:17; 11:20; 12:41 do as well.

14. See Luz, *Matthew 8-20*, 427-29. He notes that Matthew usually uses μετάνοια as *a terminus technicus* for conversion, but 18:3 has a metaphorical sense. Also, he notes that 18:3-4 points to the disciples' lowliness more than their mental humility.

15. Luomanen, *Entering the Kingdom of Heaven*, 236. However, this lifelong concept of μετάνοια does not indicate Luomanen's "staying-in" concept of Matthean salvation structure. See ch. 5 for a detailed discussion.

16. Garlington, "Who is the Greatest?," 295.

the community discourse. The commandment of turning (μετανοέω) in Matthew 18, which answers the disciples' question about who is the greatest in the kingdom of heaven, points to a new content of μετάνοια, humility like that of Jesus who become lowly through his death.

In addition, lexical and theological dictionaries note that Matthew 18:3 commands μετάνοια since στρέφω in 18:3 is a synonym of μετανοέω. Behm says μετανοέω and μετάνοια are fully synonymous with the στρέφω through which Jesus "demands radical conversion, a transformation of nature, a definitive turning from evil, a resolute turning to God in total obedience (Mark 1:15; Matt 4:17; 18:3)."[17] Moisés Silva also points out that the theme of repentance appears conceptually in the NT without the terms μετανοέω and μετάνοια (cf. Matt 18:3; Luke 14:33).[18] Louw and Nida's semantic domain for μετανοέω and μετάνοια, which are under "changing behavior" (domain 41), includes στρέφω, "change one's manner of life, with the implication of turning toward God," ἐπιστρέφω and ἐπιστροφή, "change one's manner of life in a particular direction, with the implication of turning back to God," as well as μετανοέω and μετάνοια, "change one's way of life as the result of a complete change of thought and attitude with regard to sin and righteousness."[19] Bauer defines στρέφω as "to change the position of something relative to something else by turning," "to carry something back to its previous location, bring back, return," "to turn something into something else, turn, change," "to turn away so as to dissociate one self," and "to experience an inward change, turn, change."[20] These meanings are the same as for μετανοέω and μετάνοια.

In conclusion, the community discourse begins with the commandment of turning (μετανοέω), with the word replaced by its synonym στρέφω, "turn and become like little children." The history of research on the community discourse shows that this has been a hot spot in the study of the theme of μετάνοια in Matthew. This opening demonstrates the thematic significance of μετάνοια in the discourse. I suggest that the unifying theme for the discourse is not only humility but the humility of μετάνοια. The little child represents the disciples who walk in μετάνοια. They humbled themselves by turning their lives over to Jesus and following his teachings and life. Jesus calls people to μετάνοια—to turn from the earthly value of the greatest to the new value of the greatest in the kingdom of heaven, to realize

---

17. *TDNT* 4:1003.

18. Silva, *New International Dictionary*, 3:290–91.

19. Louw and Nida, *Greek-English Lexicon*, Domain 41, 510. See also Porter, "Penitence and Repentance in the Epistles," 128–29, in which he also expands his study of repentance to the term στρέφω according to Louw and Nida.

20. BDAG 948.

that the greatest is the one who is humble and lowly to serve others just like Jesus suffered and gave his life for others (16:24; 23:11–12).

The Thematic Significance of μετάνοια in Matthew 18

This section examines the thematic significance of μετάνοια in the community discourse. As discussed previously, a heading theme of the community discourse is μετάνοια commanded in personal and social humility as well as servanthood in the church (18:1–4). Luz also emphasizes that the whole community discourse expands 18:1–4.[21] He notes "to be a Christian is to turn the world's standards upside down," that is "lowliness, scorn, poverty, humility and service" is the main theme of the discourse as the whole chapter exemplifies it in "living well together, forgiveness, and love."[22] Particularly, 18:3 echoes 4:17, and has its emphasis on the theme of humility and servanthood as one of the examples of μετάνοια.[23] Turning to little children provides a perfect visual image of μετάνοια (18:1–6). This vivid opening commandment of μετάνοια expressed in humility or servanthood shows the significance of μετάνοια in the community discourse in echoes of the thematic significance of μετάνοια in Matthew. Following this heading, each part of the discourse also demonstrates and commands the theme of μετάνοια.[24]

18:1–14—Turn to Become a Little One of μετάνοια

Matthew 18:1–4 commands turning. This heading commandment echoes the main summary statement of Jesus' ministry and teachings (4:17). As mentioned above, στρέφω in 18:3 rephrases μετανοέω from 4:17. This use of a synonym clearly shows the μετάνοια theme of Matthew 18. "Unless you turn and become like children, you will never enter the kingdom of heaven" rephrases Matthew 4:17, "Turn, for the kingdom of heaven is at hand." The two form a pair of exhortations of μετάνοια and a statement of

---

21. Luz, *Matthew 8–20*, 421.
22. Luz, *Matthew 8–20*, 430.
23. This theme of μετάνοια in not only significant in Matt 18 but also the following chapters where Jesus repeatedly commands his followers to turn away from the values of the world in terms of the first and the greatest to the last and the least (19:13–15, 21, 30; 20:16, 27–28; 23:11–12; 25:40, 45).
24. It does not have a section on how this discourse unit relates to the others (the sermon, and Matt 3, 10, and 13). Similar μετάνοια language and images will be discussed in the following discussion section. See ch. 4 for the appearance of similar language and images between Matt 3 and 18.

the consequent reward and judgment of the kingdom of heaven. Matthew 4:17 and 18:3 match exactly in their concepts of μετάνοια and their theme of entering the kingdom of heaven. Regarding the salvation structure of 18:3, Daniel Patte says, "entering the kingdom" equals "receiving Jesus," and "receiving a child" contrasts with "scandalizing a little one."[25] In relation to 4:17, 18:3 commands and explains μετάνοια and its result of entering the kingdom of heaven.

Jesus depicts an essence/content of μετάνοια through the little ones. The image of "little ones" is a perfect image of μετάνοια in the kingdom of heaven. These little ones explain what Jesus meant μετάνοια to be. A little one represents μετάνοια in meaning to turn from this world's value of greatness to the humility and servanthood of the kingdom of heaven. Jesus, the greatest in the kingdom of heaven, perfectly exemplifies this servanthood, (cf. 20:26-28).[26] He follows the Father's will as he humbles himself and dies to serve his people. Jesus calls the church to this essence of μετάνοια. This image of a little child heads Matthew 18 and shows the significance of μετάνοια in the community discourse echoing 4:17.

Matthew 18:5-14 demonstrates the importance of μετάνοια through the humility of servanthood by showing how much Jesus values the little ones who represent μετάνοια in the kingdom of heaven. Davies and Allison note that 18:5-14 shows God's concern for the little ones.[27] They are right but miss 18:3's important commandment of turning (στρέφω or μετανοέω). This parable shows God's concerns for μετάνοια little ones. Luz also argues that little ones refers 18:3-4's repentance through humility and lowliness.[28] In 18:5-11, Jesus says that receiving these little ones is receiving Jesus. He also forbids making these little ones stumble. This scene shows the great value of the little ones who turn (μετανοέω or στρέφω) through humility and lowliness. Another commandment, "do not despise or look down (καταφρονέω) one of these little ones (18:10)" also shows the great value of μετάνοια through the humility of servanthood. The following judgment sayings of Jesus—having a heavy millstone hung around one's neck and being drowned in the depths of the sea (18:6), woe (18:7), being cast into the eternal fire (18:8), and being cast into the fiery hell (18:9)—show the great importance of the one who μετανοέω (turns and becomes like a little child) in the kingdom of heaven.

---

25. Patte, "Jesus' Pronouncement," 29.

26. Davies and Allison, *Matthew 8–18*, 778. They also designate "this little one" as believers.

27. See Davies and Allison, *Matthew 8–18*, 768.

28. Luz, *Matthew 8–20*, 434.

The little ones of μετάνοια refers to the disciples (Matt 10:42) that set up a structural and thematic parallel to the previous discourse blocks in terms of μετάνοια and the disciples. Each discourse talks about μετάνοια as a significant theme, and the disciples are always there to demonstrate the theme: disciples who are called to turn (μετανοέω) (4:17—8:1); disciples who are commissioned to preach μετάνοια and a μετάνοια life style (ch. 10); disciples who as the family of God are doers of the will of the Father in heaven with the μετάνοια parables of the kingdom of heaven (ch. 13); and disciples who are commanded to turn and become like children by being humble and lowly in the kingdom of heaven (ch. 18). Some disciples wanted to be the greatest, but Jesus in the community discourse commands them μετάνοια, to turn and become like children(20:20–28).

Matthew 16:21–27 and 17:22–23 begin to emphasize the theme of humility and servanthood in its prediction of Jesus' suffering and death (16:21) and that the way to follow Jesus is by denying one's self and carrying one's own cross in humility and servanthood (16:21–28). Following the narrative context of Jesus' death and resurrection prediction, this humility and servanthood theme of the "self-sacrificing servant" continues in the community discourse. Jesus' death and resurrection show the perfect example of a child or the slave image of Matthew 18 that Jesus humbles himself and serves his people through humility and lowliness in his death. Jesus as a model of the fruitful life of the people of God commands a μετάνοια turning of the concept of greatness as the basis of the peaceful community life. This continuing theme of μετάνοια with its according judgment and reward is explicitly commanded in Matthew 18:1–10 with a little child image.[29]

In addition to μετάνοια thematic materials above, 18:1–14 contains widespread μετάνοια language and imagery that demonstrates the significance of μετάνοια in the community discourse. This μετάνοια language and imagery parallels the other discourses and shows the significance of μετάνοια in Matthew. There are largely two types of parallel language and imagery connected to μετάνοια: the commandment of turning (μετανοέω) and the judgment and reward sayings of μετάνοια. As noted above, "Unless you turn and become like children, you will never enter the kingdom of heaven" (18:3) parallels the commandment of turning (μετανοέω) and the corresponding judgment or reward language elsewhere in Matthew about entering the kingdom of heaven(4:17; 5:20; 7:21; 10:7; 19:23, 24; 25:21).

---

29. I will discuss it more in a later part of this chapter, but chs. 5 and 7 already mentioned that the image of the little one refers to Jesus' disciples. Here specifically it refers to Jesus' followers giving their life for the sake of Jesus Christ in humility and servanthood.

In 18:5, the picture of receiving a little child in the name of Jesus being like receiving Jesus shows the theme of μετάνοια playing out in receiving the disciples and their preaching of μετάνοια (Matthew 10:14, 42). Receiving and not offending the little one has a three-fold reference to μετάνοια: the receiving and offending of μετάνοια itself, of the disciples who represent μετάνοια, and of their μετάνοια message. Those who receive μετάνοια will enter eternal life and those who reject μετάνοια will enter the judgment of death (18:6–7). Matthew 10:41 and 18:5 together command receiving the prophet, the righteous, and the little child of μετάνοια.

Matthew 18:8–9 parallels Matthew 5:29–30, which gives the contents of μετάνοια.[30] Matthew 18:8–9 commands μετάνοια in order not to sin so that one may enter eternal life, not the eternal fire and the fire of hell. This reward and judgment language and images of μετάνοια repeat previous language and imagery about the commandments and judgments of μετάνοια (3:2–12; 5:22, 29, 30; 7:19; 13:40, 42, 50; 18:8, 9; 25:41, 46).[31]

In 18:14, the phrase "the will of the Father in heaven" also demonstrates the theme of μετάνοια in the community discourse. This phrase shares the meaning of μετάνοια turning one's will and life according to the will of the Father in heaven. This phrase occurs in Matthew 6:10, 7:21; 12:50; 18:14; 21:31; 26:42 to command and instruct the contents of μετάνοια indicating to what people should turn.

18:10–14—The Parable of the Wandering Sheep

In particular, this parable demonstrates the continuing theme of μετάνοια from the community discourse. The wandering sheep (18:10–14) first illustrates the little one of μετάνοια in 18:3, 10, 14. The shepherd who leaves ninety-nine sheep to search for one lost sheep shows the value of the little one who represents μετάνοια through humility and servanthood (18:3, 10, 14). The Greek verb ἀπόλλυμι, which explains the possible end of the wandering sheep (18:14), means to perish rather than to be lost. Jesus wants the wandering (πλανάω) little one (18:12) not to perish (ἀπόλλυμι) (18:14).

Also, this parable expresses that God does not want any one and any member of the community to stumble and perish but to turn (μετανοέω) and not be destroyed. This image of the shepherd who searches for the one wandering sheep, leaving the ninety-nine, demonstrates how much God always wants sinners to turn (μετανοέω) to him so that none will perish

---

30. See ch. 6.

31. For widespread parallel μετάνοια language and images that demonstrate μετάνοια as a significant theme of Matthew, see also chs. 1, 4, and 5.

(ἀπόλλυμι) (18:14). Specifically, Jesus' previous sayings regarding sin in 18:8-9 indicate that this parable describes how much God seeks sinners to turn (μετανοέω) to him. Also, in 18:15 and the following verses Jesus instructs the church to call sinners to turn from sin to righteousness. His countless illustrations of forgiveness show that this parable demonstrates God's hope for sinners to turn (μετανοέω) to him again and again. In addition, this wandering and perishing language probably reflects Jesus' hope for lost (ἀπόλλυμι) Israel to turn (μετανοέω) to him (10:6; 15:24).[32]

For reference, the same Lukan parable of the lost sheep (Luke 15:3-7) uses the term μετανοέω and μετάνοια in its interpretation: "There will be more joy in heaven over one sinner who repents (μετανοέω) than over ninety-nine righteous persons who need no repentance (μετάνοια)" (Luke 15:7). While Matthew does not use the term μετανοέω or μετάνοια in the parable, Luke helps to show the theme of μετάνοια in the Matthean parable of the wandering sheep. Luke 15:7 also explains that this lost (ἀπόλλυμι) sheep indicates a sinner who needs μετάνοια.[33] Some scholars argue that while the same parable in Luke 15:3-7 explains God's eagerness to seek sinners and his joy in their conversion, the Matthean parable explains God's care for the disciples and for rescuing believers from sin.[34] It is true, but as discussed above this parable includes the theme of μετάνοια.

In addition, the near context of the community discourse (Matthew 17:24-27) shows that this parable illustrates that Jesus does not want anyone to stumble. Jesus is rebuked for not paying the temple tax, but he finally paid it in order not to cause the tax collectors to stumble (μὴ σκανδαλίσωμεν). Jesus respects the common regulation of paying temple tax so that unbelievers will not stumble but have a chance to turn (μετανοέω) to him. The same language of σκανδαλίζω and σκάνδαλον appears in 18:6, 7, 8, 9. Jesus' action on behalf of the tax collectors shows that his community needs to do the same for the little ones in Matthew 18 and hints that the little one and the wandering sheep can be also social outcasts or the least such as tax collectors, sick, and sinners as Jesus is always with them (9:10, 11; 11:19; 17:24-27; 21:31, 32). This parallel language of σκανδαλίζω and σκάνδαλον also indicates that not causing anyone to stumble is part of the concept of μετάνοια explained in Matthew 18.

---

32. France, *Gospel of Matthew*, 689.

33. Gundry, *Matthew*, 366.

34. Davies and Allison, *Matthew 8-18*, 768. Davies and Allison say the little one in the parable is not a literal little one but a believer (771). Turner, in *Matthew*, 440, notes Matthew uses the sheep image for believer in 9:36; 10:6, 16; 12:11-12; 15:24; 18:12; 25:32-33; 26:31.

In short, the parable of the wandering sheep emphasizes Jesus' commandment of μετάνοια, to turn and become like little children (18:4) and shows that Jesus wants sinners to turn (μετάνοια) and not perish (ἀπόλλυμι).

18:15–20—the Christian Institution of μετάνοια

Matthew 18:15-20 establishes the Christian institution. The community discourse in Matthew 18 begins with the μετάνοια commandment (18:1–4) and instructs how the community should deal with sins within it. Strecker names 18:15–20 the "Christian institution of penance" that instructs the church's eschatological authority to bind and loose, in other words to admit and exclude members of the community.[35] What Strecker calls the "Christian institution of penance" is actually the "Christian institution of μετάνοια (repentance)." Penance and repentance refer to the same thing in Greek, that is μετάνοια, but we should use the term μετάνοια (repentance) rather than penance. The English word penance represented the Catholic sacrament of penance and was the English translation of μετάνοια before William Tyndale.[36]

Thus, Jesus who exhorts μετάνοια gives authority to the church to discipline members of the church according to their reactions. If members sin, the church must exhort μετάνοια, and according to members' μετάνοια response, the church can exclude or admit them. This is the Christian institution of μετάνοια (repentance) in 18:15–20.[37]

Matthew 18:15–17 instructs the church to lead sinners to turn (μετανοέω). Specifically, the church's responsibility to sin (ἁμαρτάνω), to tell one's fault (ἐλέγχω), and to listen (ἀκούω) or not to listen (παρακούω) describes the church's exhortation of μετάνοια to the one who has sinned against others. The sinner who refuses μετάνοια will be excluded from the church. This institution of μετάνοια is not only for the exclusion of sinners[38] but also to exhort and lead sinners to turn (μετανοέω).[39] The previous

---

35. Strecker, *Theology of the New Testament*, 390.

36. For a detailed discussion, see ch. 3.

37. See Gibbs and Kloha, "'Following' Matthew 18," 6–25, for a structure study of Matt 18. Gibbs and Kloha note the importance of the context to understand the institution of church. They emphasize 18:1–4 as key to the structure of Matt 18, and significant for understanding 18:15–20 in particular. The child image in 18:1–4 gives the primary idea of Matthew 18, "care for the greatest and neediest," which is highlighted in the teaching of unlimited forgiveness (18:21–35).

38. Davies and Allison, *Matthew 8–18*, 785, also says the purpose of this institution is not rebuke or condemnation but reconciliation.

39. Horning, "Rule of Christ," 69–78. Horning says the rule of Christ performs

parable of the wandering sheep and Jesus' instructions that follow about the need for boundless forgiveness, as illustrated in the parable of the debtors, shows this purpose for the institution of μετάνοια in the church.

The judgment of excommunication, "Let him be to you as a Gentile and a tax collector" (18:20), demonstrates the theme of μετάνοια in that it parallels the judgment and reward call corresponding to one's μετάνοια. The tax collector and gentile language parallels between 5:46–47 and 18:17 also demonstrate the theme of μετάνοια. While the tax collector and gentile language in Matt 18:17 proclaims judgment, 5:46–47 gives the contents of μετάνοια in that Christians must love more than the tax collectors and gentiles do. The binding and loosing language (Matt 16:19; 18:18) is a shortened form of 18:15–17.[40] Binding and loosing language elsewhere in the Synoptics also indicates overcoming the power of Satan (Matt 12:29; 13:30; 22:13; Mark 3:27; 5:3; Luke 13:16), and this church institution of μετάνοια indicates overcoming Satan's power in the church through μετάνοια from Satan to Jesus.[41]

This church institution of μετάνοια sustains one's lifelong μετάνοια. This institution of μετάνοια indicates that what we call repentance (μετάνοια) means not only to stop sinning or to change one's mind with regret, but to turn oneself and one's life from sin to righteousness under the guide of the institution of the church. This Christian institution of μετάνοια exists for the effective μετάνοια life of church members and bolsters the commandment of turning (μετανοέω) in its meaning of turning oneself and one's life to be humble like little children in the community discourse. Turner also says

---

"in the spirit of shepherd seeking his lost sheep," and the purposes are "repentance, forgiveness, reconciliation, and harmony in the church" (70). For more discussion on Matt 18:15–20 in terms of church discipline, see Duling, "Matthew 18:15–17," 4–22. Duling compares Matt 18:15–17 to Leviticus and the Dead Sea Scrolls. He notes that Matt 18:15–17 is a unique solution for conflict and confrontation by brotherhood love of forgiveness. See also Pfitzner, "Purified Community," 34–55; McClister, "'Where Two or Three,'" 549–58. McClister examines the chiastic structure of 17:22—20:19 to argue the center of the community discourse is 18:18-20, which notes the unity and reconciliation of disciples on earth (18:18–19) in relationship with Christ (18:20) (557–58). See also Carson, "On Abusing Matthew 18," 1–3, for not abusing Matt 18. And for the shekinah theme of 18:20, see Sievers, "'Where Two or Three. . .,'" 47–61.

40. Bruner, *Matthew 13–28*, 230. Bruner says it indicates the banning of sinners from the gift of life and the forgiving of the one who responds with μετάνοια to receive the gift of life. For a more detailed interpretation of binding and loosing in the Gospel of Matthew, see also Powell, "Binding and Loosing," 438–45.

41. Hiers, "'Binding' and 'Loosing,'" 233–50. Also, the disciples' power over Satan received from Jesus parallels this binding and loosing power over sinners in the community. "Binding and loosing" language basically indicate the power to judge sinners (Matt 22:13; 27:2; Mark 6:17; 15:7; John 18:12, 24).

this institution is for repentance that "leads to loosing, or forgiveness, and continued fellowship. The lack of repentance leads to binding, or retention of sin, and exclusion from the community."[42] This institution demonstrates the thematic significance of μετάνοια in the community discourse.

18:21–35—Unlimited Forgiveness for μετάνοια

The first half of the community discourse (18:1-20) commands μετάνοια as it relates to humility. The greatest of the kingdom of heaven is the one who turns to become like a little child (18:1-4), and Jesus wants this humble one of μετάνοια to be protected (18:5-14). The middle part of the discourse instructs the church institution of μετάνοια, which deals with the problem of sins in the community to lead the sinner to turn (μετανοέω) (18:15-20). The last part of the community discourse commands unlimited forgiveness of sins for church brothers and sisters (18:21-35). Therefore, the thematic structure of the community discourse is that the command to turn (μετανοέω) is followed by the promise of unlimited forgiveness of sins.

Jesus first commands μετάνοια and the church institution of μετάνοια and then assures unlimited forgiveness for those who once sinned and are now led to turn (μετανοέω), which is the purpose of the instituted church.[43] Forgiveness and μετάνοια are inseparable concepts like two sides of a coin (cf. Mark 1:4). Anderson Runesson notes the importance of repentance for the forgiveness in Matthew's Gospel. He notes, "without repentance, no forgiveness; without forgiveness no kingdom" in Matthew (3:2; 4:17).[44] He also points out that the sin is violation of the law and righteousness is the opposite.[45] If one sins, he/she needs μετάνοια, meaning to turn one's whole being and life to righteousness, and Jesus and God will forgive. Sin, turning from sin to be right, and forgiveness are all included in the theme of μετάνοια.

The parallel saying of Luke 17:3-4, "If your brother sins, rebuke him, and if he repents (μετανοέω), forgive him, and if he sins against you seven times in the day, and turns to you seven times, saying, 'I repent (μετανοέω),' you must forgive him," explains how this Matthean unlimited forgiveness

---

42. Turner, *Matthew*, 446.

43. See Gundry, *Matthew*, 358 for the flow of this discourse block: "the condition of childlikeness for entrance into the kingdom of heaven (vv 1–3); humility defines childlikeness (v 4); acceptance of childlike disciples constitutes acceptance of Jesus himself (v 5); judgment on one who causes the little people to sin (vv 6–7); self-discipline to keep from sinning (vv 8–9); the heavenly father's hope of the restoration of straying little people (vv 10–20); repeated forgiving (vv 21–30)."

44. Runesson, *Divine Wrath and Salvation*, 119, 124.

45. Runesson, *Divine Wrath and Salvation*, 122.

commandment demonstrates the theme of μετάνοια. Matthew, unlike Luke, does not use the term μετάνοια here, but he assumes it.[46] This unlimited forgiveness is for the community member who sins against brothers in the community but then μετανοέω. Peter's phrase, "my brother sins against me," indicates this commandment applies in the community. Also, the parable of the unforgiving servant shows the forgiver is a community member who has been forgiven his sins.[47]

To encourage unlimited forgiveness for those who μετανοέω, Jesus recounts the parable of the unforgiving servant (18:23–35).[48] This parable follows Jesus' commandment of μετάνοια and the institution of μετάνοια in the community/church (18:1–20) and explains and exhorts the church to offer unlimited forgiveness for those who μετανοέω from sin. This parable, therefore, insists on μετάνοια (a turning/change of heart and attitude) for the community and demonstrates the forgiveness of brothers and sisters, which is demanded by the love of God to fulfill the law—not legalistically but by God's mercy manifested in the coming of Jesus.[49]

The mercy language ἐλεέω recalls Matthew 5:7 as the contents of the fruits worthy of μετάνοια.[50] The forgiven condition of the unforgiving servant and the judgment on this unforgiving servant show the need for the unlimited forgiveness of the church toward those who μετανοέω from sin. As noted previously, Luke 17:3–4 shows that this parable of the unforgiving servant is under the theme of μετάνοια because this unlimited forgiveness is given to the one who μετανοέω. The one who is forgiven by God but does not forgive those who μετανοέω from the heart will be thrown out to the jailers. Church members who μετανοέω and have been

---

46. Hagner, *Matthew 14–28*, 536; Gundry, *Matthew*, 371.

47. There is a clear connection between the Lord's Prayer (6:12) and the commandment of forgiveness in the community discourse. Both command forgiveness, and ὀφειλέτης occurs in both places (6:12 and 18:24), the only two times in the Gospel of Matthew.

48. For interpretations of this parable, see Jeremias, *Parables of Jesus*, 210–14; de Boer, "Ten Thousand Talents," 214–32; Carter, "Resisting and Imitating the Empire"; Heil, "Parable of the Unforgiving Forgiven Servant," 96–123; Hylen, "Forgiveness and Life in Community," 146–57; Keesmaat, "Strange Neighbors and Risky Care," 263–85; Scott, "King's Accounting," 429–42. See also, Snodgrass, *Stories with Intent*, 61–76; Patte, "Bringing Out of the Gospel," 79–108; Illian, "Church Discipline and Forgiveness," 444–50. See Kuepfer, "Matthew 18 Revisited," 33–41, for recent reflection on the history of interpretation of Matt 18. He specifically reflects a Mennonite perspective on the discourse.

49. Deidun, "Parable of the Unmerciful Servant," 203–24.

50. See ch. 5.

forgiven by the love of God must in turn forgive their brothers and sisters to accomplish their μετάνοια.

On the other hand, this unlimited forgiveness by the church encourages sinners to turn (μετανοέω) because the Father in heaven and the church will forgive without limits those who μετανοέω. The Father in heaven is searching for the wandering sheep because he wants to lead him to turn (μετανοέω) and be forgiven (18:12–14). The exhortation of forgiveness is also part of the nature of μετάνοια. Any member of the church who has been forgiven a huge debt by God is exhorted in turn to forgive those who once sinned but now μετανοέω. The last summary commandment of forgiveness from the heart (18:35) demonstrates implicit connection to the heart language as part of the nature of μετάνοια throughout Matthew (5:8, 28; 6:21; 11:29; 12:34, 35; 13:15, 19; 15:8, 18, 19; 18:35; 22:37).[51]

Conclusion

Matthew 18, the community discourse, begins with the commandment of turning (μετανοέω), meaning to turn and become like little children (18:1–4). Jesus continues to command the community to receive the little one of μετάνοια and not to make them stumble (18:5–10) to emphasize the humility and servanthood of μετάνοια. He gives the parable of the wandering sheep to convey that losing the little one of μετάνοια is not the will of the Father in heaven (18:12–14). Jesus commands the institution of the church to practice μετάνοια (18:15–20). The purpose this institution is not to judge sinners but to lead them to turn (μετανοέω) again. Jesus' unlimited forgiveness commandment shows his love for the sinning community member and his hope for their μετάνοια. Anyone who sins but μετανοέω will be forgiven again and again. The purpose of this forgiveness is healing and reconciliation in the church.[52] These show the thematic and even paradigmatic significance of the humility and servanthood of μετάνοια in the discourse.

---

51. For more discussion on the heart language as content for μετάνοια in Matthew, see ch. 5.

52. Doriani, "Forgiveness," 22–32.

Chapter 11
The Thematic Significance of μετάνοια in Matthew 23–25
The Last Discourse of μετάνοια

Introduction

THIS BOOK ARGUES THE thematic and paradigmatic significance of μετάνοια in the Gospel of Matthew. Specifically, the opening commandment of turning (μετανοέω) and its reward and judgment in Matthew 4:17 indicate it. This major summary commandment and the contents of the fruit worthy of μετάνοια are evident in the book of Matthew in various ways. This chapter examines the thematic significance of μετάνοια in Matthew 23–25, the last of Jesus' five teaching blocks. Before diving into the fifth and final discourse block, this chapter will first examine the thematic significance of μετάνοια from the narrative context, the previous chapters of Matthew 18–22. Then it will examine the thematic significance of μετάνοια in the last discourse block.

The Thematic Significance of μετάνοια in Matthew 18–22

This section looks at the significance of the commandment of turning (μετανοέω) through humility and servanthood (18:3; cf. 3:2; 4:17) in the near context of the previous chapters of the last discourse (Matt 18–22) and how the fifth discourse block continues to emphasize this same message (18:1–6; 19:13–15, 30; 20:16, 26–28; 23:11–12; 25:31–36).

μετάνοια through Humility and Servanthood in Matthew 18–22

As chapter 10 noted, beginning a new phase of teaching and ministry in Matthew 16:21, Jesus predicts his death and resurrection (16:21; 17:23; 20:19) and his public ministry begins to emphasize the theme of humility and servanthood. The theme of humility and servanthood demonstrated in the predictions of Jesus' suffering and death (16:21; 17:23) begins with the admonition in 18:1–6 to turn to become like a little one of humility and servanthood. This opening focal commandment, which shows the significance of μετάνοια in the community discourse, echoes 4:17's μετάνοια commandment emphasizing its positive aspect of turning toward being humble and serving others.

This commandment of μετάνοια through humility and servanthood in 18:1–6 is not only significant in the community discourse, but also echoes in the following chapters (18–22) as well as the last discourse (Matthew 23–25) through the use of similar images, language, and parallel concepts (19:13–15, 30; 20:16, 26–28; 23:11–12; 25:31–46). The following chapters depict what the μετάνοια lifestyle looks like in humility and servanthood.

Six parallel summary phrases in the concept of μετάνοια through humility and servanthood: 18:1–6; 19:13–15; 19:30; 20:16; 20:26–28; 23:11–12 and 25:31–46. Matthew 18:1–6; 19:13–15; 19:30; 20:16; 20:26–28; 23:11–12 and 25:31–36 provide important thematic summaries for major sections of Matthew 18–25. As mentioned above, 18:1–6 is the commandment of μετάνοια through humility and servanthood. This repeats and echoes 3:2 and 4:17's commandment of μετάνοια and summarizes Matthew 18. And Matthew 19:13–15; 19:30; 20:16; 20:26–28; 23:11–12; 25:31–36 repeat and echo 4:17 and 18:1–6's commandment of turning (μετανοέω). These phrases are parallel in their shared concept of μετάνοια through humility and servanthood and work together to demonstrate the thematic and paradigmatic significance of μετάνοια in each section of 18–25. Two parallel phrases in 23:11–12 and 25:31–46 are the opening and the ending of the last discourse (Matt 23–25). Matthew 23:11–12 and 25:31–46, in turn, show the significant role of μετάνοια through humility and servanthood in the last discourse. I will discuss these passages in order.

First, Matthew 18:1–6's commandment of turning toward humility and servanthood using στρέφω, a synonym of μετάνοια, and the image of the little one[1] illustrate and echo 4:17's commandment of μετάνοια.[2] Matthew 18:1-6 leads these subsequent parallel summary phrases 19:13-15; 19:30; 20:16; 20:26-28; 23:11-12; and 25:31-46 and shows that these summary phrases echo the commandment of turning (μετανοέω) as demonstrated through the theme of humility and servanthood. The term μετάνοια or its synonyms do not occur in 19:13-15; 19:30; 20:16; 20:26-28; 23:11-12; 25:31-46, but 18:1-6 leads these subsequent parallel summary phrases by the concepts of humility and servanthood and shows that they all imitate 18:3's commandment of μετάνοια through the theme of humility and servanthood. Particularly, the words παιδίον, ταπεινόω, μικρός, ἔσχατος, διάκονος, δοῦλος, and διακονέω in each summary phrase denote the same concepts of humility and servanthood, in contrast with the terms μείζων, πρῶτος, μέγας, and ὑψόω. These verses are also parallel in the theme of entering the kingdom of heaven.

Second, the summary of the theme of humility and servanthood in 19:13-15 serves as the opening focal point for the following narrative discourse section, the story of the rich young man (19:13-30) and echoes the same theme of μετάνοια through humility of that section.[3] The image of the little one in 19:14 closes 18:1-19:12 and opens a new narrative section (19:13-19:30), indicating the importance of 18:3's μετάνοια commandment through the little one image for the following narrative and discourse.[4]

Third, "many who are first will be last, and the last first" in Matthew 19:30 and 20:16, the same repeated summary phrase for the story of the rich young man story (19:30) and the parable of the laborers in the vineyard (20:16) provide the focal point of these two stories and demonstrates the theme of μετάνοια through humility and servanthood. The contrast between the first and the last in 19:30 and 20:16 parallels the contrast between the great and the little one in 18:1-4. Thus, 19:30 and 20:16 echo 18:3's commandment of μετάνοια through humility and servanthood and show that the story of the rich young man story (19:30) and the parable of the laborers in the vineyard (20:16) continue the theme of μετάνοια through humility and servanthood.

Also, Matthew 20:27, where the same term πρῶτος occurs, shows that Jesus' saying, "many who are first (πρῶτος) will be last, and the last first (πρῶτος)" (19:30; 20:16), denotes the continuing theme of humility

1. See ch. 9 for more discussion of Matthew's use of the image of the little one or child in terms of μετάνοια.
2. See ch. 9 for a detailed argument.
3. See Luz, *Matthew 8-20*, 504-6. He also sees the thematic connection between 18:1-4 and 19:13-15.
4. See Davies and Allison, *Matthew 19-28*, 32, 35.

and servanthood echoing 18:3's commandment of μετάνοια. Matthew 20:27 uses πρῶτος and shows πρῶτος in 19:30 and 20:16 to be parallel to μέγας (great) and ἔσχατος (least), as well as to δοῦλος (slave) and διάκονος/διακονέω (servant/to serve). In other words, "many who are first (πρῶτος) will be last (ἔσχατος), and the last (ἔσχατος) first (πρῶτος)" echoes 18:3's commandment of μετάνοια in meaning to turn (μετανοέω) the first (πρῶτος) to the last (ἔσχατος) becoming a slave (δοῦλος) and being willing to serve (διακονέω). This parallelism indicates that the theme of μετάνοια appears in the humility and servanthood of 19:30 and 20:16, in the story of the rich young man (19:13–30), and in the parable of the laborers in the vineyard (20:1–16).

Fourth, 20:26–28, discussed above, the summary exhortation concerning the dispute among the disciples about who is the greatest, develops the theme of μετάνοια through humility and servanthood in this story block. It echoes 18:3's commandment. In 20:18–19, Jesus' prediction of suffering, death, and resurrection, as the opening of the dispute among the disciples, signifies the same theme of μετάνοια, because Jesus' suffering and death demonstrate the theme of humility and servanthood.

Lastly, 23:11–12, the opening for Matthew 23–25, as well as 25:31–46, which ends this last discourse block also parallels 18:3's summary phrases. These two parallel summary statements suggest humility and servanthood as a significant theme for Matthew 23–25 echoing 18:3's commandment of turning (μετάνοια) through humility and servanthood. Also, this opening (23:11–12) and ending (25:31–46) of the last discourse create an inclusio that shows the significance of μετάνοια through humility and servanthood for the discourse. These two passages will be discussed in more detail in later sections of this chapter.

μετάνοια Context in Matthew 19–22

Now, based on this contextual coherence and parallel summary phrases in Matthew 18–22, I will discuss in more detail the thematic significance of μετάνοια through humility and servanthood in the stories of the rich young man, the parable of the laborers in the vineyard, and the dispute over who is the greatest among the disciples. Also, I will include three parables of Jesus in Matthew 21–22, which are in the context of Jesus' conflict with Jerusalem's religious leaders: the parable of the repenting son, the parable of laborers in the vineyard, and the parable of the wedding banquet. I suggest that they reiterate the commandment of turning (μετανοέω) through humility and servanthood and this theme continues in the last discourse.

The rich young man (19:16–30). The rich young man story mirrors and expresses 18:3 because Jesus commands the rich young man to be humble by selling his possessions and to serve by giving his possessions to the poor and to follow Jesus in order to enter the kingdom of heaven. In directing the young man to sell everything he has, which will make him last in the eyes of the world, Jesus says he will be first (19:30). This scene conceptually expresses the theme of humility and servanthood echoing 18:3's commandment of μετάνοια.

In particular, this scene of the rich young man parallels Jesus' μετάνοια call for the disciples to enter into the kingdom of heaven and their response of turning to follow Jesus in 4:17–23—leaving everything behind. The rich young man thinks he has kept every commandment of the law, but he still lacks in regard to his wealth; therefore, Jesus calls him turn to follow him by leaving everything behind.[5] The disciples turned to follow Jesus and left everything behind, but this young man does not.

Peter's question in Matthew 19:27–30 recalls 4:17–23 and expresses the theme of μετάνοια in terms of the compensation of the disciples through humbling and serving μετάνοια. The disciples will inherit eternal life and judge the twelve tribes of Israel in the kingdom of heaven because of their life-giving μετάνοια, but the young man will not enter the kingdom of heaven because he rejects μετάνοια. This parallelism shows the thematic significance of μετάνοια through humility and servanthood in the story of the rich young man.

Scholars say the main theme of this story is "wealth and the kingdom" which has already been dealt with in the sermon.[6] As Davies and Allison note, this story illustrates many aspects of the sermon: the impossibility of serving both mammon and God (6:24), treasure in heaven (6:19–21), generosity (6:22–23), eschatological reversal (5:3–12), and perfection (5:48).[7] Luz also notes that the story of this young man illustrates the contents of the sermon such as the commandment of perfection in the antitheses.[8] In this respect, this rich young man also expresses the theme of μετάνοια by

---

5. See, Davies and Allison, *Matthew 19–28*, 41, which notes this story as a discipleship story. Matt 23:23 hints at how the young man must turn (μετανοέω), "For you tithe mint and dill and cumin, and have neglected the weightier matters of the law: justice and mercy and faithfulness." He has to show justice and mercy and faithfulness by selling all his possession to give them to the poor and by following Jesus.

6. Davies and Allison, *Matthew 19–28*, 40. For more discussion on this rich young man and a full bibliography, see Nolland, *Gospel of Matthew*, 786–87.

7. Davies and Allison, *Matthew 19–28*, 39–40, 62–63.

8. Luz, *Matthew 8–20*, 518. He notes that the perfection recalls 5:48, the Antitheses, and the love command.

illustrating many aspects of μετάνοια in the sermon[9] and shows the thematic significance of μετάνοια in the story.

In addition, as noted above, 19:30 demonstrates the theme of μετάνοια in the whole of the rich young man's story (19:16–30). Verses 19:30 summarize the story of the rich young man's rejection of μετάνοια and accords judgment on the young man as one of the last. The rich young man is first in this world with his riches. But he will be the last—in other words, he will not enter the kingdom of heaven—because he rejects Jesus' call for the μετάνοια of humility and servanthood expressed in selling his possessions and giving to the poor. Matthew 19:13–15, the opening of the story already demonstrates the theme of humility and servanthood of μετάνοια as an important theme, and the ending summary in 19:30 also demonstrates the same theme.

The parable of the laborers in the vineyard (20:1–16). We can also see that the parable of the laborers also mirrors and expresses 18:3's μετάνοια commandment through humility and servanthood. As noted above, the summary phrase of the parable, "many who are first (πρῶτος) will be last (ἔσχατος), and the last (ἔσχατος) first (πρῶτος)" (20:16), indicates that the parable of the laborers in the vineyard (20:1–16) continues the theme of μετάνοια through humility and servanthood. There are three major views on the reversal between the first and the last: "(1) a religious reversal between the Jewish religious leaders and the tax collectors and sinners, (2) a redemptive reversal between Israel and the Gentiles, and (3) an ecclesiastical reversal between the disciples and the humble ones."[10] The near and larger context of the parable, the conflict between Jesus and the religious leaders, the gentile inclusion theme of Matthew, and the dispute among the disciples about who is the greatest together all indicate that this reversal includes all three groups.

As a matter of fact, this reversal between the first and the last demonstrates the reversal of μετάνοια through humility and servanthood. As noted above, the summary phrase (Matt 20:16) expresses the theme of μετάνοια through humility and servanthood. In short, the parable says that no matter whether one is a religious leader of Israel, a sinner or a tax collector, an Israelite, a gentile, or a disciple, the one who responds in turning (μετάνοια) to Jesus through humility and servanthood will be the first in the kingdom of heaven. This parable first shows God's generous reward (kingdom of heaven)

---

9. See ch. 7, which argues for reading the sermon as the contents of μετάνοια.
10. Turner, *Matthew*, 481. See also Davies and Allison, *Matthew 19–28*, 67–71.

for undeserving sinners and tax collectors.¹¹ The workers hired first grumble against the landowner who gives mercy to those hired last illustrating that the first refuse to turn (μετανοέω) to be humble and serve the last by giving them mercy. Therefore, this parable expresses and commands the humility and servanthood of μετάνοια in connection to 18:3 and 20:16.

A dispute among the disciples and Jesus as a model of humility and servanthood (20:17–28). As Luz notes, a dispute among the disciples about who is the greatest reflects 18:3's turning (μετάνοια) commandment to become humble and serve.¹² The disciples who want to be the greatest offer a contrasting example of humility and servanthood and Jesus rebukes the disciples who dispute about who is the greatest and commands μετάνοια through humility and servanthood. The greatest in the kingdom of heaven is the one who chooses through μετάνοια to humble himself and serve others. The summary phrase of this story (20:26-28) demonstrates the significance of μετάνοια through humility and servanthood in the dispute in relation to previous parallel summary statements about the humility and servanthood of μετάνοια.

In addition, Jesus' prediction of his death and resurrection in 20:17–19 begins this story to demonstrate the theme of μετάνοια through humility and servanthood as a significant theme of the story. Also, the narrative structure, beginning with the disciples' fight about who is the greatest following on the heels of Jesus' death and resurrection prediction and further followed by 20:26–28, holds up Jesus' death as a model of the life of repentant people through humility and servanthood. Davies and Allison also say 20:17–19 illustrates 19:30–20:16 and also opens 20:20–28 as a governing theme.¹³ Jesus humbles himself and serves his people through his death serving as a contrast for his disciples. The disciples must turn from their concern over earthly prestige to the things of God (16:23) and embrace humility and servanthood.

The parable of the repenting son (21:23–32). Matthew 21:23–32, which has been called the parable of the two sons, reflects the commandment of turning (μετανοέω), because the main emphasis of this parable lies on the

---

11. Davies and Allison, *Matthew 19–28*, 70, 76. For more interpretation options, see Bruner, *Matthew 13–28*, 723; Davies and Allison, *Matthew 19–28*, 67–68; Luz, *Matthew 8–20*, 526–30, 537–38. For a full bibliography, see Nolland, *Gospel of Matthew*, 803–5.

12. See Luz, *Matthew 8–20*, 542–43.

13. Davies and Allison, *Matthew 19–28*, 82. Nolland says "the Son of Man reaches the pinnacle of greatness by giving his life as a ransom for many" (*Gospel of Matthew*, 817).

repentant (μεταμέλομαι) first son who changes his mind and does the will of the father and on the unfaithfulness of the second son toward the will of the father.[14] Μεταμέλομαι, translated as "change one's mind" (esv, niv), "regret" (nasb), or "repent" (kjv), means to change one's mind, repent, or to be sorry. This word is a synonym of μετανοέω and demonstrates the theme of μετάνοια in this parable. However, the meanings of μετανοέω and μεταμέλομαι are different; while μεταμέλομαι only means to repent and to be sorry or change one's mind,[15] μετανοέω means to turn one's mind and life from bad to right. The first son's turning his mind (μεταμέλομαι) and doing the right action by following the will of the father fully demonstrates the meaning of μετάνοια. Matthew's use of μεταμέλομαι emphasizes the internal and emotional aspect of the first son.[16]

The mention of John the Baptist in 21:25-26 and 21:32 also recalls the commandment of μετάνοια in the parable. The dispute between Jesus and the leaders of Israel about the authority of John the Baptist in the previous verses (21:23-27) reminds the reader of John the Baptist's μετάνοια preaching against the leaders of Israel and their rejection of it.[17] Snodgrass also says that this parable shows that the repentance movement begun by John the Baptist continues with Jesus and leads sinners to the kingdom.[18] In particular, 21:32, "For John came to you in the way of righteousness, and you did not believe him, but the tax collectors and the prostitutes believed him. And even when you saw it, you did not afterward change your minds (μεταμέλομαι) and believe him," clearly states the thematic significance of μετάνοια in the parable. As 21:31-32 indicates, John the Baptist commanded μετάνοια and bearing fruit worthy of μετάνοια in the beginning of the Gospel of Matthew (3:2-12), but the leaders of Israel did not believe him and refused to turn (μετανοέω). John the Baptist's

---

14. See Carter, "Parables in Matthew 21:28—22:14," 147-76; Luomanen, *Entering the Kingdom of Heaven*, 156-64; Martens, "'Produce Fruit Worthy of Repentance,'" 151-76; Przybylski, *Righteousness in Matthew*, 94-96.

15. Luz, *Matthew 21-28*, 30n44 says that μεταμέλομαι can mean both to change one's mind and to be sorry, but that here and in Matt 27:3 it probably means "he was sorry." Also, he says that μεταμέλομαι does not have "the theological weight of μετανοέω" (30n44).

16. This parable seems to contrast words (21:29) and deeds (21:30) (Turner, *Matthew*, 509), but this parable contrasts words with μετάνοια, which means to turn one's mind and accordingly to do right deeds. Matthew uses this word in the story of Judas Iscariot noting that he repents when he betrays Jesus (27:3). Judas only emotionally regrets his betrayal, but he does not μετανοέω by turning his wrong mind and action to the right one.

17. France, *Gospel of Matthew*, 801-2.

18. Snodgrass, *Stories with Intent*, 275.

commandment to turn (μετανοέω) and bear fruit worthy of μετάνοια, Jesus' parallel μετάνοια ministry, the rejection of the leaders of Israel but the acceptance of sinners and gentiles, and the corresponding judgment are the backdrop of this parable. This backdrop repeats the commandment of turning (μετανοέω) in the parable.

"Doing the will of the Father" and the righteousness language in 21:31-32 also show the thematic significance of μετάνοια in meaning to turn one's mind and deeds from wickedness to righteousness and the will of the Father in heaven.[19] Sinners and tax collectors who do μετάνοια will enter the kingdom of heaven, but the wicked leaders of Israel who reject μετάνοια will not. μετάνοια of social outcasts, tax collectors, and prostitutes demonstrate the theme of μετάνοια of humility and servanthood.

Therefore, it is likely that the first son depicts the tax collectors and prostitutes who turn (μετανοέω) their mind and life toward the will of the Father in heaven. Then the unfaithful second son depicts the unfaithful leaders of Israel who do not turn to follow the will of the Father in heaven.[20] The second son also depicts the chief priest, the elders of the people, the Pharisees, the Sadducees, and the lawyer who all reject the μετάνοια message of John the Baptist and of Jesus.[21]

In contrast to traditional understanding of Matthew, which notes the replacement of Israel with the church, Konrdt contends that in the three parables in Matt. 21:28-22:14 Matthew argues for the replacement of the authority of Israel with the disciples, not the replacement of people of Israel by the church.[22] He says, "for Matthew, the destruction of Jerusalem (22:7; 23:37-39) does not represent the condemnation of Israel but serves the evangelist as a delegitimization of the authorities."[23] He further argues that God renews and universalizes the covenant of God with Israel in Matthew. "The evangelist's central concern is to consistently locate Jesus' ministry within

---

19. See ch. 5 for the connection between μετάνοια and doing the will of the Father in heaven and between μετάνοια and righteousness in the Gospel of Matthew.

20. See Konradt, *Israel, Church, and the Gentiles*, 167-201.

21. Davies and Allison, *Matthew 19-28*, 166. Davies and Allsion note three main points for this parable: "(1) depiction of a divided Israel; (2) illustration of the first (the chief priests and elders) becoming last and the last (toll-collectors and prostitutes) becoming first; and (3) characterization of Jesus' opponents as hypocrites." They also admit the salvation-historical Jew-Gentile view (171-72).

22. See Konradt, *Israel, Church, and the Gentiles*, 167-201.

23. Konradt, *Israel, Church, and the Gentiles*, 264. Konradt argues that Israel's rejection of Jesus is not the reason of the destruction of the temple. It is not necessarily the case, because Jesus in Matthew says Israel's long history of disobedience of the will of God, the law, and the prophets, having a wicked mind and and exhibiting wicked behavior, and so on, cause the destruction of Israel, which includes its symbolic old temple.

God's history with his people Israel, on the one hand, and to link this history with Jesus' universal soteriological significance, on the other."[24]

However, as "the lost (or destroyed) (ἀπολωλότα) sheep of Israel (10:6)" reflects, it likely indicates the destruction of old Israel as people of God with its old temple (9:17; 10:28; 15:24; 21:41; 22:7; 26:52). And as this book has shown, Matthean Jesus proclaims μετάνοια not only to the leaders of Israel, but also to the people of Israel, and gentiles. And there are rejections of Jesus by both the people of Israel and the leaders of Israel, in contrast to gentile μετάνοια inclusion. This plot signifies that Jesus does not only try to replace the leadership of Israel and renew and universalize the covenant with the people of Israel, but create the new people of God, the universal church and new leadership of the twelve apostles based on Christ's role and individual's faith in him as Christ (16:18–19).

It is obvious that two parables in 21:28–46 specifically rebuke the authority of Israel and expectation of the new authority. However, Luz notes that 21:43 shows that the authority of Israel is replaced not by other leaders but by a "people." This language points to Jesus rejecting the old Israel (11:20–24; 12:22; 21:33–22:7; 23:34–39) in favor of "the new chosen people of God" including gentiles (13:12).[25] In addition, the parable of the wedding feast in 22:1–14 designates the replacement of those who were invited, not the leaders of Israel rejecting Jesus. This replacement of the guests indicates the replacement of those who reject Jesus by those who believe Jesus. Luz also notes that this parable alludes to the destruction of Jerusalem. And 23:35–36, which proclaims the judgment of God on "this generation" who rejects Jesus, points to judgment on the authority of Israel and the people of Israel (cf. 27:24–25).[26] In addition, Matthew's overall insistence on the redefinition of the people of God with gentile inclusion (3:9; 8:10–12; 21:31, 41; 22:1–14) and the replacement of Israel with the church based on faith in Jesus (16:18) widens the scope of the replacement by the new church leaders and the new people of God.[27]

---

24. Konradt, *Israel, Church, and the Gentiles*, 353.

25. Luz, *Studies in Matthew*, 246–47. See also Luz, *Matthew 21–28*, 164. Specifically, Luz notes that 23:37–39 points to the judgment on Jerusalem and therefore on all Israel.

26. Luz, *Studies in Matthew*, 246–50.

27. See ch. 5 for more discussion about Konradt's argument. Specifically, 22:1–14 clearly designates the replacement of people of Israel by those who believe in Jesus Christ. See Olmstead, "Gospel for a New Nation," 115–32. He convincingly shows that the term ἔθνος in Matt 21:43 indicates new people of the kingdom of God (not the leaders of Israel), especially in corresponding to the rejection and death of Jesus by the leaders and crowds (26:5; 27:17–24). Also, ἔθνος in Matt 21:43 does not mean the leaders but people because the term in the OT and in Matthew always refers to people or gentile people. Specifically, ἔθνος in Matt 28:19 is also used in the Abrahamic covenant

The parable of the tenants (21:33–46). The next parable illustrates that the leaders of Israel reject Jesus, their final judgment (21:41, 43, 44), and the salvation of the true people of God who bear the worthy fruit (21:43), which implies "that the entire nation (Israel) loses its election. . . and the church has taken Israel's place as the chosen people."[28] The wicked tenants probably portray how the leaders of Israel reject μετάνοια to Jesus and kill him.[29] They will be punished by a miserable death.

The closing phrase of the two parables, "the kingdom of God will be taken away from you and given to a people producing its fruits" (21:43) echoes the commandment of turning (μετανοέω) and the worthy fruit of μετάνοια in Matthew 3:2, 8. What is the fruit of the kingdom of heaven? As noted above, the previous parable has a strong connection to John the Baptist's μετάνοια preaching. This parable also connects to John the Baptist's condemnation of the leaders of Israel and his commandment of μετάνοια and of the worthy fruit of μετάνοια (Matt 3:2–12). In particular, the parallel fruit language in Matthew 3:8 shows that the fruit of the kingdom of heaven in 21:43 refers to fruit worthy of μετάνοια, which links to doing the will of the Father in heaven, righteousness, and doing good.[30]

The parable of the wedding banquet (22:1–14). Throughout Matthew, but especially in the parables of the tenants and the wedding banquet, we see Israel reject the Messiah and his call to μετάνοια.[31] The rejection of the invited wedding guests, some of whom even mistreat and kill the servants coheres Israel's rejection of Jesus and his call to μετάνοια in the narrative context of Matthew. The angry king burning and killing all the guests who rejected his invitation as well as the entire town depicts the judgment on Israel, who does not recognize Jesus as their king and rejects μετάνοια.

---

in Gen 12:2 and Exod 32:10, and indicate it is the fulfillment and replacement of the people of God. However, since the term ἔθνος means "people" or "nation," 28:19 does not exclude the ethnic people of Israel.

28. Luz, *Matthew 21–28*, 44.

29. See ch. 8, which shows the plot of Matt 4–13, from Jesus' proclamation of μετάνοια and its rejection by Israel. Davies and Allison, *Matthew 19–28*, 176–77, says that this parable has two OT themes: Israel as God's vineyard and their rejection of the prophet. This parable applies these themes to Jesus as a culmination of the revelation of God and Israel's rejection of Jesus as a culmination of the rebellion of Israel. See Nolland, *Gospel of Matthew*, 865–67, for a full bibliography for this parable.

30. See chs. 4–5. This phrase also indicates the theme of universal μετάνοια, expressed in the gentile inclusion theme.

31. See ch. 8, which shows the overall plot of Matthew. See Davies and Allison, *Matthew 19–28*, 195–97.

The worthy (ἄξιος) language in 22:8 recalls the worthy (ἄξιος) fruit of μετάνοια in 3:8 as do the previous two parables (21:1–46). This worthy language likely indicates that the rejecters of the wedding feast refer to those who reject μετάνοια and do not bear its worthy fruit. In addition, the wedding garment in 22:11–12 likely depicts the worthy fruit of μετάνοια, which Jesus commands in order to enter the kingdom of heaven (3:2, 8; 4:17). The man who does not wear proper wedding garments has to change his dirty clothes for his best, clean clothes for the royal wedding.[32] This need for changing clothes probably expresses the man's need of μετάνοια in its meaning of changing or turning (μετάνοια) his whole being and life by bearing fruit worthy of μετάνοια. Scholars say that this wedding garment indicates personal righteousness.[33] This interpretation is likely, but more precisely it refers to righteousness as the worthy fruit of μετάνοια. As noted in chapter 5, personal righteousness is included as the contents of the worthy fruit of μετάνοια in Matthew.

The invitation to all the people in the street, both good and bad (22:9–14), after the depiction of Israel's rejection of Jesus and μετάνοια (22:1–8), therefore, likely depicts Jesus' universal calling of μετάνοια toward him and into his kingdom of heaven in the previous context of Matthew. This universal calling of μετάνοια does not necessarily indicate a salvation-historical reversal of the people of God from Israel to the gentiles[34] but more likely the salvation of all nations, including sinners from both Israel and the gentiles only through μετάνοια toward Jesus demonstrated by fruit worthy of μετάνοια.[35]

Conclusion

The narrative context of Matthew 18–22 shows μετάνοια as an ongoing theme through parallel summary statements in 18:1–6; 19:13–15; 19:30; 20:16; 20:26–28; 23:11–12. Specifically, 18:1–6 begins to command

---

32. France, *Matthew*, 826–27.

33. For more discussion of the meaning of this wedding garment, see Davies and Allison, *Matthew 19–28*, 203–8; Turner, *Matthew*, 525n6; Gundry, *Matthew*, 439. For a full bibliography, see Nolland, *Gospel of Matthew*, 883.

34. See Davies and Allison, *Matthew 19–28*, 202, 207; Turner, *Matthew*, 524–25. Contra Hagner, *Matthew 14–28*, 632.

35. France, *Matthew*, 828. France says, "The chosen are the new tenants who will produce the fruit, who may be Jewish or Gentile; their chosenness does not depend of their racial origin but on their response to God's summons and their readiness to give God his due." What France says about God's summons and readiness is, I think, equal to Jesus' calling of μετάνοια and the people's bearing worthy fruit of μετάνοια.

μετάνοια through humility and servanthood and the following parallel statements—19:13–15; 19:30; 20:16; 20:26–28—reflect 18:1–6's commandment of turning (μετανοέω). Chapters 19–22 report conflict between Jesus and the leaders in Jerusalem, with their fruitlessness, wickedness, and rejection of μετάνοια. The story of the rich young man, the parable of laborers in the vineyard, and the account of the dispute among the disciples all illustrate and emphasize the commandment of turning (μετανοέω) through humility and servanthood. The parables of the repenting son, the tenants, and the wedding emphasize μετάνοια and its worthy fruit pointing to the commandment of turning (μετανοέω).[36] This theme and commandment of μετάνοια continues in Matthew 23–25, the last discourse block.

The Thematic Significance of μετάνοια in The Last Discourse

As shown above, the near context of the previous chapters (Matt 18–22) shows the thematic or paradigmatic significance of μετάνοια through humility and servanthood while Jerusalem's religious leaders' rejection of Jesus and their need of μετάνοια with worthy fruit. The fifth discourse block continues to emphasize this same message.

the Significance of μετάνοια in Inclusio Between 23:1–12 and 25:31–46

First, the opening and the ending of the last discourse, 23:1–12 and 25:31–46, create an inclusio and introduce the commandment of the humility and servanthood for the least, such as the poor, thirsty, stranger, naked, sick, and prisoner with corresponding vindication and judgment as a framing idea. Matthew 23:10–12 explains true leadership where the greatest shall be the servant, who does not exalt himself but humbles himself. Matthew 25:31–46 also advocates serving the little one (ἐλάχιστος), such as the poor, thirsty, stranger, naked, sick, and imprisoned. Both texts proclaim judgment according to humility and servanthood.[37]

Additionally, the language of sitting (καθίζω) in terms of the leadership of Israel establishes another parallel between them. Sitting language (καθίζω) occurs in 23:2, where Jesus rebukes the Pharisees and scribes who are sitting

---

36. See Luz, *Matthew 21–28*, 46–47. These three parables depict the leaders of Israel rejecting Jesus, rejecting μετάνοια, and rejecting the worthy fruit of μετάνοια.

37. See Davies and Allison, *Matthew 19–28*, 418–20, for the final judgment idea of Matt 25:31–46 as its main theme.

in Moses' seat. Jesus denounces the Pharisees and scribes as false leaders of Israel (23:10) and proclaims himself as the only true leader. Sitting language (καθίζω) also occurs in 25:31, where Jesus describes the Son of Man sitting in his glorious throne. This parallel occurrence indicates that Jesus Christ, enthroned on his glorious throne, is the only true leader of Israel.

This inclusio through humility and servanthood frames the discourse. As noted above, Matthew 23:11–12 and 25:31–46 parallel 18:1–6; 19:13–15, 19:30, 20:16, and 20:26–28 in the theme of humility and servanthood and echo 3:2, 4:17, and 18:3's commandment of μετάνοια, signifying μετάνοια's exhorting force in this final discourse.

In particular, 18:3–4 and 23:11–12 have almost same phrase. They even use the same language. "The greatest (μείζων)" and "humble (ταπεινόω)" occur in both places. "Servant (διάκονος)" and "child (παιδίον)" occur as synonyms meaning to be humble. Even though μετάνοια does not occur in 23:11–12, 23:11–12 expresses the commandment of turning (μετάνοια) following 18:3–4. Also, the other part of the inclusio (25:31–46) demonstrates themes parallel to humility and serving the least, such as the poor, thirsty, stranger, naked, sick, and imprisoned and expresses 18:3's commandment of μετάνοια through humility and servanthood.

In addition, 25:31–46 parallels Jesus equating serving him with serving the least in 18:1–6 and echoes 18:3's commandment of μετάνοια through humility and servanthood. Both passages command turning oneself to humility and serving the least, and both state that serving the least is serving the Lord himself (18:5; 25:40, 45). As the previous community discourse block of μετάνοια (18:1–10) commands μετάνοια in its meaning of turning and becoming like little ones and serving the little one, the opening of the last discourse echoes and commands 18:3's commandment of μετάνοια in meaning to turn this world's value of greatness to the humility and servanthood of the kingdom of heaven.

Besides denouncing the leadership of the Pharisees and scribes, 23:8–10 and 25:31 proclaim Jesus as the only leader of Israel and Jesus' enthroning as the only leader of Israel. These proclamations implicitly exhort the people of Israel to turn (μετανοέω) from the false leadership of the Pharisees and scribes to the only true leader of Israel, King Jesus. The contrast between the Pharisees and the scribes sitting in Moses' seat and Jesus Christ sitting on his glorious throne also implicitly expresses the Pharisees and scribes' need of μετάνοια. Also, Jesus' admonition not to do the works of the Pharisees and scribes (23:2) nor follow their wicked ways in 23:3–7 shows the negative contents of μετάνοια that the people of Israel need to turn from. The seven woes against the leaders of Israel that follow elaborate on this negative aspect of μετάνοια and provide the negative contents of μετάνοια.

In contrast, the other part of this inclusio (25:31–46) commands humility and service to the least, the positive facet of μετάνοια, which bears the fruits worthy of μετάνοια.

In addition, the humility and servanthood theme in 23:1–12 and 25:31–46 contrasts the Pharisees and scribes, who are self-exalted and served by others, sitting in Moses' seat, with Jesus who humbles himself and serves others as the king of his kingdom. Jesus proclaims himself as the only leader of Israel (23:10) replacing the Pharisees and scribes who exalt themselves to be the greatest sitting on the Moses' seat. This verse calls Israel to turn toward Jesus. Jesus humbles himself and serves his people with his life. The setting of this discourse, in which Jesus came to Jerusalem to lay down his life proves Jesus as only leader of Israel and the universe.

In conclusion, this inclusio between Matthew 23:1–12 and 25:31–46 through the themes and language of humility and servanthood echoes 18:3's commandment of μετάνοια through the humility and servanthood as a framing idea of Matthew 23–25. Also, the contrast in leadership between the Pharisees and the scribes sitting in Moses' seat, and Jesus sitting on the throne, calls people to turn to the humble servant-king Jesus as opposed to the Pharisees and scribes.[38] Matthew 23–25 also proclaims the final judgment according to this μετάνοια. These all show the thematic significance of μετάνοια in the last discourse.

Matthew 23:13–39: The Seven Woes as Negative Contents of μετάνοια

In Matthew 23 Jesus pronounces seven woes on Israel's religious leaders.[39] Jesus' statements are judgments on the scribes and Pharisees for their lack of

---

38. Besides, there is disputation about where the last discourse begins, whether in Matt 23 or 24. For scholars' further discussion on this matter, see Turner, *Matthew*, 543–44. Turner concludes that Matt 23 is the culmination of the conflict between Jesus and Jerusalem's religious leaders, functioning as a bridge or hinge for the eschatological discourse in Matt 24–25. The setting of the mount is found in Matt 24:3, but Matt 23 should be included for the following two reasons. The seven woes in Matt 23 create an inclusio between nine μακάριος in the first discourse block of the sermon (Meier, *Vision of Matthew*, 163). They give positive and negative contents for the commandment of turning (μετανοέω) (4:17). Also, in terms of the structural analysis, Matt 23:1–12 and 25:31–46 create an inclusio through the theme and language of humility and servanthood and the language of sitting (καθίζω) in Moses' seat (23:2) and Jesus' glorious throne (25:31). In this sense, Matt 23 should be included in the last discourse blocks. See also Gundry, *Matthew*, 453, where he connects Matt 23–25 to the sermon.

39. See Luz, *Matthew 21–28*, 168–77, for theological issues and discussions for Matt 23. Also, see Nolland, *Gospel of Matthew*, 919–20, 931, for full bibliography lists discussing Matt 23. See Davies and Allison, *Matthew 19–28*, 324, where they disagree that

humility and servanthood mentioned in 23:1–12. These woes reveal the negative aspects of μετάνοια (what Israel's leaders should turn (μετανοέω) from), especially as it relates to humility and servanthood (23:1–12).[40] In addition, these woes contrast to nine *makarisms* in the sermon, which demonstrate the positive aspects or contents of μετάνοια.[41] These woes and Jesus' charge of humility and servanthood parallel John the Baptist's μετάνοια commandment in 3:2, 7 (and 4:17's) for the leaders of Israel. The seven woes rebuke the Pharisees, scribes, and people of Israel, implicitly calling them to turn. Some scholars also say that the seven woes also apply μετάνοια to the church.[42]

In the opening of the seven woes, Matthew 23:11–12, Jesus calls his disciples to turn from the Pharisees and scribes to Jesus and his kingdom using parallel μετάνοια language, turning servanthood into the greatest value and reversing the usual understanding of high and low standing. In the closing of the seven woes, Matthew 23:37–39, Jesus calls Israel to turn to him through acknowledging him as their Lord.[43] Matthew 23:37 summarizes Jesus' ministry noting that he tried to gather the people of Israel, but they rejected him. Jesus' judgment of seven woes corresponds to their rejection: "Your house is left to you desolate" (23:38). Finally, in 23:39 Jesus proclaims another conceptual μετάνοια call, that if anyone says to Jesus, "Blessed is he who comes in the name of the Lord" (23:39), they will see him (Acts 3:19).[44]

---

these woes designate God's definite rejection of Israel as a whole, but only the religious leaders of Israel. They keep saying that Matt 23:39 expects "the time of repentance and reconciliation."

40. Davies and Allison, *Matthew 19–28*, 261, similarly argues the seven woes are not repentance calling, but "negative role models for believing readers." Davies and Allison understand repentance as a one-time entrance event, so they designate these woes as negative role models for believers. However, as discussed before, repentance is a lifelong event and thus these woes can be designated as the negative aspects of turning (μετανοέω).

41. Gundry, *Matthew*, 453; Bruner, *Matthew 13–28*, 430. See also Luz, *Matthew 21–28*, 114–49, which shows thematic and verbal contradictions between the sermon and the seven woe statements. See also Pennington, *Sermon on the Mount and Human Flourishing*, 41–68, 137–68. See ch. 7 for a discussion on the sermon as the contents of the commandment of turning (μετανοέω). Bruner also says the sermon teaches how to live, and the sermon of woes teaches how not to live. Bruner interestingly connects these two teaching blocks to Jesus' baptism with the Holy Spirit and fire (3:11); one saves and the other judges.

42. Bruner, *Matthew 13–28*, 428–29. See also Garland, *Intention of Matthew 23*, 23, 37, 215; Stanton, Inter*pretation of Matthew*, 14.

43. Turner, *Matthew*, 562.

44. Davies and Allison, *Matthew 19–28*, 324. In contrast, Luz argues that this phrase indicates the judgment of Israel, which corresponds to Jewish expectations about the Son of Man (*Matthew 21–28*, 164).

Matthew 23 includes parallel μετάνοια language, which underscores the theme of μετάνοια.[45] For example, the language of "serpents" and "brood of vipers" in 23:33 also recalls John the Baptist's μετάνοια preaching in Matthew 3 and demonstrates Matthew 23 as a μετάνοια discourse. Both places proclaim μετάνοια to the leaders of Israel. Matthew 23 elaborates the μετάνοια message that John the Baptist proclaimed against the leaders of Israel. In addition, parallel οὐαί language connects Matthew 23 parallels with μετανοέω in Matthew 11:21, "Woe to you, Chorazin! Woe to you, Bethsaida! For if the mighty works done in you had been done in Tyre and Sidon, they would have repented long ago in sackcloth and ashes." Matthew 11:21 announces woes (οὐαί) to the people of Israel who reject μετάνοια. Jesus declares the seven woes(οὐαί) in Matthew 23 to the un-μετάνοια leaders of Israel to turn their sins. This shows Matthew 23 is μετάνοια message. Matthew 18:6–7 also proclaims woes (οὐαί) to those who cause the little one of μετάνοια to stumble. The language of woes (οὐαί) occurs in Matthew 11:21; 18:7, and 23 and all occurrences demonstrate the theme of μετάνοια.

In short, the seven woes in Matthew 23 proclaim the negative contents of μετάνοια by showing what the leaders of Israel must turn from, and then Jesus finally calls them to turn (μετανοέω) toward him through accepting him as their Lord.

Matthew 24:1–41: Judgment for Rejecting μετάνοια and Signs of the Return of Christ

Matthew 24 is the center of the Matthean judgment sayings and language (7:15–27; 10:32–33, 39–42; 13:36–43, 47–50; 18:23–35)[46] and expands and explains the judgment of the woes (οὐαί) from the previous section. This judgment discourse proclaims the destruction of the temple and the signs of Christ's return, i.e. the end of the age (24:1–35). Matthew 24:1–41 indicates that the final judgment day is delayed to the second coming of Christ. This judgment begins with the temple destruction and will end when Christ returns.[47] The temple destruction in AD 70 anticipates the final judgment

---

45. See also Davies and Allison, *Matthew 19–28*, 307–8, for previously mentioned accusations in Matt 1–22, which also appear in these seven woes.

46. Luz, *Matthew 21–28*, 179, says Matt 24 is the center of Matthew's judgment theme (cf. 7:15–27; 10:32–33, 39–42; 13:36–43, 47–50; 18:23–35).

47. This view is called the "*preterist-futurist*" view by Turner (*Matthew*, 566–67; emphasis his). Turner explains that this view reads some verses as proclaiming the temple destruction in AD 70, and some other verses as proclaiming the final judgment. There are two other major views on Matt 24: the "*preterist* (past)" view reads all sayings of Matt 24 as fulfilled in AD 70, and the "*futurist* (future)" holds that all of Matt 24 will

at Christ's second coming.[48] In addition, Matthew 24 proclaims not only judgment but also salvation. "One will be taken and the other left" (24:40, 41) when Christ returns (24:14, 30, 33, 39).

This judgment and reward discourse echoes and parallels John the Baptist's μετάνοια commandment and judgment sayings in Matthew 3:2–12.[49] Also, this coming of the final salvation and judgment with Christ's return echoes and parallels Jesus' commandment of μετάνοια in Matthew 4:17 for the coming kingdom of heaven with judgment and salvation. As has been discussed, Jesus' teachings about salvation and judgment are inseparable to one's μετάνοια and the former encourages and emphasizes the latter. Therefore, Matthew 24 likely culminates the reward and judgment sayings of Jesus corresponding to Jesus' public ministry opening commandment of μετάνοια (4:17).[50] In this respect, this teaching of the last judgment and reward exhorts μετάνοια and the life of μετάνοια since the end of the world is imminent (3:2; 4:17).

Bruner, discussing Matthew 24, conclusively says, "When Jesus said, 'Repent for the kingdom of heaven is very near,' he meant, at least, 'Change your way of living because the end of the world is imminent!'"[51] In short, Matthew 24 explains the final judgment and implicitly exhorts μετάνοια and a life of μετάνοια in order to be saved and not to be judged at the end of the world, which is the summary of Jesus' ministry (4:17).

Matthew 23:37–39, which heads Matthew 24, shows that Matthew 24 demonstrates that Israel's judgment is the result of their rejecting the call to μετάνοια as proclaimed by prophets, wise men, and scribes (23:31, 34). In contrast, Runesson argues that Israel's rejection of Jesus is not the reason for the judgment on Israel, especially the temple destruction. He rather argues that the temple was already defiled and its destruction was evitable. Also, the temple destruction is the rationale for Jesus' sacrificial death that continues atonement of sins after the destruction.[52] It is insightful. However, as this book has shown, the plot and the judgment theme of Matthew also show

---

be fulfilled in Christ's second coming. For more discussion of different options for this discourse, see Davies and Allison, *Matthew 19–28*, 328–31. See also Nolland, *Gospel of Matthew*, 954–56, 964, 968, 977, 981–82, 986, 992, 996 for a helpful bibliography for Matt 24.

48. Davies and Allison, *Matthew 19–28*, 328–31.

49. See ch. 4 for John the Baptist's μετάνοια preaching in Matt 3:2–12 as an introduction of the whole Gospel and the parallelism between Matt 3:2–12 and Matt 24.

50. See ch. 5 for μετάνοια for a major Matthean salvation structure. Ch. 5 discusses Jesus' judgment and vindication saying in relation to μετάνοια.

51. Bruner, *Matthew 13–28*, 467.

52. Runesson, *Divine Wrath and Salvation*, 119, 126–30.

that Israel's rejection of Jesus' (and all the prophets') μετάνοια call is one of the main reasons for the judgment on Jerusalem, the temple destruction, and therefore Israel (11:20–27; 12:41–42; 19:21–24, 27–30; 23:30–39).[53] Specifically, the torn temple veil at the moment of Jesus' death points to the reason for the destruction of the temple—its defilement by the sins of Israel and the culmination of the sins of Israel, killing Jesus Christ.

Matthew 24:42–51: Being Ready and Staying Awake as Having Lifelong μετάνοια and a Focal Point for Matthew 25

Since no one knows the day and the hour of Christ's return, Matthew 24:42, 44 advises staying awake (γρηγορέω) and being ready (ἕτοιμος). These two parallel commandments—staying awake (γρηγορέω) and being ready (ἕτοιμος)—mean the same thing. Davies and Allison note that 24:42, 44 warn foolish "leisurely repentance."[54] Gundry notes these verses point to true or false discipleship, which treats fellow disciples well or abusively, and especially issues "a warning to ecclesiastical leaders... to love the little people in the Church."[55]

This commandment to be ready (and stay awake) is a repetition of John the Baptist's prepatory ministry for the coming of the Christ with the commandment of turning (μετανοέω) and producing worthy fruit (3:1–8). John the Baptist's ministry of preparing the way of the Lord in Matthew 3 complements his commandment of μετάνοια for the first coming of the Lord Jesus so that the people of Israel will not perish but enter the kingdom of heaven. This shows that what John the Baptist means by being ready (or preparing) for the coming of the Lord in 3:2–12 is to turn (μετανοέω) and produce the fruits worthy of μετάνοια. Jesus who continues John's μετάνοια ministry(3:2; 4:17) commands the same commandment to be ready and stay awake in Matthew 24:42–51 and in Matthew 25. This parallel commandment shows that Matthew 24:42–25's commandment to be ready (ἕτοιμος) and stay awake (γρηγορέω) for the coming of the Lord repeats and continues John the Baptist's commandment of μετάνοια and living a worthy life of μετάνοια.

---

53. For a full discussion and reference for the judgment of Israel because of their rejection of Jesus, see Luz, *Matthew 21–28*, 285–96. The judgment discourse obviously describes the final judgment of all nations, including Israel, at the end of the ages. In this sense, Israel's rejection of Jesus is still the reason for their judgment.

54 See Davies and Allison, *Matthew 19–28*, 383. They do not mention that 24:42, 44 are connected to 3:2, 3; 4:17, but they clearly show that 24:42, 44 implicitly command repentance before the second coming of Jesus Christ.

55. Gundry, *Matthew*, 495.

Specifically, Matthew 25 elaborates this commandment of being ready and staying awake before the second coming of the Lord through three parables of wisdom and faithfulness. Even though the term μετάνοια does not occur in these parables, the concepts of being ready and staying awake parallel John the Baptist's μετάνοια preaching as a way to be ready for the coming of the Lord (Matt 3:2–3) and echo and repeat 3:2's and 4:17's μετάνοια commandment. In short, Matthew 24:42–25 teaches its listeners to be ready for Christ's return through lifelong, wise and faithful μετάνοια in humility and servanthood. In other words, the commandment of being ready and staying awake means to have wise and faithful life worthy of μετάνοια.

John the Baptist and Jesus' Paralleled Commandment of Being Ready Through μετάνοια

Why does Jesus repeat the same commandment of being ready (and staying awake) in Matthew 24:41–25 in parallel to John the Baptist (3:2, 3, 8; 4:17; 24:41–25)? The backdrop is the delay in the full coming of the kingdom of heaven and the final judgment until the second coming of Jesus. The kingdom of heaven and the final judgment will be fully accomplished when Christ returns. While being ready language in both places (3:2–12 and 24:42–44) designates turning (μετανοέω) and having fruits worthy of μετάνοια, there is a temporal difference in that Matthew 3 awaits the first coming of Christ, but 23–25 awaits the second coming of Christ. John the Baptist proclaims μετάνοια for the people of Israel to be ready for the coming kingdom of heaven so that they will not perish but enter the kingdom of heaven. Jesus continues John the Baptist's μετάνοια ministry to make his people ready (and awake) for the complete coming of the kingdom of heaven with the second coming of the Lord Christ. In both places, Matthew uses language of being ready for the coming of the Lord with the meaning of μετάνοια.[56] This shows the thematic significance of μετάνοια in Matthew 25.

For instance, John the Baptist's misunderstanding of Jesus Christ in Matthew 11:1–6 explains this temporal gap between the first and the second coming of Christ. John the Baptist does not know about this eschatological time gap between the first and second coming of Christ. John the Baptist sends his disciple to Jesus to find out if Jesus is the One he awaits. John the Baptist expected Jesus to judge wicked Israel and vindicate the people who received him and his μετάνοια preaching, but Jesus did not. In other words, John the Baptist expected an eschatological Christ who would perform

---

56. See ch. 4 for the parallelism between John the Baptist's and Jesus' μετάνοια ministry.

the final judgment of Israel and of all nations, but the final judgment will come later—at the second coming of Christ. John should not expect the final judgment at the first coming of the Christ but the second coming. That is why Jesus says, "Blessed is the one who is not offended by me" (11:6). This scene explains the delayed coming of the final judgment till the second coming of Christ. In this delayed time frame of the end days, Jesus, just like John the Baptist, proclaims μετάνοια as being ready (and staying awake) for the second coming of Christ.

The Parable of the Wise and Faithful Servant (Matt 24:45–51)

The parable of the wise and faithful servant in 24:45–51 explains that being ready and staying awake means being wise and faithful.[57] As noted above, being ready and staying awake denote lifelong fruitful μετάνοια, and being a wise and faithful servant describes being ready and staying awake and so does lifelong fruitful μετάνοια. The servant language of the parable and the serving work of the servant taking care of the household, giving them food to eat, illustrate a coherent theme of Matthew 23–25, that is, μετάνοια through humility and servanthood and corresponding reward and judgment. Those who turn (μετανοέω) to Jesus and live a fruitful life worthy of μετάνοια are wise and faithful and are ready to enter eternal life, not the eternal fire, when Jesus returns.

In addition, μακάριος language, calling for the wise and faithful servant who is ready and stays awake in 24:46, connects this parable to the μακάριος, the contents of fruit worthy of μετάνοια in the sermon (5:3–12),[58] and demonstrates the theme of μετάνοια of the parable. "Blessed one" (μακάριος) in the sermon indicates those who turn (μετανοέω) to Jesus (4:17) and bear nine μακάριος as its fruits(5:3–12), and here also μακάριος language indicates that the wise and faithful servant who is being made ready for the coming of the Lord is the one who turns (μετανοέω) to Jesus and bears fruit in serving the household. Both the being ready language and the μακάριος language express the theme of μετάνοια in the parable.

In addition, the language of being wise parallels the parable of the wise and foolish builders in the sermon (7:24–27). The wise builder in the sermon also illustrates the one who turns (μετανοέω) to Jesus and bears worthy fruit of μετάνοια, just as the wise servant does here. Also, the contrast between

---

57. See Davies and Allison, *Matthew 19–28*, 394. They have six main points for this parable: "Division into two Groups; Delay of the *Parousia*; Ignorance of the hour; Suddenness of the end; Necessity to watch; Requirement of prudence."

58. See ch. 7 for nine *makarios* as the contents of fruit worthy of μετάνοια.

the blessed (μακάριος) servant and the evil servant and their corresponding judgment parallels the wise and foolish builder in the sermon (7:24–27).[59] In short, references to being ready, being wise, and being μακάριος express the theme of μετάνοια in the parable in its close connection to the sermon, which is μετάνοια message of Jesus.

In addition, 24:42–51 functions as the opening focal point of Matthew 25. This parable of the blessed (μακάριος) wise and faithful servant expresses μετάνοια and the fruitful life of μετάνοια and shows the thematic significance of μετάνοια in the three parables in Matthew 25 along with humility and servanthood. The three parables in Matthew 25 expand on the theme of being ready and staying awake through the lens of μακάριος wise and faithful servant. Based on 24:45 especially, the words "wise" and "faithful" govern the first two parables in Matthew 25. The wise and faithful language in 24:45 occurs in the parable of the ten virgins (25:2, 4, 8, 9) and the parable of the talents (25:21, 23) and demonstrate this governance.

Therefore, the wise and faithful one in Matthew 25 who is ready (or prepared [ἕτοιμος]) and staying awake for the coming of the Lord illustrates and exhorts the fruitful life worthy of μετάνοια, practicing humility and servanthood in preparation for the second coming or return of Christ (25:31–46). In short, the parables of the wise virgins and of the talents in Matthew 25:1–30 command hearers to be wise by being faithful in the μετάνοια through humility and servanthood till the second coming of the Lord. Additionally, the last parable of the goats and sheep depicts the final judgment according to this wise and faithful life of μετάνοια lived in humility and servanthood.

Matthew 25: Three Parables Illustrating Lifelong μετάνοια Through Humility and Servanthood

As mentioned previously, Matthew 25 is governed by 24:42–51—the wise and faithful servant who illustrates fruitful μετάνοια life as a way of being ready and staying awake before the second coming of the Lord. The parables of the ten virgins and of the talents in Matthew 25 also command believers to be wise and faithful so as to be ready (ἕτοιμος) and to stay awake by having fruitful μετάνοια life of humility and servanthood while waiting the coming of the final judgment. In other words, they promote μετάνοια and its worthy fruit until the second coming of Christ in order to enter the wedding banquet and the joy of the Lord. The parable of the goats and sheep also encourages a life of humility and servanthood and points to consequent

---

59. Luz, *Matthew 21–28*, 221 also argues for this connection.

judgment, either inheriting the kingdom and eternal life or being thrown into the eternal punishment of fire (25:31–46).

Matthew 25:1–13: The parable of ten women. The bridegroom's return will be delayed from the time of his last day on earth until the second coming of Christ and the parable of ten women commands us to be ready. As discussed above, the contents of being ready is μετάνοια, thus the parable of the ten women calls for wisdom and the need to be ready (or prepared ἕτοιμος) and stay awake (24:42, 44; 25:10, 13) through the μετάνοια life for an unknown length of time.[60]

Particularly, in the near context of the last discourse this μετάνοια life indicates the life of humility and servanthood. As mentioned in the section above, the inclusio and the closing comments of Jesus for the parables in Matthew 25:31–46 indicate that the five women who came prepared with oil illustrates wisdom, humility, and service to the least. Therefore, the five wise women's oil preparation (ἕτοιμος) expresses and echoes a μετάνοια life until the second coming of the Christ, especially demonstrated through humility and servanthood.[61] Again, the oil the five wise women prepare, the symbol of wisdom, also exhorts the need for a continuous life of μετάνοια through humility and servanthood while waiting for this delayed coming of the kingdom of heaven with the return of Christ. The five foolish virgins who are not allowed to enter the wedding banquet signify judgment for failure to prepare the oil that indicates a continuous life of μετάνοια of humility and servanthood.

Bruner says that some scholars argue for a legalistic reading of the parable that attacks the Reformation heritage of *sola fide*. However, he argues that the oil in the parable indicates the Christian life instructed in Matthew, not "conversions-only" but "a life of patient listening to the Word and of

---

60. See Blomberg, *Interpreting the Parables*, 193–97; France, "On Being Ready," 177–95; Sherriff, "Matthew 25:1–13," 301–5.

61. For a different interpretation of this oil, see Davies and Allison, *Matthew 19–28*, 396–97. They note that a common view is that the oil and lamp indicate good works. But Davies and Allison argue the oil indicates not only good works but also various obligations such as abstinence from bad behavior (15:19), love for enemies (5:44), love of other Christians (24:12), forgiveness of others (18:21–35), unhesitating faith (21:21), loyalty to Jesus (10:23), and love for God (22:37). Davies and Allison also give other different views of interpreting the oil: humanitarian acts, Christ himself, love, the Holy Spirit, grace, faith, fidelity to duty, and a personal relationship with the Lord. Also, see Luz, *Matthew 21–28*, 235–44, for a history of interpretation of this parable. One interesting interpretation is the Catholic understanding of the oil as works, thus a legalistic understanding. However, the oil, as I argue, indicates μετάνοια and its outward works according to its inward presence.

constant repenting under the conviction of the Word."[62] He says Luther even emphasizes the Christian life of μετάνοια, quoting Luther's first line of the Ninety-Five Theses, "When our Lord and Master Jesus Christ said 'repent (μετάνοια),' he intended for the whole life of believers to be a life of repentance (μετάνοια)."[63] In other words, the oil in this parable indicates a life of μετάνοια. Bruner says that although the word repentance does not occur here and not often in other parables of Matthew, many parables, especially this parable of the ten virgin women proclaims reward and judgment and seeks repentance as a key reaction.[64]

The parable of the ten virgins parallels the sermon with its use of the terms wise (7:24; 24:45; 25:2, 4, 8) and foolish (5:13; 7:26; 25:2, 3, 8).[65] Particularly, as the sermon instructs the contents of μετάνοια, parallel references to being wise (φρόνιμος) in the parable of the wise and foolish builders in the sermon (7:24–27) also show the theme of μετάνοια in this parable of ten virgins, five wise and five foolish. The wise (φρόνιμος) in the sermon indicates the μετάνοια one who turns to Jesus and follows his commandment in the sermon. Specifically, the wise (φρόνιμος) builder indicates the one who pursues the contents of μετάνοια that Jesus teaches in the sermon.[66] In this respect, the five wise virgins who prepared extra oil possibly illustrate those who do what Jesus teaches in the sermon, and especially the μετάνοια of humility and servanthood in the near context of the last discourse. The wise among the ten virgins also indicates that they turned to Jesus and followed his commandments till the second coming of Christ. The language of foolishness also parallels the last discourse as well as the sermon. The fool in the sermon is the one who does not turn to Jesus and follow his commandments. The fool in the parable of the ten virgins also illustrates those who do not turn to Jesus and follow his command to practice humble servanthood in preparation for the second coming of Christ.

Also, the parallel judgment sayings in 7:21–23 and 25:12 demonstrate a μετάνοια parallelism between the sermon and this parable.[67] Jesus will not recognize the fool in the sermon and in the last discourse and they will be taken to eternal fire and punishment, but the wise will enter the kingdom of heaven and have eternal life. As 7:21–23 rebukes those who do not have the sincere life of μετάνοια with its worthy fruit, the parallel language

---

62. Bruner, *Matthew 13–28*, 545.
63. Bruner, *Matthew 13–28*, 545–46.
64. Bruner, *Matthew 13–28*, 550.
65. See also Gundry, *Matthew*, 498–99.
66. See ch. 6.
67. France, *Matthew*, 947.

in 25:12 rebukes the foolish women. This parallel judgment language indicates that the foolish women who are not ready for the bridegroom depict those who do not have the sincere life of μετάνοια with worthy fruit.[68] In contrast, this parallel judgment language indicates that the wise women who are ready for the bridegroom illustrate those who have the sincere life of μετάνοια with its worthy fruit.[69]

Matthew 25:14–30: The parable of the talents. The parable of the talents commands faithfulness in preparing for the delayed coming of the Lord.[70] Davies and Allison also note that this parable emphasizes daily repentance for the unpredictable day of *parousia*.[71] Following 24:42–51 and the parable of the ten virgins, I suggest that this parable of the talents illustrate and exhort faithful μετάνοια life through humility and servanthood.

The three servants receive five, two, and one talents. This unrealistic number of talents represents God's gracious gifts for his people.[72] The word *talent* also occurs in Matthew 18:24 and connects the parable of the unforgiving servant with this parable of the talents. The forgiveness of a ten-thousand-talent debt indicates that the talents here also depict the grace of God. Specifically, the talents refer to the life of Jesus Christ who was humble and gave his life to serve his people and purchase their salvation. In this respect,

---

68. France, *Matthew*, 947n51 mentions a similar first-century rabbinic parable in b. Šabb. 153a, and says that "the context applies it to the danger of leaving repentance until one's deathbed." In other words, this parable demonstrates the theme of lifelong, sincere μετάνοια.

69. Many parables in Matthew point to this sincere life of μετάνοια with worthy fruit, such as the hidden treasure, the pearl, the wedding garment, the oil in the parable of the ten virgins, and so on. Bruner also connects the oil in this parable to the wedding garments, to selling one's all in the parables of the hidden treasure and the pearl, demonstrating that they all indicate the Christian life, in other words, the obedience of faith (*Matthew 13–28*, 545).

70. See Blomberg, *Interpreting the Parables*, 214–21; Carpenter, "Parable of the Talents," 165–81; Steinmetz, "Matthew 25:14–30," 172–76. Davies and Allison, *Matthew 19–28*, 402, says "the parable is more warning than encouragement."

71. Davies and Allison, *Matthew 19–28*, 411.

72. Davies and Allison, *Matthew 19–28*, 405. Luz, *Matthew 21–28*, 259, gives a historical understanding of the talent: the word of God, varying levels of understanding the Scriptures, charismata (1 Cor 12:12–31), social position, wealth and influence, a person's ability (which is not likely), and so on. Luz concludes that "the parable of talents is theologically true only when it speaks of the God of Jesus Christ, who loves people in such a way that they are indebted to him for everything that they are and that they can achieve. It is theologically true only when it speaks of his commission to love and of the gifts that are used for that purpose and not for just any human activities. It is theologically true only when it is related to the community of love that Jesus wanted" (*Matthew 21–28*, 261–62).

the talent is a symbol of Jesus' life of humility and servanthood. Jesus sows this life of humility and servanthood and asks us to do the same (25:26).

The first two faithful servants gain extra talents. They work faithfully and gain a profit as expected. Their lives, in the absence of their lord, represent the faithful life of the people of Christ who receive Jesus' commandment of μετάνοια and sincerely follow Jesus' teaching and life. Specifically, their lives illustrate practicing μετάνοια through humility and servanthood that benefits the "least among them" as indicated in the near context of the last discourse and in the ending explanation the parable (25:31–46).

The third, the unfaithful servant, is wicked and slothful. He fails to earn a profit on his talent, which illustrates an unfaithful, fruitless life without μετάνοια of humility and servanthood.[73] He will be cast into outer darkness, while the first two servants will enter into the joy of the Lord.

Matthew 25:31–46: The parable of the sheep and goats. The last section of Matthew 25, the parable of the sheep and goats (25:31–46)[74] illustrates the theme of humility and servanthood as expressed by caring for and serving the least of the world, such as the poor, thirsty, stranger, naked, sick, and prisoner. Corresponding judgment and reward are expressed by the final judgment of the whole world. This parable also embodies the μετάνοια commandment of humility and servanthood from the previous chapter. While the parables of the ten virgins and the talents illustrate μετάνοια through humility and servanthood in the picture of wisdom and faithfulness, the last parable of the goats and sheep bolsters this commandment by proclaiming humility and servanthood for the least of the world (25:31–46) and the corresponding final judgment about whether one can inherit the kingdom and eternal life or must be thrown into the eternal fire of punishment.

Also, the closing words of the last discourse (25:31–46) clarify that wisdom and faithfulness in the previous two parables illustrate a fruitful life of μετάνοια through humility and servanthood. As noted above, the ending of the last discourse block (25:31–46) creates an inclusio with the opening of the discourse (23:1–12) around the themes of enthroning and of μετάνοια through humility and servanthood. Matthew 25:31–46 ends these two parables and commands lifelong μετάνοια through humility and servanthood using the image of the goats and the sheep, which represent

---

73. He is wicked because he falsely suggests the lord has a reputation for being hard. He intentionally gives negative representation of the lord to hide his slothfulness.

74. See Court, "Right and Left," 223–33; Derrett, "Unfair to Goats," 177–78; Donahue, "'Parable' of the Sheep and the Goats," 3–31; Foster, "Making Sense of Matthew 25:31–46," 128–39; Watson, "Liberating the Reader," 57–84; Otto, "Ethical Responsibility and Human Wholeness," 79–100; Luz, "Final Judgment," 271–310; Weber, "Image of the Sheep and Goats," 657–78.

two groups of people—those who are humble and serving on the right and the others who are not humble and do not serve on the left side of the king. In particular, both Matthew18:1–6 and 25:31–46 note that to serve the least is to serve the Lord himself and command turning to humility and serving the least. To serve the least of his brothers probably indicates to serve all who do the will of the Father in heaven (12:50), no matter their ethnicity or background.[75]

The parable of the house builders in the last section of the sermon, the parable of the wheat and the weeds, and the parable of the net (Matt 13) similarly divide two groups of people, one good and the other bad. As previously discussed, they indicate whether one has μετάνοια and the fruit of μετάνοια in doing the will of the Father in heaven. In addition, the parallel language of righteousness in 25:37, 45, 46 and the works of righteousness, that is humility and servanthood for the least, show other contents of Matthean righteousness as fruit worthy of μετάνοια.[76] Jesus is always intimate with outcasts and sinners, both Jews and gentiles, this intimate language of brothers generally indicates the least ones in society regardless of their ethnicity and background.

Lastly, the theme of being ready through a μετάνοια life of humility and servanthood in the last discourse interestingly creates a large inclusio with John the Baptist's being ready through μετάνοια and his description of the fruitful μετάνοια life in Matthew 3. Matthew 3 and 23–25 parallel the theme and language of the μετάνοια life of humility and servanthood, the judgment theme involving language against Israel and the leaders of Israel, the universal salvation theme and language, and the theme of the first and the second coming of the Christ. This parallelism and inclusio demonstrate the thematic and paradigmatic significance of μετάνοια in the Gospel of Matthew.

Conclusion

Jesus' prediction of his death and resurrection in Matthew 16:21 opens a new stage of his public ministry where the themes of humility and servanthood begin to be emphasized. Matthew 18:1–6 especially begins to command μετάνοια through humility and servanthood. The following parallel summary statements (18:1–6; 19:13–15; 19:30; 20:16; 20:26–28; 23:11–12; 25:31–46) of each major section of Matthew 18–25 demonstrate the thematic significance of μετάνοια through humility and servanthood in the second phase of the Matthean narrative section, namely Matthew 16:21–25:46.

75. See Davies and Allison, *Matthew 19–28*, 428–29; France, *Matthew*, 957–60; Turner, *Matthew*, 604–7 for more information about scholarly discussion of this matter.

76. See ch. 6 on righteousness as one of the contents of μετάνοια in Matthew.

As chapter 4 argues, Matthew narrates the life of Jesus as a model of the repentant people, and the second stage of Jesus public ministry, from Matthew 16:21, demonstrates in his suffering and death Jesus' life as a model of μετάνοια through humility and servanthood (20:26-28).

The community discourse (18), the story of the rich young man (19:13-30), the parable of laborers in the vineyard (20:1-16), the dispute among the disciples about who is the greatest (20:20-28), the parable of the two sons (21:20-32), which I call the parable of the μετάνοια son, the parable of the tenants (21:33-46), and the parable of the wedding banquet (22:1-14) all illustrate the theme of μετάνοια through humility and servanthood. These stories and parables also depict the leaders of Israel's rejection of μετάνοια (through humility and servanthood) and the conflict between Jesus and these leaders.

Matthew 23 rebukes the leaders of Israel and proclaims the negative contents of μετάνοια, which they need to turn from, with seven woes in contrast to the nine μακάριος in the sermon, which give the positive contents of μετάνοια. The opening focal phrase of the last discourse block (23:11-12) echoes Jesus' μετάνοια commandment in 18:3-4. This repetition of the μετάνοια commandment demonstrates the significance of μετάνοια in the last discourse. Matthew 23:33-38 proclaims a corresponding judgment against Israel and the leaders of Israel for their rejection of Jesus' μετάνοια calling and their persecution of Jesus. This judgment proclamation (23:33-38) leads to its full contents in Matthew 24-25.

Matthew 24 explains the final judgment on Israel for rejecting μετάνοια and warns that everyone must be ready for Jesus' return by living a μετάνοια life of humility and servanthood. Matthew 24:42-51 summarizes the rest of the discourse block. Matthew 24:42-25:46 directs listeners to always be ready for Christ's return because the day of judgment has been delayed till the second coming of Christ. Such preparation requires lifelong μετάνοια and a fruitful life of μετάνοια until Christ returns. Matthew 25 commands a μετάνοια life of humility and servanthood in the language of being ready and staying awake (25:1-30). John the Baptist originally commands μετάνοια as the way to be ready (ἕτοιμος) for the first coming of Christ with his kingdom (3:2-3), and Jesus continues John's μετάνοια ministry and commands μετάνοια in the last discourse as the way to be ready (ἕτοιμος) for the second coming of Christ with his kingdom. The three parables in Matthew 25 each exhort a μετάνοια life of humility and servanthood and proclaim the final judgment according to one's μετάνοια life of humility and servanthood (25:31-46).

Chapter 12
Conclusion

THIS BOOK ARGUES THE thematic and paradigmatic significance of μετάνοια in the Gospel of Matthew. The Gospel of Matthew is Jesus' μετάνοια message. This does not mean μετάνοια is the only theme of Matthew, but it is a significant or major theme that Jesus proclaims at the beginning of his public ministry (4:17; cf. 3:2–12).

This book has examined scholarship on the theology of repentance and works as they relate to μετάνοια in the Synoptics. This research shows that this theme has been somewhat underdeveloped in Matthean scholarship. In addition, through the history of literature, I have examined a survey on the scholarship about the lexical meanings of μετάνοια, showing that μετάνοια lexically means turning (or changing) one's heart and deeds, and so one's whole being and life, from sin to righteousness, Jesus, and his teaching and life. It is a turning of the mind (or heart) and of actions, in which the outward expression and the inward turning are inseparable.

This understanding of the meaning of μετανοέω and μετάνοια reveals that the opening commandment of turning (μετανοέω) in the introductory and summarizing phrases of John the Baptist and of Jesus' public ministry (Matt 3:2–12 and 4:17) leads the whole Gospel of Matthew and shows its thematic and paradigmatic significance in Matthew. Specifically, John the Baptist's introductory μετάνοια preaching block (3:1–12) shows this significance of the commandment of turning (μετανοέω) and the fruit worthy of μετάνοια throughout the book. Much parallel language and many similar images between John the Baptist's μετάνοια preaching block (3:1–12) and the rest of Matthew show the significance of μετάνοια in John's μετάνοια and the rest of the book.

While the terms μετανοέω and μετάνοια do not occur frequently in Matthew, the essence, concepts, images, language, and their contents occur throughout the book and reveal the thematic and paradigmatic significance of μετάνοια and the fruit worthy of μετάνοια in Matthew.

Synonyms, antonyms, conceptual expressions, parables, and indirect or implicit expressions such as widespread discipleship, doing the will of God, righteousness, good works, eschatological judgment, the stories of both repentant and unrepentant people, and the Great Commission all point to the nature of the command to turn (μετανοέω) and bear fruit worthy of μετάνοια throughout the Gospel of Matthew.

The second half of this book examined the thematic and paradigmatic significance of μετάνοια in Jesus' five teaching blocks in Matthew. Each of the five major teaching discourse blocks demonstrates the significance of μετάνοια. Matthew opens Jesus' public ministry with the opening commandment of turning (μετανοέω) (4:17) and the following Matthean discourse blocks each contribute to this theme in a variety of ways. The sermon describes and illustrates the essence and contents of μετάνοια and its fruitful life. Matthew 10 commissions the apostles for universal μετάνοια mission and life. Matthew 13 figuratively depicts the mixed reception of μετάνοια and exhortation to μετάνοια. Matthew 18 teaches the community life of μετάνοια advocating turning and becoming like a little child. Matthew 23–25 reveals the negative contents of μετάνοια, the corresponding final judgment, and the wise and faithful life of μετάνοια in humility and servanthood as preparation for the second coming of the Christ.

The significant Matthean theme of μετάνοια commands and teaches both negative and positive aspects, and points to a final judgment corresponding to one's μετάνοια and fruitful life. μετάνοια in Matthew is not only a once-for-all turning, but an ongoing life of μετάνοια, following Jesus Christ's teaching and his life. People should be ready for the second coming of the Christ by practicing a fruitful life of μετάνοια.

Bibliography

Alexander, Joseph A. *The Gospel According to Matthew*. Grand Rapids: Baker, 1980.
Allison, Dale C. "The Continuity between John and Jesus." *Journal for the Study of the Historical Jesus* 1.1 (January 1, 2003) 6–27.
———. "Matthew: Structure, Biographical Impulse, and the Imitatio Christi." In *Four Gospels*, edited by Frans Van Segbroeck, 1203–21. Louvain: Peeters, 1992.
———. "Matthew 10:26–31 and the Problem of Evil." *St. Vladimir's Theological Quarterly* 32.4 (1988) 293–308.
———. *The New Moses: A Matthean Typology*. Minneapolis: Fortress, 1994.
———. *The Sermon on the Mount: Inspiring the Moral Imagination*. New York: The Crossroad, 1999.
———. "The Structure of the Sermon on the Mount." *Journal of Biblical Literature* 106.3 (September 1, 1987) 423–45.
———. *Studies in Matthew: Interpretation Past and Present*. Grand Rapids: Baker Academic, 2012.
Bailey, Jon Nelson. "Repentance in Luke-Acts." PhD diss., University of Notre Dame, 1993.
Bauer, Walter, et al. *A Greek–English Lexicon of the New Testament and Other Early Christian Literature*. 3rd ed. Chicago: University of Chicago Press, 2000.
Bauman, Clarence. *Sermon on the Mount*. Macon, GA: Mercer University Press, 1991.
Beare, Francis Wright. *The Gospel According to Matthew: Translation, Introduction, and Commentary*. Peabody, MA: Hendrickson, 1987.
———. "Mission of the Disciples and the Mission Charge: Matthew 10 and Parallels." *Journal of Biblical Literature* 89.1 (March 1970) 1–13.
Beasley-Murray, George Raymond. *Baptism in the New Testament*. London: Macmillan, 1962.
Betz, Hans Dieter. *Essays on the Sermon on the Mount*. Philadelphia: Fortress, 1985.
———. *The Sermon on the Mount*. Hermeneia. Minneapolis: Fortress, 1995.
Blomberg, Craig L. *Interpreting the Parables*. Downers Grove, IL: IVP Academic, 2012.
———. *Matthew*. New American Commentary. Nashville: Broadman, 1992.
Boda, Mark J. *'Return to Me': A Biblical Theology of Repentance*. Downers Grove, IL: IVP Academic, 2015.
Boda, Mark J., and Gordon T. Smith, eds. *Repentance in Christian Theology*. Collegeville, MN: Glazier, 2006.

de Boer, Martinus C. "Ten Thousand Talents: Matthew's Interpretation and Redaction of the Parable of the Unforgiving Servant (Matt 18:23–35)." *Catholic Biblical Quarterly* 50.2 (April 1988) 214–32.

Broadus, John Albert. *Commentary on the Gospel of Matthew*. Shanghai: China Baptist, 1935.

Brooks, Oscar S. "Matthew 28:16–20 and the Design of the First Gospel." *Journal for the Study of the New Testament* 10 (January 1981) 2–18.

Brown, Schuyler. "The Matthean Community and the Gentile Mission." *Novum Testamentum* 22.3 (July 1980) 193–221.

———. "Mission to Israel in Matthew's Central Section (Mt 9:35–11:1)." *Zeitschrift Für Die Neutestamentliche Wissenschaft Und Die Kunde Der Älteren Kirche* 69.1/2 (1978) 73–90.

Bruner, Frederick Dale. *Matthew: A Commentary: The Churchbook, Matthew 1–12*. Grand Rapids: Eerdmans, 2007.

———. *Matthew: A Commentary: The Churchbook, Matthew 13–28*. Grand Rapids: Eerdmans, 2007.

Byrne, Brendan. "The Messiah in Whose Name 'the Gentiles Will Hope' (Matt 12:21): Gentile Inclusion as an Essential Element of Matthew's Christology." *Australian Biblical Review* 50 (2002) 55–73.

Carlston, Charles E. "Metanoia and Church Discipline in the New Testament." PhD diss., Harvard University, 1958.

Carmody, Timothy R. "Matt 18:15–17 in Relation to Three Texts from Qumran Literature (CD 9:2–8, 16–22; 1QS 5:25—6:1)." In *To Touch the Text: Biblical and Related Studies in Honor of Joseph A. Fitzmyer SJ*, edited by Maurya P. Horgan and Paul J. Kobelski, 141–58. New York: Crossroad, 1989.

Carpenter, John B. "The Parable of the Talents in Missionary Perspective: A Call for an Economic Spirituality." *Missiology* 25.2 (April 1997) 165–81.

Carson, D. A. *Matthew*. In *The Expositor's Bible Commentary*, vol. 9, edited by Tramper Longman III and David E. Garland, 23–670. 13 vols. Grand Rapids: Zondervan, 2010.

———. "On Abusing Matthew 18." *Themelios (Online)* 36.1 (May 2011) 1–3.

———. *The Sermon on the Mount*. Grand Rapids: Baker, 1978.

Carter, Warren. *Households and Discipleship: A Study of Matthew 19–20*. Sheffield, UK: JSOT, 1994.

———. "Matthew and the Gentiles: Individual Conversion and/or Systemic Transformation?" *Journal for the Study of the New Testament* 26.3 (March 2004) 259–82.

———. *Matthew and the Margins: A Sociopolitical and Religious Reading*. Sheffield, UK: Sheffield Academic Press, 2000.

———. *Matthew: Storyteller, Interpreter, Evangelist*. Peabody, MA: Hendrickson, 2004.

———. "Matthew 4:18–22 and Matthean Discipleship: An Audience-Oriented Perspective." *Catholic Biblical Quarterly* 59.1 (January 1997) 58–75.

———. "The Parables in Matthew 21:28—22:14." In *Matthew's Parables: Audience-Oriented Perspectives*, edited by John Paul Heil and Warren Carter, 147–76. Washington, DC: Catholic Biblical Assoc of America, 1998.

———. "Resisting and Imitating the Empire: Imperial Paradigms in Two Matthean Parables." *Interpretation* 56.3 (July 2002) 260–72.

Chamberlain, William D. "For Deliverance and Freedom: The Biblical Doctrine of Repentance." *Interpretation* 4.3 (July 1950) 271–83.

———. *The Meaning of Repentance*. Philadelphia: The Westminster, 1943.

Charette, Blaine. "A Harvest for the People: An Interpretation of Matthew 9:37f." *Journal for the Study of the New Testament* 38 (February 1990) 29–35.

Chilton, Bruce. "John the Purifier." In *Jesus in Context: Temple, Purity & Restoration*, edited by Bruce Chilton and Craig A. Evans, 203–20. New York: Brill, 1997.

Clark, Kenneth Willis. "The Gentile Bias in Matthew." *Journal of Biblical Literature* 66.2 (June 1947) 165–72.

Clendenen, E. Ray. *Haggai, Malachi*. The New American Commentary. Nashville: B&H, 2004.

Court, John M. "Right and Left: The Implications for Matthew 25:31–46." *New Testament Studies* 31.2 (April 1985) 223–33.

Cremer, Hermann. *Biblio-Theological Lexicon of New Testament Greek*. Edinburgh: T. & T. Clark, 1872.

Croteau, David A. "Repentance Found? The Concept of Repentance in the Fourth Gospel." *The Master's Seminary Journal* 24.1 (2013) 97–123.

Davies, William David. *The Setting of the Sermon on the Mount*. Cambridge: Cambridge University Press, 1976.

Davies, William David, and Dale C. Allison, Jr. *Matthew 1–7*. International Critical Commentary. London: T. & T. Clark, 2004.

———. *Matthew 8–18*. International Critical Commentary. London: T. & T. Clark, 2004.

———. *Matthew 19–28*. International Critical Commentary. London: T. & T. Clark, 2004.

———. "Reflections on the Sermon on the Mount." *Scottish Journal of Theology* 44.3 (January 1, 1991) 283–309.

Deidun, Thomas. "Parable of the Unmerciful Servant (Mt 18:23–35)." *Biblical Theology Bulletin* 6.2/3 (June 1976) 203–24.

Deines, Roland. *Die Gerechtigkeit der Tora im Reich des Messias: Mt 5,13–20 als Schlüsseltext der matthäischen Theologie*. Wissenschaftliche Untersuchungen zum Neuen Testament. Tübingen: Mohr/Siebeck, 2004.

———. "Not the Law but the Messiah: Law and Righteousness in the Gospel of Matthew: An Ongoing Debate." In *Built upon the Rock: Studies in the Gospel of Matthew*, edited by Daniel M. Gurtner and John Nolland, 53–84. Grand Rapids: Eerdmans, 2008.

Derrett, J. Duncan M. "Unfair to Goats (Mt 25:32–33)." *Expository Times* 108.6 (March 1997) 177–78.

Dirksen, Aloys H. *The New Testament Concept of Metanoia*. Washington, DC: Catholic University of America, 1932.

Donahue, John R. *The Gospel in Parable*. Philadelphia: Fortress, 1988.

———. "The 'Parable' of the Sheep and the Goats: A Challenge to Christian Ethics." *Theological Studies* 47.1 (March 1986) 3–31.

Donaldson, Terence L. "Guiding Readers-Making Disciples: Discipleship in Matthew's Narrative Strategy." In *Patterns of Discipleship in the New Testament*, edited by Richard N. Longenecker, 41–49. Grand Rapids: Eerdmans, 1996.

Doriani, Daniel M. "Forgiveness: Jesus' Plan for Healing and Reconciliation in the Church (Matthew 18:15–35)." *The Southern Baptist Journal of Theology* 13.3 (September 2009) 22–32.

Duling, Dennis C. "Matthew 18:15–17: Conflict, Confrontation, and Conflict Resolution in a 'Fictive Kin' Association." *Biblical Theology Bulletin* 29.1 (1999) 4–22.

Dunn, James D. G. *Baptism in the Holy Spirit*. London: SCM, 2010.

———. "'Baptized' as Metaphor." In *Baptism, the New Testament and the Church*, edited by Stanley E. Porter and Anthony R. Cross, 294–310. Sheffield, UK: Sheffield Academic Press, 1999.

———. *Jesus and the Spirit: A Study of the Religious and Charismatic Experience of Jesus and the First Christians as Reflected in the New Testament*. Grand Rapids: Eerdmans, 1975.

———. "John the Baptist's Use of Scripture." In *The Gospels and the Scriptures of Israel*, edited by Craig A. Evans and William Richard Stegner, 42–54. Sheffield, UK: Sheffield Academic Press, 1994.

Dupont, Jacques. "Repentir et Conversion D'après Les Actes Des Apôtres." *Sciences Ecclésiastiques* 12.2 (May 1960) 137–73.

Edwards, R. "Uncertain Faith: Matthew's Portrait of the Disciples." In *Discipleship in the New Testament*, edited by Fernando Segovia, 47–61. Philadelphia: Fortress, 1985.

Eloff, Marvin. "Ἀπό . . . ἕως and Salvation History in Matthew's Gospel." In *Built upon the Rock: Studies in the Gospel of Matthew*, edited by Daniel M. Gurtner and John Nolland, 85–107. Grand Rapids: Eerdmans, 2008.

Etzioni, Amitai, and David E. Carney. *Repentance: A Comparative Perspective*. Lanham, MD: Rowman & Littlefield, 1997.

Evans, Craig A. "The Baptism of John in a Typological Context." In *Dimension of Baptism*, edited by Stanley E. Porter and Anthony R. Cross, 43–71. Sheffield, UK: Sheffield Academic Press, 2002.

———. *Commentary on the New Testament Use of the Old Testament*. Edited by G. K. Beale and D. A. Carson. Grand Rapids: Baker Academic, 2007.

Fitzgerald, Allan D. *The Oxford Handbook of Early Christian Studies*. Oxford: Oxford University Press, 2008.

Fitzmyer, Joseph A. *The Gospel According to Luke 1–9*. The Anchor Bible. New York: BDDP, 1979.

Flemington, William Frederick. *The New Testament Doctrine of Baptism*. London: SPCK, 1948.

Fortna, Robert Tomson. *The Gospel of Matthew: The Scholars Version Annotated with Introduction and Greek Text*. Santa Rosa, CA: Polebridge, 2005.

Foster, Graham. "Making Sense of Matthew 25:31–46." *Scottish Bulletin of Evangelical Theology* 16 (1998) 128–39.

Foster, Paul. *Community, Law, and Mission in Matthew's Gospel*. Wissenschaftliche Untersuchungen zum Neuen Testament. Tübingen: Mohr/Siebeck, 2004.

France, Richard Thomas. *The Gospel of Matthew*. New International Commentary on the New Testament. Grand Rapids: Eerdmans, 2007.

———. *Matthew: Evangelist and Teacher*. Eugene, OR: Wipf & Stock, 2004.

———. "On Being Ready (Matthew 25:1–46)." In *Challenge of Jesus' Parables*, edited by Richard N. Longenecker, 177–95. Grand Rapids: Eerdmans, 2000.

Freedman, David Noel, ed. *Anchor Bible Dictionary*. New York: Doubleday, 1992.

Garland, David E. *The Intention of Matthew 23*. Leiden: Brill, 1979.
Garlington, Don. "'Who is the Greatest?'" *Journal of the Evangelical Theological Society* 53.2 (June 2010) 287–316.
Gibbs, Jeffrey A., and Jeffrey J. Kloha. "'Following' Matthew 18: Interpreting Matthew 18:15–20 in its Context." *Concordia Journal* 29.1 (January 2003) 6–25.
Guelich, Robert A. "Interpreting the Sermon on the Mount." *Interpretation* 41.2 (April 1987) 117–30.
———. *Sermon on the Mount: A Foundation for Understanding*. Waco, TX: Word, 1991.
Gundry, Robert H. *Matthew: A Commentary on His Handbook for a Mixed Church Under Persecution*. Grand Rapids: Eerdmans, 1994.
Gutner, Daniel M., and John Nolland, eds. *Built upon the Rock: Studies in the Gospel of Matthew*. Grand Rapids: Eerdmans, 2008.
Hägerland, Tobias. "Jesus and the Rites of Repentance." *New Testament Studies* 52.2 (April 2006) 166–87.
Hagner, Donald A. "Law, Righteousness, and Discipleship in Matthew." *Word & World* 18.4 (September 1998) 364–71.
———. *Matthew 1–13*. WBC. Waco, TX: Word, 1993.
———. *Matthew 14–28*. WBC. Waco, TX: Word, 1993.
———. "Matthew's Parables of the Kingdom (Matthew 13:1–52)." In *Challenge of Jesus' Parables*, edited by Richard N. Longenecker, 102–24. Grand Rapids: Eerdmans, 2000.
———. "New Things from the Scribe's Treasure Box (Mt 13:52)." *Expository Times* 109.11 (August 1, 1998) 329–34.
———. "Righteousness in Matthew's Theology." In *Worship, Theology and Ministry in the Early Church: Essays in Honor of Ralph P. Martin*, edited by Ralph P. Martin et al., 101–20. Sheffield, UK: JSOT, 1992.
Hakh, Samuel B. "Women in the Genealogy of Matthew." *Exchange (Online)* 43.2 (2014) 109–18.
Hare, Douglas R. A., and Daniel J. Harrington. "Make Disciples of All the Gentiles (Mt 28:19)." *Catholic Biblical Quarterly* 37.3 (July 1975) 359–69.
Heil, John Paul. "Parable of the Unforgiving Forgiven Servant in Matthew 18:21–35." In *Matthew's Parables: Audience-Oriented Perspectives*, edited by John Paul Heil and Warren Carter, 96–123. Washington, DC: Catholic Biblical Assoc of America, 1998.
Hendriksen, William. *New Testament Commentary: Exposition of the Gospel according to Matthew*. Grand Rapids: Baker, 1973.
Hiers, Richard H. "'Binding' and 'Loosing': The Matthean Authorizations." *Journal of Biblical Literature* 104.2 (June 1985) 233–50.
Hood, Jason B. *The Messiah, His Brothers, and the Nations: (Matthew 1.1–17)*. Library of New Testament Studies 441. New York: T. & T. Clark, 2013.
Hooker, Morna D. "Uncomfortable Words X. The Prohibition of Foreign Missions (Mt 10:5–6)." *Expository Times* 82.12 (September 1, 1971) 361–65.
Horning, Estella B. "The Rule of Christ: An Exposition of Matthew 18:15–20." *Brethren Life and Thought* 38.2 (1993) 69–78.
Humphrey, Edith M. "And I Shall Heal Them: Repentance, Turning, and Penitence in the Johannine Writings." In *Repentance in Christian Theology*, edited by Mark J. Boda and Gordon T. Smith, 105–26. Collegeville, MN: Glazier, 2006.

Hutchison, John C. "Women, Gentiles, and the Messianic Mission in Matthew's Genealogy." *Bibliotheca Sacra* 158.630 (April 2001) 152–64.
Hylen, Susan. "Forgiveness and Life in Community." *Interpretation* 54.2 (April 2000) 146–57.
Illian, Bridget. "Church Discipline and Forgiveness in Matthew 18:15–35." *Currents in Theology and Mission* 37.6 (December 2010) 444–50.
Irons, Charles Lee. *The Righteousness of God: A Lexical Examination of the Covenant-Faithfulness Interpretation*. Wissenschaftliche Untersuchungen zum Neuen Testament. Tübingen: Mohr/Siebeck, 2015.
Jason, Mark. *Repentance at Qumran: The Penitential Framework of Religious Experience in the Dead Sea Scrolls*. Minneapolis: Fortress, 2015.
Jeremias, Joachim. *New Testament Theology: The Proclamation of Jesus*. New York: Scribner's Sons, 1977.
———. *Parables of Jesus*. London: SCM, 2003.
Kay, Christian, ed. *Historical Thesaurus of the Oxford English Dictionary: With Additional Material from A Thesaurus of Old English*. Oxford: Oxford University Press, 2009.
Keener, Craig S. *The Gospel of Matthew: A Socio-Rhetorical Commentary*. Grand Rapids: Eerdmans, 2009.
———. *Matthew*. IVP New Testament Commentary Series. Downers Grove, IL: IVP Academic, 1997.
———. "Matthew's Missiology: Making Disciples of the Nations (Matthew 28:19–20)." *Asian Journal of Pentecostal Studies* 12.1 (January 2009) 3–20.
Keesmaat, Sylvia C. "Strange Neighbors and Risky Care (Matthew 18:21–25; Luke 14:7–14; Luke 10:25–37)." In *The Challenge of Jesus' Parables*, edited by Richard N. Longenecker, 263–85. Grand Rapids: Eerdmans, 2000.
Kingsbury, Jack Dean. "Composition and Christology of Matt 28:16–20." *Journal of Biblical Literature* 93.4 (December 1974) 573–84.
———. *Matthew*. Proclamation Commentaries. Philadelphia: Fortress, 1977.
———. *Matthew as Story*. Philadelphia: Fortress, 1988.
———. "The Place, Structure, and Meaning of the Sermon on the Mount Within Matthew." *Interpretation* 41.2 (1987) 131–43.
———. "The Plot of Matthew's Story." *Interpretation* 46.4 (October 1992) 347–56.
———. "Structure of Matthew's Gospel and His Concept of Salvation-History." *Catholic Biblical Quarterly* 35.4 (October 1973) 451–74.
Kintu, Moses. "Repentance in the Sermon on the Mount." PhD diss., Trinity Evangelical Divinity School, 2014.
Kittel, Gerhard, and Gerhard Friedrich, eds. *Theological Dictionary of the New Testament*. Translated by Geoffrey W. Bromiley. Vol. 4. 10 vols. Grand Rapids: Eerdmans, 2006.
Konradt, Matthias. *Israel, Church, and the Gentiles in the Gospel of Matthew*. Translated by Kathleen Ess. Waco, TX: Baylor University Press, 2014.
Kraeling, Carl Hermann. *John the Baptist*. New York: Scribner's Sons, 1951.
Krentz, Edgar. "Missionary Matthew: Matthew 28:16–20 as Summary of the Gospel." *Currents in Theology and Mission* 31.1 (February 2004) 24–31.
Kuepfer, Tim. "Matthew 18 Revisited." *Vision* 8.1 (2007) 33–41.
Kupp, David D. *Matthew's Emmanuel: Divine Presence and God's People in the First Gospel*. Cambridge: Cambridge University Press, 2005.

Lanser, Matthew. "Repent Ye, for the Kingdome of Heaven Is at Hand: Henry Hammond's Commentary and Sermon on Matthew 3:2." *Westminster Theological Journal* 75.2 (September 2013) 279–96.
Lee, ChoongJae. "μετάνοια (Repentance) as a Major Theme of the Gospel of Matthew," *Journal of Reformed Theology* 13.2 (October 25, 2019) 149–65.
LeGrand, Lucien. "The Harvest is Plentiful (Mt 9:37)." *The Catholic Biblical Association* 17. 37 (January 1965) 1–9.
Leiva-Merikakis, Erasmo. *Fire of Mercy, Heart of the Word: Meditations on the Gospel according to Saint Matthew*. San Francisco: Ignatius, 1996.
Lohr, Charles H. "Oral Techniques in the Gospel of Matthew." *Catholic Biblical Quarterly* 23.4 (October 1, 1961) 403–35.
Long, Thomas G. *Matthew*. Westminster Bible Companion. Louisville: Westminster John Knox, 1997.
Louw, Johannes Petrus, and Eugene A. Nida. *Greek-English Lexicon of the New Testament: Based on Semantic Domains*. New York: United Bible Societies, 1989.
Luomanen, Petri. *Entering the Kingdom of Heaven: A Study on the Structure of Matthew's View of Salvation*. Wissenschaftliche Untersuchungen zum Neuen Testament. Tübingen: Mohr/Siebeck, 1998.
Luz, Ulrich. "The Disciples in the Gospel according to Matthew." In *The Interpretation of Matthew*, edited by Graham Stanton, 98–128. Philadelphia: Fortress, 1983.
———. "The Final Judgment (Matt 25:31–46) An Exercise in 'History of Influence' Exegesis." In *Treasures New and Old: Recent Contributions to Matthean Studies*, edited by David R. Bauer and Mark Allen Powell, 271–310. Atlanta: Scholars, 1996.
———. *Matthew 1–7*. Rev. ed. Hermenia. Minneapolis: Fortress, 2007.
———. *Matthew 8–20*. Hermenia. Minneapolis: Fortress, 2005.
———. *Matthew 21–28*. Hermenia. Minneapolis: Fortress, 2005.
———. *Studies in Matthew*. Grand Rapids: Eerdmans, 2005.
Marshall, I. Howard. "The Meaning of the Verb 'Baptize.'" In *Dimension of Baptism*, edited by Stanley E. Porter and Anthony R. Cross, 8–24. Sheffield, UK: Sheffield Academic Press, 2002.
———. *New Bible Dictionary*. Downers Grove, IL: IVP, 1996.
Martens, Allan W. "'Produce Fruit Worthy of Repentance': Parables of Judgment against the Jewish Religious Leaders and the Nation (Matthew 21:28—22:14 par; Luke 13:6–9)." In *The Challenge of Jesus' Parables*, edited by Richard N. Longenecker, 151–76. Grand Rapids: Eerdmans, 2000.
Marxsen, Willi. *New Testament Foundations for Christian Ethics*. Minneapolis: Fortress, 1994.
Matera, Frank J. "The Plot of Matthew's Gospel." *Catholic Biblical Quarterly* 49.2 (April 1987) 233–54.
McArthur, Harvey K. *Understanding the Sermon on the Mount*. New York: Harper & Brothers, 1960.
McClister, David. "'Where Two or Three re Gathered Together': Literary Structure as a Key to Meaning in Matt 17:22–20:19." *Journal of the Evangelical Theological Society* 39.4 (December 1996) 549–58.
McKnight, Scot. *Sermon on the Mount*. Grand Rapids: Zondervan, 2013.
Meier, John P. "John the Baptist in Matthew's Gospel." *Journal of Biblical Literature* 99.3 (September 1980) 383–405.

———. *A Marginal Jew: Rethinking the Historical Jesus*. New York: Doubleday, 1991.
———. "Nations or Gentiles in Matthew 28:19." *Catholic Biblical Quarterly* 39.1 (January 1977) 94–102.
———. "Salvation History in Matthew: In Search of a Starting Point." *Catholic Biblical Quarterly* 37.2 (April 1975) 203–15.
———. "Two Disputed Questions in Matt 28:16–20." *Journal of Biblical Literature* 96.3 (September 1977) 407–24.
———. *The Vision of Matthew: Christ, Church, and Morality in the First Gospel*. Eugene, OR: Wipf & Stock, 2004.
Merklein, Helmut. "Die Umkehrpredigt Bei Johannes Dem Täufer Und Jesus von Nazaret." *Biblische Zeitschrift* 25.1 (1981) 29–46.
———. *Exegetical Dictionary of the New Testament*. 3 vols. Grand Rapids: Eerdmans, 1990.
Michel, Otto. "The Conclusion of Matthew's Gospel: A Contribution to the History of the Easter Message." In *Interpretation of Matthew*, edited by Graham Stanton, 30–41. Philadelphia: Fortress, 1983.
Michiels, Robrecht. "La Conception Lucanienne de La Conversion." *Ephemerides Theologicae Lovanienses* 41.1 (January 1965) 42–78.
Micklem, Philip Arthur. *St. Matthew*. London: Methuen & Co., 1917.
Mitch, Curtis, and Edward P. Sri. *The Gospel of Matthew*. Catholic Commentary on Sacred Scripture. Grand Rapids: Baker Academic, 2010.
Mohrlang, Roger. *Matthew and Paul: A Comparison of Ethical Perspectives*. Cambridge: Cambridge University Press, 2004.
Morgan, G. Campbell. *The Gospel according to Matthew*. Philadelphia: Blakiston, 1929.
Morosco, Robert E. "Matthew's Formation of a Commissioning Type-Scene Out of the Story of Jesus' Commissioning of the Twelve." *Journal of Biblical Literature* 103.4 (December 1984) 539–56.
———. "Redaction Criticism and the Evangelical: Matthew 10 a Test Case." *Journal of the Evangelical Theological Society* 22.4 (December 1979) 323–31.
Morris, Leon. *The Gospel according to Matthew*. The Pillar New Testament Commentary. Grand Rapids: Eerdmans, 1992.
Mounce, Robert H. *Matthew*. New International Biblical Commentary. Peabody, MA: Hendrickson, 1991.
Mullins, Michael. *The Gospel of Matthew: A Commentary*. Dublin: Columba, 2007.
Nave, Guy D., Jr. "'Repent, for the Kingdom of God Is at Hand' Repentance in the Synoptic Gospels and Acts." In *Repentance in Christian Theology*, edited by Mark J. Boda and Gordon T. Smith, 87–104. Collegeville, MN: Glazier, 2006.
———. *The Role and Function of Repentance in Luke-Acts*. Academia Biblica Series. Atlanta: Society of Biblical Literature, 2002.
Neirynck, Frans. "Apo Tote Ērxato and the Structure of Matthew." *Ephemerides Theologicae Lovanienses* 64.1 (1988) 21–59.
Ng, Esther Yue L. "Matthew 5:17–20 and 'A Tale of Two Missions'?" In *New Testament Theology in Light of the Church's Mission: Essays in Honor of I. Howard Marshall*, edited by Ray Van Neste et al., 105–22. Eugene, OR: Cascade, 2011.
Nitzan, Bilha. "Repentance in the Dead Sea Scrolls." In *Dead Sea Scrolls after Fifty Years: A Comprehensive Assessment*, edited by Peter W. Flint and James C. Vanderkam, 145–70. Leiden: Brill, 1999.

Nolland, John. *The Gospel of Matthew*. New International Greek Testament Commentary. Grand Rapids: Eerdmans, 2005.

———. "'In Such a Manner It Is Fitting for Us to Fulfill All Righteousness': Reflections on the Place of Baptism In the Gospel of Matthew." In *Baptism, the New Testament and the Church*, edited by Stanley E. Porter and Anthony R. Cross, 63–80. Sheffield, UK: Sheffield Academic, 1999.

———. *Luke 1–9:20*. Word Biblical Commentary. Dallas: Word, 1989.

Olmstead, Wesley G. "A Gospel for a New Nation: Once More, the ἔθνος of Matthew 21:43." In *Jesus, Matthew's Gospel and Early Christianity: Studies in Memory of Graham N. Stanton*, edited by Daniel M. Gurtner et al., 115–32 Library of New Testament Studies 435. New York: T. & T. Clark, 2011.

Osborne, Grant R. *Matthew*. Zondervan Exegetical Commentary on the New Testament. Grand Rapids: Zondervan, 2010.

Otto, Dan Via, Jr. "Ethical Responsibility and Human Wholeness in Matthew 25:31–46." *Harvard Theological Review* 80.1 (January 1987) 79–100.

Owen, John J. *A Commentary, Critical, Expository and Practical, on the Gospels of Matthew and Mark*. New York: Leavitt & Allen, 1857.

Pappas, Harry S. "The 'Exhortation to Fearless Confession' – Matt 10:26–33." *The Greek Orthodox Theological Review* 25.3 (September 1980) 239–48.

Patte, Daniel. "Bringing Out of the Gospel-Treasure What Is New and What Is Old: Two Parables in Matthew 18–23." *Quarterly Review* 10.3 (September 1990) 79–108.

———. *The Gospel according to Matthew: A Structural Commentary on Matthew's Faith*. Philadelphia: Fortress, 1987.

———. "Jesus' Pronouncement about Entering the Kingdom like a Child: A Structural Exegesis." *Semeia* 29 (1983) 3–42.

Peloubet, Francis Nathan. *Suggestive Illustrations on the Gospel according to Matthew; Illustrations from All Sources, Picturesque Greek Words, Library References to Further Illustrations, Photographs of Celebrated Pictures Referred To, for the Use of Leaders of Prayer-Meetings, Christian Endeavorers, Sunday-School Teachers, Pastors*. New York: Herrick & Co., 1897.

Pennington, Jonathan T. "'Be Ye Virtuous as Your Heavenly Father Is Virtuous': Resourcing a Christian Positive Psychology from the Sermon on the Mount," Annual Meeting of the Society for Christian Psychology, Virginia Beach, VA, October 2012.

———. *Heaven and Earth in the Gospel of Matthew*. Leiden: Brill, 2007.

———. "Matthew 13 and the Function of the Parables in the First Gospel." *Southern Baptist Journal of Theology* 13.3 (September 1, 2009) 12–20.

———. *The Sermon on the Mount and Human Flourishing: A Theological Commentary*. Grand Rapids: Baker Academic, 2017.

Pfitzner, Victor C. "Purified Community-Purified Sinner: Expulsion from the Community according to Matt 18:15–18 and 1 Cor 5:1–5." *Australian Biblical Review* 30 (October 1982) 34–55.

Picken, Stuart D. B. *Historical Dictionary of Calvinism*. Lanham, MD: Scarecrow, 2011.

Porter, Stanley E. "Penitence and Repentance in the Epistles." In *Repentance in Christian Theology*, edited by Mark J. Boda and Gordon T. Smith, 127–52. Collegeville, MN: Glazier, 2006.

Powell, Mark Allan. "Binding and Loosing: A Paradigm for Ethical Discernment from the Gospel of Matthew." *Currents in Theology and Mission* 30.6 (December 2003) 438–45.

———. "The Plot and Subplots of Matthew's Gospel." *New Testament Studies* 38.2 (April 1992) 187–204.

Przybylski, Benno. *Righteousness in Matthew and His World of Thought*. Cambridge: Cambridge University Press, 2004.

Ramshaw, Elaine. "Power and Forgiveness in Matthew 18." *Word & World* 18.4 (September 1998) 397–404.

Robertson, Archibald Thomas. *Word Pictures in the New Testament*. Nashville: Holman Reference, 2000.

Runesson, Anders. *Divine Wrath and Salvation in Matthew*. Minneapolis: Fortress, 2016.

Runge, Steven E. *Discourse Grammar of the Greek New Testament: A Practical Introduction for Teaching and Exegesis*. Peabody, MA: Hendrickson, 2010.

Russel, Thomas, ed. *The Works of the English Reformers*. Vol. 2, *Tyndale and John Frith*. 3 vols. London: Palmer, 1831.

Scaer, David P. *The Sermon on the Mount: The Church's First Statement of the Gospel*. St. Louis: Concordia, 2000.

Schaff, Philip, ed. *Ante-Nicene Fathers*. Vol. 1. 10 vols. Grand Rapids: CCEL, 1885.

Schnabel, Eckhard J. "Repentance in Paul's Letters." *Novum Testamentum* 57.2 (March 19, 2015) 159–86.

Schnelle, Udo. *Theology of the New Testament*. Grand Rapids: Baker Academic, 2009.

Schonfield, Hugh J. *The Old Hebrew Text of St. Matthew's Gospel*. Edinburgh: T. & T. Clark, 1927.

Schweizer, Eduard. *The Good News according to Matthew*. Atlanta: John Knox, 1975.

Scott, Bernard Brandon. "The King's Accounting: Matthew 18:23–34." *Journal of Biblical Literature* 104.3 (September 1985) 429–42.

Senior, Donald. "Between Two Worlds: Gentiles and Jewish Christians in Matthew's Gospel." *Catholic Biblical Quarterly* 61.1 (January 1999) 1–23.

Sherriff, J. M. "Matthew 25:1–13: A Summary of Matthaean Eschatology?," In *Studia Biblica 1978, 2: Papers on the Gospels*, edited by Elizabeth Anne Livingstone, 301–5. Sheffield, UK: JSOT, 1980.

Sievers, Joseph. "'Where Two or Three . . .': the Rabbinic Concept of Shekhinah and Matthew 18:20." In *Jewish Roots of Christian Liturgy*, edited by Eugene J. Fisher, 47–61. New York: Paulist, 1990.

Silva, Moisés, ed. *New International Dictionary of New Testament Theology and Exegesis*. Vol. 3. 5 vols. Grand Rapids: Zondervan, 2014.

Sim, David C. "Conflict in the Canon: The Pauline Literature and the Gospel of Matthew." In *Religious Conflict from Early Christianity to the Rise of Islam*, edited by Wendy Mayer and Bronwen Neil, 71–86. Berlin: de Gruyter, 2013.

———. "The Gospel of Matthew and the Gentiles." *Journal for the Study of the New Testament* 57 (March 1995) 19–48.

———. "Is Matthew 28:16–20 the Summary of the Gospel?" *Hervormde Theological Studies* 70.1 (2014) 1–7.

———. "Matthew and the Gentiles: A Response to Brendan Byrne." *Australian Biblical Review* 50 (2002) 74–79.

———. "Matthew and the Pauline Corpus: A Preliminary Intertextual Study." *Journal for the Study of the New Testament* 31.4 (June 2009) 401–22.
———. "Matthew 7.21–23: Further Evidence of Its Anti-Pauline Perspective." *New Testament Studies* 53.3 (July 2007) 325–43.
———. "Matthew's Anti-Paulinism: A Neglected Feature of Matthean Studies." *Hervormde Theological Studies* 58.2 (November 3, 2002) 767–83.
———. "The Rise and Fall of the Gospel of Matthew." *Expository Times* 120.10 (July 2009) 478–85.
Smith, Ralph L. *Micah-Malachi*. Word Biblical Commentary. Waco, TX: Word, 1984.
Smith, Robert H. *Matthew*. Augsburg Commentary on the New Testament. Minneapolis: Augsburg, 1989.
Snodgrass, Klyne R. *Stories with Intent: A Comprehensive Guide to the Parables of Jesus*. Grand Rapids: Eerdmans, 2018.
Stanton, Graham, ed. *The Interpretation of Matthew*. Philadelphia: Fortress, 1983.
Stein, Robert H. "The Genre of the Parables." In *Challenge of Jesus' Parables*, edited by Richard N. Longenecker, 30–50. Grand Rapids: Eerdmans, 2000.
Steinmetz, David C. "Matthew 25:14–30." *Interpretation* 34.2 (April 1980) 172–76.
Strecker, George. *The Sermon on the Mount: An Exegetical Commentary*. Nashville: Abingdon, 1988.
———. *Theology of the New Testament*. New York: Westminster John Knox, 2000.
Talbert, Charles H. *Matthew*. Paideia. Grand Rapids: Baker Academic, 2010.
———. *Reading the Sermon on the Mount: Character Formation and Decision Making in Matthew 5–7*. Grand Rapids: Baker Academic, 2006.
Taylor, Joan E. *The Immerser: John the Baptist within Second Temple Judaism, Studying the Historical Jesus*. Grand Rapids: Eerdmans, 1997.
———. "John the Baptist and the Essenes." *Journal of Jewish Studies* 47.2 (1996) 256–85.
Thomas, David. *The Gospel of Matthew: A Homiletical Commentary*. Grand Rapids: Kregel, 1979.
Thompson, Effie Freeman. "Metanoeō and Metamelei in Greek Literature until 100 A.D.: Including Discussion of Their Cognates and of Their Hebrew Equivalents." PhD diss., University of Chicago, 1908.
Thompson, John Arthur, and Elmer A. Martens. *New International Dictionary of Old Testament Theology & Exegesis. Vol. 4*. 5 vols. Grand Rapids: Zondervan, 1997.
Thompson, William G. *Matthew's Advice to a Divided Community: Matt 17:22–18:35*. Analecta Biblica. Rome: Biblical Institute, 1970.
Trilling, Wolfgang. *Das wahre Israel; Studien zur Theologie des Matthäus Evangeliums*. Munich: Kösel, 1959.
Turner, David L. *Matthew*. Baker Exegetical Commentary on the New Testament. Grand Rapids: Baker Academic, 2008.
Tyndale, William. *Doctrinal Treatises and Introductions to Different Portions of the Holy Scriptures*. Cambridge: Cambridge University Press, 1848.
———. *Expositions and Notes on Sundry Portions of the Holy Scriptures: Together with The Practice of Prelates*. Cambridge: Cambridge University Press, 1849.
Universidad de Navarra, and Facultad de Teología. *The Navarre Bible: St Matthew, R.S.V. Text with Commentary by the Faculty of Theology at the University of Navarre*. Dublin: Four Courts, 1988.
Vincent, Marvin R. *Word Studies in the New Testament*. New York: Scribner, 1887.

Vos, Johannes Geerhardus. "The Meaning of Repentance." *Westminster Theological Journal* 6.1 (November 1943) 98–104.
Ward, Arthur Marcus. *The Gospel according to St Matthew*. Epworth Preacher's Commentaries. London: Epworth, 1961.
Warfield, Benjamin B. *Biblical and Theological Studies*. Phillipsburg, NJ: P&R, 1952.
Watson, Francis. "Liberating the Reader: A Theological-Exegetical Study of the Parable of the Sheep and the Goats (Matt 25:31–46)." In *Open Text: New Directions for Biblical Studies*, edited by Francis Watson, 57–84. London: SCM, 1993.
Webb, Robert L. "John the Baptist and His Relationship to Jesus." In *Studying the Historical Jesus: Evaluations of the State of Current Research*, edited by Bruce Chilton and Craig A. Evans, 179–229. Leiden: Brill, 1994.
———. *John the Baptizer and Prophet: A Sociohistorical Study*. Eugene, OR: Wipf & Stock, 2006.
Weber, Kathleen. "The Image of the Sheep and Goats in Matthew 25:31–46." *Catholic Biblical Quarterly* 59 (1997) 657–78.
Wenham, David. "The Structure of Matthew 13." *New Testament Studies* 25.4 (July 1, 1979) 516–22.
Weren, Wilhelmus Johannes Cornelis. "The Macrostructure of Matthew's Gospel: A New Proposal." *Biblica* 87.2 (2006) 171–200.
Wilkin, Robert Nicholas. "Repentance as a Condition for Salvation in the New Testament (metanoia, Epistrepho, Shub, Metamelomai)." ThD diss., Dallas Theological Seminary, 1985.
Wilkins, Michael J. *Discipleship in the Ancient World and Matthew's Gospel*. Eugene, OR: Wipf & Stock, 2015.
Wilkins, Michael J., and Theological Research Exchange Network. *Greek Disciples at the Time of Jesus: An Analysis of K. Rengstorf's Thesis about the Greek Background of Jesus' Disciples*. Portland, OR: Theological Research Exchange Network, 2005.
Willitts, Joel. "The Friendship of Matthew and Paul: A Response to a Recent Trend in the Interpretation of Matthew's Gospel." *Hervormde Theological Studies* 65.1 (2009) 1–8.
Wink, Walter. *John the Baptist in the Gospel Tradition*. Cambridge: Cambridge University Press, 2006.
Witherington, Ben. *Matthew*. Smyth & Helwys Bible Commentary. Macon, GA: Smyth & Helwys, 2006.
Yri, Norvald. "Seek God's Righteousness: Righteousness in the Gospel of Matthew." In *Right with God: Justification in the Bible and the World*, edited by D. A. Carson, 96–105. Grand Rapids: Baker, 1992.

www.ingramcontent.com/pod-product-compliance
Lightning Source LLC
Chambersburg PA
CBHW050848230426
43667CB00012B/2202